From the Socratics to the Socratic Schools

"Ugo Zilioli has put together an inspiring, dialogical collection of papers, which explore routes traced by the evidence for the 'other' (let's stop saying 'minor') Socratics and their heirs through many of the blank spaces left on our historical map between Plato and the Hellenistic age. At the same time as advancing our understanding of Classical metaphysics, epistemology, and ethics, the papers grapple with important questions about how we do ancient philosophy, and bring much needed critical light to categories, such as that of the 'school' itself, which shape our thinking."
—*George Boys-Stones, Durham University, UK*

In the two golden centuries that followed the death of Socrates, ancient philosophy underwent a tremendous transformation that culminated in the philosophical systematizations of Plato, Aristotle and the Hellenistic schools. Fundamental figures other than Plato were active after the death of Socrates; his immediate pupils, the Socratics, took over his legacy and developed it in a variety of ways. This rich philosophical territory has however been left largely underexplored in the scholarship.

This collection of eleven previously unpublished essays by leading scholars fills a gap in the literature, providing new insight into the ethics, metaphysics, and epistemology as developed by key figures of the Socratic schools. Analysing the important contributions that the Socratics and their heirs have offered ancient philosophical thought, as well as the impact these contributions had on philosophy as a discipline, this book will appeal to researchers and scholars of Classical Studies, as well as Philosophy and Ancient History.

Ugo Zilioli has been an Irish Research Council fellow at Trinity College Dublin, Ireland, and, more recently, a Marie Curie Intra-European Fellow at the University of Pisa, Italy. His main publications include: *Protagoras and the Challenge of Relativism* (2007; Chinese translation 2012); *The Cyrenaics* (2012; reprinted for Routledge 2014); *The Circle of Megara* (London/New York, forthcoming for Routledge).

From the Socratics to the Socratic Schools

Classical Ethics, Metaphysics and Epistemology

Edited by Ugo Zilioli

NEW YORK AND LONDON

First published 2015
by Routledge
711 Third Avenue, New York, NY 10017

and by Routledge
2 Park Square, Milton Park, Abingdon, Oxon OX14 4RN

*Routledge is an imprint of the Taylor & Francis Group,
an informa business*

© 2015 Taylor & Francis

The right of the editor to be identified as the author of the editorial material, and of the authors for their individual chapters, has been asserted in accordance with sections 77 and 78 of the Copyright, Designs and Patents Act 1988.

All rights reserved. No part of this book may be reprinted or reproduced or utilised in any form or by any electronic, mechanical, or other means, now known or hereafter invented, including photocopying and recording, or in any information storage or retrieval system, without permission in writing from the publishers.

Trademark notice: Product or corporate names may be trademarks or registered trademarks, and are used only for identification and explanation without intent to infringe.

Library of Congress Cataloging-in-Publication Data

From the Socratics to the Socratic schools : classical ethics, metaphysics, and epistemology / edited by Ugo Zilioli. — First [edition].
  Includes bibliographical references and index.
 1. Socrates. 2. Philosophy, Ancient. I. Zilioli, Ugo, 1971– editor.
 B317.F77 2015 183'.2—dc23
 2014040827

ISBN: (hbk) 978-1-84465-843-5
ISBN: (ebk) 978-1-315-71946-7

Typeset in Sabon
by Apex CoVantage, LLC

Printed and bound in the United States of America by Publishers Graphics, LLC on sustainably sourced paper.

Epigraph

Always keep Ithaca in your mind.
To arrive there is your final destination.
But do not rush the voyage in the least.
Better it last for many years;
and once you're old, cast anchor on the isle,
rich with all you've gained along the way,
expecting not that Ithaca will give you wealth.

Ithaca gave you the wondrous voyage:
Without her you'd never have set out.
But she has nothing to give you any more.

If then you find her poor, Ithaca has nor deceived you.
As wise as you've become, with such experience, by now
You will have come to know what Ithaca really means.

C. P. Cavafy (1911)

Contents

Abbreviations and Conventions		ix
Preface		xi
Introduction		xiii
UGO ZILIOLI		
1	Plato's Representations of the 'Socratics'	1
	VOULA TSOUNA	
2	The First-Generation Socratics and the Socratic Schools: The Case of the Cyrenaics	26
	CHRISTOPHER ROWE	
3	The Socratic Profile of Antisthenes' Ethics	43
	ALDO BRANCACCI	
4	Rethinking Aeschines of Sphettus	61
	KURT LAMPE	
5	Phaedo's *Zopyrus* (and Socrates' Confidences)	82
	LIVIO ROSSETTI	
6	The Sources and Scope of Cyrenaic Scepticism	99
	TIM O'KEEFE	
7	The Cyrenaics as Metaphysical Indeterminists	114
	UGO ZILIOLI	
8	Diodorus Cronus on Perceptible Minima	134
	FRANCESCO VERDE	
9	Pyrrho and the Socratic Schools	149
	RICHARD BETT	

10 Epicureanism and Socratism: The Evidence on the Minor Socratics from the Herculaneum Papyri TIZIANO DORANDI	168
11 Socrates, Alcibiades and Antisthenes in PFlor 113 MENAHEM LUZ	192
Contributors	211
Index	215

Abbreviations and Conventions

Abbreviations for ancient authors and works are those of LSJ and OLD. All Greek and Latin is translated into English. In some cases (especially in the 'philological' chapters by Dorandi and Luz), the original Greek is given with translation but with no transliteration. Bibliographical details of works cited are given at the end of each chapter.

The following abbreviations are used:

LSJ   H. G. Liddell, R. Scott, and H. S. Jones, *A Greek-English Lexicon*, 9th edition, Oxford 1940.
SSR   G. Giannantoni, *Socratis et Socraticorum Reliquiae*, Naples 1990.

Preface

This collection mainly arises from an international conference on the Socratics and the Socratic schools that was held at the Hotel Post-Victoria, Soprabolzano, in September 2013. The conference and the present collection represent one of the two main outcomes of a Marie Curie Intra-European Fellowship which I was privileged to hold during 2011–2013. I warmly thank the European Union and its FP7 scheme for the wonderful opportunity provided by the Fellowship to explore new avenues in my research.

The speakers at the Soprabolzano conference were Christopher Rowe, Kurt Lampe, Livio Rossetti, Aldo Brancacci, Tiziano Dorandi, Voula Tsouna and Richard Bett; George Boys-Stones acted as chairman. I thank all the participants at the conference, who travelled from far and wide to reach Soprabolzano: not an easy destination, but beautiful enough, I hope, to compensate them for the trouble they took to reach it. Sigmund Freud once went to Soprabolzano and immediately fell in love with it—coming back each subsequent summer to enjoy the special nature of the place and its breath-taking setting; its charms will not have been lost on any of us who were there.

In addition to the contributions by the participants to the Soprabolzano conference, the collection has been enriched and broadened by the inclusion of papers by Tim O'Keefe, Francesco Verde and Menahem Luz. I am here happy to thank them for accepting my invitation to contribute. All the contributors have been extremely supportive and collaborative in the long process of assembling the final version of the collection, always gracefully meeting the deadlines set. My particular thanks go to Christopher Rowe, who undertook the demanding task of translating the contributions by Brancacci, Dorandi and Rossetti from Italian into English, and for revising Verde's own translation. He has also substantially helped me in the revision of the Introduction. My thanks also to the two anonymous reviewers for Routledge, who have provided useful comments both on the collection as a whole and its various components.

On a more personal note, I wholeheartedly thank my wife, Cristiana, for having helped me substantially (and our children, Zoe and Delio, for their lively contributions to the occasion).

16 September 2014

Introduction

In recent decades there has been renewed interest among scholars on the Socratics and the Socratic schools. Recent studies have focused either on the Socratics or on the Socratic schools: two subjects that are closely related but also distinct. The label 'Socratics' is usually employed to refer to the immediate followers of Socrates other than Plato, such as Euclides of Megara, Aristippus of Cyrene, Phaedo of Elis, Antisthenes, Aeschines of Sphettus and Xenophon. The term 'Socratic schools', by contrast, is typically used to refer to those schools of thought that appear to have originated, more or less directly, from some of the Socratics just listed: the Megarians or Megarics (from Euclides of Megara), the Cyrenaics (from Aristippus of Cyrene), the Elians-Eretrians (from Phaedo of Elis and Menedemus of Eretria), and the Cynics (from Antisthenes – though many believe that the real founder of ancient Cynicism was Diogenes of Sinope).

1. THE SOCRATICS AND THE SOCRATIC SCHOOLS

There are then two distinct areas for investigation: the philosophical environment that grew up and flourished around and immediately after Socrates, and the enduring contribution of the immediate followers of Socrates in what Denis O'Brien has called "the two golden centuries that followed the death of Socrates." Yet, distinct as they are, these topics also constitute two sides of the same coin. As we reconstruct the different directions taken by the first-generation Socratics, we begin to see the richness and breadth that allowed the development of the 'schools' into which we are used to dividing the later 'Socratic' tradition.

What exactly it is to constitute a Socratic 'school' is a controversial issue. Are we justified in speaking of 'schools' when we refer to the Megarians, the Cyrenaics or the Cynics? If they were 'schools' at all, they were quite different from the more institutionalized schools of Plato, Aristotle, and Epicurus, each of which was located in Athens, and developed its own well-defined philosophical agenda. The Socratic 'schools' were located in cities outside

Athens, sometimes even outside the Greek mainland: in Megara, in Elis, in Eretria or in Cyrene, and on the basis of the evidence currently available, it is hard to reconstruct their particular philosophical profiles.

The school of Megara is by far the most active and diversified of all the Socratic schools. Its first members were Euclides of Megara and Eubulides of Miletus, who developed important views in ethics, metaphysics and logic. Some scholars (most notably, David Sedley)[1] have claimed that subsequent members of the Megarian school such as Diodorus Cronus and Philo are better understood as philosophers belonging to a separate school, the Dialecticians, whose philosophical activity contrasted with that of the Megarians.[2] But if it is difficult to see the Megarians as a unified group of philosophers sharing a common approach and similar philosophical views, the Cyrenaics, by contrast, can appear a rather monolithic group of philosophers who defended more or less the same views until Theodorus the Godless broke Cyrenaic orthodoxy with his new ethics of joy and grief.[3]

The Cynics are even more difficult to come to terms with. Antisthenes was undoubtedly an important and prolific philosopher who developed original views, many of them contrasting with Plato, in ethics, epistemology, logic, metaphysics and philosophy of language. Some ancient authors, and some contemporary scholars, take him to be the originator of ancient Cynicism; others believe Diogenes of Sinope to have been the actual founder of the Cynic movement. The place and authority of Antisthenes in the history of ancient Cynicism is thus problematic, and it is hard to assess the Cynic movement as a whole before understanding its proper genealogy. As for the Elean-Eretrian school, often understood as a branch of the Megarians, it is perhaps the most elusive of all the Socratic schools, and we really know very little about it.

By comparison with the Athens-based schools of Plato, Aristotle and Epicurus, the Socratic schools are thus difficult to reconstruct historically and philosophically. Tiziano Dorandi calls them 'pseudo-schools',[4] but this is probably too negative a view. The members of each of the Socratic schools will quite probably have shared common ways of life that resulted in their sharing similar philosophical approaches and basic doctrinal positions.

The contributors to the present volume take different views of the Socratic schools, and about the historical linkage between the schools themselves and the first generation Socratics. What all the contributors share, to a greater or lesser extent, is an awareness of the scope that exists for exploring the debates that flourished around Socrates, from which the Socratic schools appear to have originated. A fresh look at those debates should help us gain a wider understanding of the intellectual context in which Plato, Aristotle and the Hellenistic schools (Epicureans, Stoics and Sceptics) operated and, at the same time, while also bringing us face to face with an array of philosophers and views that often go unnoticed, but that are thoroughly worthy of exploration not only in relation to the major figures of ancient philosophy but in themselves.[5]

In short, this collection of essays does not pretend to be a comprehensive survey of the Socratics and the Socratic schools, which would require a book considerably longer than this one. The aim of the volume is more modest: to fill in some of the gaps in the existing map of the routes leading from Plato to the Hellenistic schools, by exploring the philosophical commitments of some first-generation Socratics and of some of the Socratic schools – with special emphasis, as it has turned out, on the Cyrenaics.

2. RECENT SCHOLARSHIP

Debate about the Socratics and the Socratic schools has been flourishing in the last two or three decades, thanks particularly to the appearance of Gabriele Giannantoni's monumental work on Socrates, the Socratics and the Socratic schools, *Socratis et Socraticorum Reliquiae* (henceforth 'SSR': published in Naples in 1990, in four volumes), the impact of which on the field of Socratic studies has been considerable. For the first time scholars had available a collection of the vast majority of the sources on Socrates, the Socratics and the Socratic schools, complemented by a critical scrutiny of the main scholarship on those thinkers and schools by Giannantoni himself.[6]

One cannot do justice, in a brief introduction, to all the important studies on the Socratics that have appeared since the publication of Giannantoni's work. I shall therefore be somewhat selective, briefly touching—roughly in chronological order, from 1990, when *SSR* appeared—on the contributions I believe to be the most relevant, both for the Anglophone reader and in the context of the present collection.

That year, 1990, also saw the publication of Aldo Brancacci's study on Antisthenes, *Oikeios logos: La filosofia del linguaggio di Antistene* (Naples 1990), which has now also appeared in a revised edition in French (Paris 2005). Brancacci's monograph revolutionised our understanding of Antisthenes by showing how all the various aspects of his thought converged in a systematic theory of language and predication. Then, in 1994, Paul A. Vander Waerdt edited *The Socratic Movement* (Ithaca 1994), with papers contributed by, among others, Gisela Striker, Christopher Shields, Julia Annas, Donald Morrison, Harold Tarrant and Voula Tsouna; the volume is ample testimony of the lively debate then in progress about the Socratics and the Socratic schools in the Anglophone world.[7] Another important addition to the literature was the collection of papers edited by R. Bracht Branham and Marie-Odile Goulet-Cazé, *The Cynics* (Berkeley and London 1996), a revised and expanded English version of a volume in French edited by Marie-Odile Goulet-Cazè and Richard Goulet (Paris 1993); while in 1998 Voula Tsouna published her invaluable book on the Cyrenaics: *The Epistemology of the Cyrenaic School* (Cambridge 1998). Tsouna's study is now a classic in the field, demonstrating the great originality of Cyrenaic epistemology as well as connecting it with ideas in modern epistemology.

xvi *Introduction*

Tsouna's example shows that it is possible to offer a general account of the philosophy of a Socratic school despite the extreme paucity of the available textual evidence.

In the last fifteen years, research on the Socratics and the Socratic schools has intensified further. Livio Rossetti and Alessandro Stavru have organized three international conferences on the Socratics and edited three collections of essays arising from those conferences.[8] The third conference, co-organized with Fulvia De Luise in Trento in March 2012, was particularly well attended, attracting speakers from all over the world, from New Zealand to the United States, from England to Israel, from Brazil to Iran. The proceedings of the Trento conference are now published as *Socratica III* (Sankt Augustin 2014). A brief glance at the contents—and especially the *Introduction* by Stavru—will suffice to show the presently flourishing state of Socratic studies. George Boys-Stones and Christopher Rowe have together edited *The Circle of Socrates. Readings in the First-Generation Socratics* (Indianapolis 2013), which is the first translation ever in English (with introduction and notes) of the main sources on the immediate followers of Socrates. *The Circle of Socrates* has already become standard reading for scholars working on the Socratics, both in the Anglophone world and beyond. A welcome addition on the Cynics and the Cyrenaics is the new translation of the sources on them by Robin Hard for Oxford Classics: *Diogenes the Cynic, Sayings and Anecdotes* (Oxford 2012). On Cyrenaic ethics and its later reception there is Kurt Lampe's monograph *The Birth of Hedonism: The Cyrenaic Philosophers and Pleasure as a way of life* (Princeton 2014). The Acumen Ancient Philosophies Series (now published by Routledge) has recently hosted such books as *The Cynics* (by William Desmond, 2005) and *The Cyrenaics* (Ugo Zilioli 2012). Susan Prince's fundamental and long-awaited edition of Antisthenes (*Antisthenes of Athens: Texts, Translations, and Commentary*, 824pp) was at the time of writing of this Introduction about to appear with the University of Michigan Press.

3. THE CONTENTS OF THE PRESENT VOLUME

The papers appearing in the present volume have been written specifically for it. They may be divided roughly into five sections.

First come the chapters by Voula Tsouna and Christopher Rowe, both of which deal with the Socratics and the Socratic schools in the context of Plato's dialogues. Plato is by far the most important source—more important even than Xenophon (himself now undergoing a scholarly revival)—on the Socratics of the first generation, such as Aristippus or Euclides.

In "Plato's Representation of the Socratics," Voula Tsouna contends that Plato's representation of the Socratics is very different from the way they are represented either by the ancient doxographers or by modern scholars. Through a detailed analysis of key sections of some of Plato's dialogues, Tsouna sets out to show that Plato conceived of the Socratics as a group of individuals that were influenced by Socrates but were not proper philosophers. Tsouna also examines two examples of figures often understood as Socratics, Alcibiades and Critias, showing that Plato himself did not think of them as belonging to Socrates'circle. Tsouna's chapter concludes by suggesting some reasons why Plato offers so peculiar a characterization of the Socratics within the context of his own work. The chief outcome of the chapter is that 'Socratic' is a rather more contested term than we are currently in the habit of supposing.

In "The First-Generation Socratics and the Socratic Schools: The Case of the Cyrenaics," Christopher Rowe focuses on the Cyrenaics and especially on Plato's *Theaetetus*. According to an interpretation widely accepted until some years ago, the 'subtler thinkers' of *Theaetetus* 156a3 are Aristippus and other early Cyrenaics; most scholars—Voula Tsouna among them—now reject this interpretation, and place the proper origins of the Cyrenaic 'school' two generations later. Rowe rejects both interpretations, arguing that the evidence—especially that of the *Theaetetus*, and even discounting 156a—may be good enough to justify Aristippus' reinstatement as 'founder', at least in some heavily qualified sense. Rowe's chapter bears a close relationship with those of O'Keefe and Zilioli, both of which focus on the Cyrenaics.

A second group of papers has to do with individual Socratics: Antisthenes, Aeschines and Phaedo. In "The Socratic Profile of Antisthenes' Ethics," Aldo Brancacci illustrates how ancient sources depicted Antisthenes as a fully Socratic figure who took over and further developed some key concepts of Socrates' philosophy. In particular, Brancacci insists on the fundamental idea of moral knowledge that is often, if not exclusively, understood as the kernel around which Socrates constructs his own philosophy. Brancacci argues that Antisthenes elaborated in different and original ways Socrates' idea that ethics is a form of moral knowledge.

In his chapter "Rethinking Aeschines of Sphettus," Kurt Lampe addresses the philosophical importance of a much neglected representative of the Socratics: Aeschines of Sphettus. Not much work has been done on this figure since the fundamental study by Dittmar in 1912 and some more recent papers by Livio Rossetti. It has sometimes been held that Aeschines has little to say that is of philosophical interest. Opposing this view, Lampe argues that Aeschines will have much to say if we understand him in light of the interpretative categories developed by Michel Foucault in some of his final seminars on Greek philosophy. The outcome of Lampe's argument is a thoroughly original chapter that shows the importance of both Aeschines of Sphettus as a Socratic philosopher and of Foucault as a sensitive interpreter of the Greek world.

In his chapter "Phaedo's *Zopyrus* (and Socrates' Confidences)," Livio Rossetti goes back once again to Phaedo of Elis, in particular to the *Zopyrus*, to illustrate the difference between the treatment of Socrates by other Socratics such as Phaedo (and, to a lesser extent, Aeschines of Sphettus) and his treatment by Plato. According to Rossetti, Phaedo understands Socrates not as a man who defends particular philosophical views, but rather as someone who is the master of his own passions (and resists them when they should be resisted). Rossetti concludes that if we try to reconstruct Socrates' philosophical outlook from the available evidence, we will be doomed to a failure. The proper conclusion from the evidence about Socrates is that he was a man who made self-control and rational deliberation the fulcrum of his approach to life.

A third group of chapters concerns the Cyrenaics. The two chapters belonging to this third group offer two radically alternative interpretations of the major philosophical commitments of this Socratic school.

In his paper, "The Sources and Scope of Cyrenaic Scepticism," Tim O'Keefe defends with renewed vigour the interpretation of the Cyrenaics as traditional sceptics. According to his view, the Cyrenaics deny that we can gain any knowledge of external things because of the contrast between the indubitable grasp we have of our affections and the inaccessibility of external things. O'Keefe thus maintains that Cyrenaic subjectivism is not rooted, as I myself have proposed, in the view that the world is metaphysically indeterminate. In contrast with Tsouna's and James Warren's reading, O'Keefe also argues that the scope of Cyrenaic scepticism is quite wide, including not only properties of external things, but also their identity and nature.

In my own chapter, "The Cyrenaics as Metaphysical Indeterminists," I continue to maintain my claim, *pace* O'Keefe, that the Cyrenaics may have well been metaphysical indeterminists. According to my view, the main ground for Cyrenaic subjectivism does not lie in the inevitable epistemological limitations of human beings but rather in the metaphysical structure of the external world. According to my interpretation, the Cyrenaics claim that what we are able to know is constituted solely by our affections; we cannot know the things that cause them because these lack any intrinsic ontological features of their own. I also suggest that this interpretation gives us a deeper insight into some other related aspects of Cyrenaic philosophy, in particular their invention of such neologisms as 'I am being whitened'.

The fourth group of essays deals with Diodorus Cronus and Pyrrho. In his paper "Diodorus Cronus on Perceptible Minima," Francesco Verde offers a careful investigation of the topic of perceptible minima in the atomism of Diodorus Cronus, one of the most talented members of all the Socratic schools. The question is tricky and involves a possible conceptual and historical link between Diodorus' theory of perceptible minima and Epicurus' doctrine of minimal parts. In conversation with the main interpretations available (Denyer, Sedley, Sorabji), Verde shows that a central aim of Diodorus' theory of perceptible minima could have well been to argue against the legitimacy of perceptual knowledge.

In "Pyrrho and the Socratic Schools," Richard Bett explores the reception of the Socratic schools in Pyrrho. Bett discusses the possible influence of the Megarians, the Cyrenaics and the Cynics on Pyrrho, concluding that Pyrrho was indeed influenced by the Cynics, and by some aspects of the thought of the Megarian thinker Stilpo—that is, by those aspects of Stilpo's philosophy that were themselves more Cynic-oriented. Contrary, then, to the views of some scholars, little of Socrates' thought will have come down to Pyrrho, and the little that did came through the mediation of the Socratic schools. Bett's chapter also complements those of O'Keefe and Zilioli, insofar all three pay attention to the possible mutual influence between the Cyrenaics and Pyrrho (Bett arguing for the view that there was none).

The fifth and last group of chapters is eminently philological. Recent studies of the papyrus evidence have brought to attention new material on the Socratics and the Socratic schools. Both Dorandi's and Luz's chapters explore that material, and do the hard philological work that philosophers require the philologists to do for them. Their chapters are particularly welcome in a collection on the Socratics and the Socratic schools; given the scantiness of our evidence, any additions are clearly very welcome.

Some thirty years after Giannantoni's essay,[9] "Epicureanism and Socratism: The Evidence on the Minor Socratics from the Herculaneum Papyri," Tiziano Dorandi provides us with a general overview of the evidence on the Socratics and the Socratic schools from some newly edited Herculanean papyri. In particular, Dorandi focuses on the criticism that Epicurus and the Epicureans levelled against the Socratic schools, above all the Megarians. In so doing, Dorandi not only offers new details about the philosophical commitments of the Socratic schools, but also shows how prominent those schools were in the philosophical debates of the early Hellenistic period.

Finally, in "Socrates, Alcibiades and Antisthenes in Pflor 113," Menahem Luz focuses on a second century AD papyrus roll from Egypt preserved at the Laurentian Library of Florence. The papyrus was originally edited at the beginning of last century by Domenico Comparetti, but a new appraisal is needed in light of its importance. The papyrus deals with Socrates and Antisthenes and their respective approaches to influencing the moral behaviour of a favourite pupil (most likely Alcibiades, in the case of Socrates). Luz analyses the two anecdotes and the differing views on education that lie behind them, while also trying to trace any resemblances. Luz's account of the papyrus succeeds in demonstrating its usefulness for the reconstruction of the debate about education that flourished both during Socrates' time and among his pupils.

NOTES

1. Sedley 1977.
2. I argue against this view in *The Circle of Megara*, forthcoming.
3. See Diogenes Laertius II 98. In his ground-breaking appraisal of Cyrenaic hedonism Kurt Lampe (Lampe 2014) illustrates the philosophical difference between the Cyrenaics of the first generation (Aristippus and his early followers, included his grandson) and the later sects of the Cyrenaic school, that is, the followers of Hegesias and Anniceris.

xx   *Introduction*

4. Dorandi (1999), 61.
5. A leading metaphysicians of our time, Peter Unger, has suggested that his own views were anticipated by Eubulides: "The arguments I will offer (*sc.* in his provocative essay 'There are no ordinary things') for my negative beliefs are variations upon the sorites argument of Eubulides, that incomparable Greek genius who also disclosed the paradox of the liar, the problems of presupposition and those of intentionality" (Unger 2006, 5). Diodorus Cronus' and Philo's pioneering efforts in modal and in propositional logic are often praised today by contemporary logicians: see Bobzien 1999.
6. Giannantoni's work built in part on earlier publications: for example, Giannantoni's own collection of sources on the Cyrenaics (*I Cirenaici*, Florence 1958), Decleva Caizzi on Antisthenes (*Antisthenis Fragmenta*, Milan-Varese 1966) and Döring on the Megarians (*Die Megariker*, Amsterdam 1972).
7. Other important collections on the Socratics and the Socratic schools are Giannantoni 1977 (in Italian) and Romeyer-Dherbey/Gourinat 2000 (in French).
8. See http://www.socratica.eu
9. Giannantoni 1983.

REFERENCES

Bobzien, S. (1999), 'Logic II: the Megarics' in K. Algra, J. Barnes, J. Mansfeld and M. Schofield (eds), *The Cambridge History of Hellenistic philosophy*, Cambridge: Cambridge University Press, pp. 83–91.

Dorandi, T. (1999), 'Organizations and structure of the Philosophical schools', in K. Algra, J. Barnes, J. Mansfeld and M. Schofield (eds), *The Cambridge History of Hellenistic philosophy*, Cambridge: Cambridge University Press, pp. 55–64.

Giannantoni, G. (ed) (1977), *Scuole Socratiche minori e filosofia ellenistica*, Bologna: Il Mulino.

―――― (1983), 'I Socratici minori nei papiri Ercolanesi', *Elenchos* 4: 133–46.

Lampe, K. 2014, *The Birth of Hedonism. The Cyrenaic philosophers and Pleasure as a way of life*, Princeton: Princeton University Press.

Romeyer-Dherbey G. and Gourinat, J.R. (eds) (2000), *Socrate et les Socratiques*, Paris: Vrin.

Sedley, D. 1977, 'Diodorus Cronus and Hellenistic philosophy', *Proceedings of the Cambridge Philological Society* 23: 74–120.

Unger, P. (2006), 'There are no ordinary things', in P. Unger (ed), *Philosophical Papers* II, Oxford: Oxford University Press, pp. 3–36.

1 Plato's Representations of the 'Socratics'

Voula Tsouna

Historically, when we speak of the Socratics and of the Socratic circle, we have in mind a fairly stable group of thinkers whose most prominent members were philosophers that, after Socrates' death, are alleged to have founded their own schools and who, during Socrates' life, admired and loved him, and regularly sought his company for the purpose of philosophical conversation. This is the picture emerging from the doxographers, who also attest that many Socratics, including Plato and Xenophon, wrote dialogues, the so-called Socratic dialogues, and that they shared a number of core philosophical intuitions and beliefs that have their origin in the philosophy of Socrates and have subsequently been developed by different Socratics and their schools in different ways. From a methodological point of view, a notable feature of these writings is that they are composed as *ad hoc* investigations into various subjects, conducted by means of question and answer, between two interlocutors at a time (Socrates being typically one of them), following certain dialectical rules, and with the ostensible purpose of pursuing the truth of the matter rather than of gaining victory in the debate. The protagonist of these debates is Socrates, and his interlocutors often correspond to historical personages comprising some of Socrates' companions as well.

From a philosophical perspective, interpreters generally attribute to the Socratics ethical views characterized, very broadly, by eudaemonism and also intellectualism of some sort. Regardless of ramifications and differences, all Socratics are believed to be committed to the supreme ideal of happiness, the position that virtue is an essential constituent of the good life, and the idea that virtue crucially depends or is identical with some kind of knowledge or understanding that, most of all, we ought to pursue and acquire. Historical accounts also emphasise, and rightly, the value that the Socratic writings ascribe to self-knowledge, self-control, and self-sufficiency, and also the correct understanding of virtue and of each of the five virtues belonging to the Greek canon, i.e., courage, *sôphrosynê*, justice, piety and, of course, wisdom. In metaphysics and psychology, there should be no quarrel with the historical claim that the Socratics endorse a sort of dualism involving a distinction between the body, which is related to desire and pleasure (or, as Plato sometimes argues, the irrational aspect of the *psychê*), and the soul, which may or may not be immortal and is often identified with the self. Both the major and the so-called minor Socratics recognize that, to achieve goodness, the soul must be properly educated, and this can only happen by means of philosophy; but, true pedagogy goes far beyond the traditional curriculum and may even undermine it. Besides, many Socratics problematize one form of conventional education, namely the erotic relation between a boy or youth and an older man, who is expected to play the rôle of a mentor and gradually introduce the youth to adult society and the responsibilities of a citizen. Some Socratics, notably Plato, explore *eros* as a transcendental state, while others, like Antisthenes and Aristippus detach sex from love or education, and yet others, like Xenophon, show Socrates making fun of himself by telling a prostitute that he is unavailable because of his engagement in public affairs (*Mem.* 3.11). In fact, according to the historians of philosophy, none of the first-generation Socratics was really a politician. Rather, they were interested in politics theoretically, e.g., in the sort of government that could ensure the prevalence of rationalistic ideals and the good life.

Of course, all this is well known and it indicates just the sort of approach suggested by the doxographers and developed in modern handbooks.[1] So far as it goes I believe it to be perfectly legitimate, and the same holds for endeavours to explore the philosophical engagement of various Socratics, and especially of Plato, with the views of their peers.[2] However, although the selective outline offered above serves as background for my own argument, nonetheless this latter does not have to do with the historical circle of the Socratics, but with certain interlocutors of Plato's Socrates whom I call 'Socratics' for lack of a better word, without prejudice as to whether Plato might have called them so or thought of them in that way.[3] They are characters represented as interacting with Socrates in different social occasions, geographical locations, and chronological periods. And some of them lend their name to the dialogue in which they appear—a convention followed by many authors of the Socratic circle. So, the scope of my chapter is narrow and confined within the realm of Plato's fiction: I am interested in the way in which Plato represents the aforementioned characters, not in the corresponding individuals themselves.

At the outset, it may be helpful to outline the criteria that I shall apply, jointly or severally, in order to identify Plato's Socratics. They are biographical, methodological, philosophical and psychological. In broad and general terms then, I shall call 'Socratics' the characters that, as Plato represents them, knew or liked or admired or loved Socrates; were familiar with and willing to submit to Socrates' method of cross-examination; shared with Socrates, to a greater or a lesser extent, a certain philosophical outlook; and/or indicated that they thought of themselves and of Socrates as belonging to the same circle. I aim to establish that there is a striking discrepancy between Plato's picture of the 'Socratics' and the image of the Socratics drawn by the doxographers and developed by modern scholars. While the people that the doxographers call Socratics are mainly Socratic *philosophers*, namely members of Socrates' circle who are reported to have gone on to write philosophical works and/or to found schools, the people that I call 'Socratics' are members of Socrates' circle who are influenced by Socrates but do not go on to become philosophers or teachers of philosophy. Plato, I contend, typically represents Socrates' conversations with the latter group of personages, not with the former.[4] Moreover, among the most gifted 'Socratics' depicted in Plato's dialogues are two figures conspicuously absent from the majority of historical reconstructions.

In Part I of the chapter, I argue the case at the level of drama. In Part II, I briefly outline certain philosophical views and tendencies manifest in Plato's Socratic conversations.[5] In Part III, I question the widespread assumption that Plato's representations of Critias and of Alcibiades, brilliant as they may be, nonetheless suggest that neither of these characters was an intimate of Socrates and that neither had a serious interest in Socratic philosophy and method. In Part IV, I speculate on Plato's philosophical motivation for representing the 'Socratics' in the way he does.

1. PLATO'S 'SOCRATICS' AS DRAMATIC CHARACTERS

To begin, I should like to draw attention to the following important fact. While the names of the first-generation Socratics who left behind them an institutional legacy are mentioned alongside the names of other friends of Socrates in the *Phaedo* (58c-59c), Plato never represents any major philosopher of that list as an active player in a dialectical argument. Phaedo suggests to Echecrates that he frequently participated in Socratic conversations (cf. *hôsper eiôtheimen*: 59a) but, in the narration that follows, he is mostly a listener and not a speaker. Euclides and Terpsion are, the one the putative author of the *Theaetetus*, the other the audience of Euclides' reading; however, neither of them is depicted as a conversant in the main body of the dialogue. Antisthenes and Aristippus are not identified in connection with specific philosophical views, even when it would have seemed natural for Plato to have mentioned them, nor does Plato ever depict them in debate.[6] The same goes for Aeschines. As for Xenophon, Plato does not mention him at all.[7] On the other hand, the Platonic Socrates converses with several other characters (some of whom are also found in Phaedo's list), who correspond to real people and who exhibit the behavioural and intellectual characteristics designated above, on account of which they might be considered Socratics: notably, they show familiarity and affection for Socrates, and exhibit methodological and philosophical affinities with him. Also, they seem to have some perception of themselves as Socratics in so far as some of them emphasize the fact that they are acquainted with his thoughts and methods and hold views similar to his own.[8] These are the characters that constitute my primary object of study.

At the level of drama, a first cluster of problems that arises when we try to determine who should count as a Socratic has to do with the fact that the Platonic characters under discussion strike us as quite different individuals. They are older or younger, noblemen or laymen, highly polished or rather coarse, of various professions and walks of life, with different values and aspirations, with different idiosyncrasies and characters, with a greater or lesser degree of familiarity with Socrates and his ways. How are we to decide who are Socratics and who are not? On the one hand, take the portrait of Crito, who is in Phaedo's list and is also depicted in the *Crito* in his effort to convince Socrates to escape. He strikes us as an older man (49b) of wealth and position, with a down-to-earth practical side, sensitive and decent, with the deepest affection for Socrates and the will to express that affection in deeds (45a). He tells us that he has been visiting Socrates in prison every day or almost (43a), and the shortcuts in his conversation with Socrates (47c-48b) strongly suggest that the two of them have been talking philosophy for years (cf. also 49a, e). This impression is bolstered further by Crito's unreserved assent to the principle of justice (49e). And although his philosophical credentials are controversial, nonetheless his identity as a Socratic has been unquestioned. Plato and the doxographers appear in agreement on that score.

What about Cephalus, however? Plato presents him as a very old man, who not only welcomes Socrates to his home—the setting for the *Republic*—but also regrets Socrates' rare visits and his own inability to go to Socrates more often, and urges him to 'become a companion to these lads (sc. including his own son) and frequent [the] house regarding [them] as friends and close intimates' (328d). Furthermore, by the end of *Republic* I, Socrates appears to have fulfilled Cephalus' dear wish: he has won over Polemarchus (335e) and has made Thrasymachus, who has been competing for Polemarchus' attention, abandon his case (cf. 357a). Neither the doxographers nor anyone else has placed Cephalus or Polemarchus among the Socratics. But, in my view, Plato's fiction does present them in that light. Consider Adeimantus too. Historically, he is excluded from lists of the Socratics, whereas Glaucon is included in them (D.L. II.124). Nonetheless, *Republic* II does not drive this sort of wedge between the two brothers. In fact, Adeimantus makes a major philosophical contribution, by developing further Glaucon's challenge and by enlarging the scope of the question that Socrates undertakes to answer. Their respective rôles in the argument suggest that, if the one is a Socratic, so is the other. Equally problematic is the case of Laches and Nicias, who are absent from the historical and doxographical lists, but nevertheless in Plato's *Laches* play major dialectical rôles. Both claim to be acquainted in different degrees with Socrates' personality and method,[9] and both show respect and even affection for him (and, as we shall see later, Nicias believes himself knowledgeable about Socrates' views concerning virtue as well). E.g., Laches says that Socrates 'is always spending his time wherever there is any such fine study or pursuit for young people' (180c), while Nicias adds that he too can attest to Socrates' expertise in education, since the latter has recently found an appropriate teacher for Nicias' son (180c-d).

Next, consider certain anonymous personages who make an appearance in some Platonic dialogues. The friend (*hetairos*) to whom Socrates narrates his conversation with Protagoras expresses both intimacy with Socrates and interest in the sort of conversation that Socrates had conducted with Protagoras. The two personages exchange pleasantries concerning Socrates' pursuit of Alcibiades (309a-c) and then, upon hearing that Protagoras was in town and Socrates had just left him, the friend urges him to relate what was said during that encounter (309d-310a). Clearly, there is intellectual reciprocity in this relation: Socrates says that he would be much obliged to his companion if he would listen, and the latter retorts that he would be equally grateful if Socrates would speak (310a). Even greater is the emotional and intellectual intimacy between Socrates and the 'noble friend' (cf. *gennadas*: Charm. 155d; *hetairos*: 154b) to whom Socrates reports his first meeting with Charmides and his dialectical engagement, first, with Charmides and then with Critias, the youth's cousin and guardian. Even allowing for the easy attitude of upper class Athenians towards sexual passion, Socrates' confession of what happened to him when he glanced inside Charmides' cloak has a very personal content (cf. 155b-e). And his argument with Critias is so complex and difficult that its narration would have been impossible to follow by the noble listener, unless he were deeply familiar with Socrates' way of thinking.

Turning to the age group of youths that Socrates frequents for pedagogical reasons, we find that Plato represents many of them as Socratics in the sense designated above, although later authors may or may not include them in their inventories. Of the young protagonists of the *Lysis*, Ctesippus (cf. also *Phd.* 59b) and Menexenus (also *ibid.*) often figure in the doxographical lists, whereas Hippothales and Lysis do not. In the *Lysis* however, as Socrates is making his way from the Academy to the Lyceum, it is Hippothales who summons him first to the wrestling school where he and his friend pass their time 'chiefly in conversation' (204a) under the guidance of Miccus who, as the young man reveals, is Socrates' 'friend (*hetairos*) and admirer (*epainetês*)' (204a). Socrates is close enough to Hippothales to ask him straight out whom he fancies (204b). And Ctesippus is sufficiently familiar with both to tease his friend and disclose his love for Lysis without compunction. Like their elders, they seek Socrates' company for his opinion and advice about their words and deeds—in this case, as Hippothales declares, about 'what sort of talk and what sort of action would endear one to one's favourite' (206b-c). And also, like older characters, they too as well as Menexenus, Lysis' particular friend, are eager to attend or to engage in dialogue with Socrates, who speaks, first, with Lysis on the rôle of knowledge and utility in love relationships and, second, mainly with Menexenus on the nature of friendship. Menexenus is a keen disputant (*eristikos*: 211b), whereas Ctesippus demands his share in the conversation (211c) and Hippothales listens. We cannot guess the dialectical ability of the two latter characters, but we do witness Lysis' gradual development as a conversant. At first glance at least, all four characters meet the social and psychological criteria proposed above, according to which one might say that Plato represents them as Socratics.[10] The same holds for the young protagonists of the *Euthydemus*, Hippocrates in the *Protagoras*, and Phaedrus in the dialogue bearing his name. The onus of proof should be on those who would wish to deny that these personages are represented as Socratics in a broad sense of the term.[11] To summarize my point, historians treat the above personages differently from, e.g., Crito or Glaucon, implying that the former are not Socratics but claiming that the latter are. On the contrary, Plato does not do so. Rather, he represents them all in a similar manner, as less or more sophisticated characters who converse with Socrates about all sorts of moral issues, but who are not (and not likely to become) professional philosophers in any plausible sense of the term.[12]

2. THE PHILOSOPHICAL VIEWS AND TENDENCIES OF THE 'SOCRATICS'

Let us now look more specifically at the sorts of philosophical views that Socrates examines jointly with the above characters. At the outset, it is important to stress that, with the sole exception of Crito, Plato represents *no* member of Phaedo's list as exploring jointly with Socrates central 'Socratic' topics such as the ones outlined earlier, in the introduction of this chapter.[13] Again, this fact should motivate us to revisit the common assumption that Plato gives evidence for the views of the philosophers who, after Socrates' death, founded the Socratic schools.[14]

Thus, regarding philosophical method, interlocutors friendly to Plato's Socrates appear committed to his own model of discussion: dialectical debates by question-and-answer, which have certain rules, require of the debaters to be articulate and consistent, aim to defend or refute a given claim in an effort to gain understanding, and recognise the ethical implications of that practice. Crito agrees to examine afresh the question whether or not his friend ought to escape from prison (cf. 46b-47a), although he must have known that the conclusion of the argument might well be the contrary of what he hoped for. Laches follows Socrates with some ease as he transforms the debate concerning the value of a fighting technique into a conceptual examination of the corresponding virtue (189d-190d). He gives the right sort of answer to the question what courage is (cf. 190d), answers without hesitation (though occasionally with some difficulty) the questions leading to the premises of the elenctic argument, acknowledges openly and without conceit that his definitions have been refuted and, in the end, comments about himself: 'For my part, Socrates, I am ready to continue without faltering, although I do not have the habit of such discussions. But a certain love of victory has taken hold of me with regard to what has been said, and I am truly upset if I am unable to express in just this way what I think. For I believe myself to have a conception of what courage is, but I do not know how that conception has slipped me just now, so that I have not got hold of it in speech and have not stated what it is' (194a-b). Laches then is genuine enough to admit his principal shortcoming: he has the tenacity to pursue the enquiry, but is not sufficiently accustomed to the Socratic method and does not possess a steady hold on his own thoughts. In the sense specified earlier then, he behaves like a Socratic, but nevertheless he is neither depicted as a sophisticated debater nor as being aware of the intellectualist inclinations of Plato's Socrates.

On the contrary, Nicias is represented in that manner. This second protagonist of the *Laches* says that he has often listened to Socrates (cf. *pollakis akêkoa sou legontos*: 194d), and he implicitly attributes to Socrates the idea that courage is a sort of knowledge (194c-e). Moreover, regarding ethics, Plato chooses Nicias as the speaker of the notorious passage that points to the connection between the Socratic elenchus and the examination of oneself. 'Lysimachus, you give me the impression that you only know Socrates through his father but have not associated with him except in his childhood (187e) . . . You strike me as being unaware of the fact that whoever comes very close (*engytata*) to Socrates and talks with him in person (*dialegomenos*), even when the argument may have started on a different theme, he is bound to be drawn round and round by him (sc. Socrates) in the course of the discussion until he reaches the point of giving an account of himself, both of the manner in which he now spends his days and the way in which he has lived his past life' (187e-188a). Nicias reveals that, like a true 'Socratic,' he is used to that treatment, delights in the Socratic method of investigation, and believes in the ethical benefits that derive from it (188a-c). In the same spirit, Laches says that he is willing to be cross-examined by Socrates, because he considers him a man whose words are in harmony with his deeds (188a-189b). Similar assumptions underlie Phaedo's narrative of the death scene (e.g. 88e-91c, 115a-118a), although they are not enacted in a live debate with Phaedo as a primary participant. And they are also presupposed in the pedagogical conversations between Socrates and promising youths, such as Charmides, Lysis and Cleinias.

Turning to intellectualism, which is widely believed to be a pet doctrine of Socrates and his circle, we find again the Platonic Socrates in conversation with just such men. For instance, Nicias is represented as the defender of the idea that courage is a sort of knowledge and is duly refuted by his own admissions. In the *Charmides*, as we shall see in detail, Critias advances an extreme intellectualism regarding *sôphrosynê*, temperance, that he expects Socrates to endorse but that Socrates demolishes. In a more moderate vein, Polemarchus defines justice in terms of benefiting friends whom we *know* to be good and harming enemies whom we *know* to be bad, and so he implies that that virtue is crucially dependent on a sort of knowledge; but he too concedes his errors in due course (335d-e). Besides, although many Platonic dialogues argue for the primacy of wisdom, they never represent, as it were, a professional philosopher of the Socratic circle in that rôle. Worse, Socrates debates the nature of piety with a character who is presented as an acquaintance of Socrates, but is neither socially intimate nor philosophically attuned to the latter's manner of conversation, i.e., he is not a Socratic at all in the aforementioned sense of the term. This is Euthyphro—a conceited, fanatic, and unsophisticated priest with no training in dialectical argumentation. As for another pet thesis traditionally ascribed to the Platonic Socrates, namely the unity of the virtues, matters get even more complicated, because the person with whom Socrates explores that thesis is Protagoras. I stop here, because the discussion of these last two Platonic personages is beyond the scope of this chapter. But the general point should be clear: the Platonic Socrates examines central ethical views not with the philosophers of his own circle, but with other interlocutors of all sorts; and one subcategory of these latter is the group that I summarily call 'Socratics.'

Similar remarks pertain to metaphysics and psychology. Regarding these topics too, the protagonists of Socratic conversations are not philosophers by trade, but rather more or less philosophically inclined laymen. In the *Crito*, Socrates goes quickly over well trodden ground (cf. 49a) to remind his friend of their earlier agreement that the soul is much more important than the body, is injured by the wrong but improved by the right, and hence their only concern ought to be with what is right (47a-48b). Then, relying on these assumptions, he leads Crito to reaffirm his commitment to the so-called principle of justice, which he perceives as the criterion by which one distinguishes those who think like him (i.e., the Socratics) from those who do not (49d).[15] The axiological primacy of the soul over the body plays an important rôle in Plato's representations of Socrates as a pedagogue vis-à-vis older and younger members of his circle. Nicias and Laches both concur with Socrates' contention that their current discussion concerns, really, not the technique of fighting in armour and its relevance to the optimal development of the body, but rather the correct education of the souls of their friends' sons (185c-187b). The elaborate and mystifying prologue of the *Charmides* touches upon a similar theme: beauty of the soul is incomparably more important than beauty of the body (154b-155a), and the health of the body ought to be sought as part of a holistic treatment aiming primarily at the health of the soul by means of *logoi*, arguments (156b-157c). The interlocutors use these assumptions: Critias links psychic beauty with philosophy by claiming that his ward is already an accomplished poet and a philosopher ready to engage in dialogue (154e-155a); and he also claims that Charmides possesses *sôphrosynê*, the virtue deemed equivalent to psychic health (157a). As for the youth, he shows himself eager to submit to Socrates' questioning and towards the end of the dialogue concedes that he stands in need of Socrates' incantations, his *logoi* (176b). In the second part of *Alcibiades* I, the young protagonist is led to concede that the soul rules the body and is identical with the self, self-knowledge entails knowledge of the soul (cf. 129a-131a), and self-care implies looking to the needs of the soul rather than to those of the body (132c). Furthermore, Socrates guides the lad through a short metaphysical enquiry of the self and self-knowledge (132c-133c). He suggests that the self is the better part of the soul, which is cognitive and divine, and that we know ourselves though a sort of mirroring effect, looking at the corresponding part of another person's soul and, presumably, engaging in dialogue (cf. 133b-c). The latter idea is taken up with another young character, Phaedrus, who is not listed among the Socratics either. Elements of the same idea are found in the *Phaedo* as well, where the distinction between the soul and the body and the identification of the soul with the self receive philosophical treatment. Simmias and Cebes are of course cited in the catalogues of Socratics and all three are authors of Socratic dialogues. But many think that they are not presented as Socratics within the *Phaedo*,[16] and I prefer to suspend judgement about their philosophical identity.

In politics, no one can quarrel with the historical claim that many members of the Socratic circle had a keen theoretical interest in city governance, the nature of the laws, and their relation to ethics.[17] But Plato's representations of Socrates' regular companions does not corroborate, I think, the further claim that none of his intimates had political ambitions or ever engaged actively in public affairs. On the contrary, several 'Socratics' evoked by Plato's fiction correspond to individuals with remarkable political careers. Laches was an influential aristocrat who supported the pacifist party and negotiated, together with Nicias, the six years peace bearing this latter's name; supreme commander of the Athenian fleet towards the beginning of the great war (427BC), he was subsequently prosecuted by Cleon (425BC), held high office again as general of the Athenian army and died, not ingloriously, in the battle of Mantineia (418BC). Nicias' political trajectory was similar, if more tragic. An immensely wealthy man and a redoubtable antagonist of Cleon and later of Alcibiades, he was able to overcome the pressure of the warmongers and secure the so-called peace of Nicias with the Lacedemonian coalition (421–415BC); his pacifist politics were eventually rejected by the Athenians, but even so he was appointed *stratêgos* in the Sicilian expedition and, as is well known, was executed by the enemy after the destruction of the Athenian fleet. The dramatic date of the *Laches* (*c*. 420BC) suggests that they frequented Socrates when these two men were at the height of their power (i.e., towards the beginning of the peace of Nicias). And something comparable holds, as we shall see, regarding Critias, depicted as the second protagonist of the *Charmides*, and Alcibiades, the most charismatic politician of his time. Moreover, it is not impossible that Crito had some active participation in politics on account of his social status and great wealth—features made prominent in Plato's portrait of the man. Also, we know that Phaedrus was involved in the scandal of the profanation of the

Eleusinian mysteries—probably a political act of protest—and that he was condemned to exile. Again, the *Phaedrus* represents him in conversation with Socrates at a much earlier date, when Phaedrus (allegedly, Plato's favourite)[18] appears as an impetuous youth keen on rhetoric and guided by Socrates through an amazing philosophical reflection on the nature of the soul, the transcendence of *eros*, the nature of persuasion, and the relevance of these elements to the philosophical life. There is also Chaerephon—another Socratic whom the doxographers barely mention, but whom the Platonic Socrates of the *Apology* calls 'both my own companion (*hetairos*) from youth and the companion of your democratic party, who shared this recent exile and returned with you' (20e-21a). Plato portrays him in several dialogues as fanatically attached to Socrates (*Ap.* 21a, *Charm.* 153b, *Gorg.* 447b), overfamiliar with him (*Charm.* 154d), a man of strong passions (ibid.), and an ardent democrat who took active part in the overthrow of the Thirty (*Ap.* 20e-21a).[19] To summarize, the characters I call Plato's 'Socratics,' taken in connection with their historical counterparts, suggest that the companions of Socrates did not really have a uniform attitude with regard to political *praxis*. Some of them are leaders of the oligarchic and pacifist party, others are prominent figures of the democrats, and others do not participate in high level politics at all.[20]

A word should be added about Socratic *eros*, in this context homosexual or pederastic love. We all know that the Platonic Socrates redefines this quite traditional form of early adolescent education in transcendental terms, so that the love of the older man for a beautiful youth of his choice turns to be the soul's yearning for Beauty and the other Forms. Of course, our present concern cannot be the vast subject of Plato's theory of *eros*, but only a few aspects of Plato's representations of, so to speak, Socrates' erotic inclination towards beautiful youths who have joined (or are about to join) the circle of his regular companions. In the first place, such scenes have erotic overtones, even when neither Plato's Socrates nor his object of admiration expresses the intention of entering a love relation. As Socrates confesses to his 'noble friend' in the *Charmides*, when it comes to beautiful boys, he is a 'broken stick': he cannot measure who is more beautiful because almost everyone who has just grown up appears beautiful to him (154b). In the second place, although by conventional standards older men are attracted to youths by their physical appearance, the Platonic Socrates is depicted as being far more interested in psychic beauty than in physical beauty and he suggests that, in the end, the former amounts to the extent to which a youth has a philosophical nature. Notably, in the *Charmides*, he checks Chaerephon's lustful praise of the boy's body by proposing to 'strip that very part of him (sc. the soul) and look at it first, before we look at his (bodily) form'(154e). And although he finds himself momentarily in the grip of physical desire for the lad (155c-e), nonetheless he retrieves his self-control and induces Charmides to submit to what he describes as the charm of Zalmoxis, namely the sort of *logoi* that instil temperance in one's soul (155e-157c). In similar manner, after he has stated that he is the only one of Alcibiades' lovers (*erastês*: *Alc.* 103c) who has remained, and after he has compelled Alcibiades to face his own political ambition (105a-c), Socrates urges him to attend first to his soul by 'learning what [he] ought to know before entering politics' (132b): he should endeavour, with the aid of his one remaining lover, namely Socrates himself, to be in his soul 'as handsome as he can' (131d). Plato's Socrates claims to be an expert in erotics (*Lys.* 204c) in just this sense: he can promptly recognize a lover or a beloved (ibid.) and can show the sort of conversation and conduct that improves the souls of young people (cf. *Lys.* 206b-c, 210e). Expertise in love, then, amounts to expertise in education: not the curricular education consisting in the transmission of information, but rather philosophical training helping people to think things out for themselves. Trivial as they may be, these remarks concerning Socratic *eros* crucially pertain to Plato's portraits of Critias and Alcibiades, to which I now turn.

3. PLATO'S CRITIAS AND ALCIBIADES AS 'SOCRATICS'

Are these two characters Socratics? The verdict of political history is negative, and so is the verdict of those who write the history of the Socratic circle.[21] The majority of interpreters claim that Plato's portrait of Critias in the *Charmides* is unambiguously negative and serves an apologetic purpose, namely to show that Socrates cannot have been responsible for Critias' late crimes.[22] As for the character of Alcibiades in the *Symposium*, of the great number of studies only very few highlight the emotional or intellectual links between him and Socrates.[23] On the other hand, I argue below for a different approach: in my view, both these personages are represented as 'Socratics' in the broad sense of the term that I have proposed; but also, their superbly nuanced representations point to the later development of their historical counterparts and to their future dissociation from Socrates and his circle. This section presses further the central question that I have pursued: who count as Socratics in Plato and in what way.[24]

Let us begin with the dramatic setting of the *Charmides*. In the opening scene, soon after Socrates enters the palaestra of Taureas, Chaerephon leads him to sit next to Critias. Critias then is almost the first person that Socrates greets and the one who answers Socrates' query about the current state of philosophy and of youths of great promise (153c-d). Critias' promptness to mention his ward and cousin Charmides, his easy manner when he identifies the youth's admirers, the confidence with which he tells Socrates that he will soon know how much Charmides has grown and what kind of youth he has turned to be (154b), all indicate genuine familiarity between the two men. And perhaps more than that. For Charmides remembers that, when he was but a child, he used to see Socrates in company of his own guardian (cf. *synonta*: 156a); given Critias' reputation for beauty, this remark may point not only to a longstanding friendship between the two older men, but also to an earlier love affair. In any case, Critias clearly trusts Socrates as a pedagogue, since he asks him to pretend to be a doctor and to be introduced to the lad in that capacity. He also remarks that the cure of Charmides' headache by Socrates' *logoi* will turn to be a stroke of luck for the youth; for conversation with Socrates is bound to improve his *dianoia*, his wits (157c-d). How much Critias *still* values Socrates becomes manifest in the closing scene of the dialogue as well. Despite the fact that Critias has been refuted and his *amour propre* has suffered considerably, nonetheless he urges his cousin to submit to Socrates and accept 'to be charmed by him and not forsake him through thick and thin' (176b). Equally important is the fact that Socrates appears to reciprocate. Recall his sincere and intimate encomium of his friend's forebears (cf. *ô file Critia*: 156a):[25]: given the preeminence of his ancestors, it is likely (cf. *eikotôn*: 157e), he says, that Charmides, who belongs to the same family as Critias, will be second to none.[26] For he comes from a line of poets and statesmen, whose descendants are expected to have an inclination to statesmanship as much as a sensibility to beauty.[27] Around 432 BC then, the Platonic Socrates appears to believe that Critias and especially Charmides represent a great opportunity for Athens. But he also indicates that the realization of that opportunity depends on one, important thing: the presence of *sôphrosynê* in the soul, 'from which every good and bad derives for the body and the whole of a man' (156e).

Even more manifest are the methodological and philosophical affinities between Critias and Socrates. Right from the start the former appears to recognise the importance of dialogue and its relevance to philosophy (cf. 154e-155a). And he is the only interlocutor of the so-called early dialogues represented as almost a match for Plato's Socrates. Indeed, after the round with Charmides, Socrates mentions Critias' maturity and studies (cf. *hêlêkias heneka kai epimeleias*: 162d-e) and acknowledges that he would find it much more pleasurable (*poly an hêdion*: 162e) to investigate the nature of *sôphrosynê*, temperance, jointly with Critias rather than with the younger man. If what he had hoped for was some staunch resistance to his questioning, Critias does not disappoint him. For in addition to giving yes-or-no answers, he qualifies his premises, corrects Socrates on points of method, speaks with clarity, elegance, and convincingness, and draws the red line beyond which he will withdraw his earlier assumptions and start again. An illustration is this. When Critias undertakes to defend afresh the third definition of temperance as 'doing one's own' *(to ta hautou prattein*: 161b), his first move is to reject Socrates' misleading interpretation of that definition. Next, he advances a distinction between doing (*prattein*) one's own and making (*poiein*) one's own, and he argues that the former corresponds to proper deeds (*ergon, praxis*), which are always good and pertain to virtue, whereas the latter can be shameful. Hence, he contends, there is a defensible sense in which temperance can be considered as doing one's own, namely the sense of doing good *praxeis* that benefit oneself or others

(163a-c). However, when the elenchus faces him with the choice *either* of dropping the above definition of temperance *or* of conceding that temperate people may be ignorant about the virtue that they possess (164a-c), Critias does not hesitate one moment as to what to do: 'Socrates, he says, this could never happen; but if you think that it is a necessary inference from my previous admissions, I certainly would prefer to withdraw some of them and would not be ashamed to acknowledge that my claims were incorrect rather than ever concede that a man ignorant of himself is temperate' (164c-d). Since Critias is depicted as proud and competitive, we must surmise that he has a very strong motive for admitting defeat in the argument. That motive is, in my view, his unwavering commitment to intellectualism and in particular the idea that, if we possess a virtue, we are aware of it and have knowledge (or true belief) about its nature.[28] As Socrates makes clear, the cross-examination of this sort of position lies very close to his own heart.

However, Plato's representation of the dialogue between them also highlights the telling differences in their respective approaches to intellectualism and, in general, to value. Consider the following salient features of that remarkable enquiry: on the one hand, they demonstrate Critias' consummate skill as a debater and, on the other hand, they indicate the philosophical shortcomings of his position and the inconsistencies to which he falls prey. 1. The contention under examination is that *sôphrosynê* is knowledge (or science) of itself and the other knowledges (or sciences) and of no other object (166c); in other words, it alone is a knowledge that is both reflexive and second-order. So, first, Socrates attempts to undermine the suggestion that there can be a knowledge whose object is itself,[29] by drawing analogies with other arts and disciplines and showing that they all have an object or subject matter distinct from themselves. Critias, however, successfully resists this attack. He makes the methodological point that Socrates should not have looked for *similarities* between temperance and first-order arts but for precisely the opposite, namely what is *distinctive* about temperance when it is compared with other arts (165e). He seems to be right: Socrates accepts the criticism and changes tack (166a). 2. Eventually the two characters carve out their respective positions in the debate. Socrates refers to temperance as knowledge of oneself or self-knowledge, and he intimates that this is a sort of *moral* knowledge enabling its possessor to detect *moral* knowledge or ignorance in oneself and others (167a; cf. also 174b-c). On the other hand, Critias prepares to defend in argument his contention that *sôphrosynê* amounts to a reflexive kind of knowledge: its possessor is capable of judging who is an expert and who is not, and furthermore he alone can ensure the good governance of the state (171d-172a). The knowledge of knowledge then has, as it were, technocratic as well as political aspects, but no relevance to morality. 3. There is no doubt that the Platonic Critias is deeply committed to this latter position. And moreover he has the dialectical training required in order to follow Socrates through the vertiginous twists and turns of the investigation of two major issues: the conceivability of knowledge of knowledge; and, assuming that it is conceivable, its usefulness. Here is not the place to discuss the details of this most controversial argument, which lasts almost to the very end of the dialogue. Suffice it to state that Critias' definition gets refuted for reasons having to do, specifically, with the sort of intellectualism that he espouses, i.e., the ideas that the knowledge equivalent to temperance is reflexive in the sense that it has knowledge as its object, and that, so to speak, the technocratic governance of first-order disciplines can secure happiness for its possessor and the state. However, the Socratic elenchus indicates that such reflexive knowledge is logically incoherent; and even if it were coherent, its benefits would be negligible so far as they do not pertain to good and evil, i.e., the moral dimension of human life. Nonetheless, Critias makes a final attempt to save face: assuming that the science of itself governs all other sciences, it must govern the knowledge of good and evil as well; and if so, it must be greatly beneficial (174d-e). The move is brilliant and a last tribute to Critias' intellect and skill. All the same, he is refuted: for since he has claimed that the science of science has no object distinct from itself, it cannot have as an object good and evil (174e-175a).

Enough has been said, I think, to confront again our leading question: is the Platonic Critias a 'Socratic'? I suggest that he is *no less* a Socratic than, e.g., Crito and Nicias, and in important ways he is represented as *more* familiar with the person of Socrates and his methods than they are. The Critias of 432 BC (the dramatic date of the dialogue) is an accomplished debater, with remarkable flexibility and perspicacity, with intellectualist commitments comparable to (but not identical with) Socrates' own, and with the philosophical ability to follow through one of the most complicated and difficult arguments of the Platonic corpus.[30] Socrates clearly recognizes these gifts and yields to some of Critias' interventions in a way that finds no parallel in other dialogues of the same period. Overall, Plato conveys an impression of friendship and of high quality intellectual partnership between the two men.

However, readers of the dialogue are aware of who the historical Critias was and what he did in 404 BC. And, I contend, this infamous tyrant too lurks between the lines of Plato's text and occasionally springs to the surface. (Incidentally, this holds for Charmides as well).[31] For instance, there is an unsavoury flavour in Critias' excessive praise of his young ward—'the greatest beauty' (kallistos: 154a), 'fine and good' (kalos kagathos: 154e), philosophical and most poetic (155a), and also excelling in *sôphrosynê* (157d). Such praise makes us think of unworthy lovers who flatter their beloved for their pleasure and without considering his own good. Charmides' rueful behaviour may give rise to similar thoughts. He provokes Critias by advancing the latter's conception of *sôphrosynê* without revealing his identity (161b). When he suggests that perhaps the author of the definition was really ignorant, 'he gives a sly laugh and glances at Critias' (162b). And he pushes the right button, as it were, thus forcing his guardian to take over his own rôle in the debate (162c-d). This latter could be an innocent game, but it could equally be a manifestation of a spoilt character or of supressed anger. In fact, Critias' own irascibility becomes apparent when he bursts into the conversation, abusing his ward and treating him 'the way a poet does with an actor who mishandles his verses' (162d). Later he accuses Socrates of caring about victory and not about the subject of the conversation (166c), making us wonder whether he really believes this or whether he is making some sort of psychological projection. Next, as soon as he realizes that Socrates has seriously shaken the possibility of reflexive knowledge, he tries to dodge the issue (169c). To these brushstrokes of lust, anger, pride, and ambition, finally Plato adds the language of power. In the last scene of the dialogue, the two protagonists warn Socrates that, if need be, they will use force (*bia*) to compel him to educate Charmides. But, as Socrates remarks, where force is used, it leaves no room for good counsel (176d). The upshot is that Critias' complex portrait intimates what his audience knows happened in real life: eventually, Critias severed his links with philosophy and went his own way.

Plato foreshadows a similar trajectory for the personage of Alcibiades,[32] although he depicts the latter's involvement in politics as having to do less with intellectualist beliefs and more with his ambitious drive and social arrogance (*Alc*. I 104-105e, *Symp*. 218d).[33] His early association with Socrates, his susceptibility and trust in him, Socrates' steady and affectionate guidance, and the *eros* between them were literary *topoi* for first-generation Socratics and for later authors as well. Also, there is a vast secondary literature on Plato's representation of these elements in *Alcibiades* I and, much more so, in the *Symposium*. For present purposes, I merely wish to register certain features of Alcibiades' symposiastic speech because, I believe, they lend support to the claim that he is represented as a Socratic in the sense specified above, not only in his boyhood but also in manhood, when the banquet is supposed to have taken place and the historical Alcibiades was the ascending star of Athenian politics. What is more, I submit, Alcibiades' own description of himself as one of those who 'share in the madness and Bacchic frenzy of philosophy' (*Symp*. 218b) and the contents of his speech convey the impression that, of all the characters discussed above, he is the one who has been marked by Socrates more deeply and has understood him better, although, unfortunately, not well enough.[34] His portrait in the *Symposium* leaves us with the bitter aftertaste of a lost opportunity incomparably more than in the cases of Critias and Charmides. Plato's ivy-crowned Alcibiades, in turn humorous and unbelievably moving, sets right before our eyes *both* the man he might have been *and* the reason why Plato's Socrates did bother.

He begins his eulogy in a recognisably Socratic manner, by likeness and analogy: he announces that he will only tell the truth (215a) and he famously compares Socrates to the statues of Silenus, which contain images of gods,[35] and to the satyr Marsyas, whose divine tunes had the power to entrance mankind (215a-c). However, the strange effects that he tells us he has suffered *and still suffers even now* from Socrates' *logoi* (215d) are extremely violent; no other Socratic interlocutor appears to have felt them in Plato's dialogues. When he listens to Socrates, he says, his heart leaps, his tears come forth, his soul is in turmoil, and he practically finds himself in the condition of a slave (215d-e). On the one hand, a sense of duty (cf. *dei*) and shame (*aischynesthai*) compels him to do what Socrates demands (216a-b). On the other hand, as soon as he leaves the latter's company, he is overcome by the favours of the many (216b). So he avoids Socrates like a runaway slave (216b-c), and when he sees him again he feels newly ashamed about the fact that he had admitted earlier that he is deficient and ought to take care of himself before attending to the affairs of Athens (216a). According to his account, then, Socrates stands for a moral code that the younger man does consider his own, but nonetheless regularly transgresses because of the influence of the crowd. And precisely because he finds this internal contradiction unbearable (cf. 216a), he struggles to liberate himself, shunning Socrates' presence or even wishing him dead (216c). In addition to the dominant presence of Socrates in Alcibiades' eulogy, we should also note three other elements. First, his speech is to a large extent self-referential: to praise Socrates he must talk about himself as well. Second, a feature that distinguishes him outright from other 'Socratics' in their conversations with Plato's Socrates is a high level of self-awareness: he is so very tormented because he is so fully aware (cf. *synoida*: 216b) of the conflict inside him and the reasons for it. Third, he suggests that the intensity of his suffering derives from the fact that he is unusually susceptible to Socrates' *logoi*. When he was still almost a child, he was able, as it were, to open Socrates up and see the images inside him. And, he says, 'I thought them so divine, and golden, and perfectly beautiful, and wondrous, that I simply had to do whatever Socrates bade me' (217a). Alcibiades had then decided to take Socrates as a lover for this very reason—so that the latter might help him to attain the highest possible excellence as no one else could (218c-d). In short, Plato's Alcibiades possesses this most precious gift, *a philosophical nature* (cf. 218a). It pulls him one way, the mob pulls him the other.

Alcibiades is now in his thirties and the mob has nearly won. Yet from the vantage point of his glorious maturity and transcending his own contradictions, he speaks about Socrates as none other of Plato's 'Socratics' ever did—with love, with longing, with inspiration and, most of all, with understanding. Looking back to the past and linking his memories to the present, he pierces the shell of Socrates' amorous attraction to the *kaloi*, the beautiful youths, and of his complex claim to ignorance (216d) to reveal what he has called the images of divinities within: *sôphrosynê* and Socrates' imperviousness to physical beauty (216d, 219d), his perfect indifference to externals (216e), his exemplary courage in battle (220d-221c), his endurance to cold and hunger (219e-220b),[36] but also his capacity for pleasure (220a), friendship and self-sacrifice (220d-e), his complex irony (216d-e, 218d-e), the power and tenacity of philosophical reflection (220c-d), the odd nature of his arguments (221d-222a), and their supreme value. 'When they are laid open and you get a fresh view of them from the inside you will discover, first, that they are the only speeches that have any sense and, second, that they are most divine and richest in images of virtue and intent on the most, or rather on *all* things appropriate for study for the man that is going to become beautiful and good' (222a).[37]

Alcibiades' admiration for Socrates, once at least, overcame his ambition. He reports, with clear-sighted judiciousness, that although the generals of the army were inclined to give him a prize of valour because of his social standing, he urged them to give it to Socrates instead (220e). And the latter reciprocated, pressing the generals to award the prize to the younger man (220e). More importantly, the speech suggests that, from the very beginning of their relationship, there was a genuine philosophical bond between them. For, in fact, Socrates is represented as addressing the adolescent in a more theoretical manner than other youths in other dialogues. For instance, note how he is reported to have talked to the boy when the latter confessed his feelings. Be more careful, my blessed boy: you may be deceived about me and I may be worthless. The sight of the intellect begins to see well when the sight of our eyes begins to wane. But you are far away from that point' (219a). Socrates then appears to have discerned in the boy a rare natural talent to understand this sort of talk—a promise of beauty in the soul to match his marvellous appearance. However, Alcibiades does not praise his own uniqueness but that of Socrates. 'There are many more wonderful things to find to praise in Socrates. But although there would probably be as much to say about any other of his activities and habits, this I consider the greatest miracle, that he is not like any other man, neither of the ancients nor of those now alive' (220c). Only a most intimate and insightful partner of Socrates could have summarized thus the wonder of his being.[38]

4. PLATO'S MOTIVATION IN REPRESENTING THE 'SOCRATICS': SUGGESTIONS AND REMARKS

To conclude, I wish to say something general about Plato's picture of his 'Socratics,' and also propose a tentative explanation of the disparity between that picture and the historical reconstructions of the Socratic circle. Few would disagree, I think, that the world of Socrates' interlocutors emerging from Plato's dialogues is more varied, colourful, and lively than the Socratics depicted by ancient doxographers and modern historians alike. Although several Platonic characters indicate that they perceive themselves as a group of which Socrates is the central figure (e.g., *Phd.* 59a,-c, 118a), nonetheless that group is neither static nor uniform but consists of all sorts of people and not always the same ones. Crito appears as Socrates' lifelong friend, Laches as a friendly acquaintance in irregular contact with Socrates, Critias as an intimate unlikely to remain so in the future, and so on. As for

Alcibiades, he does exactly as he pleases bursting in and out of Socrates' vicinity, drunk or sober. Regarding the discourses between Socrates and these characters, the Alcibiades of the *Symposium* is probably right to claim that they are just as entrancing when we hear them second hand, through the mouth of another, as they would have been if we attended them live (215d). Of course, all this is fiction, and my own endeavour has been to keep strictly within its constraints.

However, the point remains that the personages engaging in philosophical dialogue with Plato's Socrates do not correspond to the important philosophers whom the doxographers present as Socratics, i.e., as the followers of Socrates and the founders of the so-called Socratic schools. Rather, as documented above, the Platonic characters whom I have designated as 'Socratics' exhibit such a broad range of individuating features that it now seems questionable that they ought to be called 'Socratics' at all. To conclude, I wish to offer some tentative suggestions as to why Plato concentrated on these latter rather than on the philosophers of Socrates' circle.

In the first place, certain biographical factors may well have been relevant to his choices. His reported personal antagonism towards Antisthenes and Aristippus, as well as his literary rivalry with Aeschines and Xenophon, could explain why these people never appear in Plato's dialogues, whereas Phaedo and Eucleides do play at least honorific rôles.[39] In the second place, the discrepancy between Plato's 'Socratics' and the Socratics of other ancient authors may have to do also with the nature of Plato's literary project, as well as in his vision of Socrates and of philosophical practice. Surely, Plato must have been mindful of the reception of his dialogues by contemporary audiences. And many of his readers must have known who, e.g., Antisthenes or Aristippus were and approximately what positions they held. For just this reason the corresponding literary characters would have been, as it were, less 'plastic' than characters like Laches or Charmides, who, in the mind of Plato's public, were not associated with specific philosophical views. If Antisthenes were depicted as a participant in a dialectical argument, Plato's audience would have expected him to defend positions known to have been held by the man himself. On the contrary, Plato could mould personages like Laches, Charmides, or Phaedrus in the manner most suitable to his own philosophical purposes.[40]

In the third place, and most importantly, Plato's reluctance to show Socrates conversing specifically with the philosophers of his immediate environment is compatible with Socrates' unforgettable account of himself in the *Apology* and also with the conception of philosophy the Platonic Socrates alone appears to embody. Consider again how the doxographical and historical sources present the *Sokratikoi*, Socratics: the *followers* of Socrates, who constitute part of the Socratic succession (*diadochê*), had been taught by Socrates his ethical doctrines, and had devoted their lives to transmitting these doctrines, as each of them interpreted them, to their own pupils in their own schools. In this sort of image, Socrates appears like a guru: his words of wisdom are written down by his groupies (e.g. D.L. II. 48),[41] are received by the pupils of these groupies etc. and, in virtue of an uninterrupted line of succession, determine the Socratic identity of the latter and of their institutional establishments.

But this is exactly the kind of approach that Plato's Socrates systematically rejects. He does not lay claim to wisdom, does not hold doctrines, was never the teacher (*didaskalos*) of any student (*mathêtês*) (*Ap.* 33a), and does not conceive of philosophy as a transmission of knowledge but as a journey into one's self. His divine gift, as he often puts it, is to guide people on that journey and bring them to the point of being able to improve themselves. As we all know, in his defence speech he tells the Athenians that he has been 'searching and investigating at the god's behest anyone, citizen or foreigner' (*Ap.* 23b), has been observed carrying out that task by many regular listeners, young and old (32c)[42] and, generally, has been acting with regard to the city as a gadfly fastening upon a horse: arousing, urging, and reproaching each and every one, the whole day long, without pause (30e-31a). By his own admission then, Plato's Socrates does not set himself to converse in particular with philosophers (even philosophers sympathetic to his own outlook), but with anyone who cares to talk with him. In the dialogues discussed above, Plato illustrates just that aspect of Socrates: he shows him in dialectical conversation with all sorts of people, including the companions[43] that I have called, in a broad sense, 'Socratics.'[44]

NOTES

1. For an historical overview of the main topics and the main lines of thought of the Socratics see, most recently, Boys-Stones and Rowe 2013.
2. See, for instance, Boys-Stones 2004; Rashed 2006; and Christopher Rowe's contribution to the present volume.
3. I treat Plato's 'Socratics' as a flexible category with fluid boundaries. The reason why I use the term 'Socratics' rather than some other term is that, intuitively, it serves to drive a wedge between, on the one hand, Platonic interlocutors represented as having some familiarity with Socrates and his way of thinking (e.g., Crito, Nicias, or Glaucon) and, on the other hand, Platonic characters like Protagoras, Gorgias or Thrasymachus, who are depicted as having no regular contact with Socrates and no taste for his manner of conversation. (In my view, Euthyphro is a borderline case, whereas characters like Meletus in the *Apology* or Anytus in the *Meno* are represented as mortal enemies of Socrates and of everything he stands for). However, in the course of the chapter, it will become increasingly clear that the boundaries of the aforementioned category are so difficult to determine that it may seem preferable to abolish them altogether. The concluding section of the chapter points in just that direction.
4. Also, Plato's 'Socratics' do not behave like Socrates' pupils, whereas the doxographical accounts intimate that the Socratic *philosophers* did present themselves in that way.
5. This part of the argument harks back to the outline offered above and may prove useful for scholars who attempt to trace the views of philosophers like

Antisthenes, Aristippus or Xenophon in the dialogues of Plato. This latter, however, is not my task.
6. However, Rashed 2006 makes a very convincing case that *Phd.* 103a targets Antisthenes and, as indicated (note 2), comparable suggestions have been advanced about Aristippus, Phaedo and other Minor Socratics as well.
7. Plato's omissions on that score are consistent and systematic, and they cannot be accidental. Even if we accept that he discusses the views of, e.g., Antisthenes or Aristippus or Euclides without identifying their authors, the point remains that he does not represent these latter *in their rôle as philosophers*.
8. Phaedo's list constitutes the classic passage that doxographers and historians of philosophy have always used in order to identify the Socratics. In answer to Echecrates' query as to which of Socrates' friends (cf. *tôn epitêdeiôn*: 58c) were present in the last hours of Socrates' life, Phaedo says that, in addition to himself, 'of native Athenians there was this Apollodorus, Critoboulus and his father, Hermogenes, Epigenes, Aeschines, and Antisthenes; also there were Ctesippus from Paeania, Menexenus, and some other Athenians' (59b). Of foreigners, Phaedo mentions Simmias of Thebes, Cebes, and Phaedonides, as well as two Megarians, Euclides and Terpsion (59c). And also, he registers the absence of Plato, who, he thought, was ill (59b) and of Aristippus and Cleombrotus, who were rumoured to be in Aegina (59c). Thus the list contains fairly low-profile characters of Platonic dialogues, such as Apollodorus (narrator of the *Symposium*; cf. also *Ap.* 33e), Critoboulus (cf. *Euthydemus*), Ctesippus (cf. *Euthydemus, Lysis*), Hermogenes (cf. *Cratylus*), Terpsion (cf. *Theaetetus*), and Phaedo himself; more substantial interlocutors, such as Crito (cf. *Crito*), Simmias and Cebes (cf. *Phaedo*); Cleombrotus and Phaedonides, who are mentioned only once in the Platonic corpus, Epigenes, who is recorded twice (also in *Ap.* 33e), Menexenus, and 'some other Athenians,' who remain unnamed. Alongside them Phaedo refers to the leading philosophers of the Socratic movement, all of whom are attested to have written dialogues and most of whom (including Phaedo) are alleged to be the founders of so-called Socratic schools: Aeschines, and also Antisthenes (Cynics), Aristippus (Cyrenaics), Euclides (Megarians), Phaedo (Elians and later Eretrians), and of course Plato. Can we infer anything for the purposes of our discussion? First, it is worth noting that the catalogue is not supposed to be complete. Echecrates asks *which of* Socrates' friends were with him in prison (58c), not whether *all* of them were there. And the narrator makes clear that there were some people present whose names he does not mention. Second, Phaedo's list names people who associated with Socrates around the time of his trial and execution. Given the dramatic setting of the narrative, it would have been impossible to refer to earlier companions who had dissociated themselves from Socrates and/or who had died in the meantime. Third, I take it that one conspicuous place to look for these latter are Platonic dialogues whose dramatic date is earlier than the date of the events narrated by Phaedo, i.e., earlier than 399 BC. I want to concentrate mainly on such personages, as well as some minor figures of Phaedo's list also portrayed by Plato. On the other hand, I shall say almost nothing about the philosophers usually called 'Minor Socratics' and alleged to be the founders of the so-called Socratic schools.
9. Contrast Lysimachus and Melesias (the pair of older men in the *Laches*), who do not know much about Socrates until the conversation represented in the *Laches* takes place (180c).
10. However, Hippothales is an ambiguous character: see the analysis by Penner and Rowe 2005 *(passim)*. Also, the youth's claim that Miccus is a friend and admirer of Socrates may be ambiguous as well.

11. In other words, scholars of that persuasion would have to show, e.g., why they deny that Plato gives evidence for the Socratic identity of the aforementioned personages, but accept that he is reliable as a source for the 'Socraticism' of, e.g., Ctesippus and Menexenus (whose names occur in the doxographical lists of Socratics as well).
12. It is noteworthy that this difference is not registered in the relevant histories of philosophy. And we may well wonder why. The reason is, I think, that criteria which are external to Plato's fiction are used to assess that fiction itself as evidence for the Socratics. However, e.g., we should not infer that the Platonic Laches and Nicias are not presented as Socratics (in the sense in which I am using the term here), because they were not primarily philosophers. For Glaucon is not recorded as a philosopher either, nor is Crito, and yet we use Plato as evidence for their Socratic identity. Nor should we appeal to the fact that the former did not write dialogues, whereas the latter did (as did also Antisthenes, Aristippus, Aeschines, etc.). For even if this constitutes a criterion for the historical judgement that someone is a Socratic while someone else is not, it does not follow that that sort of criterion is applicable to Plato's representations. Therefore, we are left with the choice either of considering Socratics all the above Platonic characters in the broad and conventional sense indicated above (regardless of whether or not they occur in the doxographical sources) or, alternatively, of explaining why some of them should not be perceived in that way.
13. On the other hand, some members of Phaedo's list do occasionally explore jointly with the Platonic Socrates certain topics that appear, however, more peripheral than the ones mentioned in the introduction of this study. For instance, Ctesippus and Menexenus converse in turn with Socrates in the *Lysis*. The former also participates in the *Euthydemus*, and the latter appears in the work named after him as well. However, their dialectical rôle is not very significant and, regarding the topic of friendship, it is unclear to what extent the views examined in the *Lysis* are depicted by Plato as representative of the interests of Socrates and his closest companions. Also, we should register the protagonist of the *Cratylus*, Hermogenes, and his interest in the provenance and correctness of names. Euclides is the narrator of the *Theaetetus* (in which Terpsion also makes a brief appearance) and Apollodorus is the narrator of the *Symposium* (reported to him by Aristodemus) but, as indicated, neither has been depicted by Plato in the very act of engaging in dialogue.
14. This remark concerns Aeschines and also Xenophon, who, however, were not the founders each of his own school.
15. This is another oblique reference to the existence of a Socratic circle.
16. Some scholars believe that Simmias and Cebes are depicted as Socratics, on account of the fact that they agree with Socrates that there are Forms (a view that Plato represents as the hallmark of the Socratic circle: *Rep.* X 596a-b). Others, however, remark that the Pythagorean connection of these personages is very prominent (cf. *Phd.* 61d-e). Yet others maintain that Simmias and Cebes are represented by Plato as educated Thebans, who are familiar with Pythagoreanism and have known Philolaus during his stay in Thebes, and who are also sympathetic to Socrates' views about the nature of the soul.
17. Not only Plato and Xenophon, but also Antisthenes (*On Law* or *On the Republic, Cyrus* or *On Kingship, Menexenus* or *On Ruling, Archelaus* or *On Kingship, Statesman*), and perhaps Crito (*the Statesman, On Law*), Glaucon (*Menexenus*), and even Aristippus (*Artabazus, History of Libya* 3 vols.) wrote works on politically relevant subjects, while other members of the circle such as Euclides and Phaedo appear to have abstained from them.

18. D.L. III. 29, 31.
19. Chaerephon is also presented as the main associate of Socrates in Aristophanes' *Clouds*.
20. It is interesting that the philosophers known as the Minor Socratics probably belong to this third group. Aeschines was Athenian but, if he was active beyong his duties as an ordinary citizen, this was in the law courts (cf. his law court speeches). Antisthenes was also Athenian but his mother was a Thracian slave, and this must have precluded him from high office. Aristippus of Cyrene, Euclides of Megara, and Phaedo of Elis were not citizens of Athens and probably had no political aspirations anyway.
21. Many scholars take the evidence of Plato and the so-called Minor Socratics to corroborate the historical claim that Socrates was never closely associated with Critias or Alcibiades, was never their teacher and, philosophically, had nothing in common with them.
22. E.g., Levine 1984; Landy 1998; Schmid 1998; Lampert 2010. A notable exception is Tuozzo 2011, 52–85.
23. Exceptions include Blondell 2002, especially 93, 109; Hunter 2004, 98–112; Lane 2007; Nehamas 1998, 59–61, and 2007, 113–4, 121–2; and Nussbaum 1986, ch. 6.
24. It is useful to register the dramatic dates of the dialogues discussed below. The conversation reported in the *Charmides* is situated right after the battle of Potidaea at 432 BC, when Critias is a grown man, while the dramatic date of Socrates' narration of the dialogue to his 'noble friend' remains unclear. (The year 432 BC is also the approximate date of Socrates' dialectical encounter with Alcibiades in *Alcibiades* I, when the latter is still an adolescent). The narrative of the *Symposium* locates the events of that banquet in 416 BC, when Alcibiades was in his early thirties and had not yet been burdened by the scandal of the Eleusinian mysteries. Again, it is unclear just when the narration of sympotic entertainment in question happens, but a possible date is around 410 BC. This chronological information bears on the case made below.
25. *Contra* Van der Ben 1985, 22–23, there are no grounds for considering the encomium ironical.
26. Socrates does not express a moral imperative, but appeals to what seems likely or probable: Socrates, then, does not commit himself to the fairly common assumption that good breeding adds significantly to one's personal worth. Nor does he endorse the aristocratic ideal that the better people must come from the better families. He only articulates what society would normally expect of Charmides, but does not tell us how the matter stands according to his own judgement.
27. Cf. Tulli 2000, 260–3.
28. The exact same idea has also been expressed by Socrates early in the dialogue, when he urges young Charmides to look into himself and try to describe the virtue that he may find there (158e-159a). The gist of it is that virtue is intrinsically connected with a sort of knowledge.
29. I.e., knowledge of knowledge or science of science (cf. *epistêmê epistêmês*: 166e).
30. Of course this does not mean that he had no other affiliations, e.g., with sophists like Prodicus and with the poets of his time. So do Antisthenes, Aristippus, and other acknowledged members of the Socratic circle.
31. See also the remarks of Blondell 2002, 93.
32. The same holds probably for other Socratics as well, for many of them wrote dialogues having Alcibiades as the protagonist.
33. On the historical subtext concerning the character of Alcibiades in the *Symposium* see, most recently, Cornelli 2013.

34. However, there are crucial aspects of Socrates' personality and method that Alcibiades does not understand: e.g., see Nehamas 1998, 59–61, Hunter 2004, 107–8, and Lane 2007, who argues that, although Alcibiades' portrait of Socrates is flawed, nonetheless his encomium contains materials for the correct solution of the paradox arising from Socrates' disclaimer of knowledge.
35. However, the interpretation of Alcibiades' image is a controversial matter. On the one hand, it can be taken to point to the mistake against which much of Plato's philosophy is directed, namely the mistake of assuming that visible appearance exactly corresponds to a deeper reality. On the other hand, as Hunter 2004, 100, remarks, it is important to remember that the image of Socrates as a Silenus is Alcibiades': it is not an image which, as Alcibiades employs it, need come with special Platonic authority. Boys-Stones forthcoming (to appear in a CUP volume on the theme of the Cosmos edited by P. Horky) explores the philosophical implications of the split between outer and inner beauty suggested by Alcibiades' simile. I am grateful to the author of this latter paper for making it available to me before its publication. On the power and use of the image of Socrates as a Silenus, see Steiner 1996; and Zanker 1995, especially 32–40.
36. The argument developed by Lane 2007 indicates that these aspects of Alcibiades' encomium bridge or even undermine the outer/inner split suggested by the image of Socrates as Silenus. For the virtues that Alcibiades attributes to Socrates are virtues on display for everyone to perceive. According to Lane, they should be understood as naturalistic virtues which do not presuppose the complete control of reason over desire (as full virtue would), but result from a sort of natural energy diverted away from bodily desires and channelled towards the philosophical search for truth.
37. On the importance of what has been called Socrates' 'subjectivity,' namely the importance not only of *what* Socrates is saying but also on *how* he is saying it, see the chapters of Aldo Brancacci and of Livio Rossetti in this volume.
38. Even so, one may wonder why Alcibiades, of all people, should be the designated speaker of Socrates' eulogy? After all, despite his extraordinary beauty and natural gifts, he had been irreverent, corrupt, a traitor to Athens, and a lethal liability for Socrates. However, here too, I believe, the answer is neither historical nor biographical, but literary. Alcibiades' speech is a rhetorical *tour de force* of astonishing power and unparalleled skill. Both the eulogist and his object get under our skin so much that the speech has been standardly used as historical evidence for both Socrates and the *enfant terrible* of post-Periclean Athens. The closest comparable case of the rhetorical tradition is the *Encomium of Helen*: as Gorgias selects the most unlikely object for his *epideixis*, so Plato chooses the most unlikely subject to deliver the praise of Socrates, i.e., to use Phaedo's words, of 'the best, wisest, and most just man of his time' (118a). I owe this latter suggestion to Paul Kalligas.
39. I am indebted to David Sedley and Mauro Bonazzi for their particularly helpful remarks on this point.
40. Of course, the fact that the positions of certain philosophers were known to Plato's audience does not always deter him from portraying them in argument: Protagoras, Gorgias, Prodicus, Hippias, and also Zeno and Parmenides are cases at hand. However, these characters are represented as antagonists or critics of Socrates. They are not identifiable as his own followers. A possibility that must be considered is that, in his choice of Socrates' interlocutors, Plato may be following a sort of convention in the genre. For the philosophers who purport to be the intellectual children of Socrates rarely represent one another in conversation. One reason may be the sort of antagonism just mentioned which held, e.g., between Plato and Aristippus (see Christopher Rowe's

chapter in this volume) or between Plato and Antisthenes (see Rashed 2006). Another reason may have to do with the Socratics' intended audience. At a time when philosophy was perceived as an activity reserved for the *élite*, it might have been more appealing to depict Socrates conversing with all sorts of people, not just philosophers known to be indebted to him. I owe this latter remark to Christian Wildberg.

41. One might object that, in the *Theaetetus*, Plato represents Euclides as doing just that, namely writing down every word of Socrates, with the latter's willing help. However, Euclides does not record received wisdom, but rather a *discussion* that Socrates and Theaetetus had had and that, as Euclides judged at the time, was well worth listening to (*Tht.* 142c). It was, presumably, because he found the discussion interesting that Euclides made some notes of it when he returned to his home, then wrote it out at his leisure, and then endeavoured to polish the details of his account by asking Socrates repeatedly about the points that he could not remember (143a).
42. No philosopher other than Plato is mentioned by Socrates in his own list of friends present at his trial (*Ap.* 33d-34a).
43. I.e., not, as it were, philosophers by trade.
44. I read an earlier version of this chapter at a conference on the Socratics which took place at the small town of Soprabolzano in the Dolomites, in 26–28 September, 2013. I am very grateful to the organizer, Ugo Zilioli, and to all the participants for their comments during the session and for much extracurricular discussion outside the conference room. Also, warm thanks to Chloe Balla, Mauro Bonazzi, Myrto Hatzimichali, David Konstan, Richard McKirahan, David Sedley, and Christian Wildberg for written comments on the earlier draft. I presented the penultimate version of the chapter at the Bay Area Colloquium in Ancient Philosophy (UC Davis, November 2014), and I thank the participants and especially my commentator Christopher Buckels, for their remarks. A modern Greek translation of that version has been published in Φιλοσοφία (the journal of the Research Centre for Greek Philosophy of the Academy of Athens), and I owe a debt to the director, Dr Maria Protopapa, and the researchers of the Centre for their imput. The central argument of the chapter took its final shape after many hours of discussion with Paul Kalligas. As always, I have drawn much benefit from his suggestions and from the gift of his time.

REFERENCES

Blondell, R. (2002) *The Play of Characters in Plato's Dialogues*, Cambridge: Cambridge University Press.

Boys-Stones, G.R. (2004) 'Phaedo of Elis and Plato *on the Soul*,' *Phronesis* 49: 1–23.

Boys-Stones, G.R. (forthcoming) 'The Myth of "Inner Beauty" in Plato' (to appear in a volume edited by P. Horky on the theme of the cosmos, Cambridge: Cambridge University Press).

Boys-Stones, G.R. and Rowe, C. (2013) *The Circle of Socrates. Readings in the First-Generation Socratics*, Indianapolis/Cambridge: Hackett.

Cornelli, G. (2013) 'He longs for him, he hates him and he wants him for himself: The Alcibiades Case between Socrates and Plato,' in G. Cornelli (ed.), *Plato's Styles and Characters, Archai Supplementa* III, 140–63.

Hunter, R. (2004) *Plato's Symposium*, Oxford Approaches to Classical Literature, Oxford: Oxford University Press.

Lampert, L. (2010) *How Philosophy Became Socratic: A Study of Plato's Protagoras, Charmides, and Republic*, Chicago: University of Chicago Press.
Landy, T. (1998) 'Limitations of Political Philosophy: An Interpretation of Plato's *Charmides*,' *Interpretation: A Journal of Political Philosophy* 26 (2): 183–99.
Lane, M. (2007) 'Virtue as the Love of Knowledge in Plato's *Symposium* and *Republic*,' in D. Scott (ed.), *Maieusis: Essays in Ancient Philosophy in Honour of Myles Burnyeat*, Oxford: Oxford University Press, 44–67.
Levine, D.L. (1984) 'The Tyranny of Scholarship,' *Ancient Philosophy* 4: 65–72.
Nehamas, A. (1998) *The Art of Living: Socratic Reflections from Plato to Foucault*, Berkeley: University of California Press.
Nehamas, A. (2007) 'Beauty of Body, Nobility of Soul: The Pursuit of Love in Plato's *Symposium*,' in D. Scott (ed.), *Maieusis: Essays in Ancient Philosophy in Honour of Myles Burnyeat*, Oxford: Oxford University Press, 97–135.
Nussbaum, M. (1986) *The Fragility of Goodness*, Cambridge: Cambridge University Press.
Penner, T. and Rowe, C. (2005) *Plato's Lysis*, Cambridge: Cambridge University Press.
Rashed, M. (2006) 'Platon, Sathon, Phedon,' *Elenchos* XXVII fasc. 1: 117–22.
Schmid, W.T. (1998) *Plato's Charmides and the Socratic Ideal of Rationality*, Albany NY: SUNY Press.
Steiner, D. (1996) 'For Love of a Statue: A Reading of Plato's *Symposium* 215A-B,' *Ramus* 25: 89–111.
Tulli, M. (2000) 'Carmide fra poesia e ricerca,' in T.M. Robinson and L. Brisson (eds.), *Plato: Euthydemus, Lysis, Charmides, Proceedings of the V Symposium Platonicum, Selected Papers*, Sankt Augustin: Akademia Verlag, 259–64.
Tuozzo, T.M. (2011) *Plato's Charmides*, Cambridge: Cambridge University Press.
Van der Ben, N. (1985) *The Charmides of Plato: Problems and Interpretations*, Amsterdam: Gruner.
Zanker, P. (1995) *The Mask of Socrates*, Berkeley: University of California Press.

2 The First-Generation Socratics and the Socratic Schools
The Case of the Cyrenaics

Christopher Rowe

This chapter will be mainly about Aristippus (the elder) and the Cyrenaics. I begin, however, with two more general questions, about our use of the term 'school.'

1. ON 'SCHOOLS'

(a) Why do we not speak of a School of Socrates; and (b) why, conversely, *do* we speak of 'Socratic schools'?

(a) Let us suppose, as it appears presently to be becoming the norm to suppose, that there are two conditions for a collection of philosophers to constitute a 'school': first, the substantive views they severally hold must be at least broadly similar, or not radically inconsistent on fundamental points (or . . . ?); and second, if we follow the lead of Pierre Hadot,[1] they will share a 'way of life.' The first-generation Socratics fail to fulfil the first of these conditions—and by Hadot's argument, that their 'philosophical discourse' ought to support, and be designed to support, their 'way of life,' they are therefore likely also to fail to fulfil the second condition. My first contention in this chapter is that to a degree the first-generation Socratics do in fact, in a way, fulfil the second condition, even while patently not fulfilling the first: i.e., that they 'share a way of life' insofar as they share a common commitment to the importance, for life, of dialogue and argument. Our evidence, such as it is, is that both before and after Socrates' death the Socratics were preoccupied with argument, whether with each other, with Socrates, or with anybody and everybody else.[2] According to the doxographic tradition, they—and their successors—reached different conclusions, at a greater or lesser distance from any views that Socrates may himself have held, and lived more or less differently from him and from each other (whether their choices of life preceded their philosophical reasonings, à la Hadot, or followed them). But they all had from Socrates a common taste for, and habit of, argument. I am not hereby proposing that we should after all begin talking about a 'School of Socrates'; I am merely pointing out a possible common aspect of the first-generation Socratics that I believe may help to answer my second question:

(b) Why do we talk of 'Socratic schools,' plural (when we do not talk of a 'school of Socrates,' singular)? The 'Socratic schools' may be schools, perhaps, because to a greater or lesser extent they fulfil both the conditions Hadot proposes: the members of each separate 'school,' whether Megarian, Cyrenaic, Cynic, or whatever, share roughly the same views, and—in one way or another—they share a choice of life. But they will not all fulfil this second condition without the extension to the notion of 'sharing a choice of life' that I have just proposed; an extension that probably in any case stretches it beyond breaking-point. The Cynics fit Hadot's specifications pretty exactly: they choose and live a certain way of life, which they seem to call and/or think of as Socratic, and use philosophical discourse—to the extent that they do use it—to justify their choice. The same seems hardly true, however, of the Megarians and the Elian/Eretrian schools. Admittedly, we know even less about the Elians than we do about most of the Socratic schools, but they appear to be close in some respects to the Megarians, and like them seem to have little in the way of substantive doctrines that one could actually live by, in the way that the Cynics, or after them those other Socratics, the Stoics, live by theirs. The Megarians, for their part, seem to have been *defined* (or at some stage to have come to be defined) by their preoccupation with argument: they are the 'Eristics' and/or the 'Dialecticians.' That may be seen as another way of living Socratically; for example, we might try thinking of it as reflecting what Plato has Socrates describe as the ideal of an 'examined life.' But this is not, I think, a 'way of life' of the sort Hadot had in mind.[3]

The Socratic schools, I propose, are related to each other by family resemblance. Pierre Hadot's description fits the Cynics. The Megarian and (perhaps) the Elian 'schools,' on the other hand, are composed of individuals who are essentially defined (1) by their commitment to argument; (2) by the fact that they generally share, and work on, certain broad ideas—Megarians with each other, Elians both with each other and (perhaps, in some cases) with Megarians; and (3) by a *location*, or in the case of the Elians/Eretrians, two locations. Athens, the philosophical metropolis, would have been the exception, hosting philosophers and philosophies, from time to time, of all descriptions; some other cities, by contrast, seem to have come to host particular traditions of philosophy, in the same way that they might have their own way of making pots, or cooking, or their own types of wine. Ephesus, according to the satirical account given by Theodorus (of Cyrene) in Plato's

Theaetetus,[4] is full of fluxing Heracliteans, mimicking their great predecessor, and the cases of Megara and Elis, at least, look like more serious versions of the same phenomenon: at Elis, the *Phaedo* seems to tell us, there is already a group, maybe contemporaries, around Phaedo himself, with similar interests and a similar concern for Socrates.[5]

2. ON ARISTIPPUS THE ELDER AND (OTHER?) CYRENAICS

But what, then, about the Cyrenaics? Here the answer has to be more complicated. There used to be a vigorous dispute, recently revived,[6] about whether the Cyrenaic school could properly be said to have begun with its putative 'founder,' Aristippus the elder, evidently an established member of the Socratic circle. The predominant view now seems to be that so-called 'Cyrenaic' views, as reported by Diogenes Laertius and others, owe their formulation as such to Aristippus' grandson of the same name.[7] My own proposal is that the older Aristippus was indeed the founder of the Cyrenaic school, insofar as he was responsible, *to one degree or another* (an important qualification, as will become clear), of those ideas typically thought of, both by members of the school and by others, as 'Cyrenaic.'

The basis for this proposal is simply stated. Beneath all the potential confusions of the tradition, induced or increased by the fact that two of the main players shared the same name, there seems to be on the one hand a distinctive, indeed colourful, picture emerging from those sources that specifically mention the elder Aristippus, and, on the other, a different but rather less colourful picture that emerges from the sources that talk about 'the Cyrenaics,' or 'those following Aristippus.' At the same time, however, these two pictures—the one of the older Aristippus, the other of his grandson and the other 'Cyrenaics'—have connections with one another that are close enough to show that they are somehow related: genetically related, that is, and not just in the literal sense of 'genetically,' i.e., that some of the protagonists actually belong not just to the same city, but to the same family.

Take as a starting-point the following general statement of the philosophical views held by 'the Cyrenaics,' which I use for convenience, and to avoid any charge of bias; the author, Tim O'Keefe, holds himself aloof from any judgement about how much these views owe to Aristippus the elder.

> The Cyrenaics are notable mainly for their empiricist and skeptical epistemology and their sensualist hedonism. They believe that we can have certain knowledge of our immediate states of perceptual awareness, *e.g.*, that I am seeing white now. However, we cannot go beyond these experiences to gain any knowledge about the objects themselves that cause these experiences or about the external world in general. Some of their arguments prefigure the positions of later Greek skeptics, and their distinction between the incorrigibility of immediate perceptual states

The First-Generation Socratics and the Socratic Schools 29

versus the uncertainty of belief about the external world became key to the epistemological problems confronting philosophers of the 'modern' period, such as Descartes and Hume. In ethics, they advocate pleasure as the highest good. Furthermore, bodily pleasures are preferable to mental pleasures, and we should pursue whatever will bring us pleasure now, rather than deferring present pleasures for the sake of achieving better long-term consequences.[8]

Now let us suppose, with those who adopt a minimalist position on Aristippus, and refuse to attribute to him anything more than can be immediately read off from passages like the following (some of the most important testimonia for the present context), which attribute ideas and positions to him individually:

A. [Aristippus] was good at adapting to any place or time or person, and molding himself to fit any situation; which was why he was in greater favor with Dionysius [tyrant of Syracuse], as he always made the best of everything that happened to him. *He used to take pleasure in whatever was currently available, and did not go in for laboriously hunting down the enjoyment of things that weren't*; all of which explains Diogenes' labeling him the "king's cur." Timon sneered at him for having no backbone, and said something like this about him: "An effeminate nature like Aristippus,' *telling false from true | By groping.*"[9]

B. Aristippus seems to have spoken with very great vigor, passing on the message to people *not to labor either with going over the past or with working for the future*; behaving that way would be a sign of cheerfulness and the proof of a happy mind. He told us to keep our mind on the day, and again within the day on that part of it in which each of us acts or thinks. For only the present is ours, he claimed, not what has gone by or what is to come, for the one has passed away, and it is uncertain that the other will be.[10]

C. And whole schools of philosophers contended for the choice of a life of luxury; one of which was the so-called Cyrenaic school, which took its rise from *Aristippus the Socratic*, who *accepted the experience of pleasure and went on to say that this was the end*, and that happiness is built on it. *He said it belonged to the moment*,[11] and like the profligate he thought neither the memory of past enjoyments nor the expectation of future ones were anything to him, making the present the one and only criterion of the good, and regarding past and future enjoyments as nothing to him because the first no longer existed and the second did not yet exist and it was uncertain that they would; which is the sort of way luxurious livers behave, thinking that it's the present that does them good.[12]

If we compare these three passages, taken exactly as they stand (I have italicized some of the most important elements), with the preceding summary of 'Cyrenaic' ideas (which may or may not be Aristippean too), I think it emerges clearly enough that the ideas contained in that summary, when filled out in the necessary detail, promise just the kind of philosophical backing Aristippus' radical hedonism would require, if it is not to descend into the mere crudity[13] and opportunism with which his opponents labelled it. Either he developed these ideas, or somebody else/others did it for him.

The obvious suspects, if we adopt the second alternative, are Aristippus' philosophical successors in Cyrene. These included—so says Diogenes Laertius—his daughter Arêtê, Aethiops from nearby Ptolemaïs,[14] and Antipater of Cyrene, all taught by Aristippus himself. Arêtê taught her son Aristippus the Metrodidact, who in turn taught Theodorus [nicknamed] "the Godless, later God"; Antipater taught Epitimides of Cyrene, who taught Paraebates, who taught Hegesias "the advocate of suicide" and Anniceris "who ransomed Plato."[15] Theodorus, Hegesias and Anniceris are all said to have had their own disciples/sects. If these later figures consorted with prostitutes, as Aristippus *grand-père* supposedly did,[16] or went in for other such alleged pleasures, we do not hear about it, except as an inference from their brand of hedonism;[17] they appear, as a group, to be treated—unlike him—as developing and purveying views, rather than as choosing and living a particular lifestyle. That is, they seem to have satisfied themselves with setting out an intellectual stall, selling ideas that—so far as we can tell—have only a historical link, through the first Aristippus, to any kind of practice.[18]

But this is too simple. The state of affairs as presented to us by our meagre sources—Aristippus the elder living a certain sort of life, his successors providing some sort of theoretical backing for such a life—has two possible explanations. Either Aristippus was indeed so busy living out his ideal that he failed to justify it philosophically; or our sources, having latched on to what could be presented (perhaps by Aristippus himself) as a shockingly radical choice of life, preferred not to complicate their picture with the detail of his more technical philosophical thinking. In the first case, the credit would go to his daughter Arêtê, grandson Aristippus and others; in the second, the grandfather would at least have begun the process. Whichever alternative is correct, I think it quite incontrovertible that what we find attributed to the elder Aristippus and the epistemology attributed to 'the Cyrenaics' are, as I put it, genetically related: the first, somehow and at some point, gives birth to the second.

3. THE CYRENAICS AND PLATO

As I have said, current scholarship tends to take a different view, treating the Cyrenaic school as taking its definitive shape not before the second half of the fourth century BC, with the younger Aristippus.[19] An older generation thought differently,[20] opting heavily in favour of identifying the 'subtler' thinkers of Plato, *Theaetetus* 156a with the Cyrenaics, and therefore placing the emergence of the latter, as a recognisable group, well before 350.[21] But opinion seems to have turned decisively against this identification, thus at a stroke removing what might have been the fullest, or at least most interesting, testimonium by far available to us on the school.[22] This is partly explicable as a change of fashion, away from the kind of educated but optimistic guesswork favoured by earlier generations, towards a greater conservatism which is at the same time, within its own limits, a greater realism: if one looks carefully at what our other sources tell us about Cyrenaic views, there appear to be sufficient differences from what appears to be attributed to the 'subtler' thinkers of the *Theaetetus* to make their identification with Cyrenaics look at best speculative. Thus there is no indication in our other sources (1) that Cyrenaics "held the metaphysical doctrine of perpetual flux,"[23] as those "more subtle" people allegedly do; or (2) that, like these thinkers, they denied the duration over time of the identity of both objects and perceivers; or (3) that, as by extension the *kompsoteroi* will have done, they—the Cyrenaics—"entertained doubts about the nature of collections and our knowledge of them."[24] Indeed, at least in the second and third cases our independent evidence positively suggests that they rejected the 'subtler' thinkers' views.[25]

There are, however, at least two objections to this kind of argument, one general and the other more specific. The general objection is that it identifies the Cyrenaics too closely with a single, fixed set of doctrines (give or take the innovations of a Theodorus, a Hegesias or an Anniceris). This is the way of the ancient doxographers, the only difference being that the modern interpreter looks for the hand that did the fixing (belonging, allegedly, in this case to Aristippus the younger, mainly because there is supposed not to be enough evidence for his grandfather's having done it). But there is no reason why we should here mimic the methods of ancient doxography. Why should we suppose that the Cyrenaics plumped for a set of doctrines and stuck by it willy-nilly? That may be the style of some schools (the early Epicureans, for example), but we have no reason to assume that the Cyrenaics, or anyone else, operated in the same way. Why should we presume that they became so un-Socratic, at whatever point in their short history, as to stop thinking and start merely preaching? The idea of a monolithic Cyrenaic credo is, I would guess, a convenient fiction, reducing complex, shifting thoughts, reached through extended and continuing reflection, to a few 'opinions.' What lists of *doxai* miss out, and what we therefore miss out on,[26] is the process by which those opinions evolved, and the variations they may have gone through and/or went on going through,[27] even while in the best case the basic characterization required and produced by the doxographer may remain accurate enough to capture the eventually dominant features of a school or individual. And in the case of the Cyrenaics, there seems to me to be no good reason not to suppose that that process of evolution at least *began* with, of from, the elder Aristippus himself. According to Diogenes, there was no break between this Aristippus and his successors; if he needed a defence, especially in the form of a worked-out epistemology, who knows when that work may have started?

I myself believe, *pace* those who adhere to the current consensus, that the *Theaetetus* offers positive evidence that it had indeed already started (which would be enough for us to say, with Diogenes, that a 'Cyrenaic school' existed even in the first half of the fourth century), whether with the elder Aristippus or not.[28] The evidence consists in Socrates' presentation in the *Theaetetus* of the idea of the incorrigibility of our immediate perceptions, attributed to unnamed 'subtler,' *kompsoteroi*, thinkers—not, as I shall go on to explain, that I think these thinkers actually *are* Cyrenaics: the truth, once again, is more subtle. I cite part of the main relevant passage:

> Their starting-point . . . was that everything was motion and that there was nothing besides motion; and of motion there were two kinds, each unlimited in plurality but with different powers, one to act, the other to be acted upon. From the coming together of these two kinds of motion, and the friction of one against the other, offspring come into being—unlimited numbers of them, but twins in every case, one twin being what is perceived, the other a perception, emerging simultaneously with what is perceived and being generated along with it. Well, for the perceptions we possess names such as seeing, hearing, smelling, cooling down or burning up; the perceptions we call pleasures and pains, too, desires and fears, and others besides—an unlimited number that lack names as well as a huge range that are named. As for what is perceived, it shares its birth with the perception, so that colours of all different varieties come to be with different seeings, sounds similarly with hearings, and the other kinds of things perceived with the other kinds of perceptions, kindred births in every case.
> (*Theaetetus* 156a3-c3)

The basic idea here, of our immediate perceptions as the sole criteria of truth (if we leave aside the theory of motions in which it is dressed), and the extension of this basic idea to include pleasures and pains,[29] already in my view take us close both to what is required for Aristippus' defence and to what the Cyrenaics did at some point offer. Close enough, in any case, for it to be plausible to suppose some sort of link with thinking in Cyrene; for nobody that we know of apart from them[30] proposed anything like such an epistemology. Of course Plato might have made it up out of his own head. But if he did make it up, I think he might well himself have had Aristippus in mind; and if Aristippus and his successors read the *Theaetetus*, as they might well have done, they might then have taken a leaf from it . . . The more economical hypothesis, however, will be that they were already working in the same direction; I shall follow up this suggestion presently.

What I have called the 'more specific' objection to the case against finding engagement with the Cyrenaics in the *Theaetetus* is that it is at least partly aimed at the wrong target. Here is the way the *Theaetetus* passage just cited is introduced:

SOCRATES . . . Let me ask: do you now understand why the things in question [some puzzles that have been raised] are as they are, from what we're claiming our friend Protagoras says—or are you not yet there?
THEAETETUS I don't think I am, yet.
SOC. So I'll be doing you a favour if I help you sniff out the hidden truth in the mind of a famous man—or rather, famous men?
THEAET. You certainly will—a very big favour.
SOC. Then take a look round and make sure none of the uninitiated is listening in on us. The people I have I mind are those that think there is nothing in the world except what they can grasp firmly in their hands, and refuse to accept an action or a coming to being, or anything that can't be seen, as part of what is.[31]
THEAET. What an obstinate and thick-skinned sort of person you're describing, Socrates!
SOC. Yes, my boy, because they're quite without any cultivation at all. But others are much more subtle, and it's their mysteries I'm going to tell you about. Their starting-point, on which hangs everything we were talking about just now, was that everything was motion and that there was nothing but motion, etc.

(*Theaetetus* 155d5–156a3)

The 'mysteries' of the 'much more subtle' others are things that they never actually spelled out, but are necessary to explain (or capable of explaining) what they did spell out; similarly with 'the hidden truth,' in Protagoras' mind and the minds of other famous men, that Socrates suggests he might help Theaetetus to 'sniff out' a few lines before. In fact I think the logic of the context shows that the 'more subtle' people referred actually *are* Protagoras and the other, unnamed, famous men.

> "Shall we sniff out the hidden truth [let me call this 'the first mysteries'] in the minds[32] of Protagoras & Co.?" "Yes." "Watch out that those uninitiated [in the first mysteries] aren't listening—people who think that only what they can grasp in their hands is real." "Numbskulls!" "But not everyone is so obstinate—and it's their mysteries ['the second mysteries'] I'm going to tell you about."

This exchange, it seems to me, only makes a decent sense if the second 'mysteries' are actually the same as the first;[33] and the 'mysteries' of perpetual flux, with its corollaries, which Socrates immediately goes on to describe, do in fact turn out to be part of the truths that have already been said to be in the minds of Protagoras and other big names. These other big names are Heraclitus, Empedocles, and everyone else who was said at 152d-e to believe in flux;[34] none of them spelled out the theory of perception Socrates will expound, but it was, nevertheless, he suggests, what they had in mind. (Or as we might gloss this suggestion, it is what they need to complete their theory/make it stand up/square with actual experience.) In short, the question about the identity of the *kompsoteroi* of 156a2 reduces to the question about who the plural *andres onomastoi*, the 'famous men,' at 155d9–10 are, apart from Protagoras, and this latter question is readily answered, by reference to 152d-e.

At first sight this conclusion might appear to damage the case for a Cyrenaic presence in the *Theaetetus*, in that Plato will now no longer here be dangling some specific but unnamed grouping before us, and inviting us to guess its identity.[35] However I think the case remains strong: that is, for supposing that Cyrenaics, if not 'the Cyrenaic' position as formulated by our ancient sources, were at least part of what Plato had in his sights when he set out, in this section of the *Theaetetus*, to examine the equation of knowledge and perception—using the idea of flux, and the special theory of quick and slow motions he has Socrates build on top of it, in order to give it the best run he could for its money.[36]

Moreover, I think that a Cyrenaic presence here in the *Theaetetus* would help provide an answer to a fundamental puzzle about Plato's general strategy in dealing with knowledge as perception. Protagoras' theory, which Plato has Socrates use in order to investigate this answer to the question about the nature of knowledge, is not, of course, a theory about perception as such. It is rather, as Socrates's own presentation of it suggests, a *general* theory. If according to that theory perceptual appearances are all true (for the perceiver), so are non-perceptual appearances, for example about good and bad, just and unjust;[37] but if so, perception will not be the whole of knowledge, and it was an account of *that* which Socrates was asking for. From Protagoras' perspective, perceptual appearances will only be examples of knowledge,[38] not knowledge, and Socrates has already rejected an account of this sort from Theaetetus. So why should he, himself, use Protagoras to represent the thesis that knowledge is perception?

Here is my proposal: that Plato adopts this strategy because he has in mind not just Protagoras himself, but another form of Protagoreanism—or what he sees as another form of Protagoreanism—that actually does appear to have restricted, or at some point tried restricting, truth to perceptual experience; namely Protagoreanism in its Cyrenaic form; or, alternatively, if Plato thought of it first, what would become its Cyrenaic form.[39] That is, Plato was setting out to confront a mode of thinking that threatened to locate truth exclusively in the present perceptual experience of the individual, and thereby to rob the world of stability, predictability and order even more completely than Protagorean relativism in its original form;[40] hardly less completely, indeed, than the extreme Heracliteans satirised by Theodorus, but with the crucial difference that it was based in argument and not just in some local fashion (if there really were Ephesians who behaved as Theodorus describes).[41] One may add, finally, that the connection between the *Theaetetus* and Cyrenaic ideas was already made in late antiquity; it is by no means a modern invention.[42]

Let me clear about what exactly, in the *Theaetetus*, on my account, has Cyrenaic provenance or pedigree. Certainly not the metaphysics of flux, or the detailed theory of perception, because I take it that these would be as much 'hidden truths,' or 'mysteries,' for the Cyrenaics as they are for Protagoras and the rest (i.e., things it would allegedly be either useful or necessary for them to believe, according to Socrates, even if they didn't recognise the fact). As to whether Socrates is thinking of Cyrenaics when he has the thinkers he is criticising "den[y] the duration over time of the identity of both objects and perceivers," or "entertain doubts about the nature of collections and our knowledge of them,"[43] I am agnostic.[44] It may be that these too are Platonic inventions, designed like the others to bring out the full force and import of the thesis he is criticising (in which case, later Cyrenaics may or may not have taken them on); alternatively, Plato is reproducing or referring to things that he has heard are, or might be, taking shape in Cyrene. On the whole, given the state of our evidence, it seems safer to opt for the first alternative (giving the responsibility to Plato). What I would wish to insist on is that we should not underestimate either Plato or the Cyrenaics: Plato, by supposing that he would not have been as aware of, or curious about, contemporary developments in philosophy as he represents as his Socrates as being;[45] and the Cyrenaics, by supposing that they only properly existed when they had a written-up, systematised body of doctrine, and that their raison d'être was merely to hand that body of doctrine dutifully down through the generations. Plato, as I have argued, certainly did not underestimate them, using as he did (or on my analysis will have done) almost two-thirds of a long dialogue, in part, to respond to them and what he would rightly have seen as a revival of Protagoreanism.

A final question: if the Cyrenaics are as important to the *Theaetetus* as my hypothesis suggests, why is it that they are so thoroughly hidden under the camouflage of 'famous men' of the past, and not somehow picked out—with whatever degree of circumspection might be needed to avoid anachronism? I speculate that Plato so disliked Aristippus, and his blatantly and unashamedly hedonistic attitude to life, that he generally preferred to avoid even the most indirect reference to him and his kind. One thinks of *Phaedo* 59c3–4, when Plato has Phaedo remark that Aristippus, and one other, "were said to be in Aegina" at the time of Socrates' execution. This is surely a genuine slight, as our ancient sources say. We may contrast the case of Phaedo in the *Phaedo*, or that of Euclides and Terpsion, the Megarians drafted in, one as the putative author of the *Theaetetus*, the other as the audience for Euclides' reading; it is no accident, surely, that Euclides is said to have held some views not so very far from Plato's own (as, it seems, did Phaedo, or the Elians/Eretrians).[46]

4. CONCLUSION

Although I end with the Cyrenaics and the *Theaetetus*, that is not the intended focus of the present chapter. My subject is rather the nature and development of one 'minor' Socratic school, which begins from an allegedly 'crude' but actually quite nuanced hedonism, and either merges with or ends in an epistemology that, while providing a theoretical justification for hedonism, and while being itself of considerable philosophical potential,[47] succeeds in leaving out the nuances of the elder Aristippus' original, hedonistic position. The result, ironically, is to give him philosophical respectability, but at the cost of making his choice of life actually unliveable. An unqualified recommendation to "pursue whatever will bring us pleasure now"[48] is hardly a helpful guide for a human life. But then, if I am right, "the Cyrenaics" never themselves intended to live by it anyway.[49]

A last, and provocative, proposal, at which I have already hinted. Suppose we decide that there is just not enough evidence to allow the placing of the evolution of Cyrenaic epistemology prior to the writing of the *Theaetetus*. In that case, I suggest, given the close connection of the *Theaetetus* with that epistemology (that is, the basic model, without any extra bits tacked on), and given that a copy of the *Theaetetus* might well have made its way to Cyrene, it would not be in the least fantastical to imagine that it was actually Plato who formulated Cyrenaic epistemology; rather in the way that Euclides is supposed to have written the *Theaetetus*—except, of course, that we know that that *is* a fiction.

NOTES

1. In order to save space (since Hadot's ideas are not my main focus), I cite from Donald Zeyl's useful summing up of Hadot 2002, in the first paragraph of Zeyl 2003:

    "Philosophical discourse [Hadot says, describing Greco-Roman philosophy] . . . originates in a choice of life and an existential option—not vice-versa . . . This existential option, in turn, implies a certain vision of the world, and the task of philosophical discourse will therefore be to reveal and rationally to justify this existential option, as well as this representation of the world" (p. 3). Moreover, philosophy both as a way of life and as its justifying discourse is not the attainment and deployment of wisdom, but "merely a preparatory exercise for wisdom" which "tend[s] toward wisdom without ever achieving it" (p. 4).

2. For the evidence in relation to the first-generation Socratics, see Boys-Stones and Rowe 2013 (hereafter 'BSR'), especially chapter 10.

3. If the 'choice of life' on the part of the Megarians, say, is precisely 'philosophical discourse,' the task of that discourse is scarcely, either in principle or in fact, to justify their choice. Hadot appears to fit Socrates himself into his scheme only by attributing to him an absolute 'will to do good' (which is then subserved by philosophical endeavour). But as Zeyl suggests in his 2003, this assimilation to Kantian doctrine is "historically anachronistic and seriously misleading"; the best that can be said for it is that it is consistent with Hadot's own thesis, which is itself questionable—as a general thesis about 'ancient philosophy'—on other grounds.
4. *Theaetetus* 179e-180a.
5. This is of course not in the least to suggest that even in smaller cities philosophers all sang to the same tune: Theodorus of Cyrene, for example, is presented in the *Theaetetus* as a 'friend,' and/or pupil, of Protagoras of Abdera (friend: 161b, 168c, 168e, 171c [where Theodorus describes himself as such], 183b; pupil: 179a), whom Socrates expects him to defend (as his *epitropos*, a role Theodorus prefers to assign to Callias son of Hipponicus: 164e-165a); and he is happy to praise Theaetetus of Athens over any currently budding talent in Cyrene (143d-e). Equally, while Democritus of Abdera has some ideas that overlap with Protagoras', he is hardly in the same tradition—or, if he is, he was not seen as such by Plato (see note 41 below). City loyalty, nevertheless—stemming perhaps from a natural pride in local figures who had made their intellectual mark, especially in the ambit of the great Socrates?—seems to have been a significant factor in philosophical choices in the post-Socratic period.
6. Especially by Ugo Zilioli, in his 2012.
7. Voula Tsouna agrees: "Aristippus the Younger . . . was born around 380 BC and . . . is usually considered the first epistemologist of the Cyrenaic school" (Tsouna 1998, 129 n.18; Tsouna is evidently accepting this 'usual' view). See also, and especially, Giannantoni 1997.
8. O'Keefe 2005 (cited from the opening paragraph of the entry 'Cyrenaics').
9. BSR 2.7 = Diogenes Laertius 2.66 = Aristippus [*SSR* IV A] 51.
10. BSR 2.8 = Aelian, *Historical Miscellany* 14.6 = Aristippus [*SSR* IV A] 174.
11. I.e., was *monochronon*—translated by Ugo Zilioli, following Tsouna, as "occupying one temporal unit" (Zilioli 2012, 107-8, 155-6)—further glossed, by Zilioli, as "time-limited."
12. BSR 2.9 = Athenaeus, *The Learned Banqueters* 12, 544A-B = (continuation of) Aristippus [*SSR* IV A] 174.
13. Of which Tim O'Keefe, in the continuation of the passage from his 2005 cited above, tends to accuse the Cyrenaics in any case: "their iconoclastic and 'crude' hedonism," he says, "stands well outside the mainstream of Greek ethical thought," sc. by comparison with the 'moderate' Epicureans. Aristippus' own reputation for self-indulgence—though no doubt encouraged by the fact that his ideas endorsed the enjoyment of physical pleasure, and that he made no apology for enjoying it himself—may well have been less than fully deserved; for he also insisted on the importance of staying in control, and training oneself to do so. For the first idea, see n.18 below; on training, BSR 3.10 (= *Vatican Sayings* 34 = Aristippus [*SSR* IV A] 124).
14. That is, presumably, the city that became Ptolemaïs in the Hellenistic era.
15. Diogenes Laertius II.85-6 Here, evidently, is a real confusion in Diogenes: of the philosopher Anniceris with an earlier Anniceris, also from Cyrene—a wealthy charioteer who, according to Aelian, had once attempted vainly to impress Plato with his skill (Aelian, *Historical Miscellany* II.27). But Diogenes' mistake is useful in reminding us that Plato had a close link with Cyrene

in the 380s. "Some say," Diogenes reports elsewhere, that the same Anniceris who apparently paid for Plato's release also helped bankroll his new school, by buying for him "the small garden in [the suburb of Athens called] *Akadêmeia*" (Diogenes Laertius III.20) where "the Academy" was set up.

16. Though in fact the stories centre on just one liaison of his, with the apparently notorious Laïs (see, e.g., BSR 6.24 [for which cf. n.18 below]: "in response to the accusation that Laïs didn't love him, he said he thought the wine and the fish didn't love him either, but he enjoyed having both of them.").
17. This may be a tendentious way of putting it. We actually hear very little about Aristippus' successors at all, and especially about their manner of living; the real point is that our relatively extensive sources on the elder Aristippus emphasise both his personal commitment to the enjoyment of physical pleasure and the public nature of that commitment (for which see, e.g., the beginning of passage B = BSR 2.8 cited above: "Aristippus seems to have spoken with very great vigor."). But see following note.
18. The elder Aristippus is also decisively separated from those who came after him by his idiosyncratic take on virtue. The key to virtue, he apparently held, lay in self-control: taking advantage of opportunities for pleasure, but without ever being pleasure's slave (see, e.g., Plutarch, *Dialogue on Love* 750D-E = BSR 6.24; Diogenes Laertius 2.74–5 = BSR 3.43). There is little or no trace of such a view in accounts of 'Cyrenaic' ideas; its implication of the supremacy of reason may, perhaps, be part of what connects him with Socrates—from whom, in truth, (later) 'Cyrenaic' ideas seem in most respects utterly removed. (So much, one might say, for 'the Cyrenaics' as a 'Socratic' school, even a minor one. But as I shall continue to argue, a link still remains in their commitment to dialogue and/or argument, as well as in their continuity with the first Aristippus.)
19. See note 7. The importance attributed to the younger Aristippus, it has to be said, is purely speculative, resting on an assumed confusion in the ancient sources between him and his grandfather rather than on any concrete information on those sources themselves.
20. As amply documented by Giannantoni 1997.
21. See Tsouna 1998: "The prologue of the *Theaetetus* is situated in 369 BC and the actual year of [the] composition [of the dialogue] was probably close to that date" (p. 129, note 18). (For comparison, Aristippus the elder's dates are around 435–356; his daughter Arêtê was born, say, around 400, her son Aristippus around 380.)
22. No matter where exactly that testimonium was supposed to begin and end: see further below.
23. Tsouna 1998, 130. My whole list here in fact derives from Tsouna's argument against a Cyrenaic presence in the *Theaetetus* (behind those 'subtler' thinkers) on the grounds that it contains the most powerful and most complete statement so far of the opposition case.
24. Tsouna 1998, 132.
25. Or so Tsouna claims; but her claim is especially vulnerable, I think, to the general objection I raise in the following paragraph.
26. That is, because we rely mainly on the writers of 'opinions,' or reports derived from these; for bigger groupings, like Platonists and Stoics, we often have other and richer documentation to make up for the simplifications of collections of *Doxai*.
27. That is, apart from the divergencies the doxographers do note, as in the case of the later Cyrenaic sects; but here too a dynamic process is reduced to immobility.

28. His death in fact seems to have postdated the writing of the *Theaetetus*; but maybe he was otherwise engaged, or just disinclined—or just too doddery—to do the philosophical work?
29. On the Cyrenaics and what they may or may not have said about the potentially complicated relationship between perceptions of hard, white, loud, etc. and perceptions of pleasure and pain, see esp. Zilioli 2012, ch. 5.
30. Even Protagoras (see further below).
31. These, I take it, are the atomists, Leucippus and Democritus; see note 41.
32. Or 'of the thought': *tês dianoias*.
33. This seems also to be the way Anne Balansard takes it in her (2012, 198), if I have correctly understood her exposition of the text. (A similar interpretation may perhaps also lie behind Schleiermacher's and Burnet's uneasiness about the received text at 156a2, where the first reads *all'hoide* for the MSS' *alloi de*, the second *halloi* (=*hoi alloi*) *de*.) Contrast David Sedley's analysis of the context (Sedley 2004, 46 n. 9), which accepts Voula Tsouna's case against the identification of the *kompsoteroi* with Cyrenaics, but goes on to treat them as purely fictional. "And in fact [Sedley comments] they resemble in a non-accidental way the equally fictional reformed Giants of the *Sophist*, who, much as [the *kompsoteroi*] do, replace a crude reduction of being to corporeality with an ontology that makes interactive power (*dunamis*) the hallmark of being (*Sophist* 247c9-e6; cf. *Theaetetus* 156a6-7)." This is an important observation—one that, given my own analysis, will tend to give the Cyrenaics a toehold in the *Sophist* as well as the *Theaetetus*.
34. Hence the philosophical imperfect (implied in the Greek, in 156a4–5, by the *ên* in a6): "Their starting-point, on which hangs everything we were talking about just now, *was* [we said] that everything was motion and that there was nothing but motion."
35. But see the reference to Protagoras' 'pupils' (*mathêtai*) at 152c10 ("Has he given us this [i.e., the thesis about the infallibility of perception] as a riddle for the common riff-raff, while revealing the truth [about flux, etc.] to his students, *mathêtai*, in secret?"; cf. also the reference at 154b8 to "Protagoras and everyone who tries/sets out to say the same things as him"), as well as the singling out of the idea of the incorrigibility of present perceptions as being particularly hard to "convict of untruth" (179c-d; see n. 39 below).
36. Cf. Tsouna 1998, 125–9, which puts the best possible case for finding the doxographers' Cyrenaics in the *Theaetetus* before setting out to demolish it; and Zilioli 2012, which rejects Tsouna's demolition. My own purpose, as should by now be clear, is to bypass this dispute.
37. See, e.g., *Theaetetus* 166d ff.
38. That is, insofar as a relativist like Protagoras would accept that there was such a thing as knowledge at all—which Socrates takes the licence to imagine him as doing.
39. Some, e.g. Voula Tsouna, have insisted that there are large differences between Protagoras and the Cyrenaics. This may or may not be true, but it seems to me plain that *Plato* either did not see the differences Tsouna identifies, or chose to ignore them in constructing the *Theaetetus*. Or rather: on the account I am proposing, Plato did see one difference between Protagoras and the Cyrenaics, namely that their thesis is narrower than his. This difference is finally marked in the text, perhaps, at 179c:

"There are plenty of other ways too, Theodorus [says Socrates], of catching out the sort of claim that says any belief anyone has is true. But if one sticks to what each individual experiences in the immediate present, which gives rise to perceptions and the corresponding beliefs, it is harder to convict these of untruth. But perhaps I'm talking nonsense. Maybe they are simply unassailable, and those who claim that they are evident, and cases of knowledge, maybe are saying what is the case—and Theaetetus here was not off the mark when he proposed that perception and knowledge were the same thing." (179c1-d1)

Similarly at 183b: "So we're finished with your friend, Theodorus, and we're not yet conceding to him that every individual is a measure of all things, unless he has some sort of wisdom; nor shall we be conceding that knowledge is perception, at any rate if you pursue the thesis along the line that everything is in motion, unless Theaetetus here has something different to say" (183b7-c3). Socrates said that "there's no small battle over ['this idea of being as motion' (179d3)], and there are more than a few combatants" (179d4–5). To this Theodorus responds by identifying the idea as Heraclitean, "or Homeric, as you say, or even earlier" (179e3–4), and claiming that it is presently much in vogue, especially in Ionia, around Ephesus; but Socrates, I suggest, is still extending it (as a "secret truth") to Cyrene too.

40. That the Cyrenaics at some stage took up such a position is, I think, close to being beyond dispute (see, e.g., Sextus Empiricus *Against the Professors* VII.191–200, VI.52–3); and it is not impossible, as Aldo Brancacci suggested to me in discussion, that they adopted the label of neo-Protagoreans for themselves. Giannantoni, 1997, 197, refers (not necessarily on his own behalf) to a "contradiction between the definition of the *Theaetetus* [i.e., perception = knowledge] and the Cyrenaic principle, reported to us by Diogenes Laertius [II.93], that 'perceptions do not always tell the truth [*tas aisthêseis mê pantote alêtheuein*].'" But this 'principle' as reported by Diogenes is part of a longer sentence, the other part of which may well affect its sense; even if it does not, it is possible to think of more than one way that the Cyrenaics could consistently have held *both* that all perceptual experiences are infallible *and* that "perceptions do not always tell us the truth": thus, e.g., even if my perceptions are infallible, they do not tell me anything about yours.

41. Some have found connections in this part of the *Theaetetus* with the atomists. Thus, e.g., Francesco Ademollo writes, in his 2011, "Democritus held *both* that physical objects are constituted by ever-moving atoms *and* that sensible qualities are subjective and 'customary.' Thus he could be legitimately regarded as embodying the very convergence of flux and relativism that characterizes the *Theaetetus*' theory [sc. of perception?]" (p. 227). However (1) it is far from clear that Democritus' atoms are in fact 'ever-moving' (so that his membership of the community of fluxers is at best dubious); (2) that Democritus says sensible qualities are 'customary' hardly makes him a relativist (the point being, at least in relation to senses other than sight, that they reduce to properties of atoms: "by convention sweet [etc.], in truth atoms and void," fr.9); and (3), as Ademollo himself acknowledges (p.227, n.103), there are two other theories (Empedocles', and Timaeus', in the *Timaeus*) that seem to share the general shape of the *Theaetetus*' and the Democritean accounts of vision, and will need ultimately to be taken into account in the interpretation of the *Theaetetus* context. (I myself think it quite likely that the general idea that vision involves the active participation, as it were, of both observer and object was in the air in the fifth/fourth centuries, along with some version of flux theory: Socrates in the *Theaetetus* is not, I think, just making it up when he says more or less *everybody*, except the Eleatics, is a fluxer of some kind—as even he himself is, up to a point, in the *Symposium* . . .) (4) [still *contra* Ademollo] I think we need Democritus to play the role of the 'uninitiated' at

Theaetetus 156e, as he can if we follow Aristotle at *Metaphysics* A4, 985b4–5: "Leucippus and ... Democritus say the elements of things are the full and the empty, calling the one being and the other non-being"—and if we suppose that in "those that think there is nothing in the world except what they can grasp firmly in their hands, and refuse to accept an action or a coming to being, or anything that can't be seen, as part of what is" [*Theaetetus* 156e4–6] we are to supply "anything [*like actions, etc.*] that can't be seen" (I note too that for Democritus all perception will, in effect, reduce to touch, or something analogous to touch: contact between collections of atoms). Finally (5), a last point against Ademollo, it would be odd to have Democritus turning up in any substantial way among the chorus adduced, in whatever way, to support the identification of knowledge with perception, when his fr.11 specifically says that perception is only a *skotiê* kind (*idea*) of knowledge (*gnôsis*), as opposed to the genuine (*gnêsiê*) kind, which is presumably an understanding of what underlies perception; final proof, surely, that he was no relativist, and that Plato would have had little reason to treat him as such.

42. See the anonymous *Theaetetus* commentator (the relevant material is conveniently supplied in Tsouna 1998, 147–8). There is also a certain amount of circumstantial evidence: (1) the choice of Theodorus of Cyrene as Socrates' initial, and recurring, interlocutor; (2) Socrates' *praeteritio* on the subject of philosophical developments in Cyrene (143d); and (3)—perhaps, though this is entirely speculative—Socrates' mention of his mother's name, Phaenaretê, at the beginning of his discussion with Theaetetus: if Plato is at least in part talking about Aristippus and his successors, it creates a nice parallelism that one of the latter, and his daughter, should be called Arêtê (Platonic puns can survive change of length in a vowel: see *Phaedrus* 244c-d). Socrates' description of his activity as midwife, and his mother's son, would also be given extra point by the implicit contrast with Aristippus', and his daughter's, role as teachers.
43. See the first paragraph in the present section.
44. Both positions, I note, are independent of flux and the fluxing theory of perception, which so far as the *Theaetetus* is concerned remain 'hidden truths' or 'mysteries,' introduced and/or invented for the occasion.
45. I.e., at the beginning of the conversation in the *Theaetetus*, written down by Euclides.
46. E.g.: "Euclides used to apply Parmenidean ideas ... He claimed that the good was one thing called by many names: sometimes wisdom. Sometimes god, at other times intellect, etc. What was opposite to the good he eliminated, saying that it [what was opposite to the good] didn't exist" (Diogenes Laertius II.106 = BSR 2.33); "The Eretrian philosophers ... placed all good in the mind, and in that acuteness of the mind by which the truth is discerned" (Cicero, *Academica* II.42, tr. Yonge).
47. Recognized by Plato—on the account I have offered —as a threat needing to be countered; but see also, and more positively, O'Keefe 2005 (as cited above, p. 528), and Zilioli 2012, which sees the Cyrenaics as espousing a version of metaphysical indeterminism; for a recent epistemological approach with more than a passing resemblance to what the Cyrenaics' either was or could be, see Galen Strawson, "Real naturalism," *London Review of Books* vol. 35 No. 18, 28–30 (26 September 2013).
48. I cite again from O'Keefe's summary of the Cyrenaic position (see the first section of the present paper).
49. My thanks to all those present at the original colloquium at Soprabolzano for their comments on the first draft of this chapter, which they will find altered in some respects beyond recognition. (I also thank Terry Penner, in particular,

for his lucid response to a second draft.) The chief burden of the objections made by Richard Bett and Voula Tsouna to the first draft was that I took too little notice of the detail of ancient reports about Cyrenaic doctrine; and I have made significant concessions in this regard. But I am not inclined to retreat at all from my contention that it is misleading to give too much attention to attempts—like those in modern encyclopaedias—to summarize a school in terms of set doctrines, when especially in the period in question criticism, counter-argument, reformulation and evolution would have been likely to make any statement of a group's position always potentially subject to revision and restatement. I admit, of course, that doubting the accuracy of even those very meagre sources that we possess may mark the beginning of a slippery road. But I am unrepentant about trying to guess at something of the larger picture that in my view undoubtedly lies behind them.

REFERENCES

Ademollo 2011. Francesco Ademollo, *The* Cratylus *of Plato: A Commentary*. Cambridge: Cambridge University Press.
Balansard 2012. Anne Balansard, *Enquête sur la doxographie platonicienne dans la première partie du* Théétète. Sankt Augustin: Akademia Verlag:.
Boys-Stones and Rowe 2013. George Boys-Stones and Christopher Rowe, *The Circle of Socrates: Readings in the First-Generation Socratics*. Indianapolis: Hackett.
Giannantoni 1997. Gabriele Giannantoni, 'Il concetto di *aesthesis* nella filosofia cirenaica.' In Giannantoni and Michel Narcy (eds), *Lezioni socratiche*, 179–203. Naples: Bibliopolis.
Hadot 2002. Pierre Hadot, *What Is Ancient Philosophy?* Translated from the French by Michael Chase. Cambridge, MA: Harvard University Press.
O'Keefe 2005. Tim O'Keefe, *Internet Encyclopaedia of Philosophy, s.v.* 'Cyrenaics'.
Sedley 2004. David Sedley, *The Midwife of Platonism*. Oxford: Oxford University Press.
Tsouna 1998. Voula Tsouna, *The Epistemology of the Cyrenaic School*. Cambridge: Cambridge University Press.
Zeyl 2003. Donald Zeyl, Review of Hadot 2002. *Notre Dame Philosophical Reviews*, 9 June.
Zilioli 2012. Ugo Zilioli, *The Cyrenaics*. Acumen: Durham, UK. Reprinted for Routledge, 2014.

3 The Socratic Profile of Antisthenes' Ethics

Aldo Brancacci

Because of his philosophical authority and recognized philological skills, Panaetius' judgement on the Socratic dialogues available to him was famous in antiquity, though its correct interpretation has long been the subject of controversy: "of all Socratic dialogues, Panaetius believes that Plato's, Xenophon's, Antisthenes' and Aeschines' dialogues are *aletheis*; he is in doubt about Phaedo's and Euclides' dialogues; he rejects all the others."[1] It is interesting to note here that in the first part of this statement the four major Socratic philosophers are mentioned in a particular order: Plato, the most important philosopher, Xenophon, the most important scholar, Antisthenes, the second most important philosopher, and Aeschines of Sphettus, the second most important scholar. One controversial aspect of the first part of the statement is the use of the adjective *aletheis* in place of the more common *gnesioi*, the term more often employed by the ancients when discussing the authenticity of literary works. Some scholars have interpreted *aletheis* as substantially equivalent to the latter, while others have wanted to give it the meaning of "reliable."[2] The entire structure of Panaetius' judgement, however, with its characteristic tripartition into works he accepts, works he is in doubt about, and works he rejects, clearly has to do with judgements about authenticity. The characteristic division of the latter two groups of dialogues into "uncertain" and "spurious" (where the use of technical philological vocabulary is evident) is clear evidence that the label *aletheis* similarly refers to the issue of authenticity. If we were to suppose that *aletheis* meant "reliable" (though in fact *pistos* would be more normal in this sense), the presence of the second category, "doubtful" dialogues, would be hard to explain—a point that seems to me not to have been raised in previous discussions of the issues. In fact, generally speaking, "doubt" in such contexts tends to refer to the authenticity rather than to the reliability or otherwise of a text. But did Panaetius have at his disposal hermeneutic criteria that were advanced enough to allow him to distinguish between Socratic dialogues that were reliable and those that were not, and then to go on to declare certain dialogues "dubious" from this point of view? It is hard to believe so, both for intrinsic reasons and, above all, because a real debate about Socrates and his legacy, of the sort familiar in the modern era, did not exist in antiquity. One could translate *aletheis* more simply as "truthful," and suppose Panaetius to be saying that the Socratic conversations reported or created by Plato, Xenophon, Antisthenes and Aeschines were truthful in terms of their content, style and character: that he had doubts about the truthfulness in this sense of the productions of the second group of authors; and that he rejected those of the authors in the third group. While this seems to me a better solution, it is liable to the same difficulty as the first one, and in a way collapses into it. But that first solution is, in this version, at least theoretically possible. Certainly, one could pose the question whether dialogues that seemed to Panaetius doubtful or to be rejected altogether, so far as concerned their claim to being "truthful," despite their being dialogues attributed to Socratics, could then still have appeared to him as properly authentic. A third possibility would be to understand "truthful" in its ordinary sense, but also as linked with "authentic": truthful because authentic. In any case the tripartite structure of Panaetius' judgment corresponds too closely with the standard ancient division of works into genuine, disputed and spurious for that fact to be ignored. Plato and Xenophon, joined also by Antisthenes, and occasionally Aeschines, are much the most quoted sources in all of ancient literature for Socrates' life and thought. So far as concerns the use of *aletheis* in place of *gnesioi*, one may note that here, as in all places where we find similar terminology, the talk is obviously not about Socrates' own works (since he wrote nothing), but about works written by other authors in which Socrates is a protagonist; and from this perspective, *aletheis* could well have been a more appropriate term to use than *gnesioi*.

Panaetius then most likely wants to say that, among the large collection of Socratic dialogues at his disposal, only Plato's, Xenophon's, Antisthenes' and Aeschines' were written by the authors whose names they carried, and are to be treated as truthful, *aletheis* for this reason; the Socratic dialogues attributed to Phaedo and Euclides appear to him to be of doubtful authenticity, and all the others—for example, those that Diogenes Laertius suggests can be attributed to Crito, to Simon and to other characters belonging to the Socratic circle—are spurious works, not written by recognised Socratics but by some other unidentified authors.

I have quoted this testimony (many others could be added), because it reminds us that Antisthenes was an author of Socratic dialogues, of sufficient repute for Panaetius not just to place him in the company of figures of such calibre as Plato and Xenophon, but to mention him just after them. In fact, Antisthenes was the author of a particularly large number of dialogues, as is shown by the catalogue of his writings transmitted by Diogenes Laertius (and probably compiled by a Stoic living in the Hellenistic era).[3] It is legitimate to identify the division of Antisthenes' works that Diogenes Laertius gives us with that known to and accepted by Panaetius. It contains as many as sixty-three titles, and even if occasionally there are works that belong to a different formal genre (the two surviving discourses, *Ajax* and *Odysseus*, an *Apology of Orestes*, a book of *Problems*), most of them are

Socratic dialogues, as the indirect tradition concerning such works confirms. An examination of the catalogue shows that Antisthenes' literary production had a slant that was predominantly ethical (volumes two to five in Diogenes' arrangement contain ethical and political dialogues) and logical-dialectical (volumes six and seven), but he was also interested in rhetoric, and in *phusika*, that is, in theology and in eschatology, and also in issues of a literary-critical sort, especially to do with Homer.

Antisthenes' thought stems from, and bears the mark of, Socrates' philosophy. It is generally recognised that the link between ethics and knowledge so fundamental to Socratic philosophy is also the focus of discussion in Plato's early dialogues, even if in terms that ultimately justify the claim Plato himself attributes to Socrates, most notably in the defence speech in the *Apology*, namely that he was never anybody's teacher, and never taught or transmitted doctrines to any student.[4] In an earlier period, well before the composition of Plato's earliest dialogues,[5] the same link between ethics and knowledge appears in Antisthenes' own philosophy, where it leads to the elaboration both of a concept of knowledge and of ethical reflection of a distinctive sort, the character of which is confirmed by a significant number of fragments and testimonia. Founded on the function of *logos* as the only instrument we have for grasping, implementing and transmitting the truth, Antisthenes' approach involves a "dogmatic" interpretation of Socratic *dialegesthai* as opposed to the "aporetic" interpretation proposed by the early dialogues of Plato.

The reconstruction of these issues takes us back to the contentious nature of the debate about the education of the young and the role of philosophy in political life. From a theoretical point of view, it is important in highlighting an original and significant outcome of the Socratic view on knowledge; from a historical point of view, it has the merit of reminding us that there were many participants in the debate: first and foremost Plato, but also Isocrates, and, in a far from insignificant role, Antisthenes himself. It is also a fact that in the period immediately after Socrates' death, Antisthenes was considered the most representative member of the Socratic circle, as is evident from Xenophon's testimonies in his *Symposium*.[6] And it should be noted that he was considered such both by his supporters, who saw in him the outstanding representative of Socraticism,[7] and by his detractors, who argued vigorously against him for the very same reason. It is also revealing that Antisthenes should be the only one among the Socratics who in his turn wrote polemical works explicitly directed against the sophists, against Isocrates and against Plato.[8] Immediately after Socrates' death, he was again the only Socratic to open a school in Athens, as is shown particularly by polemical references in Isocrates, who gives pride of place in the proems to a series of his works (particularly *Against the Sophists*, dated to about 393 BC, and *Helen*, dated around 385 BC) to attacks on Antisthenes and his teachings. And after all Euclides lived, not in Athens, but in Megara; and it was to Megara that Plato thought it opportune, after Socrates' death, to retire for a period of time.⁹ Aristippus did not open a school, but instead travelled incessantly,[10] while Aeschines of Sphettus is known throughout the ancient tradition for not having founded a school and not having professed any sort of teachings.[11] At a time when the star of Plato had not yet risen, it was Antisthenes, whether because of his age (he was seventeen years older than Plato), his more consistent previous relationship with Socrates, or the fact of his having opened a school in Athens,[12] who seems to have appeared as the Socratic closest to the master and as his designated successor, in a way that would subsequently be made part of the official record by Xenophon's depiction of him in the *Symposium*.[13]

I have reconstructed elsewhere the contents of Isocrates' testimony, in relation both to his attacks on Antisthenes and to the controversial relationship between Antisthenes himself and Isocrates. I shall therefore restrict myself to repeating that Isocrates launched numerous and prolonged attacks on Antisthenes, the oldest of which is contained in the introduction to *Against the Sophists*. There Isocrates reacts polemically to a work of Antisthenes in a way that allows us to reconstruct some aspects of the work. The term *epangelma*, which in sophistic culture defines the programme governing the teaching of a single person or a group,[14] is here used several times to indicate the structure of Antisthenes' teaching. When one also takes into account how specific Isocrates' polemical references are, it is hard not to believe that in the introduction to his work Isocrates had in mind a particular work by Antisthenes, most probably *Truth*, on whose title Isocrates appears to play in an allusive fashion,[15] pouring scorn on the search for the truth as conducted by his competitor, and returning with ironic intent to the same theme several times over.[16]

The markedly direct tone of Isocrates' references, laying out a series of educational concepts typically adopted and developed by his adversary, makes it relatively straightforward to reconstruct Antisthenes' *epangelma*. The whole introductory part of Isocrates' work is built on the criticism of Antisthenes' concept of knowledge and of the distinction between opinion and truth that underlay it. If one takes Isocrates' references together as a whole, it is clear that this distinction operated both in the logical-dialectical sphere, insofar as it was involved in the discussion of contradiction in speech-making, and in the ethical sphere, where it led to the identification of truth with the "science of things practicable."[17] Such a science was taken as the goal of a search aimed at grasping the truth, and was then identified with virtue, itself considered as the *sine qua non* of happiness. In light of this significance, both logical and ethical, of the concept of science, the other two central themes in Antisthenes' *epangelma* against which Isocrates directs his barbs reveal themselves: the teachability of virtue, and the consequent promise to "make immortal" the recipients of such teaching. Antisthenes uses the same term, "immortal," elsewhere too, to describe those who find themselves in an indefeasible moral condition.[18] From an important testimony in Dio Chrysostom, we can infer that the theme of the pursuit of truth in Antisthenes was linked to that of a man's search for the way to achieve perfect virtue, or *kalokagathia*; and that this search was identified by Antisthenes with doing philosophy. Thus the concept of science, which according to Isocrates' testimony has as its subject the very general field of "things practicable," is more precisely an exaltation of what must be known to be a man of "perfect virtue." From this perspective a man is uneducated not when he is ignorant of the contents of a traditional education, but when he lacks moral knowledge.[19] From this, it follows that the "search for truth" pursued by Antisthenes was fully identified with *philosophein*, and treated as inseparable from the notion of science or *episteme*. The latter, in turn, was based in logical-dialectical study, but has an ethical goal, given that its possession would guarantee the formation of the virtuous man. In this sense, it represented the condition of that logical-rational foundation of education by means of *logos* and, more specifically, through the theory of the *oikeios logos* to which numerous Antisthenean fragments refer.[20]

Obviously, this *logos* of Antisthenes' was neither the sophistic *logos* nor the instrumental, creative *logos* celebrated by Isocrates as the "guide of all actions and all thoughts," but rather a *logos* able to reveal rational structures where ordinary language remains at the level of the equivocal and incorrect; it thus fundamentally excludes the possibility of a conception of education, *paideia*, that does not identify it with *philosophein*. Antisthenes' account of knowledge and education, which was presumably expounded and justified in *On Education* or *On Names*, in five books, is expressed tersely in a fragment restored from Epictetus, where we find the formula "the beginning of philosophical education is the examination of names."[21]

I have shown elsewhere that the doctrine of *episkepsis ton onomaton* was the interpretation Antisthenes offered of Socratic *exetazein*, making it equivalent to an analysis of terms that aimed, by the end of the dialectical process, to determine their meanings and provide proper definitions. This is in accord both with our doxographical information, which records Antisthenes as the first philosopher who offered a definition of *logos*, and with the theory of the *oikeios logos*, insofar as this can be reconstructed on the basis of the testimonies of Isocrates and of Aristotle and his commentators.[22]

It is important to emphasise how different Antisthenes' conception of the dialectical method is from that attributed to Socrates by Plato, in two fundamental respects.[23] For the Platonic Socrates the starting point of the process of examination or *exetazein* is the response to the request for a definition, understood as a concrete dialogical situation in which the fundamental ethical principle is implemented—the principle, that is, that *dialegesthai* is itself the highest good.[24] The process, on this account, will go on renewing itself indefinitely. According to Antisthenes, by contrast, the *oikeios logos* came to represent the final step in the *episkepsis ton onomaton*, and as such would close the discussion once and for all. Thus the *exetazein* that the Platonic Socrates identifies with *dialegesthai* was for Antisthenes an appropriate method, not itself identical with the highest good, but understood rather as the founding principle of philosophical education. There was, accordingly, no absolute identification of the sort made by the Platonic Socrates between *exetazein* and *dialegesthai*. Alongside a theory of dialectic, Antisthenes developed a related but distinct theory of rhetoric, whose model was Odysseus, understood as the versatile or *polutropos* hero, able to converse with his fellow human beings by the varied use of his powers of expression.[25] Hence, too, Antisthenes' elaboration of a theory of the wise man, from which there derived, above all, the distinction between the knowledgeable and the ignorant, paralleling that between *spoudaioi* and *phauloi*, and the consequent requirement of the former to transmit their knowledge to the latter.[26] This is an outcome which, while representing the opposite pole to the positions attributed to Socrates by Plato, is no more than we should expect in light of the preeminent role attributed by Antisthenes to *phronesis*, that is, to the cognitive-rational element in man.

The very close connection between dialectic and logic, on the one hand, and ethics on the other is also shown by the fact that it is the same conceptual distinction, between *oikeion* and *allotrion*, that governs both fields. This distinction replaces the traditional distinction between true and false in the first field, while it combines and overlaps with that between good and bad in the second. Ancient tradition has passed down to us different formulations of Antisthenes' fundamental ethical *diairesis*, though all are strictly binary: there are two ethical principles, and between them *tertium non datur*. The principle is passed on from Antisthenes to the Cynics: as Diogenes Laertius tells us in the appendix to Book VI dedicated to illustrating the views common to Antisthenes, Diogenes and the Cynics (and also the links between Cynicism and Stoicism), "like Aristo of Chios, they [sc. the Cynics] consider indifferent all that is intermediate between virtue and vice."[27] This doctrinal view is well illustrated by the use of the famous Homeric verse *Odyssey* IV.392, also attributed to Socrates and Aristippus, and is also documented by Diogenes, and it is very likely, so far as the Cynic tradition is concerned, that such a use derives directly from Antisthenes.[28] The late but precious source Arsenius tells us that when "asked to say what things one should learn [*manthanein*] from Homer, Antisthenes answered 'what has happened for good and bad within the house' [= *Odyssey* IV.392]."[29]

Antisthenes specialised in Homeric studies, as attested both by the titles of the writings listed in Diogenes' catalogue and by a number of fragments. The answer attributed to him by Arsenius is explained by the fact that the Homeric verse contains, in a way, his fundamental ethical distinction, grounded on the two-term opposition between *agatha* and *kaka*; one also has to keep in mind that on his view the objects of *manthanein* (a verb that for Antisthenes has strong ethical connotations, as a function of *episteme*) were the fundamental truths of ethics, the study of which he identifies with the doing of philosophy.[30] It is thus easy to understand the verse's being chosen by Antisthenes to represent the primacy and the goal of ethical investigation. This accords with the fact that Antisthenes devotes a work specifically to the very episode of Proteus from which the verse comes: the *On Proteus*, a work listed in the ninth volume of Diogenes' catalogue.[31]

Antisthenes' *diairesis* is represented sometimes by the simple opposition between *oikeion* and *allotrion*, that is, between what is "appropriate" and what is "extraneous" to man, sometimes in the more complete and precise formulation transmitted to us by Diogenes Laertius, on Diocles' authority: "good things are fine, bad things shameful. Think of everything that is bad as alien."[32]

The concepts of good, bad, fine and shameful define the field of ethics for Antisthenes, and the relationships that Antisthenes establishes between them are emblematic of Socratic philosophy. On this point Antisthenes and Plato are in full agreement, as is shown by comparing Antisthenes' formula with Socrates' *Apology*, where the Platonic Socrates sets out the same things as constituting the ethical field.[33] Antisthenes sets up an opposition between *agathon* and *kakon* that also holds between *kalon* and *aischron*; he then goes on—and this is the fundamental point—to identify *agathon* with *kalon* and *kakon* with *aischron*. It is this second move that properly defines Socratic ethics, safeguarding as it does the absoluteness of moral value and cutting off at the root any deviation towards relativism or, still worse, immorality. On this point too there is full agreement between Antisthenes and Plato, as is evident as soon as one compares Plato's *Gorgias*, from which it also becomes clear that the main aim is to counter the sophists.[34] Polus there explicitly rejects the identification of fine with good and of bad with shameful,[35] and the theoretical reasons behind such a rejection are developed by Callicles, whose intervention turns out to represent the paradigm of the sophistic account of virtue and excellence. (There is a similar, though partial, correspondence on this point between Antisthenes and Xenophon.)[36] We have a fragment from Themistius too, very probably drawn from the *Archelaus*, which helps clarify further the meaning of Antisthenes' fundamental ethical distinction. In this text, in response to an interlocutor who asks him what happiness for man consists in, Antisthenes' Socrates answers that happiness lies

> "in knowledge (*scientia* = *episteme*), in a correct grasp (*prudentia recta* = *phronesis*), and in truth (*veritas* = *aletheia*); in an understanding of what is and of what is not in one's power; in an understanding of what one must study to make things so [i.e., in one's power], and what one must practise in order to avoid their not being so."[37]

Knowledge, wisdom and truth are here mutually entailing. The fundamental point at which they converge is the knowledge of what is in man's power: such knowledge requires effort and commitment, to allow one's grasp to remain "correct," and to ensure a continuing awareness not only that rational activity alone is in one's power, but also that nothing else is. The requirement is to adapt to both these facts, the second no less than the first, and to keep both firmly in view in one's attitudes and in one's behaviour, even when this may be supremely difficult to achieve. The fundamental point is that things are *allotria* in relation to the only thing that is *oikeion*, belonging or appropriate, to man: *phronesis*, or more generally, the values represented by the rational principle that allows one to act appropriately in the face of external reality, which, in itself is "alien." In this sense, and for all the reasons stated, *phronesis* is a matter not only of awareness or recognition of this principle but of its actual implementation.[38] So far as *episteme* is concerned, the definition given in the Themistius passage fits with the sense of the term that emerged from the testimonies of Isocrates and Dio Chrysostom, with their characteristic linking of the cognitive and the ethical.

The third term mentioned in the passage is truth, a recurrent term in Antisthenes' works, and a very important one; so important, indeed, that it forms the title of one of his Socratic dialogues. Given that in Antisthenes truth is obviously contrasted with *doxa*, one assumes that just as the latter stands for appearance/opinion,[39] truth would generally indicate the possession of knowledge, and so, in the final analysis, the awareness that one knows; which in its turn, for the reasons stated, is also moral certainty. I believe that Antisthenes' "truth" is, then, ultimately both what is true and also what, for that reason, "matters."

The treatment in the appendix to Diogenes Laertius, Book VI, of the affinity between Cynicism and Stoicism traces Cynicism back to Antisthenes as well as to Diogenes. This link is confirmed not only by an established biographical and doxographical tradition, but by direct references from a number of Stoics, who often referred to Antisthenes, whether in their treatment of logic or of ethics, in the context of the interpretation of the poets or in that of theology, thus showing that they regarded him as an important *auctoritas*. The connection is also demonstrated by Antisthenes' formulation of the end in ethics. This is reported to us in two different forms: according to Diogenes Laertius, "the Cynics concede that the end is to live according to virtue, as Antisthenes says in the *Heracles*; similarly to the Stoics, for there is a certain affinity between these two schools."[40] We might be tempted to treat this formulation of the end as a retrojection to Antisthenes of a concept properly belonging to Hellenistic philosophy (though in fact it is already in Aristotle). From this perspective, one might think of the formulation attributed to Antisthenes as having been manufactured by taking an ethical concept that is central for Antisthenes—that is, of virtue—and inserting it into the later doxographical framework of the definition of the highest good, or end. Yet any such hypothesis neglects an important fact. Plato's Socrates, in the *Apology*, also speaks of the highest good, and does so in a theoretical context crucial for understanding the significance he attaches to the proper choice of the philosophical life:

> "If I say to you that *this* is the greatest good for a man—to discuss virtue every day, and those other things about which you have heard me

conversing and testing myself and others, and if I say that the unexamined life is not worth living for a man, you will believe me even less."[41]

Even if this passage is much richer in detail than the blunt formulation attributed to Antisthenes by the doxographers, one notes that here too the content of the highest good is located in daily discussion of virtue. Moreover the concept of life, *zên*, so important in Antisthenes' formula, has several parallels in this and other passages of the *Apology*, in which Socrates speaks insistently of living, and of living a life of philosophy, before introducing the climactic, and indubitably Platonic, concept of the *anexetastos bios* as one that is not truly liveable for a human being. This concept is in its turn consistent with that of the kind of *exetazein*, understood as an endless and indefinite process, which is fundamental for Plato's interpretation of Socrates; whereas Antisthenes, as we have seen, considered *exetazein* as an instrument leading us to the conquest of truth and the firm establishment of science or knowledge. In line with this, in the *Odysseus* Antisthenes presents the *amathia* from which Ajax suffers as the worst evil for man.[42] The reliability of Diogenes Laertius' testimony about Antisthenes' formulation of the highest good is further confirmed by the fact that it cites a work by Antisthenes, the *Heracles*, which was a highly important source for the doxographers on Antisthenean and Cynic ethics. And since we know that the *Heracles* was a Socratic dialogue, it is legitimate to suppose that the context from which the doxographical evidence was taken would have been similar to that of Plato's *Apology*: one in which Antisthenes' Socrates will have explained the significance of his choice of a philosophical life by establishing the primacy of the concept of virtue. The formula of the end transmitted by Diogenes Laertius also allows us to make a connection between Antisthenes' position and that of the Stoics. It is the same Diogenes Laertius who reports for us Zeno's definition of the end: "Thus Zeno was the first, in his work *On the Nature of Man*, to define as end a life in conformity with nature, that is to say, a life according to virtue, because nature leads us to virtue."[43] As this says, Zeno considered "living in harmony with nature" as equivalent to "living according to virtue"; that is to say, equivalent to Antisthenes' conception (the rest of the Zenonian formulation revealing a further elaboration of the concept of nature to which Zeno probably arrived as a consequence of his polemical exchanges with Polemon).[44] Stobaeus attributes a slightly different formulation to Zeno, *homologoumenos zên*, which may perhaps be considered as the original wording, "with nature" representing a later, or clarifying, addition made by Zeno himself.[45] In fact, since *logos* represents the true nature of the man, the formulation *homologoumenos zên têi phusei* could equally express the idea of *homologoumenos zên* in the—clearly Socratic— sense of living in harmony with one's own *logos*. And in this connection, it is interesting to note that the Socratic principle of living consistently with yourself and your own *logos* is expressed by Antisthenes himself, both with the concept of *homonoia heautoi*, "unanimity with oneself," and with the claim that the greatest advantage deriving from philosophy (a concept close to that of end) was *to dunasthai heautoi homilein*, "the ability to converse with oneself."[46]

On the other hand, we learn from Clement of Alexandria and Theodoret that for Antisthenes the end consisted in a *bios atuphos*.[47] Quite probably the two formulations, the one reported by Diogenes Laertius, the other reported by these two later but doxographically important authors should not be considered as alternative but rather as complementary; it is also to be supposed that the two quotations come from similar contexts, if not from the very same context.[48] As a matter of fact, we know Antisthenes claimed that "obscurity (*adoxia*) was a good thing, equal in rank with labour," giving Cyrus and Heracles—obviously in his works on the two figures—as models of the life of labour.[49] The analogy between *adoxia* and *atuphia*, "lack of arrogance," is evident; these concepts, and that of *ponos* too, should be considered as complementary features of the central concept of *aretê*, giving it a peculiarly Antisthenean slant.

Antisthenes' conception of virtue is complex and cannot be completely reconstructed here; that would require a separate study. Nonetheless, it is possible at least to highlight the key features of Antisthenes' teaching on the subject, the starting point of which is the Socratic equation of virtue with knowledge. This equation explains both the principle that virtue depends on *phronesis*, and the consequent idea of the teachability of virtue. And this means that virtue for both women and men is one and the same, a thesis whose cultural significance should not be underestimated. The other characteristic element of Antisthenes' conception deriving from the same equation is the principle according to which it is logical-dialectical investigation that allows the isolation and definition of moral concepts, by acquiring in each case the corresponding *oikeioi logoi* that in the ethical context represent the *analotoi logismoi*, the impregnable reasonings capable of guaranteeing the immovability of moral convictions and the correct understanding of things. It follows from this that once acquired, virtue cannot be lost; and it is worth noting here that the problem whether virtue can be lost would be discussed by the Stoics too, and that Cleanthes would adopt Antisthenes' position on the matter.[50] For these same reasons, virtue is an *anaphaireton hoplon*, "a weapon that cannot be taken away,"[51] a thesis that develops, and makes more radical, the Socratic principle that the one who knows the good always acts accordingly. Antisthenes' ethical doctrine is, as all this suggests, predominantly intellectualist; how could it be otherwise with a Socratic philosopher? From this point of view Antisthenes' position is not in principle different from Plato's, despite all the many differences between them. However the actualisation, the practical realisation, of virtue for Antisthenes also requires the presence of a certain moral tension, labelled *Sokratikê ischus*, "Socratic strength,"[52] or simply "effort" (*ponos*), which adds a thoroughly ascetic element to the intellectualist analysis. Contrary to what is usually believed, or used to be believed, such an element is governed by *phronesis*, just as the whole movement towards the actualisation of virtue is governed by the principles theoretically defining it; it does not constitute value in itself, but only insofar as it is aimed at an ethical goal, which is again only possible under the directing role of *phronesis*. This emerges with particular clarity from a long fragment from Themistius, relating to the meeting between Prometheus and Heracles, the central part of which, after a eulogy of *phronesis*, and of the preeminent role accorded to *phronesis* in Antisthenes' philosophy, runs as follows:

> Antisthenes says that Prometheus told Heracles 'your efforts are devoid of any value, because you look after human things and have neglected to take care of what is more important than they are. In truth, you will not be a man of complete virtue until you learn those things that are higher than men. If you learn those things, then you will know human things too; but if you learn only human things, you will go wandering like a brute animal.'[53]

Weber supposed many years ago that the characters had been switched in Themistius' Syrian version, and that in Antisthenes' original version it was Heracles who was admonishing to Prometheus.[54] Weber thus showed his failure to understand that this fragment captured Heracles in the initial phase of his own "wandering," and that the lessons he was receiving from Prometheus were in fact precisely those by means of which Antisthenes intended to change, and radically change, the meaning of the *ponoi* that an old tradition attributed to the son of Alcmene and Zeus.[55] The change consisted in transforming physical trials, expressions of pure physical strength, into trials aimed at precise goals of an ethical order, and so expressions of *phronesis*:[56] ethical goals without which the *ponos* or labour has nothing whatever to do with the "Socratic strength" celebrated by Antisthenes in another fragment,[57] and without which, indeed, it is in itself *vilissimus*.[58]

Here, in effect, Antisthenes was dealing with the theme of conversion from a state of lower consciousness to a state of higher consciousness, which is also the great theme of philosophical erotics,[59] and is ultimately connected with the justification of the equation between *agathon* and *kalon*, characteristic of Socrates' thought and then also explicitly adopted by Antisthenes. In the *Heracles*, once having identified the simple emotional drive of a *ponos* unshaped by clear goals, but still a powerful motor of human action, Prometheus indicates the way that leads to the sublimation of *ponos* and diverts human inclinations away from material or morally neutral and meaningless goals, redirecting them instead towards the desire for the fine and the good. This is the meaning of the equation *agathon* = *ponos* that the doxographers tell us was to be found in the *Heracles*.[60] A further confirmation of this is provided by a small but important fragment, generally neglected, in which Antisthenes is quoted as saying "those who mean to become virtuous must exercise their body with physical exercises, the soul with reasoning."[61] Here it should be noted that the higher level of "exercise" (*askein*) has as its object the soul itself, and it is the soul, as Antisthenes himself makes clear in his long self-presentation in Xenophon's *Symposium*, that is for him the most precious and privileged element in man.[62] Such "exercise" thus becomes substantially the same thing as *philosophein*. This is the source of the theory of the wise man (which the Stoics inherit from Antisthenes), based as it is on the same close relationship between the cognitive-rational and the ethical underlying Antisthenes' particular understanding of the notions of knowledge and education. The attribute constantly identified in the wise man is that of his *knowing*, and this knowledge of his turns out to cover the two fundamental areas on which Antisthenes' concept of science or *episteme* is focused: it is only the wise that are skilled in dialectic, only the wise that are virtuous. For this reason "whatever the wise man does, he does it virtuously."[63] At the same time, the wise man is infallible, and only he is able to teach his knowledge to others. The opposition between opinion and truth is mirrored by that between the mass of ordinary men and the wise, between the ignorant and the knowledgeable: equipped as he is with the knowledge of what is *oikeion* and what is *allotrion*, of what needs to be done and what needs to be avoided, the wise man appears endowed with perfect spiritual balance, a model of all the virtues.

I believe the present study shows the positive and strongly assertive character of Antisthenes' moral thought. It is this that explains the warm reception given to Antisthenes' Socrates by Stoicism,[64] while an Arcesilaus will find his inspiration in the Platonic Socrates, albeit one passed through the sieve of a reading that will brutally transform his tendency to *aporia* into "withholding of judgment," *epoche*.[65] However, this general picture lacks nuance, and needs qualification. Truth was always for Antisthenes the object of a search (*zetein*), as Isocrates tells us, and Dio Chrysostom too speaks of a quest for the way to becoming fine and good. "One must build walls in one's own impregnable reasoning,"[66] says one of most characteristic propositions of Antisthenes' ethics, reminding us how, while the logical-dialectical approach may formulate the *oikeioi logoi*, still it requires knowledge in all its aspects to transform the *oikeioi logoi* into walls high enough to keep out epistemological relativism,[67] and how this is also, still, a matter of individual, personal effort (note the reference to 'one's own' reasoning in the passage just cited). Similarly, in the passage from Themistius, the final clauses, "*to make things so . . . in order to avoid their not being so*," indicate the need for a personal engagement, as does the reference to "study" and "exercise"; one notes, too, the imperative "*Think* of everything that is bad as alien" in that formulation of Diocles' reported by Diogenes, which gives it a distinctly protreptic tone of advice or prescription. In Antisthenes' ethical fragments there are many imperatives, gerundives, modal verbs, all expressing the identification of the possible as the norm, the discovery that moral value consists in possibilities not yet realised. Antisthenes is clear that "virtue is something that has to be worked at,"[68] a principle that could appear at first glance to contradict that ubiquitous intellectualism of his, whereas in fact it is no more than its necessary complement, expressing as it does an awareness that value has to be realised in material action. There is thus a path to be travelled on man's part, between knowledge and virtuous action itself, a path that on each occasion reaffirms and realises the value of truth. This is the space in which ethics emerges in its theoretical dimension, which seems to me to carry a double connotation, and in the light of which it I think it would be interesting to re-read all of Antisthenes' fragments, including those that are most well-known: on the one hand those that express the motif of the stability of a virtuousness thought of as actually achieved, and on the other, those that reveal how virtue, even when rationally grounded, still requires effort—because ethics itself is a process, an aspiration, ultimately involving something that *should* be done but is yet to be done.

NOTES

1. Diogenes Laertius II 64.
2. For an overview of the various views on this matter, see Alesse 1997, 280–7.
3. See Patzer 1970, 127.
4. See Plato *Apology* 33a-b.
5. As for Antisthenes' chronology, see Giannantoni 1990, volume IV, 199–201. The most likely and commonly accepted dates for the philosopher's birth and death are 444 and 365 BC respectively.
6. See Eucken 1983, 26.
7. See the appreciative judgement of the historian Theopompus of Chios cited at Diogenes Laertius VI 14 (= SSR V A 22 = 115 F 295 *FGrHist* II B 600). For further information about Theopompus and his relationship to Antisthenes' thought, see Brancacci 1992b, 4052 n. 10; 4053 n. 11. For Antisthenes' influence on Theopompus, see Momigliano 1931.
8. The *Peri ton sophiston phusiognomonikos*, of which we have a single fragment (= SSR V A 62), was directed against the sophists. The *Satho* was directed at Plato: see Brancacci 1993a for further information about Antisthenes' arguments against Plato. As for the works against Isocrates and the logographers, they range from the more general *Peri ton dikographon*, which seems to have taken up a general stance opposed to the writers of forensic discourses, to '*Isographe or Lysias and Isocrates*' (combining polemic and sarcasm directed against Isocrates and Lysias), to *Pros ton Isokratous amarturon*: all these works are aimed at ridiculing Isocrates' activity as a logographer and at drawing the attention of the Athenian people to a period of the rhetorician's activity that he considered, or wanted to be considered, permanently over. See Brancacci 2011a.
9. There are two chronologies relating to Euclides, arising from contrasting ancient testimonies: according to one he was born in 450 BC and died around 380 BC, while according to the other his death occurred between 368 BC and 360 BC. See Döring 1972, 73–74 and 88 (Döring supports a chronology between 435 BC and 365 BC); Montoneri 1984, 39–44; Giannantoni 1990, volume IV, 33–36.
10. See Giannantoni 1990, volume IV, 139, for the evidence relating to these travels.

11. For Aeschines' biography, see Natorp 1984a and Humbert 1967, 214–21. See also Themistius, *Oration* XXXIV 5 (= *SSR* IV A 166), where he claims that Aeschines, being interested only in ethics, remained a member of "the true Socratic chorus"—in which, besides Aeschines, Cebes, Phaedo and Aristippus were also included. Antisthenes is, one notes, implicitly excluded from this grouping, since his philosophy was not restricted to the ethical. See Giannantoni 1990, volume IV, 585–96. On the new fragments of the *Miltiades* restored from the Oxyrhynchys papyri, see Lausdei-Rossetti 1981.
12. The ancient tradition indicates the Cynosarges as the school where Antisthenes taught: see Diogenes Laertius VI 1. The connection made by the same ancient tradition with the later Cynic school (starting from the name of the Cynosarges gymnasium itself) is, however, highly dubious. As for the Cynosarges itself, which is likely to have existed at least since the second half of the fifth century BC, and which a well-attested tradition says was frequented by those not of pure Athenian blood (of which Antisthenes was one), see Billot (1993), who has shown, on the basis of a new examination of the documents, that nothing prevents us from supposing that Antisthenes actually taught at the Cynosarges.
13. Cf. Xenophon, *Symposium* 4, 61–4 (= *SSR* V A 13).
14. See, e.g., Plato, *Protagoras* 319a, *Euthydemus* 274a; Xenophon, *Memorabilia* 1.2.7; Aristotle, *Nicomachean Ethics* X.9, 1180b35.
15. On this work, see my note in Brancacci 1990, 25–27.
16. That Antisthenes was the object of Isocrates' polemic in paragraphs 1–8 of *Against the Sophists* is an old assumption, beginning with Usener 1856, 12 and Überweg 1861, 257. Already a widely accepted view, supported by Reinhardt 1873, 24–28, Natorp 1894b. 2540, Raeder 1905, 138, and others, it was then taken up and discussed by Münscher 1916, with agreement from Wilamowitz-Moellendorff 1919 (II 108 s.) and Burk 1923, 33–34, 51. For further clarification, and a qualification, see Brancacci 2011a.
17. See in particular Isocrates, *Against the Sophists* 1–6 (= *SSR* V A 170).
18. See Diogenes Laertius VI 5 (= *SSR* V A 176).
19. See Dio Chrysostom *Oration* XIII 27–28 (= *SSR* V A 208).
20. For a more detailed examination of Isocrates' and Dio Chrysostom's testimony, see Brancacci 1990, 97–104, and Brancacci 1990, 85–118 for Antisthenes' theories of education and of wisdom. On *Oration* XIII, see Giannantoni 1990, volume. IV, 350–3, and Moles 2005, 117–20.
21. Epictetus, *Discourses* I 17.12 (= *SSR* V A 160).
22. For the doctrine of *episkepsis ton onomaton*, see the reconstruction presented in Brancacci 1990, 119–46. For the definition of *logos* and the testimonia in Diogenes Laertius VI 3 (= *SSR* V A 151) and in Alexander of Aphrodisias' commentary on Aristotle's *Topics* (42, 13–22 = *SSR* V A 151), see Brancacci 1990, 199–226. For the theory of the *oikeios logos*, 227–262.
23. For the Platonic-Socratic conception of *dialegesthai*, see Giannantoni 2005, in particular 216–20.
24. See Socrates' important statement in Plato, *Apology* 38A 1–6, on which see also note 41 below.
25. For the difference between Antisthenes' concept of *dialegesthai* and that of the Platonic Socrates, see Brancacci 2005a, 137–8. For Antisthenes' theory on the *aner polutropos*, see Porphyry *Questions on Homer's Odyssey*, on *Odyssey* I, 1 (= *SSR* V A 187). For the relationship between dialectic and rhetoric in Antisthenes' thought, see Brancacci 1996, 359–406. On Socratic-Platonic *dialegesthai*, see Giannantoni 2005, 141–195 e 197–256.
26. For the wise man, see Brancacci 1990, 114–17.

27. Diogenes Laertius VI 105 (= *SSR* V A 135).
28. For Aristippus see [Plutarch] *Patchworks* 9 (Eusebius *Preparation for the Gospel* I 8.9 24 B = *SSR* IV A 166 = fr. 144 Mannebach); for Diogenes (according to Diocles; Socrates according to others) see Diogenes Laertius VI 103 (= *SSR* V B 161); for Socrates also see Diogenes Laertius II 92.
29. Arsenius *Violetum s.v. Antisthenous* (lacking in *SSR*).
30. Diocles: Diogenes Laertius VI 12 (= *SSR* V A 134); also Phaenias, at Diogenes Laertius VI 8 (= *SSR* V A 172). For *manthanein*, see Dio Chrysostom *Oration* XIII 27–28 (= *SSR* V A 208).
31. See Diogenes Laertius VI 17: see also Lulofs 1900, 54–56.
32. Diogenes Laertius VI 12 (= *SSR* V A 134). See also Epictetus *Discourses* III 24.67 (= *SSR* V B 22). For "fine," *kalon*, see also Plutarch, *How the Young Should Listen to Poetry* 33 C (= *SSR* V A 195) and my comment in Brancacci 1990, 70 and 76–79; the fragment is directed against the ethical relativism of the sophists.
33. See Plato, *Apology* 29b8–9 for the opposition between *agathon* and *kakon* (in parallel with that between *diakion* and *adikon*), and 28c-d for the opposition between *aischron* and *kalon* (the latter term is not explicitly introduced, but the *kalon* is paradigmatically represented in the passage by the figure of the hero Achilles).
34. Aristophanes, *Clouds* 1020–21 is relevant here: Right ends his presentation of its own values by saying that "[Wrong] will make you think everything shameful is fine, and that the shameful is fine."
35. See Plato *Gorgias* 474c13-d2, *Protagoras* 332c. Cf. *Hippias Major* 299a, for the difficulty Socrates' interlocutors have in rigorously defining what is beautiful.
36. See Xenophon, *Memorabilia* III 8.5: "And you think, resumed Socrates, that good is one thing, fine another? Don't you know that, in relation to the same things, all things fine are also good? In the first place, virtue is not good compared with some things, fine compared with others; then again, men are said to be 'fine and good' in the same respect and in relation to the same things."
37. Themistius, *On virtue* 34.10–35.9 Mach : [. . .] *in scientia et in prudentia recta et in veritate; in eo, ut homo sciat, quid sit, quid non sit in sua potestate; cui rei, ut ita sit, studendum, cui rei, ne sit, sibi operam dandam*. Themistius' speech has survived in a Syriac translation, which the most recent editor has rendered into Latin. On this fragment see Brancacci 1992a, 3323–5 and Brancacci 2000.
38. See Brancacci 2005b.
39. It should be noted that *doxa* means appearance or opinion in an epistemological context but, as in later Cynicism, also superficial and deceitful opinion in the ethical context. In Cynicism, the latter meaning will be linked with the theme of life as immersed in appearance, and thus to the theme of human folly: on the latter, see Goulet-Cazé 1986, 17–22.
40. Diogenes Laertius VI 104 (= *SSR* V A 151). See also Suda *s.v. kunismos* (n° 2712) (= *SSR* V A 135).
41. Plato *Apology* 38a1–6. On this passage, see Calogero 1942, 112–5.
42. See Antisthenes, *Odysseus* 13 (= *SSR* V A 54).
43. See Diog. Laert. VII 87 (= fr. 179 *SVF* I).
44. See Ioppolo 1980, 146.
45. See Stobaeus II 7.6a, 75.11 (= fr. 179 *SVF* I). The bibliography on Zeno's formulation of the end, and on the relationship between the testimonies of Stobaeus and Diogenes Laertius, is huge; I will just mention Romeyer-Dherbey 2005, Annas 2007, Sellars 2009, pp. 47 ff. See also Bett 2010 (which I have

not seen). The less recent bibliography includes: Pearson 1891, 14 and 153; Dyroff 1897, 29 ff.; Bréhier 1952, 220; also Long 1967, 61 and nn.7–8; Gould 1970, 163; Rist 1977, 170 ff.; Ioppolo 1980, 142–6.
46. See Diogenes Laertius VI 6 (= *SSR* V A 100). For Antisthenes' concept of *homonoia* see Diogenes Laertius VI 6 (= *SSR* V A 108, 100); Stobaeus III 1,28 (= *SSR* V A 125); Dio Chrysostom *Oration* XIII 19 (= *SSR* V A 208). More recently, see Brancacci 2011b, which offers a new interpretation.
47. See Clement of Alexandria, *Patchworks*. II XXI 130,7; Theodoret, *Cure of the Greek Maladies* XI 8 (= *SSR* V A 111).
48. Here I have abandoned the view expressed in Brancacci 1992b, 4073, in which I completely endorsed Diogenes Laertius' testimony.
49. Diogenes Laertius VI 11 and 2 (= *SSR* V A 97). For Heracles and Cyrus, see Höistad 1948.
50. See Diogenes Laertius VII 127 (= fr. 237 *SVF* III; fr. 568 *SVF* I); Diogenes Laertius VII 128 (= fr. 569 *SVF* I).
51. Diogenes Laertius VI 12 (= *SSR* V A 134).
52. See Diog. Laert. VI 11 (= *SSR* V A 134).
53. Themistius, *On Virtue* 43 Mach (= *SSR* V A 96).
54. See Weber 1887, 242.
55. On the crucial stages of this tradition see Höistad 1948, 22 ff.; Detienne 1960.
56. This fundamental distinction would be inherited by Cynicism: see Diogenes Laertius VI 71 (= *SSR* V B 291).
57. See Diogenes Laertius VI 11 (= *SSR* V A 134). For the exact meaning of this fragment, see Brancacci 1990, 92 n.19.
58. For another occurrence in Antisthenes of the term *ponos* in a negative sense, because lacking in ethical value, see Xenophon, *Symposium* 4.35 (= *SSR* V A 82).
59. See Brancacci 1993c.
60. See Diogenes Laertius VI 2 (= SSR V A 97).
61. *PKöln* 66 II 2, in *Corpus dei papyri filsofici greci e latini*, I 1*, Florence 1989, 237 (Antisthenes 1 T). Cf. Stobaeus II 31.68 (= *SSR* V A 163).
62. See Xenoph. *symp.* 4, 34–44 (= *SSR* V A 82).
63. Anonymous scholium to Homer, *Iliad* XV 123 (= *SSR* V A 192).
64. See Brancacci 1990, 114 on the theory of the wise man, and 147–164 on the wise man as both skilful dialectician and skilful rhetorician); also Brancacci 2005c. Cf. Alesse 2000, *passim*.
65. See Ioppolo 1995, 89–123.
66. Diocles *ap*. Diog. Laert. VI 13 (= *SSR* V A 134).
67. See Höistad 1948, 111 Nr 6, and Oehler 1962, 44 Nr. 1.
68. Diogenes Laertius VI 11 (= *SSR* V A 134).s

REFERENCES

ALESSE 1997: F. Alesse, *Panezio di Rodi. Testimonianze, Edizione, traduzione e commento* (Napoli, Bibliopolis).
ALESSE 2000: F. Alesse, *La Stoa e la tradizione socratica* (Napoli, Bibliopolis).
ANNAS 2007: J. Annas, "Ethics in Stoic philosophy," *Phronesis* 57 (2007), 58–87.
BETT 2010: R. Bett, Beauty and its relation to goodness in Stoicism, in A. Nightingale& D. Sedley (eds.), *Ancient models of mind: Studies in human and divine rationality*, Cambridge: Cambridge University Press, pp. 130–152.
BILLOT 1993: M.-F. Billot, "Antisthène et le Cynosarges dans l'Athène des Ve et IVe siècles," in M. Goulet-Cazé & R. Goulet, *Le Cynisme ancien et ses prolongements*, Actes du Colloque International 1991 (Paris, PUF), pp. 69–116.

BRANCACCI 1990: A. Brancacci, *Oikeios logos. La filosofia del linguaggio di Antistene* (Napoli, Bibliopolis).
―――― 1992a: A. Brancacci, "Struttura compositiva e fonti della terza orazione 'Sulla regalità' di Dione Crisostomo: Dione e l'"Archelao' di Antistene," *Aufstieg und Niedergang der römischen Welt II*, 36.5 (1992), 3308-3334.
―――― 1992b: A. Brancacci, "I koinêi areskonta dei Cinici e la koinonia tra cinismo e stoicismo nel libro VI (103-105) delle 'Vite' di Diogene Laerzio," *Aufstieg und Niedergang der römischen Welt II*, 36.6 (1992), 4049-4075.
―――― 1993a: A. Brancacci, "Antisthène et la tradition antiplatonicienne au IVe siècle," in M. Dixsaut (ed.), *Contre Platon, tome I: Le platonisme dévoilé* (Paris, Vrin), pp. 31-51.
―――― 1993b: A. Brancacci, Erotique et theorie du plaisir chez Antisthène, in M. Goulet-Cazé & R. Goulet (eds.), *Le Cynisme ancien et ses prolongements*, Actes du Colloque International 1991 (Paris, PUF), pp. 35-55.
―――― 1996: A. Brancacci, "Dialettica e retorica in Antistene," *Elenchos* 17 (1996), 359-406.
―――― 2000: A. Brancacci, "Temistio e il cinismo," *Elenchos* 21 (2000), 381-396.
―――― 2005a: A. Brancacci, *Antisthène. Le discours propre* (Paris, Vrin) [= trad. fr. di Brancacci 1990]. 23
―――― 2005b: A. Brancacci, "Episteme and Phronesis in Antisthenes," *Méthexis* 28 (2005), 7-28.
―――― 2005c: A. Brancacci, "Antisthène et le stoïcisme: la logique," in G. Romeyer Dherbey (dir.) & J.-B. Gourinat (ed.), *Les Stoïciens* (Paris, Vrin), pp. 55-73.
―――― 2011a: A. Brancacci, *L'elogio di Isocrate nel Fedro, la chiusa dell'Eutidemo, e la polemica isocrateo-antistenico-platonica*, in *Il Fedro di Platone: struttura e problematiche*, a cura di G. Casertano (Napoli, Loffredo).
―――― 2011b: A. Brancacci, "Antistene e Socrate in una testimonianza di Filodemo (T 17 Acosta Méndez-Angeli)," *Cronache Ercolanesi* 41 (2011), 83-91.
BRÉHIER 1952: E. Bréhier, *Chrysippe et l'ancien Stoïcisme* (Paris, PUF).
BURK 1923: A. Burk, *Die Pädagogik des Isokrates als Grundlegung des humanistischen Bildungsideals: im Vergleich mit den zeitgenössischen und den modernen Theorien dargestellt* (Würzburg, Becker).
CALOGERO 1942: G. Calogero, "Socrate," in G. Calogero (ed.), *Scritti minori di filosofia antica* (Bibliopolis, Napoli), 106-126 [first edition in *Nuova Antologia* 90 (1955), 291-308].
DETIENNE 1960: M. Detienne, "Héraclès héros pythagoricien," *Revue d'Histoire des Religions* 158 (1960), 19-53.
DÖRING 1972: K. Döring, *Die Megariker. Kommentierte Sammlung der Testimonien* (Amsterdam, Grüner).
DYROFF 1897: A. Dyroff, *Die Ethik der alten Stoa* (Berlin, Calvary).
EUCKEN 1983: C. Eucken, *Isokrates. Seine Position in der Auseinandersetzung mit den zeitgenössischen Philosophen* (Berlin-New York, de Gruyter), p. 24.
GIANNANTONI 1990: G. Giannantoni, *Socratis et Socraticorum reliquiae, collegit, disposuit, apparatibus notisque instruxit* (Napoli, Bibliopolis).
GIANNANTONI 2005: G. Giannantoni, *Dialogo socratico e nascita della dialettica nella filosofia di Platone* (Napoli, Bibliopolis).
GOULD 1970: J.B. Gould, *The Philosophy of Chrysippus* (Leiden, Brill).
GOULET-CAZÉ 1986: M.-O. Goulet-Cazé, *L'ascèse cynique. Un commentaire de Diogène Laërce VI 70-71* (Paris, Vrin).
HÖISTAD 1948: R. Höistad, *Cynic Hero and Cynic King. Studies in the Cynic Conception of Man* (Lund, Bloms).
HUMBERT 1967: J. Humbert, *Socrate et les petits socratiques* (Paris, PUF).
IOPPOLO 1980: A.M. Ioppolo, *Aristone di Chio e lo stoicismo antico* (Napoli, Bibliopolis).

―――― 1995: A.M. Ioppolo, "Socrate nelle tradizioni accademico-scettica e pirroniana," in G. Giannantoni *et al.* (eds.), *La tradizione socratica* (Napoli, Bibliopolis), pp. 89–123.
LAUSDEI-ROSSETTI 1981: C. Lausdei-L. Rossetti, "P.Oxyr. 2889 e il «Milziade» di Eschine Socratico," *Rheinisches Museum* 124 (1981), 154–165.
LONG 1967: A.A. Long, "Carneades and the Stoic Telos," *Phronesis* 12 (1967), 59–90.
LULOFS 1900: A. Lulofs, *De Antisthenis studiis rhetoriciis*, diss. Amsterdam.
MOLES 2005: J. Moles, "The Thirteenth Oration of Dio Chrysostom: Complexity and simplicity, rhetoric and moralism, literature and life," *Journal of Hellenic Studies* 125 (2005), 112–138.
MOMIGLIANO 1931: A. Momigliano, "Teopompo," *Rivista di Filologia e di Istruzione Classica* 9 (1931), 230–232, e335–353 [now in A.M., *Terzo contributo alla storia degli studi classici e del mondo antico*, Roma, Edizioni di storia e letteratura 1966, vol. I, 367–392].
MONTONERI 1984: L. Montoneri, *I Megarici. Studio storico-critico e traduzione delle testimonianze antiche* (Catania, Università di Catania).
MÜNSCHER 1916: K. Münscher, s.v. "Isokrates" (n° 2), in RE IX 2 (1916), 2172–2173.
NATORP 1984a: P. Natorp, s.v. "Aischines" (n° 14) in RE I 1 (1894), 1058–1060.
―――― 1984b: P. Natorp, s.v. "Antisthenes," in RE I 1 (1894), 2538–2545.
OEHLER 1962: K. Oehler, *Die Lehre vom noetischen und dianoetischen Denken bei Platon und Aristoteles. Ein Beitrag zur Erforschung der Geschichte des Bewußtseinsproblems in der Antike* (München, Beck).
PATZER 1970: A. Patzer, *Antisthenes der Sokratiker. Das literarische Werk und die Philosophie, dargestellt am Katalog der Schriften*, diss. Heidelberg.
PEARSON 1891: A.C. Pearson, *The Fragments of Zeno and Cleanthes*, with introd. and expl. notes by A.C. Pearson (London, Clay).
RAEDER 1905: H. Raeder, *Platons philosophische Entwicklung* (Leipzig, Teubner).
REINHARDT 1873: K. Reinhardt, *De Isocratis aemulis*, diss. Bonn (Bonn, Georgi).
RIST 1977: J.M. Rist, "Zeno and Stoic Consistency," *Phronesis* 22 (1977), 161–174.
ROMEYER-DHERBEY 2005: G. Romeyer-Dherbey, "Vivre en accord avec la nature" ou "vivre en accord avec Zénon," *Philosophie Antique* 5 (2005), 49–64.
SELLARS 2009: J. Sellars, *The Art of Living : The Stoics on the Nature and Function of Philosophy* (London, Duckworth, Second Edition).
ÜBERWEG 1861: F. Überweg, *Untersuchungen über die Echtheit und Zeitfolge Platonischer Schriften und über die Hauptmomente aus Plato's Leben* (Wien, Gerold).
USENER 1856: H. Usener, *Quaestiones Anaximeneae* (Göttingen, Dieterich) [also in H.U., *Kleine Schriften*, vol. I, Leipzig–Berlin, Teubner 1912, 1–49].
WEBER 1887: E. Weber, "De Dione Chrysostomo Cynicorum sectatore," *Leipziger Studien zur classischen Philologie* 10 (1887), 77–268.
WILAMOWITZ-MOELLENDORFF 1919: U. von Wilamowitz-Moellendorff, *Platon, vol. II: Beilagen und Textkritik* (Berlin, Weidmann).

4 Rethinking Aeschines of Sphettus

Kurt Lampe

1. INTRODUCTION

Aeschines of Sphettus is an odd omission from most recent Anglophone histories of philosophy. Even specialists in Greek philosophy might be forgiven for thinking that none of his writings survive, or that no scholarship has been devoted to them. In fact the last century has added several important papyri to what was already the largest collection of verbatim quotations from any Socratic author other than Plato and Xenophon.[1] This in itself testifies that unlike the vast majority of ancient philosophical works, his continued to be read throughout antiquity. Furthermore, although he has been the topic of little Anglophone scholarship, German and Italian scholars in particular have significantly increased our understanding of the characters, plots, themes and style of several his dialogues.[2]

So why does Aeschines continue to be ignored? Beyond the difficulty of the evidence, the major problem may be that he seems to have nothing philosophically interesting to say. For example, the substantial fragments and testimony from his *Callias*, *Telauges*, *Miltiades*, *Aspasia* and *Alcibiades* contain neither the definitional inquiries of the early Plato nor the elaborate theorizing of the late Plato. Hence, although they obviously touch upon questions of ethics and politics in particular, they may appear to have nothing to contribute to the history of philosophical thinking about these topics.

My suggestion is that we will find Aeschines more interesting if we change our interpretive framework. Rather than looking for carefully delineated concepts and rigorous arguments, I suggest we engage cautiously with the interpretive categories which Michel Foucault began to develop during his final three seminars.[3] It should be said right away that Foucault left this research in an incomplete state with numerous loose ends. Moreover, although he is fascinated by Socratic philosophy, which he connects with a perceived crisis in Athenian politics and education,[4] he focuses overwhelmingly on Plato;[5] Aeschines is left entirely out of account. This chapter will therefore also provide the basis for supplementing his historical claims.[6]

2. FOUCAULT'S INTERPRETIVE MODEL

I will begin with a very brief summary of Foucault's major interpretive terms. The most fundamental change he introduces is to shift the focus from philosophical theories to philosophical practices and experiences. (In this he was influenced by Pierre Hadot.[7]) He is particularly concerned with ethics and politics; there is little question of physics, although a sort of metaphysics—what he calls "ontologies of true discourses"—appears at the margins of his project.[8] Three concepts dominate his approach to ethics and politics. The first is truth-telling or "veridiction." Rather than asking what philosophers believe to be the truth about souls, actions, or cities, Foucault asks under what conditions they are authorized to know, speak, and act on the truth about these things. Thus Foucauldian "truth" is intersubjectively and historically constituted. The second is self-fashioning or "subjectivation." In place of asking about the nature of virtue or vice, Foucault asks through which behaviours philosophers make themselves who they are. The third is the exercise of power or "governmentality." In place of asking about formally established laws and institutions, Foucault asks about the normative frameworks through which people exert power on both others and themselves. Finally, it should be emphasised that these three domains of practice and experience (veridiction, subjectivation and governmentality) are interlocking, and that their interface produces numerous subtle variations. Even though Foucault is given to both neat schematizing and to grand historical narratives, the details of his careful analysis of evidence always reveal much more fluid and shifting terrain than his schemes or narratives suggest.

A quick example will make this clearer. Let us take the domain of Freudian psychoanalysis.[9] Here it is easy to identify various modes of veridiction. Most obviously, through testing and training the psychoanalyst is accredited and authorized to tell the truth about her own psyche, about psychological structure and pathology in general, and eventually about the neuroses of particular patients. But it is also through sustained engagement with the psychoanalyst that the patient will be enabled to tell and act upon the truth about himself—in other words, he will remember repressed memories or emotions. These processes of veridiction are simultaneously processes of subjectivation: the patient is becoming who he is. For it is only through the ritual of precisely choreographed daily meetings, the recollection and analysis of dreams, the exercise of free association, and the discovery of formative events, which must be "worked through," that the patient comes to "know who he really is."[10] Finally, these are processes of governmentality. Some level of knowledge about psychoanalysis has led the patient to come to therapy, or perhaps induced his relatives to send him. He then develops a powerful relationship with the therapist. And even after his analysis has concluded, he continues to monitor *himself* for the recrudescence of neurosis. In all these ways psychoanalysis impacts other people's guidance of his actions and his own guidance of himself. Thus veridiction, subjectivation,

Rethinking Aeschines of Sphettus 63

and governmentality overlap; or, as the earlier Foucault would say, knowledge always generates fields of power.

3. AESCHINES ON VERIDICTION, SUBJECTIVATION AND GOVERNMENTALITY

This brings us back to Aeschines. I will begin with the fragments of his *Miltiades*, *Telauges* and *Callias*, which collectively permit us to see how the Foucauldian framework illuminates Aeschines' criticism of several of his contemporaries. For the analysis of the *Miltiades* I am particularly indebted to Andreas Patzer and the two collaborative articles of Livio Rossetti and Claudio Lausdei.[11] The dramatic framework and thematic preoccupations of this dialogue are established by an Oxyrhynchus papyri that came to light in the 1970s. Papyrus 2889 tells us: "It happened to be the day of the Great Panathenaic procession, and Hagnon the father of Theramenes, Euripides the poet and I were sitting in the Stoa of Zeus Eleutherios. Suddenly Miltiades walked by, almost as if by design" (*SSR* 6a.76).[12] Hagnon was an influential statesman: he held the office of *strate͞gos* in 440 BC, 431 BC, and 429 BC; he was a signatory to the peace treaty with Sparta in 421 BC; and he was elected to the council designated to respond to the Sicilian catastrophe in 413 BC.[13] Euripides, of course, was a famous tragedian. Thus in Socrates, Hagnon and Euripides we have a trio of influential Athenians from three different walks of life. Miltiades is certainly a descendant of the legendary general credited with the victory at Marathon. He seems to have been involved in setting up the short-lived and infamous oligarchy of the "Thirty Tyrants" of 404–403 BC, although he was not one of the thirty (Lys. 12.72). Given the theme of the other fragments, which we will see in a moment, it is tempting to see him as one of those young aristocrats whose aspirations motivate so many Socratic conversations.[14]

For it becomes explicit on this same papyrus that the main topic of this conversation is education (*paideia*) and its goals. On the front of Oxyrhynchus papyrus 2890, which is too lacunose to translate with any confidence, we can nevertheless discern that many people have sailed from their homes to Greece (*oikothen . . . [pe]pleukasin*) in order to spend time (*sungenesthai*) with whoever is wisest (*tōi sophōtatōi*) in the education of a human being (*paideusai anthrōpon*) (*SSR* 6a.79). On the back of this same papyrus Socrates says,

> It won't be at all strange if the problem that stumps us doesn't stump him. For it's no surprise that, if I asked Euripides which craftsman he should spend time with in order to deliberate best about making shoes, he could answer "cobblers"; or which he should spend time with in order to deliberate best about building houses, he could answer "architects." But now . . .
>
> (*SSR* 6a.80).[15]

Here the papyrus breaks off, but clearly Socrates goes on to ask Euripides with whom Miltiades should spend time in order to deliberate best about justice, virtue, political governance, or something like that. It will be a question of who can teach someone like Miltiades how to achieve what he wants, which is to develop certain personal qualities, exercise a certain influence in the polis, and guide the polis toward certain goals.

Note two items in the vocabulary of this passage. First, the verb *sungenesthai* reappears twice as *sunōn*, the participle of *suneimi*. These verbs signal that Socrates is concerned with the interpersonal dimension of education, the "being-with" of the student and the teacher.[16] The specific modality of this being-with will invite analysis in terms of Foucauldian governmentality. Second, note the insistence on the word *bouleuomai*, which is all the more conspicuous because it is somewhat out of place with reference to cobbling. Whether we look backward to Homeric *euboulia* or forward to Aristotelian *bouleusis*, this insistence calls into question the ability to give the correct or "true" counsel (*boulē*) to yourself, your friends and dependents, and your political community.[17] This corresponds primarily to Foucauldian veridiction. The entire passage raises questions of Foucauldian subjectivation as well, not only because the three processes typically overlap, but specifically because *paideia* involves becoming a certain sort of person.

Let us now turn to another long fragment, which will allow us to ask how these three Foucauldian processes play out later in the dialogue. This fragment describes Miltiades' upbringing. Aeschines has probably put it in the mouth of Hagnon, who is responding to a question from Socrates about the young man walking past:[18]

> This is Miltiades the son of Stesagoras. When he was a boy he trained for the Olympics, and was more eager to undertake strenuous exercise than his trainer was to assign it! There he defeated boys who were bigger and older than he was. When competing for prizes he never wanted to follow his trainer from the field. He had guardians of various ages and characters, but he obeyed all of them. The pedagogue who attended him wasn't a very good man, but he never opposed him in any way. This is how he behaved as a boy. When he became an adolescent he decided silence was a fine thing. He's been quieter than bronze statues. He also decided it would be a fine thing to care for his body, and he's cared for it so well that his body's in the best shape of any man his age.
> (SSR 6a.77 = Stob. 2.31.23)

The primary characteristics of the education outlined here are competition (*agōnizomenos huper tou stephanou*), obedience (*katēkoos, ouden pōpote ēnantiōthē*), silence (*siōpān*) and strenuous exertion (*ponous ponōn*), which is connected with care of the body (*tou sōmatos . . . epimeleisthai*). Previous scholars have noted that this constellation suggests Miltiades sympathizes with Spartan culture.[19] Criticism of Miltiades could thus represent an implicit disagreement with Aeschines' Laconizing fellow Socratic, Xenophon.[20] What the Foucauldian perspective permits is a more comprehensive analysis of what is wrong with the Spartan model.

First, the passage implies a model of subjectivation. Previous scholars have conjectured that Socrates must have criticized Miltiades' excessive emphasis on the body, perhaps arguing that true "care of the self" (*epimeleia heautou*) concerns the soul.[21] This is plausible, especially since the passage ends with the assertion that "he's cared for it (*epimemelētai toutou*) so well that his body's in the best shape of any man his age." But the issue is more complex than this simple body-soul dichotomy. According to the *Constitution of the Lacedaemonians* ascribed to Xenophon, the Spartan *paideia* is an entire system of behaviour designed to produce men who are, among other things, tolerant of exertion, in control of their appetites, honour-loving, obedient and respectful (*Lac.* 2.1–4.7). Miltiades has obviously imposed a similar set of exercises on himself: through his bodily exertion, competition for honour, docility, and silence he hopes to develop precisely the virtues reiterated throughout the *Constitution*—to become *eupeithēs*, *enkratēs*, *aidēmōn*, and generally *kalos kagathos*.[22] But even the scanty remains of Aeschines' dialogue signal that he calls this mode of self-fashioning into question. In order to see how, it will be best to turn to the dialogue's models of veridiction and governmentality, which will allow us to explain how these exercises fail to produce the desired characteristics.

Let us begin with veridiction. The goal of the Spartan education is of course to raise citizens who will think and speak intelligently for themselves, their fellow citizens, and the polis. Somewhat paradoxically, in order to do this they are encouraged to be silent during their adolescence. As the *Constitution* puts it in famous passage,

> Because [Lycurgus] wanted to implant a strong sense of shame in them, he ordered [adolescents] to keep their hands in their sleeves when on the road, to walk quietly, and to look in neither direction, but rather to gaze at the ground in front of their feet. . . . You'd sooner hear a sound from stone statues than from them, sooner turn the eyes of bronze statues . . . And when they come to the communal meal, it's enough if you can get them to listen to a question.
>
> (*Lac.* 3.4–5)

The point is that it is more important for young Spartans to develop a strong sense of shame and obedience than to develop their own ideas. Passive absorption of what they hear from their elders, who are collectively authorized to speak by their upbringing and battlefield bravery, is supposed to turn these adolescents into men capable of making the right decisions in the Assembly or on the battlefield.

Miltiades' deliberate exercise of silence (*siōpān kalon hēgēsato einai*) signals his implicit allegiance to this model of veridiction. Hagnon's description of Miltiades as quieter than bronze statues strongly recalls the *Constitution*'s image of stone and bronze statues, perhaps with a touch of authorial parody. As Rossetti and Lausdei have rightly noted, this model of education is incompatible with Socratic conversation. For example, Xenophon's claim that Spartan youths will scarcely even listen to a question (*to erōtēthen akousai*) marks a strong contrast with the open exchange of opinions required by Socratic dialectic. Hence Rossetti and Lausdei rightly adduce a passage from Apuleius,[23] which may be a reminiscence of a lost passage from our dialogue:

> When Socrates saw a modest young man keeping silent for a little too long, he said, "say something, if you want me to see you." Because Socrates couldn't see someone who was silent: he thought people should be contemplated with the gaze of the mind and the vision of the intellect, not the eyes.
>
> (*Fl.* 2.1–5)

Regardless of whether this genuinely derives from our dialogue, certainly Socrates must have questioned whether Miltiades' self-imposed silence could ever lead to the ability to "deliberate as well as possible."

This is not to insist that Aeschines' position was as simple as preferring speech to silence. In a passage preserved by Plutarch we have a very balanced appraisal of the value of silence:

> Everywhere silence is a certain ornament for a young man, especially when he's listening, so that he doesn't get upset or interrupt angrily at every point. Even if he doesn't like what's being said, he should wait for the speaker to pause, and when he has paused, he shouldn't object immediately, but rather, as Aeschines says, wait a bit, in case the speaker wants to add something to what he's said or change or subtract something.
>
> (SSR 6a.78 = Plut. *Mor.* 39b-c)

Here the claim "Everywhere silence is a certain ornament for young men" probably belongs to Plutarch, not Aeschines. What remains could be a tactfully sympathetic reaction by Socrates to Hagnon's initial description of Miltiades' silence. This is what we might expect from Aeschines, who reportedly asserted that "he learned from Socrates not only how to speak, but also how to be silent" (Stob. *Anth.* 3.34.10).[24] In the atmosphere of masculine competitiveness and rhetorical loquacity that reigned in early fourth-century Greece, respectful listening would be as important as intelligent speech. But this probably was not Socrates' final word on the matter. Rather, I conjecture that Socrates began with this qualified sympathy, which already departed significantly from the radical silence practiced by Miltiades, and then moved into an argument about the need for an open exchange of opinions. This tactful approach would be in keeping with the less aggressive tone of Aeschines' Socrates vis-à-vis those of Plato or Xenophon.[25]

This brings me to the last Foucauldian approach to this passage, which is governmentality: the way in which its participants exert power and influence on each other and on themselves. In the case of Spartan education governmentality and veridiction are tightly connected, since the regime of respectful silence, which is designed to nourish veridiction, also involves conspicuous relationships of power. These are embodied by officers such as the Child-Minder (*paidonomos*) and the Whip-Bearers (*mastigophoroi*), although all adult Spartan citizens are authorized to punish any child (*Lac*. 2.1–2, 2.10, 6.1–2). Each of these adults obviously exercises influence over the children. At the same time, the weight of tradition, the authority of the legendary Lycurgus, and the politico-military needs of Sparta exercise influence over those adults. They treat the children as they do because this is the time-honoured way of creating the next generation, because Lycurgus ordained this behaviour, and because Sparta needs hardened soldiers both to keep control of the Helots and maintain its military preeminence across Greece. So there is a complex and coherent network of power relations expressed through the entire Spartan *paideia*.

Aeschines' dialogue must have more or less explicitly called into question the value of such a systematic discipline. Since he has highlighted Miltiades' submission to guardians of diverse ages and characters (*oute tas autas hēlikias ekhontes outa tous autous tropous*) and a pedagogue who was "not entirely virtuous" (*ou panu spoudaios*),[26] it seems likely his Socrates went on to interrogate the Spartan ideals of docility and obedience. Here we should remind ourselves that Miltiades later became complicit in the Spartan-supported oligarchy of the Thirty Tyrants. So did Hagnon's son Theramenes, who was mentioned at the outset of this dialogue. Socrates was blamed for "corrupting" these young aristocrats and thus being responsible for the disaster they caused. In the remainder of the dialogue, Aeschines must have shown that Socrates was very far from encouraging the ethical and political models that led not only to tyranny in Athens, but also to his own execution.

Miltiades' Laconophilia is not the only systematic and coherent model of subjectivation, veridiction, and governmentality presented and implicitly criticized by Aeschines. Athenaeus reports that in Aeschines' *Telauges*, about which practically nothing has been written, he "mocks Telauges himself for hiring the robe he wore from the fuller for half an obol a day, wrapping himself in a sheepskin and tying his shoes with rotten cords" (Athen. 220A = SSR 6a.84). Only three people named Telauges appear in the massive *Lexicon of Greek Personal Names*. Two appear in third and second centuries BCE on inscriptions from northern Asia minor.[27] Before these the only Telauges is the legendary son of Pythagoras.[28] Scholars have thus reasonably assumed that Aeschines' Telauges is one of the so-called "Pythagorists" who appeared in mainland Greece at the end of the fourth century BC,[29] such as Diodorus of Aspendus. Diodorus supposedly grew his beard long, wore filthy clothes, and went barefoot, all of which recalls Telauges' appearance in Aeschines' dialogue (Athen. 163D-64A, D.L. 6.13). We know very little about these Pythagorean ascetics,[30] so it is regrettable that we have so little of this dialogue. In it Socrates must have interrogated Telauges about his unusual behaviour and beliefs. Here we should note that Athenaeus' testimony, which appears in an anti-philosophical diatribe, probably misrepresents Aeschines' tone. According to Demetrius' less polemical testimony, "People often speak ambiguously. . . .[31] [T]here's an example in Aeschines' *Telauges*. Practically the whole description of Telauges makes you wonder whether it's expressing amazement or ridicule" (Demetr. *Eloc.* 291 = SSR 6a.89). The allusion to "practically the whole description of Telauges" (*pasa skhedon hē peri ton Tēlaugē diēgēsis*), which contained enough detail to express both "amazement" (*thaumasmos*) and "ridicule" (*khleuasmos*), suggests that Aeschines said a significant amount about Telauges' extraordinary lifestyle.

Like the Spartan *paideia* admired by Miltiades, Telauges' Pythagorean lifestyle represents a coherent and systematic model of behaviour. First, it obviously involves a series of ascetic exercises, which is why Telauges does not own a robe (he has to rent one) and wears decrepit shoes and animal skins. The object of this asceticism, as of the "countless prohibitions and obligations" that are well-documented for the Pythagoreans,[32] was purification of the soul.[33] It is therefore a system of practices of subjectivation. These rituals were ordained by the unquestionable authority of the *akousmata*, or oral teachings, which the Pythagoreans ascribed to their legendary founder. And they must have been transmitted through some combination of textual study and oral indoctrination. This would be a system of governmentality. Finally, this purification of the soul through observation of rituals promised the practitioner the capacity to perceive the truth about correct behaviour, the nature of souls, and perhaps even ultimate reality. This would be a game of veridiction. Aeschines' dialogue must have called all of this into question, since Demetrius says that his portrayal of Telauges lies between "amazement" and "ridicule." Two final fragments from this dialogue allow us to glimpse Aeschines' ambiguous criticism in action: "Let's enjoy some of the benefit of your mind, since it has become so virtuous"; "'Just as with Solon the law-giver,' I said, 'though he is now dead, we still enjoy great benefits'" (Priscian 18.189 = *SSR* 6a.88). Probably these ironic questions were put in the mouth of Socrates, and signalled the beginning of his interrogation of Telauges' ostensibly "virtuous mind" (*tēs sēs dianoias spoudaias genomenēs*).[34]

Finally, we should quickly note that in Aeschines' *Callias* there was a discussion of sophistic *paideia*. The dialogue reportedly contained

> mockery of the sophists Prodicus and Anaxagoras. For Aeschines says that Prodicus produced Theramenes as his student, and the other produced Philoxenus the son of Eryxis and Ariphrades the brother of the

kitharist Arignotus. From the vice of those mentioned and their lust for vulgar pleasures he aimed to illuminate the instruction offered by their teachers.

(Athen. 220B-C = SSR 6a.73).

Here again we have a discussion of *didaskalia* and *paideia*: Aeschines wanted "to illuminate the instruction offered by their teachers" (*thelōn . . . emphanisai tēn tōn paideusantōn didaskalian*). This "illumination" must have included relations of influence, modes of speech, and exercises of self-fashioning. Unfortunately, the details are entirely lost.[35]

So far I have focused on the models of subjectivation, veridiction, and governmentality of which Aeschines' Socrates is critical. I now want to turn to Aeschines' *Aspasia* and *Alcibiades*, which will permit us to say more about the positive side of Aeschines' Socratic model. Since Barbara Ehler's seminal monograph it has been common to treat the *Alcibiades* as a protreptic dialogue, in which Socrates' primary accomplishment is to puncture his interlocutor's conceit, while the *Aspasia* provides a better picture of Aeschines' thinking about constructive pedagogy.[36] This approach, I suggest, is misguided: given the vastly greater supply of exact quotations from the *Alcibiades*, which a Foucauldian analysis can turn to good account, it is with the latter that our discussion should culminate.

The *Aspasia* returns to the figure of Callias, who is looking for a teacher for his son.[37] In other words, the framing issue for the dialogue is once again the aims and mechanisms of subjectivation. Unfortunately few verbatim quotations survive from this dialogue; we have to piece together its structure from Athenaeus' claim that "in the *Aspasia* [Aeschines] calls Callias' son Hipponicus a blockhead" (*SSR* 6a.61)[38] and Maximus of Tyre's apostrophe to Socrates: "You even encourage Callias to send his son, a man, to the house of Aspasia of Miletus, a woman" (6a.62). Of course, this becomes a commonplace in Socratic literature: Socrates claims that he himself learned from Aspasia, the (in)famous lover of Pericles, and suggests that others should do the same.[39] In Aeschines' *Aspasia*, as in Plato's *Menexenus*, her particular area of expertise is rhetoric. Hence Philostratus claims that "Aspasia of Miletus sharpened Pericles' tongue with Gorgias' style" (*Ep*. 73 = *SSR* 6a.65), and even quotes what must be a sample of her Gorgianic oratory: "Aeschines didn't hesitate to gorgianize in his discussion of Thargelia, where he says, 'Milesian Thargelia coming to Thessaly lived with Antiochus of Thessaly, king of all Thessalians'" (ibid.).[40] This is designed to titillate Callias, to whom Socrates probably addresses the following quotation: "You seem to me to emulate the people who compete in court on their own behalf and on behalf of others" (*SSR* 6a.69).[41] In other words, Socrates calls attention to Callias' interest in the power of rhetoric, which is exemplified by the ability to contend successfully in court (*tous en dikastēriōi . . . agōnizomenous*); and he uses this to propose Aspasia—ostensibly a master of rhetoric—as a teacher for his son Hipponicus.

In this summary we begin to glimpse the model of governmentality Aeschines' Socrates prefers. Rather than colluding in Callias' belief that he or someone he knows has expertise in education, which would generate a cascade of power effects (influencing Callias' choice of a teacher, Socrates' manner of teaching, and Hipponicus' manner of formulating and developing skills and traits), Socrates instead begins to draw out and interrogate Callias' own interests—in this case, his interest in rhetoric. The foregoing quotation hints that Callias has forensic applications in mind. (Note that Callias' grandfather faces a capital charge in Aeschines' *Callias*.)[42] In other testimony Socrates probes Callias' interest in politics: "Aeschines says that Lysicles the sheep-dealer was transformed from his ignoble and humble status into the first of the Athenians by consorting with Aspasia" (Plut. *Per.* 24.4); "Aspasia made Lysicles a terrific orator, just as she had trained Pericles in addressing the people, according to Aeschines the Socratic in *Aspasia*" (schol. in Pl. *Men.* = *SSR* 6a.66). From these testimony we can infer that Socrates attempts to support his proposal by arguing that Aspasia can not only teach Hipponicus to win in court, but also to speak influentially in the Athenian Assembly. These promises on Aspasia's behalf push Callias to articulate for himself which abilities he wants his son to learn rather than receive this articulation from Socrates' educational authority.

We should also note the density of Socrates' irony in this dialogue, which enlarges his interlocutor's agency in a conversation that, whatever Callias' original intention, has obviously become a complex philosophical inquiry.[43] The proposal of Aspasia as an educator is deliberately provocative, as Callias must realize as easily as Plato's *Menexenus* (249d1-e7). Moreover, Gorgias' conspicuously stylized oratory, as exemplified by the Thargelia quotation, would be effective in neither the courts nor the Assembly.[44] Socrates cannot seriously be advising Callias either to send Hipponicus to Aspasia or to develop a full-blown Gorgianic style. So what *is* he advising? In the space created by this enigma Callias and Hipponicus will have to think for themselves about the sort of rhetoric they want to learn and what sort of teacher, what sort of relationship, and what sort of conversational exercises can help them.

The remaining testimony from the dialogue revolves around a particular aspect of educational relationships, namely eros. Cicero preserves in Latin translation an extended quotation between Aspasia, Xenophon, and his wife, which must come from a conversation Socrates relates in order to exemplify Aspasia's educational prowess:

"Tell me, wife of Xenophon, if your neighbor had a better gold necklace than you have, would you prefer it or your own?"
"That one," she said.
"What if she had more expensive clothes and other feminine adornments than you have? Would you prefer yours or hers?"
"Hers," she answered.

"Come then," she said. "What if she had a better husband than you have? Would you prefer your husband or hers?"

Here Xenophon's wife blushed, but Aspasia began a discussion with Xenophon himself. "Dear Xenophon," she said, "if your neighbor had a better horse than yours, would you prefer yours or his?"

"His," he said.

"What if he had a better farm than you have? Which farm would you then prefer?"

"The other," he said, "because it's better."

"What if he had a better wife than you have? Would you prefer yours or his?"

Here Xenophon too fell silent.

Then Aspasia said, "Since the only question each of you refused to answer is the only one I wanted to hear, I myself will say what you both think. You, wife, want to have the best husband, and you, Xenophon, want to have the most excellent wife. So unless you make sure that there's neither a more excellent man nor woman on earth, you'll undoubtedly always lack most of all what you think best of all."

(Cic. *Inv.* 1.51–52 = SSR 6a.70)

In this quotation the issue has obviously expanded from narrowly forensic or political rhetoric to holistic self-development and its interpersonal contexts. Those contexts are erotically charged, both because of the involvement of Aspasia, who was Athenian literature's most powerful symbol of erotic femininity,[45] and because of the marital connection between Xenophon and his wife.[46] In fact, scholars have generally taken this passage to communicate love's power to bring about ethical improvement. However, they have been perplexed by the absence of clear indications of how this works.[47] Granted, Aspasia suggests that in reciprocal loving relationships, each partner stands to benefit by making the other as good as possible. Furthermore, it can be inferred that all people should improve themselves in order to make themselves lovable. This would be useful for both politicians and legal pleaders.[48] But how exactly do lovers improve themselves or one another? We can expand this question by returning to the Foucauldian interpretive framework: What are the modes of influence employed between lovers? How does love enable true speech between lovers? Finally, how do these modes of influence and speech contribute to self-development?

In order to answer we will have to turn to the richer remains from the *Alcibiades*, which furnishes by far our most extensive verbatim quotations from Aeschines.[49] In the longest of these excerpts, which is preserved by Aelius Aristides, Socrates tries to impress upon Alcibiades the moral conveyed by the life of Themistocles (*Or.* 3.348–9 = SSR 6a.50). As in the Platonic dialogue of the same name, Alcibiades obviously aspires to political preeminence. So Socrates reminds him of the extraordinary talents and accomplishments of the statesman and general Themistocles, and how even these talents and accomplishments were not enough to save him from political reversals. He concludes: "So consider, Alcibiades, that even such a man, with such great understanding, wasn't able to avoid exile and dishonor at the hands of his polis. His understanding failed him. So what do you think happens to useless people, who take no care of themselves?" (Aristid. *Or.* 3.348 = SSR 6a.50) Note the emphasis on the sort of person Themistocles was (*ekeinōi toioutōi onti*), which is spelled out in terms of the magnitude of his "understanding" (*hē epistēmē tosautē*). Elsewhere in the same fragment we have repeated allusions to his being "earnest" (*andri . . . spoudaioterōi*; *spoudaioteroi en aretēi*), to his ability to "take thought" (*tōi phronein periegeneto*), and to his ability to deliberate (*bouleusaito*). All of this vocabulary picks out the attributes and capacities which made Themistocles the exemplary individual he was—even if he wasn't quite earnest, thoughtful, or prudent enough for his own good. The question Socrates implicitly puts to Alcibiades is how he can become as good or better than Themistocles.

The key to the answer is in the words I have already quoted: "So what do you think happens to useless people, who take no care of themselves" (*tois . . . en mēdemiai epimeleiai heautōn ousin*)? Alcibiades must take "care of himself" (*epimeleia heautou*); he must identify and undertake a system of exercises in order to become a certain kind of subject. The question is, what are those exercises?

Given everything else we have seen in Aeschines, we should expect the foregoing question to be linked with questions about modes of influence and speech. These connections are in fact highlighted in the other extended quotation preserved by Aristides, which appears to be the dialogue's conclusion:[50]

> As for me, if I thought that I could help through any craft, I would consider myself guilty of great foolishness. But as it is, I thought that this <power> over Alcibiades was given to me by divine dispensation, and there's nothing amazing in that. After all, many sick people become healthy by human craft, but others by divine dispensation. Physicians are responsible for those who are healed by human craft, but those who are healed by divine dispensation are led to what will help them by their own desire. Thus they wished to vomit when it would help, and to go hunting with hounds when exercise would help. As for myself, because of the love I felt for Alcibiades, my experience was just like that of the Bacchants. For when the Bacchants are divinely inspired, they draw honey and milk from places where others can't even get water from their wells. So it was with me: though I had neither learning nor understanding by which I might benefit someone in teaching them, nevertheless I thought that because I loved him, I could make him better by associating with him.
>
> (Aristid. *Or.* 2.61–4, 74 = SSR 6a.53).[51]

As in the *Aspasia*, here we see the issues of ethical improvement and love connected. But once again the nature of the connection is not immediately clear. How, we must ask, can Socrates' love help? Moreover, since we have just seen that Alcibiades needs to care for himself, how does love relate to self-care?

This is not the only enigma suggested by this fragment. Socrates' comparison of himself to the celebrants of Dionysus might dispose us to believe that we are dealing with a form of divine inspiration that transcends any sort of purposeful activity on the part of Socrates or Alcibiades.

In fact we can illuminate both of these enigmas by attending more carefully to the interplay of governmentality, veridiction, and subjectivation in these fragments. I will begin by analysing the second analogy in the preceding quotation, which compares Socratic eros to medicine. This analogy is constructed around an opposition between craft (*tekhnē*) and divine dispensation (*theia moira*). Socrates says that some sick people are cured by the craft of physicians. In this case, we may assume, physicians apply the sort of theories we read about in the Hippocratic corpus to the empirical symptoms of the patients. Here we should emphasize both the physicians' pretention to knowledge and the authoritarian model of their influence. The physicians supposedly understand illness and the body, and because of their faith in this knowledge, the patients accept the physicians' recommendations. It is worth noting that this parallels the disciplinary spirit of Miltiades' Laconizing self-culture and Telauges' allegiance to the *akousmata* of Pythagoras. By contrast, when sick people improve by divine dispensation, they experience a change in their own desire (*epithumia*). It is by an internal transformation that they make themselves better.

Socratic eros works in a similar way, although there is a complication. Socrates does not help by craft, which again would presumably mean by combining pedagogical theory with empirical observation of Alcibiades. Rather, he helps through the mechanism of desire. Note that in the first part of the quotation Socrates says he helps by *theia moira*, not by *tekhnē*; and in the second part he says he helps by *erōs*, not by *epistēmē* or *mathēmata*. His lack of understanding and learning is obviously correlated with his lack of craft, and his eros is correlated with divine dispensation. More exactly, just as inspired patients lack craft but by divine dispensation possess the right *epithumia*, so Socrates lacks craft but by divine dispensation possesses the right eros. That is all there is to the divine intervention here.[52]

Now we must ask how we can get from Socrates' divinely inspired love to an improvement in Alcibiades. Must we have recourse to some sort of immediate daemonic stimulus, analogous to the inspired patients' urge to vomit or exercise precisely when it will be therapeutic? On the one hand, I do not want to rule that out. As I have argued elsewhere, such subtle forms of divine intervention appear less outlandish in late classical Athens, even in Socratic circles, than they do to secular rationalist philosophers today.[53] After all, this was a man who claimed to receive prophetic dreams, oracles, and individual divine signs. Perhaps a god inspires Socrates to say the right thing to Alcibiades at precisely the right time. This could be what he's getting at when he compares himself with maenads drawing honey and milk from dry earth. It is hard to be certain, especially since this rhapsodic peroration partakes of the irony we have identified in the *Aspasia*.

But Aeschines may also have in mind a more everyday sort of miracle, one that revolves around interpersonal rather than divine influence. As Foucault emphasizes more effectively than most, a fundamental complement to the care of the self throughout Greco-Roman antiquity was a relationship with a guide or "master."[54] As he says with reference to the Socratic phase of this relationship,

> The master is the person who cares about the subject's care for himself, and who finds in his love for his disciple the possibility of caring for the disciple's care for himself. By loving the boy disinterestedly, he is then the source and model for the care the boy must have for himself as subject.[55]

I want to focus for the moment on the idea of "disinterested love," which is a potentially misleading phrase. The point is not that the lover has no personal interest in the beloved's education, which, as we have seen, is belied by Aeschines' *Aspasia*. Rather, the point is that the primary object of the lover's desire is the beloved's moral improvement. It is not the beloved's adulation, body, possessions, or political influence. For this reason the lover's behaviour will be entirely oriented toward motivating the beloved to recognize and remedy his shortcomings. He wants to help the beloved care about himself in the same way *he* cares about him. If we contrast this with the idealization of pederasty from Pausanias' speech in Plato's *Symposium*, where education is exchanged for sexual favours, not to mention the determined effort to deglamourize pederasty in the first two speeches of the *Phaedrus*, we can see in what sense it is a sort of "miracle."

Finally, in order to explain how this divinely inspired "disinterested love" actually profits Alcibiades, let us look at the way their conversation unfolds. The dialogue begins with Socrates and one or more unnamed companions sitting in the Lyceum, where Alcibiades passes by on his way to the assembly.[56] Someone comments that Alcibiades was the sort of person "who would happily have found fault even with the twelve gods" (Aristid. *Or.* 3.575 = *SSR* 6a.46). This hubristic pride is obviously the trigger for Socrates' line of questioning on this occasion. Socrates reports that he "noticed that [Alcibiades] admired Themistocles" (Aristid. *Or.* 3.575 = *SSR* 6a.49), so he introduces a discussion of Themistocles' life. Vestiges of this conversation are preserved in a papyrus. First he brings up Themistocles' shameful dispute with his own father, who supposedly disowned him. To this Alcibiades responds,

Well, *this* I wouldn't have expected: that Themistocles was disowned by his father. That's really stupid. It's the sort of thing that happens to a useless person, to end up having such fights and extraordinary enmity with his own par-ents. Even a little child . . . [end of fragment].
(Pap. Ox. 1608 = SSR 6a.48).[57]

Socrates may have two aims here. First, he provokes Alcibiades to reflect on his own youthful hubris by getting him to criticize Themistocles' foolish and arrogant behaviour as a young man. Second, through this criticism he sets up an unfavourable comparison between Alcibiades and his idol. Hence another fragment begins, "Since you've taken it upon yourself to find fault with Themistocles' life, consider what sort of man you resolved to criticize" (*Or.* 3.348 = SSR 6a.50).

In this same papyrus we have the following exchange of question and answer: "And do you think people must first be cultured, or without culture?" Socrates asks. "And must they first be accustomed to riding horses, or unaccustomed to it?" "I think they must first be uncultured and unaccustomed to riding," Alcibiades answers. We can see that the issue here is education. In order to become *mousikos* you need teachers and you need to exert yourself in training; the same goes for becoming *hippikos*. Although the precise connection between this exchange and Themistocles' shameful relationship with his father is unclear, the point must somehow have been that Themistocles required training and exercise in order to develop his eventual attributes, to become the sort of person he was said to be (*hoiōi andri epitimān ēxiōsas*). This brings us back to Socrates' contrast between Themistocles and "the useless people who take no care for themselves." Obviously Alcibiades is supposed to include himself in this number. The tables have turned: it is not Themistocles who was "useless" (*phaulos*), as Alcibiades thought, but arrogant and negligent people like Alcibiades himself. This lesson hits home with Alcibiades, whom we next see "crying with his head on his knees, upset because he was nowhere near as well prepared as Themistocles" (Aristid. 3.575 = SSR 6a.49).

I want to emphasize four points about this conversation. First, Socrates' disinterested love for Alcibiades has facilitated his veridiction as master. He has not shied away from implicitly communicating some very harsh truths. Hence Plutarch praises him for the free speech (*parrhēsia*) he employs in this conversation (*Mor.* 69e-f = SSR 6a.51). This is because those truths were necessary to achieve Socrates' only desire, which is Alcibiades' moral improvement. A stranger would probably have avoided such social awkwardness, while a less disinterested lover would have flattered Alcibiades' vanity. Second, as elsewhere in Socratic literature, Socrates has brought Alcibiades to these intellectual and emotional conclusions through the revelation of Alcibiades' own beliefs. While Socrates obviously plays a role in the articulation of those beliefs, he does not tell

Alcibiades what to believe or feel. This model of governmentality is collaborative rather than apodictic, because neither member of the relationship possesses the knowledge toward which their dialogue is oriented. Third, one of the principal topics throughout the conversation has been subjectivation: not only what sort of subject Themistocles was as a young man and then as a mature statesman, but also what sort of "care for himself" enabled him to became that sort of person. Note also the reference to "preparation" (*paraskeuē*) in the last passage I quoted, which in Hellenistic philosophy is one of the key words used to designate the battery of attitudes, propositions, and arguments which enable the educated person to cope successfully with the world.[58] Fourth, nowhere in the fragments or testimony for this conversation do we have any real definition or investigation of the specific attributes Alcibiades ought to acquire. In fact, nowhere in any of the fragments of Aeschines' dialogues do we have any clear reference to the canonical moral virtues, much less any attempt to define them. In this respect Aeschines appears to put more emphasis on the processes of governmentality, veridiction, and subjectivation than on theorizing the goals of these processes. Those goals remain open-ended. Presumably it is through continued Socratic conversations, undertaken in loving relationships, that they are to be approached.

4. CONCLUSION: THE PHILOSOPHICAL SIGNIFICANCE OF AESCHINES

It is time to pull together some conclusions. If we look for the philosophical significance of Aeschines, where are we to find it? Of course, we should mention that he was probably an important dialectical partner for Antisthenes, Xenophon and especially Plato. Thus he was important for the historical development of philosophy. We should also remember the inexplicable hostility displayed toward him by Menedemus of Eretria, who insisted Aeschines got his dialogues from Xanthippe and passed them off as his own (D.L. 2.60–1 = *SSR* 6a.22). Even more oddly, the Stoic Persaius claims that the dialogues ascribed to Aeschines were actually written by Menedemus' disciple, the Eretrian philosopher Pasiphon (ibid.). Some sort of engagement with Aeschines' ideas probably lies behind these attacks on the authenticity of his dialogues. Lamentably, we can no longer even conjecture what it was.

If, on the other hand, we want to address Aeschines as a thinker of more than historical interest, where should we begin? Since the evidence for his dialogues contains no subtle theorizing about ethical, epistemological, or metaphysical questions, scholars have sometimes damned him with faint praise: he lacks the ability or aspirations for profound thought, but he is a very faithful disciple of Socrates.[59] Or else his dialogues may be categorized with the mildly pejorative labels of "pedagogical" and "protreptic" rather than "investigative" or "constructive." What I have suggested here is that, without inflating our estimation of Aeschines to a degree the evidence does not merit, we might nevertheless find in Foucault an interpretive framework which will make Aeschines' fragments more philosophically significant. For Foucault is unquestionably an important contributor to contemporary philosophical debates. He engages with canonical "big questions" in the field of ethics, politics, and epistemology. But in place of virtue, constitutions, and knowledge his final work focuses on subjectivation, governmentality, and veridiction. In this chapter I have suggested that Aeschines too is thinking about the interconnections among these processes, although of course he does not use these words. In fact I hope to have shown that an interpretation framed by these categories can both knit together Aeschines' disparate fragments more effectively than has hitherto been accomplished and support a detailed discussion about their precise wording. Aeschines can therefore be used to qualify and enrich Foucault's investigation of the Greek and Roman tradition, to which he should be considered a significant contributor.

NOTES

1. See the papyri first discussed by Grenfell and Hunt 1919: n. 1608, Lobel 1972: n. 2889–2890. For the rest of the fragments of Aeschines, see Giannantoni 1990.
2. See esp. Dittmar 1912, Ehlers 1966, Allman 1972, Patzer 1974, Rossetti and Lausdei 1979 and 1981.
3. Foucault 2005, 2010, 2011.
4. 2005: 36–37. On this crisis in the Athenian democratic model of subjectivation/veridiction/governmentality, see also 2008: 180–208.
5. Foucault returns to this body of texts in almost very lecture from 1981 to 1984. Passages he analyses in some depth come from the *Alcibiades*, *Apology*, *Crito*, *Phaedo*, *Phaedrus*, *Gorgias*, *Laches*, and the fifth, seventh, and eighth Platonic letters. He also discusses the Neoplatonic commentaries on the *Alcibiades*.
6. The most thorough examination of Foucault's final three seminars of which I am aware is McGushin 2007. Nehamas 1998: 157–88 also contains a brilliant discussion of Foucault's handling of Plato in these seminars. See also Miller 1994: 354–74. (Nehamas, McGushin, and Miller all had access to transcripts of the final seminars before their publication.)
7. He explicitly cites Hadot at 1990: 8 and 2005: 387, 417–8
8. See, for example, Foucault 2010: 309–10.
9. Foucault discusses the exemplarity of Freudian psychoanalysis at various points in *The Will to Knowledge* (e.g. 1998: 112–14, 129–31, 58–9), but the following elaboration is my own.
10. In fact, while Freud tends to consider whatever neurosis he "discovers" a given, Lacanian psychoanalysts admit that the core "fantasy" behind neurotic behaviour is actually something *constructed* during the course of analysis (Fink 1997: 70).
11. Patzer 1974, Rossetti and Lausdei 1979, 1981. Slings 1975 is also of some use for the philological reconstruction of the papyrus.
12. The only uncertain part of this passage is the ending, for which I follow the reconstruction of Rossetti and Lausdei 1981: 155: παρῆλ[θεν] οὖν παρ' αὐτοὺ[ς] ἡμᾶς ἐξ[αίφνης Μι]λτιάδης, [ὥσπερ ἐπί]τηδες.

13. Thuc. 1.117.2, 2.58.1, 2.95.3, 5.19.2, 5.24.1, 6.31.2, 8.1.3; Lys. 12.65. All references from Will 2013.
14. On Miltiades' identity and age, see Patzer 1974: 274 n. 12, followed by Rossetti and Lausdei 1981: 157; Nails 2002: 207–8. It is not clear why Nails dates Miltiades' birth to around 470 BC. Our only evidence about him, except for this dialogue, is Lysias' testimony that he and Philochares helped the Spartan Lysander get approval for the regime of the so-called "Thirty Tyrants" (Lys. 12.72). Philochares became one of the Thirty; it is not clear why Miltiades did not. In any event, this hardly proves that Miltiades was old at this time, since many of the Thirty were relatively young. It seems best to me to revert to the assumption of Slings 1975: 305–7, that Miltiades is a young man in need of education.
15. I follow the reconstruction of Rossetti and Lausdei 1979: 47 of this admittedly difficult passage: οὐ[δὲν ἂν εἴη τοῦτό γε] δεινόν, ἔφην ἐγώ, [εἰ περὶ ὧν ἡμεῖς μὲν ἀ]ποροῦμεν, ἐκεῖ[νος δὲ περὶ τούτων] οὐκ ἀπορήσει· θαῦ[μ᾽ οὐδὲν γὰρ ὅτι, εἰ μὲ]ν ἠρόμην Εὐριπί[δην δημιουργῶν] ὅτωι ξυνῶν ἂν Μιλ[τιάδης ἄριστα] β[ου]λεύοιτο ὅπως χρὴ [ὑποδήματα] ποιεῖν, εἶ[χ]εν ἄν μοι λέ[γειν ὅτι τοῖ]ς σκυτοτόμοις, ἢ ὅτωι ἂν [ξύνων ἄρ]ιστα βουλεύοιτο ὅπως [χρὴ οἰκία] ν οἰκοδομεῖν, καὶ τοῦτ᾽ εἶ[χεν ἂν λέγ]ειν ὅτι τοῖς τέκτοσιν· νῦν [. . .] Xen. Mem. 4.4.5 contains an extremely similar argument (Rossetti and Lausdei 1979: 50).
16. Regarding *sunousia* as an essential element of Socratic pedagogy, compare Pl. *Tht.* 150d2-d6 and [Pl.] *Thg.* 129e1–31a10 with Tarrant 2005, Lampe 2013; Pl. *Ep.* 7.341b7-d2 with Foucault 2011: 245–57.
17. Regarding Homeric *euboulia*, see the classic discussion of Schofield 2001; regarding Aristotelian *boulē* and *bouleusis*, see *EN* 3.3 1112a18–13a14.
18. Rossetti and Lausdei 1981: 157–8.
19. Rossetti and Lausdei 1981: 157.
20. As Rossetti and Lausdei 1981: 163 note, there may also be a criticism here of Antisthenes' penchant for exertion. However, D.L. tell us that Aeschines himself was *ek neou philoponos* (2.60).
21. Slings 1975: 306–7, Rossetti and Lausdei 1981: 159.
22. See esp. 2.14: "I've now discussed the education of the Lacedaemonians and that of the other Greeks. Let anyone who wishes judge which produces men who are more obedient (*eupeithesteroi*), respectful (*aidēmonesteroi*) and appropriately self-controlled (*hōn dei enkratesteroi*)." The words *eupeithēs* and *enkratēs* do not appear elsewhere in the work, but the concepts are ubiquitous. The words *aidōs*, *aidēmōn*, and *aideomai* appear frequently.
23. 1981: 159–60.
24. *Pace* Rossetti and Lausdei 1981: 162, I do not believe this *khreia* is "completamente estraneo al nostro dialogo."
25. Rossetti and Lausdei 1979: 52.
26. I take this to be an ironic way of saying the pedagogue was downright bad. See LSJ s.v. πάνυ def. 3, re οὐ πάνυ: "sts. with litotes, not *quite*, implying 'not *at all*.'"
27. Fraser and Matthews 2010: 428.
28. Fraser and Matthews 1987: 434.
29. Taylor 1928: 23.
30. See Burket 1972: 198–208, Kahn 2001: 49, Reidweg 2005: 106–8.
31. I omit the following crux: †τοῖς ἐοικέναι εἴ τις ἔθελοι καὶ ψόγους [εἰ καὶ ψόγους εἶναι θέλοι τις].
32. Riedweg 2005: 67.
33. As Aristophon fr. 12 (Kassell and Austin 1983: 10) clearly implies.
34. Cf. Taylor 1928: 25, who plausibly suggests that Socrates was situated between the dissolute luxury of Critobulus and the radical asceticism of Telauges.

35. For a creative reconstruction see Allman 1972. While the story of the cock fight between Callias and Meidias at D.L. 2.30 would add a fascinating element to this dialogue, I am not persuaded by Allman's arguments that it derives from Aeschines.
36. Ehlers 1966, followed implicitly by Döring 1984, Kahn 1990: 291, 1994: 93. Gaiser's review of Ehlers (1969: 200–206) is the exception.
37. My summary of this dialogue's structure is indebted to Ehlers 1966: 35–100, Döring 1984: 22–5, and Kahn 1994: 94–103.
38. Athenaeus' testimony here is highly tendentious; see my comments earlier in the article about his description of the *Telauges*.
39. Cf. Pl. *Men.* 235e3–36c4, 249d1-e7; Xen. *Oec.* 3.14, *Mem.* 2.6.36 = SSR 6a.66, 71, 72.
40. Θαργηλία Μιλησία ἐλθοῦσα εἰς Θετταλίαν ξυνῆν Ἀντιόχῳ βασιλεύοντι πάντων Θετταλῶν.
41. Priscian provides this quotation without any hint of context (*Inst.* 18.296).
42. He escapes not by his artful speaking, but by the testimony on his behalf by his cousin, Aristides "the Just" (*SSR* 6a.75).
43. Cf. Gaiser 1969: 202–3, 206; Kahn 1994: 102.
44. See Porter 1993 and especially Gagarin 2001.
45. See Henry 1995 for Aspasia' history and literary legend.
46. The thematic connection encompassing rhetoric, eros, and self-improvement is not random: Plato combines the same elements in the *Phaedrus*.
47. Ehlers 1966: 93, Kahn 1990: 291–3, Kahn 1994: 100–103. Döring 1984: 22–5 argues that erotics and dialectic are "two sides of the same coin," which is plausible (see below); but as I argue in Lampe 2010: 196, Döring fails adequately to explain what is erotic about Aspasia's or Socrates' dialectic. The reconstruction of Gaiser 1969: 205–6 is the best currently on offer, but is too reductively schematic.
48. Gaiser 1969: 205.
49. On the interpretation of the *Alcibiades* see most recently Döring 1984, Kahn 1994, Lampe 2010: 194–9.
50. Immediately after this quotation Aelius Aristides comments, ἐνταῦθα τελευτᾷ τῶν διαλόγων (*Or.* 2.74).
51. Here I re-use my translation from Lampe 2010: 195.
52. For the insight that Socrates' eros should be "subsumed under the generic term *epithumia*" see Joyal 1993: 266.
53. Lampe 2013.
54. See especially 2005: 37, 58–9, 127–67, 395–411. This issue goes out of focus in Foucault's final two seminars, but they still contain many relevant discussions, e.g. 2008: 225–97, 2011: 57–94, 231–305. Even in scholarship on Socratic eros the importance of interpersonal emotional dynamics is often neglected, as I have argued in Lampe 2010.
55. Foucault 2005: 59.
56. The quotation in *SSR* 6a.43 = Dem. *Eloc.* 205 almost certainly represents the dialogue's opening words, beginning with *ekathēmetha men*. Alcibiades probably appeared in the *de* clause. The particulars of Alcibiades' movements may be conjectured from Maximus of Tyre's testimony in SSR 6a.42 = *Phil.* 7.7.
57. Regarding Alcibiades and his father, compare Plut. *Them.* 2.6. While Giannantoni prints a question mark at the end of the last sentence, this appears to be a typo (and would be unintelligible); Grenfell and Hunt print a semicolon.
58. Foucault 2005: 320–7.
59. Ehlers 1966: 23.

WORKS CITED

Allman, H. 1972. "Über die beste Erziehung: Zum Dialog Kallias des Sokratikers Aischines." *Philologus* 116: 213–53.

Burkert, W. 1972. *Lore and Science in Ancient Pythagoreanism*. Trans. E. L Minar, Jr. Cambridge, MA: Harvard UP.

Dittmar, H. 1912. *Aischines von Sphettos. Studien zur Literaturgeschichte der Sokratiker: Untersuchungen und Fragmente*. Berlin: Weidmann.

Döring, K. 1984. "Der Sokrates des Aischines von Sphettos und die Frage nach dem historischen Sokrates." *Hermes* 112: 16–30.

Ehlers, B. 1966. *Eine vorplatonische Deutung des sokratischen Eros. Der Dialog Aspasia des Sokratikers Aischines*. Munich: C. H. Beck.

Fink, B.. 1997. *A Clinical Introduction to Lacanian Psychoanalysis: Theory and Technique*. Princeton: Princeton University Press.

Foucault, M. 1998. *The History of Sexuality Volume 1: The Will to Knowledge*. Trans. R. Hurley. London: Penguin.

———. 2005. *The Hermeneutics of the Subject. Courses at the Collège de France 1981–1982*. Ed. F. Gros, trans. G. Burchell. New York: Picador.

———. 2010. *The Government of Self and Others. Lectures at the Collège de France 1982–1983*. Ed. F. Gros, trans. G. Burchell. New York: Picador.

———. 2011. *The Courage of Truth: The Government of Self and Others II. Lectures at the Collège de France 1983–1984*. Ed. F. Gros, trans. G. Burchell. New York: Picador.

Fraser, P.M. and E. Matthews, eds. 1987. *A Lexicon of Greek Personal Names. Volume I. The Aegean Islands. Cyprus. Cyrenaica*. Oxford: Clarendon.

———. 2010. *A Lexicon of Greek Personal Names. Volume VA. Coastal Asia Minor: Pontos to Ionia*. Oxford: Clarendon.

Gaiser, K. 1969. Review of Ehlers 1966. *AGPh* 51: 200–209.

Gagarin, M. 2001. "Did the Sophists Aim to Persuade?" *Rhetorica: A Journal of the History of Rhetoric* 19.3: 275–91.

Grenfell, B.P. and A.S. Hunt, eds. 1919. *The Oxyrhynchus Papyri Part XIII*. London: Egypt Exploration Fund.

Henry, M. 1995. *Prisoner of History: Aspasia of Miletus and Her Biographical Tradition*. Oxford: Oxford UP.

Joyal, M. 1993. "The Conclusion of Aeschines' *Alcibiades*." *RhM* 136: 263–8.

Kahn, C. 1990. "Plato as a Socratic." In P. Bourdieu et al., eds., *Hommage à Henri Joly*, 287–301. Grenoble: Université des sciences sociales de Grenoble.

———. 1994. "Aeschines on Socratic Eros." In *The Socratic Movement*, ed. P. Vander Waerdt, 87–106. Ithaca: Cornell UP.

———. 2001. *Pythagoras and the Pythagorans: A Brief History*. Indianapolis: Hackett.

Kassell, R. and C. Austin, 1983. *Poetae Comici Graeci vol. 4: Aristophon-Crobylus*. Berlin: De Gruyter.

Lampe, K. 2010. "Socratic Therapy from Aeschines of Sphettus to Lacan." *Classical Antiquity* 29.2: 181–221.

———. 2013. " Rationality, Eros, and Daemonic Influence in the Platonic *Theages* and the Academy of Polemo and Crates." *AJP* 134: 383–424.

Lobel, E., ed. 1972. *The Oxyrhynchus Papyri Volume XXXIX*. London: Egypt Exploration Society.

McGushin, E.F. 2007. *Foucault's Askēsis: An Introduction to the Philosophical Life*. Evanston: Northwestern UP.

Nails, D. 2002. *The People of Plato: A Prosopography of Plato and Other Socratics*. Indianapolis: Hackett.

Nehamas, A. 1998. *The Art of Living: Socratic Reflections from Plato to Foucault.* Berkeley: UC Press.
Patzer, A. 1974. Αισχίνου Μιλτιάδης. *ZPE* 15: 271–87.
Porter, J. 1993. "The Seductions of Gorgias." *ClAnt* 12.2: 267–99.
Reidweg, C. 2005. *Pythagoras: His Life, Teaching, and Influence.* Trans. S. Rendall. Ithaca: Cornell UP.
Rossetti, L. and C. Lausdei. 1979. "Ancora sul *Milziade* di Eschine socratico: P. Oxy. 2890 (Back)." *ZPE* 33: 47–56.
———. 1981. "P. Oxy. 2889 e il *Milziade* di Eschine Socratico." *SIFC* 124: 154–65.
Schofield, M. 2001. "*Euboulia* in the *Iliad*." In *Oxford Readings in Homer*, ed. D. Cairns, 220–59. Oxford: Oxford UP.
Slings, S. R. 1975. "Some Remarks on Aeschylus' *Miltiades*." *ZPE* 16: 301–8.
Tarrant, H. 2005. "Socratic *Synousia*: A Post-Platonic Myth?" *Journal of the History of Philosophy* 43:131–55.
Taylor, A.E. 1928. "Aeschines of Sphettus." In *Philosophical Studies*, 1–27. London: Macmillan and Co.
Will, W. 2013. "Hagnon." In *Brill's New Pauly*, ed. H. Cancik and H. Schneider. Accessed 22 September 2013. <http://referenceworks.brillonline.com/entries/brill-s-new-pauly/hagnon-e501580>.

5 Phaedo's *Zopyrus* (and Socrates' Confidences)

Livio Rossetti

1. SOME PRELIMINARIES

The figure of Phaedo, the Socratic from Elis, has been drowned out by the success, over the centuries, of the Platonic dialogue named after him. A significant reawakening of interest in him as an author, in the period 1970–1990, and some more recent studies (in particular Kahn 1996, Sellars 2003, Boys-Stones 2004, Boys-Stones 2007), have hardly saved him from his traditional banishment to the corner. He remains little more than the beautiful youth whose hair Socrates strokes, at *Phaedo* 89b-c; a colourful but secondary figure in the context of the death of the great man himself.

If nothing much has changed in relation to our sources of information about Phaedo, a change has certainly occurred in the way we think of the so-called 'Minor Socratics.' Recent years have witnessed a complete rediscovery of Xenophon and his *Socratica*,[1] and the beginnings of a treatment of the Socratic circle not as Plato's little brothers but rather as his travelling companions, friends or erstwhile friends, and of an appreciation of the fact that each one of them contributed both to the building of the posthumous image of Socrates and to the immediate fate of Socraticism.[2] It was Gabriele Giannantoni who first suggested that the first-generation needed to be studied independently of the formation of philosophical schools inspired by their teachings, so "giving back to Euclides, to Phaedo, to Aristippus and to Antisthenes their true character as authentic Socratics"; it was a mistake, he proposed, "to interpret their thought in light of the later history of their so-called schools."[3] His propensity for cutting the "umbilical cord" tying each Socratic to the school he would go on to found has continued to create the conditions for starting to recognise the Socratics of the first generation as a relatively homogeneous and close-knit group, though one that would very soon split apart.

Notwithstanding some promising developments in this direction, the tendency has continued of treating the severer form of Socraticism found in Antisthenes and its hedonistic counterpart in Aristippus as the two extremes on a scale of values with which to measure the positions taken by the other Socratics; so too of devoting close attention to the few remaining fragments of certain dialogues of Aeschines' and Phaedo's while leaving aside all the highly informative testimonia we have about them, thus failing to see what invaluable evidence these provide, certainly in relation to Socrates. It is this that explains the way scholars persist in talking of a supposed incommensurability between testimonies, the impossibility of arriving at the real, historical Socrates, and so on, and end up once more taking refuge in the familiar Platonic account. But it is hard to contest, and properly speaking needs no proof, (1) that Aeschines and Phaedo give well articulated and unequivocal testimony on the subject of Socrates—a testimony which, besides not depending either on Plato or on Xenophon (and even less on Aristotle or Aristophanes), has the great merit of revealing Socrates' inner self, to an extent that other sources do not; and (2) that their evidence allows just the kind of confrontation between different testimonies, and the kind of opportunity for independent confirmation, that modern interpreters insist on treating as "unfortunately impossible." A renewed attention to the dialogues of these two authors, along with the external evidence, will be sufficient, I suggest, to prompt a comprehensive re-thinking of the figure of Socrates—and equally a rethinking, even more overdue, of the so-called "Socratic question."[4]

2. THE SOCRATES OF THE *ZOPYRUS*

Those who have paused on the story of Zopyrus have generally treated the Socrates-Zopyrus episode as an excuse for trying to extract an impression of Phaedo's own supposed philosophy. My own view, however, is that we need to ask ourselves what we learn from *Zopyrus* about *Socrates*. As it happens, there is a well connected set of testimonia that allows us to form a quite precise idea of the story as narrated in the dialogue. Let me then outline this story, assuming that a reliable enough account of what happens is available. Socrates' companions come face to face with Zopyrus, who professes to be able to read off people's characters from their facial features. They show him a portrait of Socrates, perhaps to put his claim to the test. In the person represented in the portrait Zopyrus finds an essentially stupid individual who is also lustful, and possibly a pederast, all of which arouses indignation in the Socratics. But Zopyrus insists that his diagnosis is no hasty one, and asks for a personal meeting with Socrates. The meeting happens, and he immediately confirms his diagnosis: he has perfectly understood the kind of person Socrates is. Socrates' friends become even angrier with him, but at this point the master intervenes with the words "Stay calm, my friends! For I really am the kind of man he found in me; but I control myself" (that is, I control myself so effectively that none of you, for all the time you have been with me, has ever noticed).

Although certainty on the matter is impossible, it is at least probable that the plot ended with a eulogy of philosophy as capable of improving even those who cannot boast a good character or education. In his *On Fate*, Alexander of Aphrodisias concludes his short re-evocation of the Zopyrus story with the words "Socrates did not contradict Zopyrus; he said that that *was* what he was like, so far as his nature was concerned, unless through the *askêsis* that comes from philosophy he had become better than his own nature."[5]

This declaration is important from many points of view. To begin with, Socrates says he will not contradict Zopyrus, admitting that his nature is exactly as it has just been described, but then going on to say that he would have remained such, and the vices identified by Zopyrus would have revealed themselves, except for the fact that he has become a better person thanks to *askêsis* and, ultimately, thanks to philosophy. Thus Alexander's report presents a Socrates (1) who admits he is not, by nature and instinct, as his disciples know him, and (2) who assigns his present condition (of an intellectual who is both respectable and respected) to philosophy, or more precisely to the kind of *askêsis* offered by philosophy: that is—or so we may suppose—to the results obtained from exercise, labour, effort, and a commitment to improve himself under the impulse and guidance of philosophy.

With Alexander's report we may link the testimony provided by the Emperor Julian in one of his letters (*SSR* III A 2): "Phaedo of Elis . . . thought there was nothing that was incurable by philosophy, and that thanks to philosophy it is possible for all to purify themselves of any kind of life, habit, passion, and other things of that sort. For if it was useful only to those with a good character and education, there would be nothing exceptional in it; but if it enlightens even those who are in such a condition (. . .), then it is something truly prodigious." According to Boys-Stones (2004, 9) and others "There is no way of telling upon which of Phaedo's works Julian based his assessment," but there is more than enough in it to give us reason to disagree: the sentiment reported by Julian comes from the *Zopyrus*. There is, after all, considerable conceptual proximity between "becoming better thanks to philosophy" and "being purified by philosophy," as there is between the unattractive initial dispositions Socrates admits to having had and the similarly unattractive initial conditions of which some are said to be "purified" by philosophy. This agreement between Alexander and Julian also fits well with the fact that Socrates' admissions about his character will very likely have given rise to further comment; indeed, it is virtually impossible that the meeting concluded with Socrates' unexpected confession. It seems probable that Julian is in fact alluding to a concluding statement, in *Zopyrus*, about the benefits that can come from philosophy, as in Socrates' own case, which functions as it were as the moral of the story.

Support for this conjecture, which of course remains speculative, can be found in the analogous concluding reflections in the *Alcibiades* of Aeschines of Sphettus (fr. 11 Dittmar = *SSR* VI A 53), insofar as the sentence reported by Julian too seems clearly to represent the crowning of the narrative. It is thus reasonable to suppose that the *Zopyrus* emphasized the power of philosophy, as capable of purifying and offering redemption even in the most desperate cases; and it is not only possible but probable that with his phrase "to people who are in such a condition" Julian intended an allusion to the supposedly bad natural dispositions of Socrates.[6] The convergence of the evidence is so clear as not to leave room for reasonable doubt.

With all this in mind, I propose now to focus briefly on another detail, the *portrait* of Socrates that figures in the story of the *Zopyrus*. There are only three texts, all from the Arabic world (numbers 20–22 R., not in *SSR*), that have anything to say about this portrait; but it fits well in the setting of the story, usefully heightening the tension before the arrival of Socrates himself. In fact, without the splitting of the story into two stages (first a diagnosis based on the portrait, then a diagnosis based on direct observation), the whole is exceedingly banal. In particular, the surprise and indignation of Socrates' pupils would be hard to understand: if Socrates had been present from the beginning, we would have to ask ourselves what he would be doing while the disciples were getting upset—would he have waited, cruelly, until misunderstanding provoked a physical confrontation before intervening? I note, in passing, that our other sources offer an abstract of the story reduced to the minimum, and it is not unreasonable to suppose that one of its two phases will have been suppressed in the interests of brevity. As for the likelihood that a portrait of Socrates would have been made when he was alive, I limit myself to the observation that there could be some foundation to the report, even in the absence of any known parallel, in view both of the notoriety of the person in question, and of his ties with wealthy people.

When it comes to the identification of the defining traits of the Socratic *ethos*, Boys-Stones (2007, 23) has rightly pointed out that the information given by fragment 6 R. (Cicero, *On Fate*, using the terms *stupidus* and *bardus*) is not in conflict with the generality of our other sources, which, depending on the case, speak of *vitia* (fr. 7 R., from Cicero), Socrates as *libidinosus* (fr. 8 R., from pseudo-Plutarch), strange things (*atopa*) (fr. 10 R., from Alexander of Aphrodisias), pederasty (fr. 11 R., from John Cassian), Socrates as full of eros (fr. 12 R. from Adamantius), *amator* (fr. 15 R., from an anonymous *On Physiognomy*), *amans coitum* (fr. 16 R., from Polemon), *lascivior* (fr. 20 R., from the Constantinopolitan epitome), *fraudolentus, deceptor, amans coitum* (fr. 21 R., from the *Secret of Secrets*), *luxuriosus, deceptor, amans coitum* (fr.22 R., from another version of the *Secret of Secrets*). The discrepancy is easily resolved as soon as we understand that a thick neck is supposed to indicate stupidity, the set of the eyes traits of a sexual nature. So, while the observation of what may be indicated by a thick neck gives us clear reason for saying that Zopyrus was capable of being analytical, and noting non-convergent indications, the other group of attributions points unequivocally in the direction of a supposed hypersensitivity on Socrates' part to the allures of sex. These indications find their confirmation in a range of texts, from the discourse of Alcibiades in Plato's *Symposium*, and a well known passage in the *Charmides* (154b-d), to the topic of the "kissing of the beautiful" in Xenophon's *Symposium* (4.23–27; cf. *Mem.* II 6.28; see also I 3.8–14, I 6.13); and one should recall in this context a recent book by Gabriel Danzig which concludes from a reconsideration of the testimonia that the Socratics felt the need to present the sexual life of their master in a more favourable light, making every effort particularly, in the face of the charge that Socrates corrupted young men, to avoid any appearance that he indulged in unlicensed sexual intercourse.[7] There is also, of course, that report that Socrates might have come across Phaedo in a brothel. In general, there is plenty to reassure us of the reality of the "unmentionable inclinations" that Zopyrus in all probability saw in Socrates, to the surprise and indignation of his friends.

Some attention deserves to be paid to the implicit conclusion of the story. Socrates might have added "so well do I control, *contineo*, what you have not noticed at all." His disciples, in their turn, might on the one hand have commented "True, but now we begin to understand a whole series of details and episodes," and on the other have congratulated themselves along with Zopyrus, acknowledging that he was right, "though we never would have suspected," and so on. This detail is quite significant, insofar as it allows us a glimpse of a kind of hoping for the best on the part of Socratics, who suspect nothing, cannot believe it, and so on.

There are many aspects that may help us to understand such an attitude. In the first place, I observe that such attitudes may also reflect a new emphasis on respectability, observable in the behaviour of Athenians of the time: while during the long years of the Peloponnesian War sexuality was experienced and represented in the most exotic variety of forms, in the first half of the fourth century we seem to find an increasing sensitivity to the idea that the diffusion of reports about some example or other of excessive sexual "licence" could endanger one's respectability.[8] Thus, behind the chorus of indignation of Socrates' friends at what Zopyrus says, we can see not so much the models of behaviour belonging to the end of the fifth century as those of a time some decades later.[9]

This brings us to the story of the liberation of Phaedo, according to which he found himself a prisoner of war, then a slave in a brothel; while he was still there, so the story continues, somehow or other Socrates himself discovered him, recognized his worth, fell in love with him, then ransomed him (or arranged to have him ransomed). It has often been thought that this story was told by Phaedo himself, and that the references to the redeeming power of philosophy were intended to allude to his own personal experiences. But this is doubtful on many grounds. Phaedo could not have been introducing such an autobiographical note into the *Zopyrus*: there is an obvious contrast, in the tale about Zopyrus, between the surprise that greets the report of Socrates' weakness for dubious pleasures and the essential presupposition of the story about the ransoming of Phaedo, namely that Socrates and his friends were regular visitors to the brothel, so that they could get to know the young slave and appreciate his qualities. Such a story does credit to

Socrates, but only at the cost of throwing a less than reassuring shadow not only on Phaedo but on other Socratics who would apparently be frequenting the brothel along with their master. It is thus hardly likely that the story was brought into the open by the very person most implicated in it, namely Phaedo, at least in the contest of *Zopyrus*. Other alternative hypotheses are available: it is possible, for instance, that the story—too ugly, surely, not to have originated as a slander—was first reported by Aristoxenus, for example, or by Phaenias of Eresus. There are in fact analogies between the adventures of Phaedo and other romanticised fictions that were given credit around the same time by authors such as Theopompus.

It thus seems appropriate to dissociate these biographical (and scandalous) reports clearly from the dialogue presently under examination.

3. SOCRATES' CONFIDENCES IN THE *ZOPYRUS*

The observations and inferences offered in the preceding section have already contributed towards establishing certain aspects of the *Zopyrus* and, in particular, in the matter of the image of Socrates that the *Zopyrus* intended to project. However, I believe we have not yet addressed the essential and defining aspect of the dialogue. As I have already indicated, the primary contribution of the *Zopyrus*—as of the *Alcibiades* of Aeschines of Sphettus—is its attempt to reveal something of Socrates' inner self. To all appearance, this is no mere detail.[10] To establish the point one needs only to recall how Plato, for example, tends to give us a Socrates that sets up and guides a relationship, a Socrates caught as he acts, speaks, creatively moulds his interlocutors, in other words a Socrates observed in action, understood through the logic of his actions: a Socrates seen, observed, scrutinised, studied by someone who wants to discover his secret while remaining other—in short, a Socrates that is an object of observation, not a subject prone to lift the veil on his inner self. This is particularly evident in Socratic dialogues like those of a Plato with Socrates as narrator: he tells us what he has said, heard or done, not what he wanted or the goal he had in mind; he does not say things like "I am glad that" / "what a pity that"; he is given no opportunity to pronounce on the meaning, for him, of what has just happened. Again, as narrator, he gives no opinion on the person, or people, he has met and talked to for long periods.

What fails to happen in Plato's dialogues (we will see later one or two small exceptions in Xenophon) does, however, occur in that wonderful ending to Aeschines' *Alcibiades*, in which Socrates directly expresses his amazement at the emotions he has succeeded in evoking. He asks himself "how could this happen?," and offers the following answer:

> "If I thought that I could be of any help through some art (*technê*), I would convict myself of very great stupidity. As it is, I thought this had

been granted me, in respect to Alcibiades, by divine gift ... The genuine love that I had for Alcibiades made me no different from the Bacchants. For whenever the Bacchants become inspired, sources from which others cannot even draw water allow *them* to draw honey and milk. Just so I have no knowledge of any subject that I can benefit a person by teaching him, and yet I thought that by being with him I would make him better, through my loving him."[11]

The striking feature of these declarations is that Socrates does not just relive the event and set out to interpret it, trying to understand what really happened and ending by asking himself how on earth the proud Alcibiades could ever have dissolved into tears. He has no hesitation in admitting that it all happened by virtue of a special emotional tension, a tension which—as he explicitly says—transcends the sphere of expertise, even the art of communication, rhetoric, itself; he even admits that he himself felt it as much as did Alcibiades. This admission clearly is not tinged with any *eirôneia*, because there is no affectation in it, only an intensity of felt emotion; it marks a virtually unique moment of tranquillity, in which Socrates is not proving something (and indeed no longer has any need to prove anything), but can instead allow himself some confidences, insisting that what has happened owes nothing to his presumed cleverness. All of which is quite unusual, from many points of view. But since the focus of the present notes is not Aeschines' *Alcibiades* but Phaedo's *Zopyrus*, I shall here limit myself to registering the word "confidences," observing that the *Zopyrus* too ends with, and is characterized by, certain important "confidences."

As I have already said, the whole situation in the *Zopyrus* is conceived in such a way as to make Socrates able to say words to the effect of "My friends, stay calm, and stop being angry, because this foreigner, Zopyrus, is quite right. I am in fact the kind of man he says, only I contain myself."[12] That is, the situation is designed to prepare for a revelation, building up to the unexpected moment when Socrates reveals his cards and says who really he is. For the reasons indicated above, we may suppose that, in revealing his cards, he used the opportunity to mention the battles he fought to achieve this *epechein*, this keeping under control (or—as we might say—repression) of instinctive impulses —impulses that he does not deny he not only has had but has, and that Zopyrus has identified by carefully observing his face, and, given his impartiality, could call by their name.[13] As Cristiana Caserta has recently written, "The topic of the encounter with Zopyrus also confirms that the problem of self-knowledge was one that Socrates put to himself, not just to his interlocutors."[14] This is a good observation, and I record that it is not so much Xenophon or Plato that allows us to make it as Phaedo and his *Zopyrus*.

Phaedo in fact starts from a well known aspect of Socrates' lifestyle, his *enkrateia*, to allow us to deduce, as George Boys-Stones says, that "Zopyrus' diagnosis must be wrong. The whole episode is a typical example of a sophist stopped in his tracks; of a false pretence of knowledge that crumbles. But there is a surprise in store."[15] This is the way Phaedo prepares the way for the memorable moment when Socrates confesses and makes the admission he does, when his friends' anger threatens to degenerate into an actual beating.

This confession—we may call it a confidence—serves not just to relax the tension or round off the narrative: it allows us at the same time to understand Socrates from his own point of view, and to see that while he controls himself, and cares about controlling himself, he is very aware that he is keeping in check a set of instincts that—we are invited to suppose—continue to cause him trouble. I speak of "confidences" in this context because the Socratics are not represented as knowing already, for themselves, what impulses Socrates was engaged in governing or repressing, particularly since, as the story encourages us to suppose, they had noticed no dissonant aspects in the personality, or the behaviour, of the master. Thus what we have is a frank confidence, one that clarifies but also, in a certain way, embarrasses: this, at least, is the logic that seems to guide the course of events described in the *Zopyrus*.

That it allows us access to a confidence of Socrates' potentially makes the dialogue a document of the highest value, indeed a unique value, in comparison with those most comparable to it. While Plato offers us, at most, Alcibiades' confidences *on* Socrates,[16] Xenophon in his *Symposium* finds a way of having Socrates admit that he was shoulder to shoulder with Critobulus, and "it was as if I had been bitten by a wild animal—my shoulder smarted for more than five days . . . So now, Critobulus, before all these witnesses I warn you not to lay a finger on me until you have as much hair on your chin as you have on your head" (4.27-8). This too is not an admission that has been solicited, and so constitutes a confidence, but in comparison with what we find in the *Zopyrus* it is much more filtered and circumspect. What makes the difference is that, in Xenophon's *Symposium*, the discussion prevents any special emphasis on the story of two bare shoulders touching. Similarly, in the Platonic *Charmides* (155e), Socrates tells he was seriously disconcerted by the sight of the young man's nudity. But once more the impact of the incident is immediately lessened by the fact that is treated as a mere detail in the context of a discussion that far transcends it, so disconnecting itself from the revealing confidence. The *Zopyrus*, by contrast, far from treating its moment of revelation as a mere detail, puts it at the very centre of the whole narrative.[17]

One deduces from this that the "confidences" in the *Zopyrus*, and in Aeschines' *Alcibiades*, are given much greater emphasis, and bear all the marks of telling the truth about Socrates. Both authors, to say what sort of man Socrates is, resort to using his own confidences. So, if some tens of Socratic dialogues, Platonic or otherwise, show us a Socrates acting in recognizable ways (even if new differences of detail are understandably always bursting through), while other dialogues present doctrines often reflecting the author's thoughts much more than they do the thoughts of the main character, the *Zopyrus* gives us a Socrates who, for once, does not take the situation in hand except at the end, and only for a moment, but does so in a highly revealing way.

Even the discontinuity between these confidences and everything we know of the literature of the time is worth noting: does the world of embarrassing confidences perhaps originate with Socrates, and most particularly with these two dialogues? It is possible that these two Socratics, Phaedo and Aeschines, invented a new model for communication—and why else if not to evoke situations that were deeply impressed in their memories? Since our other testimonia make it impossible to treat these "confessions" as mere narrative fictions, what they contain comes with the highest grade of authenticity.

Some reflections on the general importance of this conclusion will be in place here. If out of the maelstrom of our supposedly chaotic and incommensurable sources on Socrates two turn out to be more than reliable, and capable of adding significantly to our understanding of who Socrates really was, then the terms of the dispute about the so-called "Socratic question" are immediately changed. The idea that the sources were irreducibly diverse took hold in the course of the twentieth century, when it became the standard view, especially in the form proposed by Dorion, who claimed that it is simply impossible to reconstruct the thought—the philosophy—of Socrates because there exists no workable criterion to help us resolve the impasse.[18] But this is simply not the case.

I do not of course mean to maintain that Phaedo and Aeschines give us the quintessence of truth; I have pointed out myself the signs of a certain re-reading of the figure of Socrates aimed, for example, at removing any impression that he indulged in unlicensed sex. My claim is simply (1) that it is useful to *begin* by comparing the image of Socrates offered by Plato and Xenophon with what emerges from Phaedo and Aeschines, and (2) that, if this is possible, and practicable, the decision to pronounce on the subject of Socrates without making these and other comparisons is neither justified nor justifiable.

4. COMMUNICATING AND INSPIRING WITHOUT TEACHING

A further and important point is that Socrates was immersed in a culture in which, even among *sophoi* and *sophistai*, a confirmed aversion to elaborating and expounding a fixed corpus of doctrines was widely shared: that is to say, intellectuals practised authorial withholding in the same way as poets and writers for the theatre. From Zeno to Plato, including especially those authors of discourses of an unequivocally antilogical character (Protagoras, Antiphon, Prodicus, Gorgias, Antisthenes himself), Greece went through a long period characterized by a passion for intellectual provocation. The opposite tendency—the effort to assemble systematic and connected sets of answers: theory, wisdom, doctrines, philosophies and a corresponding concern to assert one's paternity of them—preceded and postdated this phase (from Anaximander to Democritus, then from Aristotle on). One may ask how it could be that scholars should have failed to notice such an important oscillation;[19] not to take it into account is in any case rather dangerous, because it leads interpreters to busy themselves with trying to discover the *doctrines* of Socrates (or of Plato, of Gorgias . . .) and, once they have failed to find such things, systematised *more Aristotelico*, to maintain that we are just not in a position to acquire such knowledge of Socrates (or Plato, or Gorgias . . .).

Socrates was, however, one of those intellectuals, active between the middle of the fifth and the middle of the fourth centuries, who did nothing at all to expound and establish any doctrines, and it is therefore quite possible that to search for them is to labour in vain. This is because he communicated in other registers, for example through his behaviour and by promoting an innovative idea of excellence. A particular idea of excellence can be transformed into a doctrine, but it can also arise and establish itself as a way of being and a style of living without immediately becoming a doctrine in the process. It is no accident that our sources frequently, and in my view unequivocally, converge on just these points.[20] Consequently, what we need is not to give up trying to say who the real Socrates was, but rather to give up searching for what he did not care to leave to us, namely well worked doctrines.

One needs to be clear that to adopt, or to represent, a way of behaving behind which one can detect a rule of life inspired by *enkrateia* is not the same thing as offering a theory, or at least contains only a germ of a theory (of the kind that there is, for example, in the claim that the soul of a harmonious person is *sôphrôn* and courageous, whereas the soul of a person lacking in harmony is bad, even savage: Plato, *Republic* IV 411a). As opposed to an illustration of correct behaviour, in the first case, the second proposes permanent relationships between concepts, relationships that aspire to be universal. Again, in the first case, ideas are suggested without being developed (though they *could* be developed), while the second sets aside the present, contingent event and proceeds to connect notions already subject to generalization. The difference between the two cases is clear enough to make it easy to conclude that while Plato may have devoted himself to establishing permanent relationships between concepts, and so too some other Socratics, Phaedo (and Aeschines) did not—and neither did Socrates.

If then the Socrates of the *Zopyrus* proposes and values a style of life without giving any teaching or occupying himself with generalizations, it is up to us to make specific comparisons within this same field, without slipping into that of conceptual elaboration. That is easy enough, given the great variety of statements and anecdotes pointing in this direction:[21] the *logos proteptikos* in Plato's *Apology* (29d-30a), the *Clitophon*, the

Symposium, with its narrative of Alcibiades' confusion and shame, and so on. There are many occasions on which Socrates seems occupied with inculcating a style of life that generates self-esteem (or what we have come to call self-esteem) through the experience of shame. Alcibiades, for instance, is induced to despise himself and feel shame for being the person he is, but this psychological pressure is brought into play on the assumption that if he decided to change his life (that is, if he succeeded in controlling his instinctive impulses), then he would be content to live in a different way. Here Socrates is used exactly as a living example of success in the control of emotions and passions.

We may further compare the fragment in which Antisthenes ends by declaring that he would willingly kill Aphrodite, if he could, when he thinks of the many girls from good families that she has corrupted and ruined, and goes on to declare that he would prefer madness to the enjoyment of eros.[22] The most intuitive interpretation of this is that Socrates knew how neutralize Eros very well, even to the point of immunizing himself (and without any real fight). Also worth mentioning are the dozens of anecdotes connected with the name of Aristippus,[23] because this whole collection of witticisms serves to justify his behaviour by attributing to him an unexpected *freedom from* passions, pleasures and luxury even if he does not abstain from them. They strongly suggest that Aristippus too practises *epechein*, i.e. *enkrateia*, but without emphasizing the fact, and above all without denying himself many ways of gratifying his desires (within certain limits and under certain conditions). Thus his aphorisms too contribute towards establishing the exemplary nature of the Socratic commitment to *epechein*. The comparison with Aristippus also serves to bring out the point that Socrates is never said himself to have set a positive value on the idea of *ponos* or that of *hêdonê*. Rather, his behaviour always speaks to us of *enkrateia*, manifestly a quite different notion. It is exactly on this latter that the *Zopyrus* turns the spotlight, while at the same time suggesting intuitive connections with other texts on Socrates' style of life. The dialogue thus contributes towards an outline of an idea of Socrates that is rock solid, not least because the sources are in perfect agreement about it.

I observe, moreover, that from this connected set of testimonies there emerges a picture of a style and a life, and a proposal for living, that are profoundly innovative; indeed it would be vain to search for precedents.[24] And obviously the lack of precedents itself offers some reassurance that we are indeed in a position to know something about Socrates.

5. THE *ZOPYRUS* AS A SOURCE OF KNOWLEDGE

The time has come to ask ourselves whether perhaps we learn something else from the *Zopyrus*—or more precisely, from the story we have been discussing up to this point. One might have the impression that, in light of the preceding, the answer must in the nature of things be no, but as always, the reality is little more complicated. Let us try then to ask whether, in the case of the *Zopyrus*, the representation of the rule of life by which Socrates lives is positively connected with any more or less embryonic theoretical elaboration. For this purpose we need to review the relevant sources.

Fr. 7 R. In *Tusculans* IV 80 Cicero observes that, when Zopyrus recognised in Socrates a combination of many vices, the philosopher declared that they were "innate in him, but kept down by him through reason" (*illa sibi insita, sed ratione a se deiecta*). We may hypothesise here that the reference was to vices innate in Socrates, not necessarily in man as a species; and that the idea of vices being "kept down" by the intervention of reason is linked to what Zopyrus claims about Socrates. It is thus doubtful whether there is any room here for a theory about the nature and function of reason, even apart from the fact that we have no means of judging the authenticity or otherwise of the term used (i.e., *deicere*).

Fr. 6 R. In Cicero, *On Fate* 10, the narrative introduces the figure of Zopyrus who, having found in Socrates the signs of obtuseness, "added that he was a lover of women, at which Alcibiades broke into hollow laughter" (*addidit etiam mulierosum, in quo Alcibiades cachinnum dicitur sustulisse*). Then Cicero observes "But these vices can be born in us from natural causes; as for extirpating them and getting rid of them altogether, so that they very person prone to them is steered away from such great failings, *that* is not within the realm of natural causes, but in that of will, application and discipline" (*Sed haec ex naturalibus causis vitia nasci possunt; extirpari autem et funditus tolli, ut ipse qui ad ea propensus fuerit a tantis vitiis avocetur, non est id positum in naturalibus causis, sed in voluntate, studio, disciplina*). The trio of will, application and discipline is thoroughly Ciceronian, and it seems fairly unlikely that Phaedo could have been moving towards the kind of generalisation Cicero is making, not least because the Greek equivalent of *vitia* (that is, in the plural) is for the most part absent from pre-Aristotelian literature, and rare even in Aristotle himself.

Fr. 8 R. Scholium to Persius, *Satires* 4.80: "It is for me/in my power to defeat pleasure itself" (*meum est ipsam libidinem vincere*). That Phaedo could have spoken about the possibility of, or the need for, defeating, controlling or overcoming eros is obviously possible.

Fr. 9 R. The Syriac text of pseudo-Plutarch does not say anything about the end of the story but, before relating the anecdote, it observes that Socrates showed that desires can be defeated if one takes appropriate care. Again, it is not impossible that Phaedo said something of the sort.

Fr. 10 R. Alexander of Aphrodisias, *On Fate* 6 (already cited): Socrates acknowledges he is by nature as Zopyrus says he is, "unless through the *askêsis* that comes from philosophy he had become better than his own nature." There is certainly here the germ of a theory about the connection between *askêsis* (exercise or practice) and philosophy, to the effect that philosophy functions as a kind of motor for *askêsis*. Thus there is here an embryonic idea of a non-generic connection between two potentially universal notions, although it must be stressed that there are no indications to show that the sentence in question is in fact closely related to Phaedo's text. At the same time there is a noticeable proximity between "through the *askêsis* that comes from philosophy" and "kept down by him through reason" (fr. 7 R.).

And that is all. Unless I am mistaken, the documentation available on the *Zopyrus* offers no other useful clue that would enable us to sketch a *doctrine* of Phaedo's own. Thus in my view the conditions do not exist for to inferring, from the above that

> [T]he evidence . . . attributes the following claims to Phaedo: (1) that each person has a 'nature' which encompasses their irrational impulses; (2) that this "nature" is related to the body in such a way that an expert in the matter could deduce the former from the appearance of the latter; and (3) that one's "nature" does not determine behaviour.[25]

In fact, from what we know of the *Zopyrus* there emerge no systematic theories, only premises that *might* have been developed into the form of a systematic doctrine. Something is potentially stirring, but no actual theory is documented in our texts. There is proof of this, if proof were necessary, in the doubts surrounding the precise significance of the "*askêsis* that comes from philosophy" (or more generally, guided by reason): it is not clear if this kind of action produces a mere containment, or repression inspired by the aim of a complete uprooting. The available testimonia do not permit us, then, to say whether Phaedo wished and was able to express a specific teaching on the subject of erotic impulses and how to restrain them, or, if so, what that teaching was. Boys-Stones is particularly concerned to extract from the story a precise and articulated theoretical construct, but it has to be admitted that any such thing is present, if at all, only in a virtual sense, even if, in the abstract, it is quite compatible with what little we know of the *Zopyrus*. But was the purpose of the story to give us a better understanding of Socrates and of his value to us, or was it to impart a doctrine? Nothing by way of a *theory*, so far as we can tell, actually takes shape in the dialogue.[26]

For the same reasons, I suggest that it would not make any sense to talk of an "Antisthenising" Phaedo. That Phaedo shows a propensity for a fundamental distrust of the passions, and in favour of their containment, however this is understood, is undeniable. But for it to be possible to deduce that he sympathises with Antisthenes' moralizing, we would have to suppose that he had just two alternatives: i.e., taking inspiration either from Antisthenes, or from Aristippus. But in this case *tertium datur*: Phaedo could have focussed on what he remembered of the real Socrates.

6. THE *ZOPYRUS* AND PHILOSOPHY

We need still to ask what the *Zopyrus* leaves us to understand, or to conjecture, about philosophy. It is no mere secondary matter to discover that documentation of the use of word "philosophy" in the first decades of the fourth century BC extends beyond occurrences of the term itself and its derivatives in Plato, Xenophon and Isocrates: it extends to Phaedo too. There is no shortage of indications that other Socratics too are to be considered as philosophers but, unless I am mistaken, documentary proof is available only for Phaedo, and the nature of that documentation makes the fact highly significant.

We should note too the connection which seems to be made between philosophy and Socrates. If in the concluding parts of the *Zopyrus* Phaedo really did write of the beneficial effects of philosophy (and I have examined the evidence for this above), it would follow that, in his view, the beneficial effects of philosophy were apparent above all in the person of the master. In that case Socrates would have been presented as a living and paradigmatic example of a person improved—or better, profoundly altered—by philosophy.

As for the idea of philosophy Phaedo favours, the indications are that he had developed an essentially therapeutic conception. We find him representing philosophy as able to release positive energies whatever a person's natural leanings may be. Socrates is the living example of the way in which one can conduct a more than respectable life even if one's starting conditions are not in the least favourable. This emphasis, for all that we know, seems to be original, only we have no basis for conjectures about the frame in which it was set, or to guess at the justifications Phaedo might have introduced in support of his eulogy of philosophy.

We might, all the same, risk the proposal that the *Zopyrus* could have offered Phaedo an excellent opportunity to dissent from Plato, when the latter makes Socrates say, in the case that we need to find young men to make fit for governmental, that we must prefer "those specimens who are the most stable and the most courageous, so far as possible the best looking, and so on. But we need to add to this list: the people we're looking for mustn't just be upstanding and enterprising characters, they'll also need to possess the natural traits that are conducive to the kind of education we're talking about" (*Republic* VII 535a-b, tr. Rowe). However, we do not know if there was disagreement on the subject (there is no indication of it), and it would be fruitless to try to imagine a way in which Phaedo might have constructed arguments against Plato.

More significant is the sense that Phaedo has sympathy for a philosophy that helps us to live better (in fact, a philosophy that heals). One would therefore like to know whether he had any idea of philosophy as wisdom, and as a set of theories, and if so what he thought of it; but we lack the evidence to enable us to offer any useful answers. We do know that the school he founded had a short life and no great success, and it would be interesting to know if his particular idea of philosophy contributed to the limited vitality of what we call the school of Elis.

We would like to know. Considering the many things we do *not* know about him, it seems to me appropriate to recognise in those "confidences" of Socrates—and in the idea itself, of a character who gives such confidences—one of the most conspicuous legacies of Phaedo (and of Aeschines of Sphettus).

7. CONCLUSION

I conclude, as I must, by returning to the theme of philosophical importance. Limiting myself, on this occasion, to the *Zopyrus* alone, I would claim to have adduced arguments for saying that on this particular dialogue we know too much of importance to continue to show so little interest in it. It is not true that we know nothing of value about Phaedo. I have tried to demonstrate that from his *Zopyrus* we learn important things—indeed, things of first importance—both about Socrates' personality and about the beginnings of philosophy in Greece. Phaedo's *Zopyrus* offers us key testimony on both points. First, his Socrates dares to speak about himself, and to reveal an aspect of his nature that Phaedo presumes to have gone completely unseen even by the master's habitual followers. Second, here and at the end of Aeschines' *Alcibiades* we find the earliest evidence of a person giving confidences, and of confidences treated as revealing of, and as revealing very important things about, the person who gives them. Thirdly and finally, one observes that, other than Plato and Xenophon, only Phaedo among the Socratics seems to have written anything on the subject of philosophy (neither Aristippus and Antisthenes do so, for example). We are dealing here with affirmations that are anything but negligible, insofar as we witness here taking shape an idea of philosophy the value of which is made to depend on its potentiality for affecting our life and our actions, and not (also) on certain doctrines, or on the value of such doctrines. Its novelty is such as to require us to rethink our views about the different ideas of philosophy that took shape among the Socratics, before the advent of Aristotle.

NOTES

1. Xenophon has been the object of intense study in every issue of *Socratica* (see www.socratica.eu); see also Narcy and Tordesillas 2008, Hobden and Tuplin 2012, various books by Vivienne Gray, and a penetrating article by David O'Connor in Morrison 2011; also Dorion 2013.
2. See Rossetti 2008.
3. *SSR* IV, p.14.

4. Hence the fact that although its main focus is on Phaedo's *Zopyrus*, there will be plenty of references in the present paper also the final part of Aeschines' *Alcibiades*.
5. Fragment 10 Rossetti (henceforward 'R.'; the fragment is not found in *SSR*).
6. I shall discuss in a moment the alternative view, adopted by many, that the statements in question referred to Phaedo's own obscure personal history.
7. Danzig 2010, esp. chapters IV-V.
8. Practically nothing has been written about this change in taste. Its clearest expression is in Aristophanes, that is, in the difference between *Wealth* and the comedies preceding it; also in the changed political-cultural climate. Could the brazen arrogance of an Alcibiades have manifested itself after Aegospotami? Plato and other Socratics certainly describe such instances, but only in the context of a projection into the past, when there was a more relaxed attitude towards such behaviour.
9. Cf. Danzig's conclusions (Danzig 2010) about the careful way Plato and Xenophon appear to distract attention away from allegations against Socrates of a sexual nature.
10. This appears to me an aspect almost totally neglected in the literature, and I myself have struggled to take proper account of it. I confess, with regret, that I failed to pay proper attention to the subject either in my 2010 or in my 2011.
11. Aelius Aristides, *In Defence of Oratory* 61 and 74 (= *SSR* VI A 53).
12. *Quiescite, o sodales: etenim sum, sed contineo*: John Cassian, *Conferences* XIII 5.3 (= fr. 11 R., missing in *SSR*).
13. In our own times, we readily recognise that our fundamental traits have a tendency to express themselves whether we wish it or not, thanks to the way certain types of emotion involve the body.
14. Caserta 2013, 301–2.
15. Boys-Stones 2007, 23.
16. Such a comparison weakens the presumption that Alcibades in this context is not to be taken seriously (as proposed in Narcy 2008).
17. In the case of Aeschines' *Alcibiades* too, attention is notoriously focused on the moment of crisis that gives rise to the philosopher's confidences, with the result that these acquire a paradigmatic value.
18. See most recently Dorion 2010. It will suffice to cite his p. 19: "we must abandon the project of faithfully reconstructing the historical Socrates' ideas, so desperately out of reach."
19. In fact I seem to be the only one to have drawn attention to it (most recently in Rossetti 2013, 307–8, n.4), but I remain convinced that my position is well founded.
20. See my arguments in Rossetti 2010.
21. Note the iterative aspect of this passage (29d6); for testimonia of a similar kind, see Capizzi 1971.
22. Theodoret, *Cure for Greek Maladies* III 53 (= *SSR* V A 123).
23. See especially *SSR* IV A 35–100.
24. See further Rossetti 2010.
25. Boys-Stones 2007, 27 (also Boys-Stones 2004, 13).
26. "There is, of course, no reason at all to suppose that Phaedo ascribed to Zopyrus a theoretical view of the soul's relationship with the body, or that this is what Socrates was supposed to be in agreement with him about. In fact the dynamic of the dialogue would be better explained if Zopyrus had no *theory* at all" (Boys-Stones 2007, 25). In my view it is not just the figure of Zopyrus, but the dialogue as a whole that fails to give us a theory of the option for *enkrateia* that is floated before us.

WORKS CITED

G. Boys-Stones, "Phaedo of Elis and Plato on the Soul," *Phronesis*, 49, 2004, 1–23.
———, "Physiognomy and Ancient Psychological Theory," in S. Swain (ed.), *Seeing the Face, Seeing the Soul. Polemon's Physiognomy from Classical Antiquity to Medieval Islam* (OUP, Oxford 2007), 19–124.
A. Capizzi, *Socrate e i personaggi-filosofi di Platone* (Edizioni dell'Ateneo, Roma 1971).
C. Caserta, "Per un approccio comunicazionale al *logos sokratikos*: Le Dialogue socratique di Livio Rossetti," *Nova Tellus* 30.2, 2013, 275–306.
G. Danzig, *Apologizing for Socrates* (Lexington Books, Lanham MD 2010).
L.-A. Dorion, "The Rise and Fall of the Socratic Problem," in D. Morrison (ed.), *The Cambridge Companion to Socrates* (CUP, Cambridge 2010), 1–23.
F. Hobden and C. Tuplin (eds), *Xenophon: Ethical Principles and Historical Inquiry* (Brill, Leiden 2012).
Ch. H. Kahn, *Plato and the Socratic Dialogue: The Philosophical Use of a Literary Form* (CUP, Cambridge 1996).
E.L. McQueen and C.J. Rowe, "Phaedo, Socrates, and the Chronology of the Spartan War with Elis," *Méthexis* 2, 1989, 1–18.
D. Nails, *The People of Plato* (Hackett, Indianapolis-Cambridge 2002).
M. Narcy, "Socrate nel discorso di Alcibiade (Platone, *Simposio*, 215a-222b)," in L. Rossetti and A. Stavru (eds.), *Socratica 2005. Studi sulla letteratura socratica antica* (Levante, Bari 2008), 287–304.
M. Narcy and A. Tordesillas (eds.), *Xènophon et Socrate* (Vrin, Paris 2008).
D. O'Connor, "Xenophon and the Enviable Life of Socrates," in D. Morrison (ed.), *The Cambridge Companion to Socrates* (CUP, Cambridge 2010), 48–74.
L. Rossetti, "Ricerche sui dialoghi socratici di Fedone ed Euclide," *Hermes* 108, 1980, 183–200.
———, "Introduzione," in L. Rossetti and A. Stavru (eds.), *Socratica 2005. Studi sulla letteratura socratica antica* (Levante, Bari 2008), 11–18.
———, "Socrate, questo sconosciuto," *Peitho. Examina antiqua* 1, 2010, 13–30.
———, *Le dialogue socratique* (Paris, Les Belles Lettres, 2011).
———, "Riflessioni sulle vostre osservazioni," *Nova Tellus* 30.2, 2013, 307–315.
J. Sellars, "*Socraticorum Maximus*: Simon the Shoemaker and the Problem of Socrates," *Pli. The Warwick Journal of Philosophy* 11, 2003, 253–269.

6 The Sources and Scope of Cyrenaic Scepticism

Tim O'Keefe

INTRODUCTION

Although we possess no primary texts by the Cyrenaics and must rely on later reports to reconstruct their views, these reports firmly establish their epistemological subjectivism and scepticism. On the one hand, my subjective affections (*pathê*, singular *pathos*) are obvious to me, e.g., the sweet sensation when I eat some honey, and I cannot be mistaken about my present affections (Sextus Empiricus *Against the Professors* 7 193–5, Plutarch *Against Colotes* 1120e-f). This doctrine is often reported using the technical vocabulary that I "grasp" or "apprehend" (*katalambanô*) my *pathê*. This cognitive grasp, however, is confined to what is immediately given in my experience, and the Cyrenaics were infamous for coining locutions such as the person eating honey being "sweetened" or the person seeing a wall being "yellowed," rather than simply saying that the honey seems sweet or the wall yellow to him, in order to report only this immediate, indubitable content. On the other hand, our *pathê* are not sufficient evidence for judgments about the external objects that produce them (*Against Colotes* 1120d), and when we overstep our present *pathê* and make such judgments we are liable to error (*Against Colotes* 1120f). A *pathos* reveals nothing more than itself (Sextus Empiricus, *Against the Professors* 7 194), and external objects are inapprehensible (*akatalêpton*, Sextus Empiricus, *Outlines of Pyrrhonism* 1 215).

But this still leaves open important questions about what exactly the Cyrenaics' 'scepticism' amounts to. The Cyrenaics assert that we cannot apprehend external objects, and they recommend that we cease making judgments concerning them. But what is the *source* of this scepticism? I explore this question in the first part of this chapter and argue that their scepticism is grounded in our limitations as epistemic *subjects*, rather than (as has been argued) being based upon any metaphysical thesis about the nature of the external world as an inapprehensible *object*.[1] In the second part of the chapter, I turn to the question of the *scope* of the Cyrenaics' scepticism. Our sources are inconsistent on this issue. Some report doubt about whether the external world exists at all, others doubt about the identity of objects in the external world, e.g., whether the object that heats me is fire, and others merely doubt about the properties of objects in the external world, e.g., whether the fire that heats me is really hot. I argue that the Cyrenaics are dubious about both the properties and identity of the cause of each particular *pathos*: my being heated has *some* cause, but I cannot grasp whether this cause is really hot or whether it is a fire. I close the chapter with a consideration of whether the Cyrenaics' scepticism involves just the identity of particular objects or extends as a global thesis about the structure of the world.

I. THE SOURCES OF CYRENAIC SCEPTICISM

Zilioli argues that the Cyrenaics' scepticism is based upon an ambitious metaphysical thesis about the nature of the external world, that it is in constant flux and contains no proper objects with determinate properties (Zilioli 2012 and 2015b). Let us call the view "metaphysical indeterminacy." I believe that ultimately metaphysical indeterminacy is inconsistent with the reports we have on the Cyrenaics, but I will first spell out what the view is and how it does comport with many of our *testimonia*.

According to Zilioli, the Cyrenaics think that the external world exists "as an indeterminate substratum, made up of no discrete and distinct objects" (Zilioli (2012) 78), which is similar to the metaphysical view of the "subtle thinkers" allied with Protagoras and Heraclitus in *Theaetetus*156a3–160c who advance a doctrine of radical flux (Zilioli (2012) 50). The Cyrenaics' restriction of knowledge to our affections is grounded on their view that the external world contains no determinate objects or essences to be grasped by us.

It may seem immediately inconsistent for sceptics like the Cyrenaics to advance an ambitious metaphysical thesis about the world: to maintain both that we cannot grasp the ways things external to us are, and that the external world is an indeterminate substratum containing no distinct objects in constant flux. But this charge is too hasty. As Zilioli notes, to say that the external world has no determinate nature is a peculiar sort of claim, which allows the Cyrenaic on his interpretation to avoid inconsistency (Zilioli (2012) 84). But before we examine how advancing a positive doctrine of metaphysical indeterminacy can coexist with scepticism, let me discuss a simpler (but pertinent) parallel example.

Suppose that somebody is a Berkeleyan idealist, holding that only minds and their contents exist. This qualifies as an ambitious metaphysical thesis. But on its basis, one could certainly maintain the sceptical thesis that we cannot grasp the essences of mind-independent physical objects, for the simple reason that no such objects exist to be grasped.[2] And in fact, one report in Sextus Empiricus seems to ascribe such a position to the Cyrenaics. In order to argue against musical theory, Sextus makes a case that musical notes don't exist. (This is relevant because notes make up melodies, the subject matter of musical theory.) He writes, "the Cyrenaic philosophers claim that only the *pathê* exist, and nothing else. So, since sound is not a *pathos* but rather something capable of producing a *pathos*, it is not one of the things that exist. To be sure, by denying the existence of every sensory object, the schools of Democritus and of Plato deny the existence of sound as well, as sound is taken to be a sensory object" (*Against the Professors* 6 53).[3]

Now, we have excellent reason not to trust this report. It is inconsistent with all of our other reports on the Cyrenaics, including other reports in Sextus. As Tsouna notes (Tsouna (1998) 80), whereas elsewhere Sextus is concerned to "present an accurate and detailed outline of Cyrenaic doctrine," here his purpose "is dialectical and consists in attacking the implicit belief of the professors of the art of music in the existence of sound." So accuracy is not an important *desideratum* of the report, and this disregard for accuracy is shown by his sloppy "misconstrual of the positions that he ascribes to Democritus and Plato for the same purpose" (Tsouna (1998) 81). But if the Cyrenaics *did* hold such a position, it would form a solid basis for denying that we can grasp the external things.

Returning to the metaphysical indeterminacy thesis, a similar manoeuvre defuses the charge of inconsistency against it. According to Zilioli, the Cyrenaics hold that the external world exists, but as something with no determinate essence for us to grasp, or for us to accurately describe as being one way rather than another. He draws a parallel between the Cyrenaics' position and that of Pyrrho of Elis, at least as construed by Richard Bett (Zilioli (2015b) 118–9). Bett states, "Pyrrho answered the question, 'what is the nature of things?' by saying 'things are in themselves indeterminate,' and on that basis recommended a withdrawal from all opinions about how things really are that ascribe fixed and definite characteristics to those things" (Bett (2015) 159).[4] And Bett also correctly notes (*pace* O'Keefe 2013) that somebody holding such a position would avoid, as hopeless, studies that attempt to pin down the way things are, so that the Cyrenaics' refusal to engage in physics because of its uncertainty (*DL* 2 92) does not count against the metaphysical indeterminacy thesis (Bett (2015) 160 and 166).

While the metaphysical indeterminacy thesis is consistent with maintaining that the external world is ungraspable, it cannot be reconciled with the reports we have concerning the particular arguments the Cyrenaics give for scepticism or the way they describe our resultant ignorance. Sextus reports that we all make mistakes regarding the external object and cannot grasp the truth regarding it because "the soul is too weak to distinguish it on account of the places, the distances, the motions, the changes, and numerous other causes" (*Against the Professors* 7 195), firmly placing the responsibility for their scepticism on our epistemic limitations rather than on the nature of the world (or lack thereof).

The Cyrenaics' sceptical arguments start from noting cases in which an object appears F to one percipient and not-F to another, depending upon the percipients' condition, e.g., something that appears white to me may seem yellow to a fellow with jaundice and red to a chap with ophthalmia. From such cases, it's plausible to suppose that an object that isn't F can appear F to somebody (Sextus Empiricus *Against the Professors* 7 192–3, 197–8). As noted above, our *pathê* are not sufficient evidence for judgments about the external objects that produce them (Plutarch *Against Colotes* 1120d), and when we overstep our present *pathê* and make such judgments we are liable to error (1120f). This is because a *pathos* reveals nothing more than itself, and we have no criterion by which we could judge which of the conflicting claims regarding the objects is true (Sextus Empiricus *Against the Professors* 7 194–5).

So, say the Cyrenaics, we sense only that we are affected in a certain way, and we do not know whether something has a particular colour or sound (Cicero *Lucullus* 76). When we are burnt or cut, we know we're undergoing something but cannot tell whether what is burning us is fire or cutting us is iron (Aristocles, quoted by Eusebius, *Preparation for the Gospel* 14.19.1). The Cyrenaics do not merely assert that we cannot grasp the essence of things—which could be squared with the view that things have no such essence to be grasped. Instead, they say that we cannot know *whether or not* the object really is the way it appears to us. That leaves open the possibility that the object burning us is really hot, or is really a fire—and this possibility cannot be squared with the metaphysical indeterminacy interpretation. If the Cyrenaics were committed to the thesis that no objects such as fires exist, they could know that the feeling of hot was not caused by a fire.

Since the metaphysical indeterminacy interpretation is inconsistent with the fullest reports we have on the Cyrenaics' position, we should be loathe to accept it absent powerful countervailing considerations. But the evidence in its favour is thin. Zilioli (2015b) mentions several passages to support it.

The first is the passage from Sextus about the non-existence of sounds discussed above. On its face, it does not support the metaphysical indeterminacy interpretation, as it denies that anything other than the *pathê* exist, rather than asserting that the external world exists but as something indeterminate. Zilioli, however, reads it as asserting that "sound does not *properly* exist" (emphasis mine; Zilioli (2015b), 120), presumably meaning that sound (alongside everything other than the *pathê*) does not exist as a proper or determinate being, while allowing that it exists indeterminately. But there is nothing in the context of this passage to indicate that *hyparchein* is being used in some sense analogous to the way Plato uses *einai* when discussing the lovers and sights and sounds and the objects of knowledge and opinion. And so we should retain the straightforward reading of the report as denying that anything other than the *pathê* exists, and we should disregard it for the reasons Tsouna gives.

The second passage is Sextus *Against the Professors* 7 193–4, which Tsouna translates: "Hence, if one must speak the truth, only the *pathos* is actually a *phainomenon* [i.e., something apparent] to us. But what is external and productive of the *pathos* perhaps exists (*tacha estin on*), but it is not a *phainomenon* to us." As with the first passage, Zilioli reads this in terms of types of existence, rather than existence *tout court*. He translates the second sentence: "What is external and productive of the affection perhaps is a being, but it is not a *phainomenon* for us," and he goes on to say, "This means that things in the world perhaps are not, properly speaking, existing items; that is, material things, as individual items, may well be not existent." (Zilioli (2015b), 120–1). Again, I am suspicious of reading the passage as doubting a certain *type* of existence. But even if we grant Zilioli this point, this passage does not support the metaphysical indeterminacy thesis, as in it the Cyrenaics are asserting that we *cannot know* about the being of external things, rather than asserting that external things *are not* proper beings.[5]

The final passage is a badly damaged Herculaneum papyrus (probably by the Epicurean Philodemus) discussing the ethics of some philosophers, most likely the Cyrenaics. After mentioning some people who deny that it is possible to know anything, and others who have selected the *pathê* of the soul as the ends of action, Philodemus goes on to say, "And yet others held the doctrine that what our school calls grief and joy are totally empty notions because of the manifest indeterminacy (*aoristia*) (of things)." Zilioli takes this an explicit attribution of the metaphysical indeterminacy thesis to the Cyrenaics (Zilioli (2015b), 124–6). But as Bett points out (Bett (2015), 166, n. 42), the indeterminacy view is attributed to "others," so Philodemus here may not be referring to the Cyrenaics. And even if he is, I think that, absent further context, the claim that "things are indeterminate" can with equal plausibility be read as making either a metaphysical claim ("Things in themselves have no determinations") or an epistemological one ("We are unable to determine how things are").[6]

II. THE SCOPE OF CYRENAIC SCEPTICISM

So, I think we have excellent grounds for accepting the epistemic limitations interpretation and rejecting the metaphysical indeterminacy interpretation. But this still leaves open the scope of the Cyrenaics' scepticism. Let us imagine that a Cyrenaic accidentally puts his hand into a fire and burns it. He can apprehend his own *pathos*, that he is being burnt, while he refrains from making judgments about the external object that causes the affection. But how radical is his scepticism? We can distinguish three types:

- *Object property scepticism*. The Cyrenaic refrains from judging that the fire that burns him is really hot. (And likewise, that the honey he tastes is really sweet, and the wall he sees really red.)
- *Object identity scepticism*. The Cyrenaic refrains from judging that the object that burns him is a fire. (And likewise, that the thing that sweetens him is honey, or the thing that reddens him a wall.)

- *External world scepticism.* The Cyrenaic refrains from judging that there is any object external to him that burns him (and likewise for cases of his being sweetened or reddened).

Against External World Scepticism

Unfortunately, the *testimonia* on the Cyrenaics point in different directions on this issue, with passages supporting each type of scepticism. Still, we can quickly rule out external world scepticism. In its support there is a single report in Sextus Empiricus on the Cyrenaics, which we have already mentioned in connection with the metaphysical indeterminacy interpretation: "Hence, if one must speak the truth, only the *pathos* is actually a *phainomenon* to us. But what is external and productive of the *pathos* perhaps exists (*tacha estin on*), but it is not a *phainomenon* to us" (Sextus Empiricus *Against the Professors* 7 193–4). This seems to raise the possibility that the external cause of the *pathos* may not even exist. But all of the other reports on the Cyrenaics have them thinking that our *pathê* have *some* sort of external cause, so we should be suspicious of this report and opt to explain away the appearance of external world scepticism if we have a plausible way of doing so.[7]

Tsouna's analysis of the passage (Tsouna (1998) 54–61) is convincing: the talk about what is *phainomenon* to us is distinctive to Pyrrhonian scepticism, not the Cyrenaics. So we should think that this passage is a sceptical interpretation and not a faithful reporting of the Cyrenaics' views, as Sextus blurs the distinction between the *pathê* for the Cyrenaics and the sceptical *phainomena*.[8] She also notes that even if we think that Sextus' report can be attributed to the Cyrenaics, it need not express a doubt about the existence of the external world. Instead, it can be read as a "dialectical concession: let us admit for the sake of the argument that the external cause of the *pathos* exists, even so, it is not a *phainomenon* to us" (Tsouna (1998) 78).

For Object Property Scepticism

This leaves us to decide between object property scepticism and object identity scepticism. Tsouna and Warren give a number of considerations in favour of restricting the Cyrenaics' scepticism merely to the properties of objects. Tsouna notes (Tsouna (1998) 75–6) that the Cyrenaics sometimes use common nouns to denote the external objects that are the causes of my *pathê*, e.g., they speak of the fire that burns me (Anonymous commentator on Plato's *Theaetetus* 152b col. 65–29.39), the honey which sweetens me, and the young olive shoots which bitter me (Plutarch *Against Colotes* 1120e). Tsouna writes, "Such passages indicate that that the Cyrenaics conceived of the ontological structure of external reality in a fairly conventional way: what they questioned was not whether things or classes of things in the world exist, but only whether they have the properties that an individual perceiver may attribute to them." (Tsouna (1998) 76) Similarly, Warren claims that the report "it is non-evident whether the fire is such as to burn" by the anonymous commentator "explicitly rules out" object identity scepticism (Warren (2013) 415).

On the other hand, the Cyrenaics often refer to the causes of our *pathê* in much vaguer and non-committal terms. Tsouna usefully catalogues these (Tsouna (1998) 76–7). Sometimes they indicate that that these causes are external things in some general manner but shy away from labelling them with the names of particular objects, instead talking about "the external objects" (*ta ektos hupokeimena*, Sextus *Outlines of Pyrrhonism* 1.215) or "the things outside" (*ta exôthen*, Anonymous 65.31–2). Other times the external objects are characterized entirely by their effect on the percipient, e.g., "that which is burning us" (*ta kaion*, Eusebius 14.19.1). Such passages may seem to point toward the Cyrenaics eschewing judgments about the identity of external objects, but Warren rightly resists this implication. These indeterminate expressions, he writes, are just "an expositional convenience" to explain the Cyrenaics' claims in broad terms that can be filled in later with specific items (like the fire that burns me), and we shouldn't take them as committing them to a significant philosophical position (Warren (2013) 415).

But two passages do explicitly commit the Cyrenaics to object identity scepticism. Colotes the Epicurean, as reported by Plutarch, says that the Cyrenaics would refuse to say that there is a man or a horse or a wall, but instead assert that they're being walled or horsed or manned (*Against Colotes* 1120d). And Aristocles the Peripatetic, as quoted by Eusebius, says that the Cyrenaics, when they're being burnt or cut, know that they're undergoing something but cannot tell whether the thing that is burning them is fire or the thing that is cutting them is iron (Eusebius *Preparation for the Gospel* 14.19.1).

Given these conflicting reports, Warren claims that on grounds of charity we ought to favour those that ascribe to the Cyrenaics a limited object property scepticism and disregard those that commit them to an object identity scepticism. That's because the wider scepticism would leave them open to the *apraxia* objection—that their doctrines would make it impossible to act and live—whereas on the more limited property scepticism, they have the epistemic resources to get by. As Warren puts it, a Cyrenaic might "feel that his commitment to there being an external world populated by various external objects including, for example, a wall in front of him at the moment, would allow him sufficient grounds for living a life even though he will not affirm for sure that the wall is, for example, rough or painted red" (Warren (2013) 414).

The *apraxia* objection also allows us to explain, and explain away, the reports committing them to object identity scepticism. Both Colotes and Aristocles wish to paint the Cyrenaics in the least flattering light by exaggerating their scepticism and its unpalatable consequences (Warren (2013)

416). We have further reason to doubt the accuracy of Colotes' report—Plutarch reprimands Colotes for satirizing the Cyrenaics with his mocking coinages like "I am horsed" and "I am walled." They never said such things, reports Plutarch, instead confining themselves to locutions like being sweetened, chilled and warmed (*Against Colotes* 1120de, noted in Warren (2013) 416 and Tsouna (1998) 86–7).

For Object Identity Scepticism

Despite the arguments above, I think that ascribing object identity scepticism to the Cyrenaics is both more charitable and more in accord with the reports we have on them. That is because (1) it is unclear that object property scepticism fares any better than object identity scepticism with regard to *apraxia* objections; (2) restricting their scepticism only to objects' properties is unjustifiable; (3) restricting their scepticism only to objects' properties is inconsistent with the arguments the Cyrenaics give for their scepticism; (4) the reports that Tsouna and Warren take to support a limited scepticism can be accommodated within object identity scepticism, so object identity scepticism requires us to reject or explain away fewer of our reports. Let me present my arguments for (1)-(3) first, as they hang together, and then turn to (4).

Warren claims that the Cyrenaic can live his life well enough by knowing, at least, that there is an external world populated by objects such as the wall in front of him at that moment, even if he cannot affirm that it has properties such as being rough or being red. But what *can* the Cyrenaic know about the wall in front of him? If, for *every single* property F that the wall appears to me to have, I can know only that the wall moves me F-ly, and not that the wall itself is F, it's unclear what useful information I have about the wall that allows me to act.

Perhaps what Warren has in mind is that I can grasp infallibly only my own *pathê*, and I have no idea what *sensible* properties objects have (such as the wall being red or the honey sweet), but on the basis of my *pathê*, I somehow have reason to infer other things about the external world and the objects around me right now—e.g., that the object in front of me is a wall, that it's solid, and that it's about five feet in front of me. And this gives me reason to act—e.g., to stop running so that I don't slam into it and break my nose.

I can imagine an epistemological position of this sort, but I do not think it can be ascribed to the Cyrenaics. Consider the following report on the Cyrenaics—a sympathetic one, where there seems to be no motive for exaggerating the extent of their scepticism:

> What do you think of the Cyrenaics, by no means contemptible philosophers? They deny that there is anything that can be perceived from the outside: the only things that they do perceive are those which they sense

by internal touch, for instance pain or pleasure, and they do not know whether something has a particular color or sound, but only sense that they are themselves affected in a certain way.

(Cicero, *Lucullus* 76)

Cicero here does not explicitly ascribe to the Cyrenaics a wider object identity scepticism. But he does say that, for the Cyrenaics, we perceive only our own *pathê*—particular pleasures, pains, colours, tastes, etc.—and nothing external to ourselves. Plutarch characterizes the Cyrenaics as "shut[ting] themselves up within their *pathê* as in a state of siege" (*Against Colotes* 1120d). These reports don't comport with a modest scepticism merely about sensible properties but which allows a wide range of justified beliefs concerning other properties of external objects.

Plutarch does criticize Colotes for mischaracterizing the Cyrenaics with his satirical coinages like "being walled" rather than sticking to their actual terminology of "being reddened" and the like, but he admits that the philosophical point that Colotes is making with those coinages—that the Cyrenaics cannot affirm that there are horses, men, or walls in front of them—is correct (*Against Colotes* 1120d). And it's easy to see why. If all we have cognitive access to are our own *pathê*, and these *pathê* reveal to us nothing about the properties of their causes, then we have no information to use by which we could judge what sorts of items in the external world—horses, men, or walls—are causing our *pathê*.

And this is not some *recherché* point that would be noticed only by critics of the Cyrenaics. It's already front and centre in their own sceptical arguments. According to these arguments, it's not just that the same horse may appear white to me but yellow to a chap with jaundice, but that, on the basis of my *pathê*, it may appear to me that there is a horse out there, while to another person it may look like it's a cow, and we'd have no basis to judge which (if either) of our opinions is accurate. The Cyrenaics themselves raise the example of a madman who sees an object like the sun doubled (Sextus Empiricus *Against the Professors* 7 192–3), and around the time of the Cyrenaics Epicurus mentions the case of Orestes, who thinks that the Furies are pursuing him when there were really no solid bodies out there causing his sensations (Sextus Empiricus *Against the Professors* 13 63).[9] So, the Cyrenaics are far from thinking that I can at least have some confidence that there is a solid wall in front of me, although maybe not that it is red. The Cyrenaics' arguments imply, and would have been seen by them to imply, that I should not judge e.g., that there are two objects in front of me, although it appears that there are two, or that the object in front of me is a solid body, although it seems like it is.

Let's return to Plutarch's famous simile of the Cyrenaics as shut up inside their *pathê*. It occurs in Plutarch's own introduction to the views of the Cyrenaics, prior to discussing Colotes' *apraxia* objection against the Cyrenaics. Plutarch says,

[The Cyrenaics], placing all *pathê* and all sense-impressions within themselves, believed that the evidence coming from them is not sufficient regarding assertions about external objects. Instead, distancing themselves from external objects, they shut themselves up within their *pathê* as in a state of siege, using the formula 'it appears' but refusing to affirm in addition that 'it is' with regard to external objects.

(*Against Colotes* 1120c-d)

The most natural way to read this passage, especially given Plutarch's assertion that the Cyrenaics distance themselves from external objects and shut themselves up inside their *pathê*, is that the Cyrenaics believe that the *pathê* give insufficient evidence regarding assertions about external objects *tout court*. While it's possible for claims of this sort to have an implicit scope restriction, in this case I think it would be strained to read Plutarch as attributing to the Cyrenaics merely that "the evidence coming from the *pathê* is not sufficient regarding assertions about [the sensible properties of] external objects."

So on grounds of charity, I think we should ascribe a wider object identity scepticism to the Cyrenaics, since restricting their scepticism merely to the properties of objects would be unjustifiable given their other well-attested commitments. And if our reports on the Cyrenaics were inconsistent, it would be preferable to reject or explain away those that commit them merely to object property scepticism. But as a matter of fact, those reports give, at best, only weak support to a restricted scepticism. Those two reports are:

[The Cyrenaics] say we are being sweetened and bittered and chilled and warmed and illuminated and darkened, each of these *pathê* having within itself its own evidence, which is intrinsic to it and irreversible. But whether the honey is sweet or the young olive-shoot bitter or the hail chilly or the unmixed wine warm or the sun luminous or the night air dark, is contested by many witnesses, [wild] animals and domesticated animals and humans alike, for some dislike honey, others like olive-shoots or are burned off by hail or are chilled by the wine or go blind in the sunshine and see well at night.

(*Against Colotes* 1120e)

[T]he Cyrenaics claim that the *pathê* alone are apprehensible but the external object is inapprehensible, for, they say, I apprehend that I am being burnt, but it is non-evident whether the fire is such as to burn.

(Anonymous commentator on Plato's *Theaetetus*
p. 152b col. 65.29–39)

The first thing to note is that, *pace* Warren, the passage from the anonymous commentator does not explicitly rule out object identity scepticism.

Let us suppose that object identity scepticism is true and I cannot tell whether or not the object that burns me is a fire. Then the statement "the fire is such as to burn" is *also* going to be something that isn't evident to me—after all, it isn't even evident to me whether the object is a fire, much less whether it is such as to burn! Likewise with the report from Plutarch: object identity scepticism is perfectly compatible with being unable to tell whether or not the honey is sweet, the hail chilly, etc. At best, a statement like "We cannot know whether or not the fire is such as to burn" conversationally implicates that there is an object, the fire, whose nature we cannot know; it does not entail it.

But I don't think that in this context there is much if any conversational implicature of this sort going on. A parallel case from the Pyrrhonian sceptics will help us see why. The sceptic lives his life in accordance with the way things appear to him, e.g., that the honey appears sweet. But unlike the *pathê* for the Cyrenaics, statements about appearances (*phainomena*) are usually a matter of describing how the *object* seems to be, not merely the internal states of the percipient. As Hankinson puts it, "When Sextus does wish to refer to purely mental phenomena, he employs the language of impression, *phantasia* (see [*Outlines of Pyrrhonism* 1 19]), and *phantasiai* are caused by the *phainomena*, which are their intentional objects. An appearance, then, is not something we have of objects: it is something that objects themselves have (as I might compliment you upon your appearance)" (Hankinson (1995) 25).

Everson (1991) believes that these "objective appearances" commit the Pyrrhonian sceptic to the existence of objects like the honey: I may wonder whether the honey *is* as it *appears* to be, but to believe that the honey appears sweet presupposes that the honey exists. But Gail Fine points out that these statements require only an "ostensible object." She gives the example of Macbeth saying that the dagger's handle seems to be pointed toward his hand, while still doubting that there really is a dagger there. Likewise, the Cyrenaic is free is talk about the properties that an object like fire seems to have, while still being dubious about whether the thing he's perceiving really is a fire (Fine (2003) 350-1).

I think that these determinate ways of referring to the causes of our *pathê* are, as Warren puts, merely "an expositional convenience." When initially setting out sceptical arguments from perceptual relativity, it is more vivid to use concrete examples like the wine that is warming to one person and cooling to another. This also lets the Cyrenaics make their point that that is only the *pathê* of being warmed, cooled, bittered, etc., that we can apprehend, and not the corresponding sensible properties of the objects—their warmth, coolness, or bitterness. Once this central epistemological point is appreciated, however, they can note that their arguments also call into question the identity of the objects that move us—that we cannot tell whether the object that burns us is fire, or the one that cuts us iron.

Global Object Identity Scepticism

My argument so far, if it is successful, shows that the Cyrenaics' scepticism extends to the identity of the particular objects that cause our particular *pathê*. That is, for any particular *pathos*, let us say of sweetness, the Cyrenaic refrains from judging not only that the honey he tastes is sweet, but also from judging that the object causing his *pathos* is honey. But this leaves open the question of whether this object identity scepticism extends to the structure of the world in general. That is, do the Cyrenaics believe in a common-sense way that the world is populated by objects like fires, honey, and so forth, or do they countenance the possibility that reality may well be some sort of indeterminate substratum in constant flux, containing no proper objects, even though (*pace* Zilioli) they would not *subscribe* to that view?

I believe that we should remain agnostic about this final question, given our lack of evidence. As I indicated above, the mere fact that the Cyrenaics sometimes designate the causes of our *pathê* using common nouns like honey, fire, and olive-shoots does not commit them to the existence of such items. Likewise, Warren is right that the more non-committal ways that the Cyrenaics describe these causes, although it is *compatible* with a wider scepticism about their identity, doesn't entail such scepticism.

Hankinson thinks Sextus' report in *Outlines of Pyrrhonism* 1 215 regarding how Pyrrhonian sceptics differ from Cyrenaics precludes a global object scepticism. He first gives the passage: "Furthermore, while we suspend judgment in regard to the essence (*logos*) of external objects, the Cyrenaics assert that they have a nature which is inapprehensible (*akatalêpton*)," and he then writes that the Cyrenaics apparently "combine a general dogmatic ontological claim ('objects have essences') with negative E-dogmatism about them taken as particulars ('we can never know what those essences are')" (Hankinson (1995) 57). So the contrast between the Pyrrhonians and the Cyrenaics, on Hankinson's reading, involves the Cyrenaics making a judgment about the general structure of reality that the Pyrrhonians eschew.

But this is not the only plausible reading of the passage. Tsouna's translation of it runs "Besides, we suspend judgment about the external objects, as far as the arguments go. The Cyrenaics, on the other hand, affirm that the external objects have an inapprehensible nature." As far the Greek goes, either translation is fine. Tsouna's translation suggests, although it does not require, that the difference between the Cyrenaics and the Pyrrhonian sceptics is epistemological, not ontological. That is, neither the Pyrrhonian nor the Cyrenaic makes claims about the nature of things, but the Cyrenaic goes on to say that external objects "have an inapprehensible nature," i.e., that we are unable ever to apprehend their nature, unlike the Pyrrhonian. The contrast, then, would the same as the one Sextus makes at the start of *Outlines of Pyrrhonism* between the sceptic and Academics like Carneades: the sceptic continues investigating, with no opinions of his own either about the subject of his investigation *or* about whether the investigation will be successful, whereas the Academics assert that things cannot be apprehended (*Outlines of Pyrrhonism* 1 1–3).

On the other hand, a passage that would support attributing global object identity scepticism to the Cyrenaics is *Against the Professors* 7 194, if we accept Zilioli's reading of what's going on. Recall that Zilioli takes Sextus to be attributing to the Cyrenaics the thesis that the cause of our *pathos* "perhaps is a being" [*tacha men estin on*], which means that these causes may not be determinate individual material things that exist, properly speaking. This reading has two troubles, though. First, as Tsouna explains, we have good reason to be suspicious of the accuracy of this report. Secondly, absent some surrounding context to establish that being is used in a technical sense to contrast proper beings with processes, indeterminate substrates, or whatever, the more natural way to read the passage is as asserting that these causes perhaps exist.

So no texts bear much weight in determining whether or not the Cyrenaics subscribed to global object identity scepticism. Considerations of charity likewise do not get us far. One could try to argue as follows: the Cyrenaics subscribe to object identity scepticism about the particular cause of each particular *pathos*. Furthermore, they were probably aware of the possibility that the external world is metaphysically indeterminate, with no proper objects, as this thesis had been put forward in the *Theaetetus* and (perhaps) by Pyrrho. Given this, and their further thesis that we apprehend only our *pathê*, they would have no justification for thinking that our common-sense view of the world is true rather than the metaphysical indeterminacy thesis, and they should have subscribed to global object identity scepticism.

Perhaps. On the other hand, the metaphysical indeterminacy thesis is strange enough that I can imagine somebody rejecting it as incoherent or self-contradictory without claiming to know the determinate properties or identity of any particular object in the world. And in any case, we have no textual evidence that the Cyrenaics concerned themselves with this issue. The *testimonia* allow us to answer, though not definitively, many of our questions concerning the Cyrenaics' scepticism, but on this question we should suspend judgment.[10]

NOTES

1. A little terminological housekeeping: when I talk about the Cyrenaics' "scepticism," I am referring to their denial that we can apprehend external objects and their recommendation that we eschew making judgments regarding them. For Sextus Empiricus, such a stance is not properly sceptical, since it involves a sort of (negative) epistemological commitment. It is for this reason that Hankinson labels the Cyrenaics as "negative E [i.e., epistemological] dogmatists" (Hankinson (1995) 13–18), although Sextus does not use that terminology. In

Zilioli's chapter in this volume, he labels the sort of position I endorse as the "sceptical interpretation" because of its stress on our epistemic limitations, which he contrasts with his own "metaphysical indeterminacy" interpretation. These labels are fair enough, but the way I am using terms, both would qualify as sceptical interpretations, as both acknowledge that the Cyrenaics deny we can apprehend external objects, although they differ on the reasons the Cyrenaics do so, and so I label my view the "epistemic limitations" interpretation, while retaining "metaphysical indeterminacy" for Zilioli's view.
2. Berkeley and his ilk, of course, would typically deny that ordinary physical objects *are* mind-independent, opting instead for some sort of phenomenalist reduction of physical objections to actual or possible patterns of sense-data, but the point about mind-independent physical objects still stands.
3. Unless otherwise noted, all translations are from the appendix to Tsouna (1998).
4. Bett (2000) 14–62 contains his arguments for this construal.
5. Similar considerations apply to Zilioli's discussion of *Against Colotes* at pp. 186–9.
6. See chapter 3 of Zilioli (2012) for his arguments that Aristippus and other early Cyrenaics were the subtle thinkers who advanced the flux doctrine of the *Theaetetus*, and O'Keefe (2013) for my criticisms. Briefly: while the Cyrenaics and the subtle thinkers each characterize our infallible acquaintance with our *pathê* similarly, this on its own gives us little reason to attribute the metaphysical doctrine of flux to Aristippus, especially if (as I have argued) this doctrine conflicts with the reports we have on the Cyrenaics. In this volume, Rowe argues that Aristippus is the unnamed source of many of the ideas advanced (and then criticized) in the *Theaetetus*, although not the metaphysics of flux.
7. We have no reports on why the Cyrenaics think this, but Tsouna plausibly speculates that the Cyrenaics "may presuppose the use of some version of the causality principle: if I am feeling burnt, there is something over there which is burning me" (Tsouna (1998) 77 n. 5). See also Burnyeat (1982) more generally on (the absence of) idealism as a live option in ancient philosophy.
8. See O'Keefe (2011) for more on how these things differ. Hankinson (1995) 58) also thinks that the "genuine scepticism of [this passage] is a Sextan intrusion."
9. For Epicurus himself, Orestes' delusional perceptions themselves are nonetheless true, insofar as his senses were moved by something existent, and it's only his judgment that the Furies are solid bodies that's false.
10. I would like to thank Ugo Zilioli for his generosity of spirit in inviting me to contribute to this volume after reading my often critical review of his book on the Cyrenaics in *Notre Dame Philosophical Reviews*, and for sharing with me drafts of his paper and the other papers appearing in this book. Some of the material in this paper in its introduction and discussion of the metaphysical indeterminacy thesis is adapted from that review.

WORKS CITED

Bett, R. 2000. *Pyrrho, his Antecedents, and his Legacy*. Oxford and New York: Oxford University Press.
Bett, R. 2015. "Pyrrho and the Socratic schools," in Zilioli (2015a).
Burnyeat, M. 1982. "Idealism and Greek Philosophy: What Descartes Saw and Berkeley Missed," *Philosophical Review* 91: 3–40.

Everson, S. 1991. "The objective appearance of Pyrrhonism," in *Psychology. Companions to Ancient Thought 2*, ed. S. Everson. Cambridge: Cambridge University Press, 121–147.

Fine, G. 2003. "Sextus and External World Scepticism," *Oxford Studies in Ancient Philosophy* 24: 341–385.

Hankinson, R.J. 1995. *The Sceptics*. London and New York: Routledge.

O'Keefe, T. 2011. "The Cyrenaics vs. the Pyrrhonists on Knowledge of Appearances," in *Essays on Ancient Pyrrhonism*, ed. D. Machuca. Leiden: Brill, 27–40.

O'Keefe, T. 2013. "Review of Ugo Zilioli, *The Cyrenaics*," *Notre Dame Philosophical Reviews*, November 4, 2013 (http://ndpr.nd.edu/news/39081-the-cyrenaics/).

Rowe, C. 2015. "The First-Generation Socratics and the Socratic Schools: the case of the Cyrenaics," in Zilioli (2015a).

Tsouna, V. 1998. *The Epistemology of the Cyrenaic School*. Cambridge: Cambridge University Press.

Warren, J. 2013. "Cyrenaics," in *The Routledge Companion to Ancient Philosophy*, eds. F. Sheffield and J. Warren. London and New York: Routledge, 409–422.

Zilioli, U. 2012. *The Cyrenaics*. Durham: Acumen; reprinted in London and New York: Routledge, 2014.

Zilioli, U., ed. 2015a. *From the Socratics to the Socratic Schools*. London and New York: Routledge.

Zilioli, U. 2015b. "The Cyrenaics as Metaphysical Indeterminists," in Zilioli (2015a).

7 The Cyrenaics as Metaphysical Indeterminists

Ugo Zilioli

1. THE SCEPTICAL INTERPRETATION

According to the sceptical interpretation, the Cyrenaics defended a kind of strict subjectivism with regard to our own private affections and, at the same time, discharged as hopeless the possibility that we may come to know what causes them.[1] A crucial passage by Sextus Empiricus is usually taken to show the point:

> (191) The Cyrenaics hold that affections [*pathē*] are the criteria [of truth] and that they alone are apprehended and are infallible [*kai mona katalambanesthai kai adiapseusta tunchanein*]. None of the things that have caused the affections [*tōn de pepoiēkotōn ta pathē*] is, on the contrary, apprehensible. They say that it is possible to state infallibly and truly and firmly and incorrigibly that we are being whitened or sweetened [*oti men gar leukanometha, phasi, kai glukazometha, dunaton legein adiapseustōs kai bebaiōs kai alēthōs kai anexelenktōs*]. It is not possible however to say that the thing productive of our affection [*to empoiētikon tou pathous*] is white or sweet (192), because one may be disposed whitely even by something that is not-white or may be sweetened by something that is not-sweet.
> (*M*. VII 191–2=*SSR* IV A 213).[2]

In the passage, Sextus reports the kernel of Cyrenaic subjectivism: for the Cyrenaics we may truly and infallibly affirm that we have an affection of white but we cannot say that what we perceive as white is white in itself. Things in the world—"things that have caused the affections"—are not apprehensible or infallible, while our affections are such that we cannot be mistaken about them. The contrast here is, the sceptical interpretation goes, between *infallible affections* and *unknowable items* in the world (causing affections in us). The contrast is traditionally sceptic: we know how things appear to us, but not how things are in themselves.[3] The Cyrenaics took this contrast and stretched it at a full extent by coining neologisms such as 'to be whitened, sweetened,' to express the full epistemological privacy of our affections. In adopting such a position, like other sceptics, the Cyrenaics cannot be credited with any interest in metaphysics, since they openly profess things in the world to be unknowable.

The sceptical reading of the Cyrenaics I have just summarily reconstructed is at the root of the interpretation I wish to resist. In this paper I will construct the best case I can to show that a rival interpretation of Cyrenaic philosophy is available. According to this rival interpretation, the Cyrenaics had metaphysical commitments that went parallel to their epistemological subjectivism and that will explain some features of their philosophy in a more convincing way.

2. THE ALTERNATIVE INTERPRETATION

Let us begin with a preliminary remark about the Cyrenaics' attitude towards metaphysics. In this connection, Sextus reports the following view:

> (11) The Cyrenaics appear to confine themselves to ethics only, and to dismiss physics and logic as contributing nothing to the happiness of our life. Some, however, have suggested that this view about them is actually refuted by the very fact that the Cyrenaics divided ethics into sub-branches: one having to do with what has to be done or avoided; another dealing with affections; a third one on actions; the fourth concerned with causes; and a final one dealing with arguments
> (*M.* VII 11=*SSR* IV A 168; see also Sen. *Ep. ad. Lucilium* XIV 1, 12=*SSR* IV A 165).

The passage seems to lend support to the sceptical interpretation of the Cyrenaics in so far as it begins with a rather peremptory statement about the exclusive interest in ethics the Cyrenaics appear to have had. According to one possible reading of the passage, for the Cyrenaics no metaphysics and no other branch of philosophy apart from ethics will be ever contributing to the happiness of life. Yet, the support that the passage may offer to the sceptical interpretation is only apparent. If properly understood, in fact, it offers arguments *against* that interpretation. The passage insists that the Cyrenaics had wide interests for every branch of philosophy, since ethics was further divided by them in sub-branches that correspond roughly to ethics proper, epistemology, theory of action, metaphysics and logic. This passage, therefore, confirms that the Cyrenaics had interest also for epistemology and metaphysics, not only for ethics. This is one first difficulty for the sceptical interpretation: how could any interest of the Cyrenaics for metaphysics be explained if they believed metaphysical knowledge to be wholly unattainable? It seems that the sceptical interpretation has close analogies with old-fashioned readings of the Cyrenaics, for which Aristippus' followers were understood as ultra-hedonists, with no other proper philosophical views to defend, not even the original epistemology on which scholars have focused in the last decades.

The sceptical exegete of the Cyrenaics may well insist that Sextus openly says that "none of the things that have caused the affections [*tōn de pepoiēkotōn ta pathē*] is, on the contrary, apprehensible (*mêden katalêpton*) or infallible." Sextus reports the same view when he distinguishes the Cyrenaics from the Sceptics in *PH* 215: "[The sceptics] suspend judgement—as far as the argument goes—about external things, while the Cyrenaics assert that they have an inapprehensible (*akatalêpton*) nature." The term Sextus uses in both passages is the canonical term '*katalpêton*,' which the sceptics usually employ to express the epistemological apprehensibility of things.[4]

Now, what could it mean that, in contrast with infallible affections, things are inapprehensible? I see two possible explanations: either that we are epistemologically incapable to arrive at the very nature of things for a variety of reasons, such as those that the ancient sceptics have usually brought to attention with the modes of suspending judgement; or, alternatively, things are inapprehensible because *by their own nature* they are not knowable, that is, there is nothing determinate there to be known for us. The sceptical exegete of the Cyrenaics takes them to be committed to the first explanation: the Cyrenaics claim that only our affections are apprehensible exactly because we cannot grasp the ontological features of the things that cause affections in us. I will defend the second explanation: the Cyrenaics claim that we know our affections, not things in the world because the latter are metaphysically indeterminate. Even more radically, I will try to show that the Cyrenaics may have ventured to stretch their metaphysical views to the point where material things are denied to be existing.

In other words, what I suggest is that the Cyrenaics endorsed a metaphysics of indeterminacy, which I also take to be working at the root of their epistemological subjectivism. On the basis of this interpretation, the Cyrenaics declare the exclusive apprehensibility of our affections because there is widespread indeterminacy in the world and there are no determinate objects there to be apprehended for us. On this understanding, we can simply know how things appear to us, not how they really are, because material things are metaphysically indeterminate.

3. METAPHYSICAL INDETERMINACY IN CONTEMPORARY PHILOSOPHY

From a purely philosophical standpoint, is the claim that things are inapprehensible because ultimately indeterminate a plausible one? What does it mean to say that things are indeterminate? In her critical survey of antecedents of scepticism in early Greek philosophy, Mitzi Lee insists that some predecessors of ancient scepticism conceived of things as inapprehensible for ontological reasons (among those predecessors, however, she does not include the Cyrenaics), such reasons being the following ones: contradictionism (the view that everything is both F and not-F), flux (the view that everything is always changing from F to not-F) and indeterminacy (the view that nothing is anymore F or is determinately F to any greater extent that it is not-F). She rightly remarks: "If then all of nature is fundamentally indeterminate, and nothing that exists has a definite nature, then it will be impossible to say how things are, since my attempt to do so will vainly try to pin things down as being one way rather than another."[5]

I claim the Cyrenaics to be committed to the third of Lee's options, that is, indeterminacy. I make the additional claim that the Cyrenaics may have embraced both the kind of indeterminacy Lee refers to and another version of it, more radical, which account for the denial of the proper existence of objects. Contemporary speculation helps us to understand more appropriately what metaphysical indeterminacy amounts to in philosophical terms, as well as teaching us that even the most disturbing idea that there are no proper objects in the world could be accommodated within a credible theory of the material world.

Alongside with neo-Aristotelian theories of the material world such as that defended by e.g. David Wiggins in *Sameness and Substance* (Cambridge 1980; revised edition, Cambridge 2000), current debates in analytic metaphysics are focused on three views that all challenge, although in different ways, our commonsensical understanding of the material world: (1) four-dimensionalism, that is, the view that material objects have temporal parts, in addition to spatial parts; (2) an appropriately revised version of four-dimensionalism, that is, stage-theory, namely the view that material objects are the sum of spatial and temporal stages; (3) metaphysical vagueness and indeterminacy.[6] For the purposes of this contribution, I will briefly concentrate on vagueness and indeterminacy. Among the flourishing scholarship on metaphysical vagueness, there is an important contribution by Rosen and Smith, where the authors classify the different kinds of metaphysical indeterminacy that are currently discussed. They single out two versions of metaphysical indeterminacy that well suit our discussion. The former version (let us call it 'mild indeterminacy') maintains that material objects are indeterminate in their secondary qualities (hotness, redness, etc.); the latter one (let us call it 'radical indeterminacy') maintains that the world itself is indeterminate and deprived of material objects.[7]

If metaphysical indeterminacy is mild, we will be confronted with a vast array of material objects that are in themselves neither hot nor cold, neither sweet nor bitter, and so on. If metaphysical indeterminacy is radical, we will be confronted with a vast array of undifferentiated matter, truly devoid of material objects. There are at present two well-known (and different) theories of radical indeterminacy. One is that defended by Peter Van Inwagen in *Material Beings* (1990), where he advances the view that what exists is either a living organism or a simple (that is, the basic constituent of matter, arranged in different fashion, on different occasions). Since material objects are neither living organisms nor pure simples, they are, strictly speaking, non-existent. Along similar lines, in *Objects and Persons* (2003) Trenton Merricks defends a theory of the material world that allows for the existence of both animate items and extended material stuff devoid of material objects, yet displaying non-redundant casual powers.[8]

4. METAPHYSICAL INDETERMINACY IN ANCIENT PHILOSOPHY

Contemporary speculation helps us gain a much deeper understanding of what metaphysical indeterminacy actually amounts to in philosophical terms. At the same time, recent studies in ancient philosophy have shown that metaphysical indeterminacy was also present in Greek thought. Richard Bett's book on Pyrrho has demonstrated with amplitude of details that Pyrrho was committed to metaphysical indeterminacy, as well as offering further help in locating traces of that indeterminacy throughout ancient philosophy. To motivate his innovative interpretation of Pyrrho as a non-sceptic (since, on Bett's understanding, Pyrrho is truly committed to holding a metaphysical thesis), Bett offers a refreshing interpretation of a crucial passage of Aristocles on Timon on Pyrrho (Aristocles, fragment 5 Chiesara=Eusebius, *PE* 14.19.1–5). According to Bett, in that passage Pyrrho is ascribed the view that "things are equally indifferent and unstable and indeterminate (*ep'isês adiaphora kai asthamêta kai anepikrita*)."[9]

By commenting on Aristocles' passage, Bett further specifies the metaphysical view he attributes to Pyrrho: "to say that things are 'indifferent' presumably means that they are not, in their real natures, any different from one another—no doubt because they do not have any real natures of a sort that would permit such differentiation; to say that are 'unstable' must mean that they do not have any fixed natures; and to say that they are 'indeterminate' must mean that they do not have definite natures. Clearly all these features are closely related, and for convenience I shall speak from now on (. . .) simply of the 'indeterminacy thesis'" (Bett 1999, 28–9). Bett rephrases the indeterminacy thesis as the view that "there is absolutely nothing that we can say about the object—or at least absolutely nothing definite; all we can say is that it is no more F than not F or both or neither" (Bett 1999, 36). Bett identifies traces of indeterminacy in other ancient texts, such as significant sections of Plato's *Theaetetus* and *Republic*, and in the thought of some ancient thinkers (not in the Cyrenaics though).[10] I have argued elsewhere in support of Bett's claim that metaphysical indeterminacy was a respectable and fairly widespread view in ancient philosophy; against his judgement on this, I have also included Aristotle's discussion of the principle of non-contradiction as further evidence of ancient commitment to indeterminacy.[11]

Do current conceptions of metaphysical indeterminacy (namely those briefly referred to in section 3) overlap with the ancient one? The kind of indeterminacy Bett discusses in connection with Pyrrho may in principle accommodate both mild and radical indeterminacy. When things are said to be no more F than not-F or both or neither—as Pyrrho appears to be saying on the basis of Bett's interpretation—it is just another way to say that things are indeterminate in their secondary properties (mild indeterminacy). But even radical indeterminacy may easily come in the picture: on Bett's understanding, for Pyrrho material objects are not defined and are so undifferentiated one from the other that they can not be regarded as properly existent. In his book, Bett tends to focus on what I have called 'mild indeterminacy,' although I suggest that also radical indeterminacy may be implicitly allowed to.[12]

The option of radical indeterminacy has been brought to scholarly attention, exactly in connection with the Cyrenaics, by another important book, that is, Voula Tsouna, *The Epistemology of the Cyrenaic school* (Cambridge 1998). In her book, Tsouna suggests three metaphysical options to be potentially present in the philosophy of the Cyrenaics: idealism, the commonsensical view on whose basis the world is made up by ordinary objects and states of affairs; 'radical indeterminacy' (she refers to it as the view that "[the material world is] an undifferentiated substratum affecting us in various ways").[13] As far as the metaphysics of the Cyrenaics is concerned, Tsouna rules out the idealist option, and I fully follow her lead on this.[14] She defends the second option, whereas I will defend the third one. What I am about to do in the next sections is to take up both Bett's and Tsouna's leads (but in contrast with their overall understanding of the Cyrenaics), to see whether a credible case could be made to argue that the Cyrenaics were metaphysically committed to indeterminacy. In addition, while I construct a case for attributing indeterminacy to the Cyrenaics, I try to answer, mainly in the footnotes, to the criticism O'Keefe levels against the metaphysical reading of the Cyrenaics I advance.

5. SEXTUS AND COLOTES

After this brief survey into ancient and current conceptions of metaphysical indeterminacy, let us now go back to the passage of Sextus I have quoted at the opening, that is, *M*. VII 191–2. Let us briefly recapitulate where we were. The sceptical exegete of the Cyrenaics maintains that in that passage we are plainly given, by Sextus' own words, the essential details of Cyrenaic epistemology: for the Cyrenaics we know truly and infallibly how things appear to us, but not how things are in themselves. The contrast here is between infallible affections and inapprehensible items in the world. I have suggested that there are two possible ways to understand the claim that things are inapprehensible: either things are inapprehensible because we are

120 *Ugo Zilioli*

distorted in our apprehension of them for a variety of factors (sceptical interpretation) or, alternatively, things are inapprehensible because by their own nature they are not determined, that is, there is nothing determinate there to be known for us (metaphysical interpretation).

On my interpretation, Sextus' passage does not rule out any of the two interpretations. It simply insists that for the Cyrenaics affections can be known, while material things causing them cannot.[15] There is, however, another passage by Sextus that may support the indeterminacy reading of the Cyrenaics I suggest. The passage goes thus:

> Cyrenaic philosophers hold that affections alone exist [*mona huparchein ta pathē*] and nothing else. Since it is not an affection but rather it is something capable of producing an affection [*hothen kai tēn phōnēn mē ousan pathos, alla pathous poiētikēn*], sound is not one of the things that exist [*mē gignesthai tōn huparktōn*].
>
> (*M*. VI 53=SSR IV A 219)

In this passage, Sextus reinterprets the Cyrenaic position on affections in metaphysical terms: the Cyrenaics grant existence to affections alone, whilst they deny proper existence to those things that cause our affections. We have sound-affections, but sound does not properly exist.[16] This passage is not usually given great importance because to deny existence to sensory-objects seems to be a rather awkward view to defend. But Sextus takes that view seriously and attaches it not only to the Cyrenaics, but also to Plato and Democritus.[17] In addition, few lines after the long extract of Sextus I have quoted at the beginning of this article Sextus reports the same suspicion, from the Cyrenaics' part, about the actual existence of material objects. By reproducing the same dichotomy between affections and things that we have seen displayed in the opening lines of *M*. VII 191–2, Sextus remarks:

> We must therefore say either that the affections are *phainomena* or that the things productive of the affections are *phainomena*. If we say that the affections are *phainomena*, we will have to maintain that all *phainomena* are true and apprehensible. If, on the contrary, we say that the things productive of the affections are *phainomena*, all *phainomena* will be false and not apprehensible. The affection occurring in us tells us nothing more than itself. If one has to speak but the truth, the affection alone is therefore actually a *phainomenon* for us. What is external and productive of the affection [*to d'ektos kai tou pathous poiētikon*] perhaps is a being [*tacha men estin on*], but it is not a *phainomenon* for us.
>
> (*M*. VII 194=SSR IV A 213)

What causes our affections "perhaps is a being". This means that things in the world perhaps are not, properly speaking, existing items; that is, material things, as individual items, may well be not existent after all. After our survey into the notion of indeterminacy, to deny proper existence to material objects is to be understood as a quite serious philosophical view: we may think that in the two quoted passages, Sextus is ascribing to the Cyrenaics a form of radical indeterminacy, on whose basis there are no proper objects (to be perceived) in the world.[18]

Is Sextus alone in attributing the Cyrenaics such a radical view? Not quite so, I claim. The oldest source on the Cyrenaics, a lengthy passage from the work of the Epicurean philosopher Colotes as preserved by Plutarch, suggests that the Cyrenaics may have embraced radical indeterminacy. I quote most part of the passage:

> He [Colotes] aims, I suspect, to refute the Cyrenaics first, and then the Academy of Arcesilaus. The latter school was of those who suspended judgement on everything; whereas the former, placing all affections and sense-impressions within themselves, thought that the evidence derived from them was not enough, as far as assertions on external objects are concerned. Distancing themselves from external objects, they shut themselves up within their affections as in a siege. In doing so, they adopted the locution 'it appears' but refused to say in addition that 'it is' with regard to external objects. This is the reason why—Colotes says—the Cyrenaics cannot live or cope with things. In addition, he says (making fun of them), that 'these men do not say that it/there is (*anthrôpon einai*) a man or a horse or a wall, but that they themselves are being walled or horsed or manned' [*toichousthai kai hippousthai kai anthrôpousthai*].
> (Adv. Col. 1120c–d=SSR IV A 211)[19]

According to Plutarch, in his book entitled "On the point that conformity to the views of other philosophers actually makes it impossible to live" Colotes singles out the Cyrenaics as a group of philosophers who make life impossible to live because of the doctrines they endorse. By granting epistemological infallibility to affections alone, the Cyrenaics shut themselves into a siege, distancing themselves from the external world. As Kechagia has observed, the Greek in the expression "these men do not say that it/there is a man" (*anthrôpon einai*) is ambiguous and can be rendered with two different translations, depending on how one construes the verb '*einai*': either 'there is a man' in the existential sense of 'a man exists' or, alternatively, 'it is a man,' meaning 'the thing here is a man.'

The ambiguity in the text provides us with two philosophical alternatives. Given the infallibility they grant to affections alone, the Cyrenaics refuse to say either that what causes our affections actually exists or, alternatively, that what produces in us an affection of sweet is, for instance, really honey. On the former alternative, Colotes would be denying existence to material objects; that is, he would be restating the same view that, at least on my interpretation, Sextus expresses in the two passages just quoted (hence committing the Cyrenaics to radical indeterminacy). On the second alternative, Colotes would be suggesting that the Cyrenaics cannot identify an external object as the kind of thing it is.[20]

Both Tsouna and Kechagia remark that both alternatives are present in the text: Tsouna opts for the latter while Kechagia highlights the close philosophical linkage between the two options.[21] It is true that to refuse to identify an external object as the kind of thing it is is different from saying that material things as such do not exist, but the former option may be understood as leading, more or less naturally, to the latter. If in my affection of sweetness, I refuse to say that what produces in me that affection is really honey or a bar of chocolate; if in my affection of whiteness, I refuse to say whether it is either a table or a stone that produces that affection of white in me; what view of the material world could I end up to have? The most natural answer I can think of is that of a view of the world where objects play no part at all—since I cannot identify them for what they are. According to this view, we are confronted with an undifferentiated lump of matter, fully devoid of discrete items. And this is metaphysical indeterminacy, of the radical kind.

Colotes' reference to Cyrenaic neologisms (such as 'to be horsed,' 'manned'), leads Plutarch to complain that Colotes had not been historically accurate in reporting the doctrines of the Cyrenaics, since they are uniformly reported to have used neologisms referring to sensible qualities. While he recognizes that Colotes had actually put the fingers on the philosophical fulcrum of Cyrenaic philosophy, Plutarch insists to be able to expound such philosophy in more historically trustworthy terms.[22] But, I suggest, Colotes' real point has little to do with historical accuracy, much more with philosophical acumen. By using a slightly mocking tone, Colotes has correctly identified the main metaphysical feature of Cyrenaic philosophy, that is, the total absence of any reference to objects in their philosophy and in their philosophical language. If they want to make life possible, Colotes tells us, the Cyrenaics should restore in their philosophy the very notion of object, which they appear to have wholly dispended with. Instead of using expressions referring to secondary qualities alone and, while retaining their original neologisms, the Cyrenaics should bring in expressions actually referring to objects, such as horse and man. Otherwise, their philosophy would be completely untenable and make life actually impossible to live. This is, I claim, Colotes' quite sensitive appraisal of the Cyrenaics.

To avoid any reference to objects as such and to refer to the world of undifferentiated matter we are confronted with by indicating only secondary properties is exactly the best characterization of metaphysical indeterminacy according to what Aristotle says in *Metaphysics* 4, sections 5 and 6. When he deals with those who deny the principle of non-contradiction, Aristotle clearly shows that the principle of non-contradiction can be denied coherently only by those who assume that reality is ontologically indeterminate.[23]

He suggests that those who deny the principle of non-contradiction and assume that reality is indeterminate get rid of, among other things, the notions of essence and substance, thus maintaining that everything has to be predicated *per accidens*. As Aristotle puts it:

> And in general those who use this argument [i.e. those who deny the principle of non-contradiction] do away with substance and essence. For they must say that all attributes are accidents, and that there is no such thing as being essentially man or animal. For if there is to be any such thing as being essentially man this will not be being not-man or not being a man (yet these are negations of it); for there was some one thing which it meant, and this was the substance of something. And denoting the substance of a thing means that the essence of the thing is nothing else. But if its being essentially man is to be the same as either being essentially not-man or essentially not being a man, then its essence will be something else. Therefore our opponents must say that there cannot be such a definition of anything, but that all attributes are accidental; for this is the distinction between substance and accident—white is accidental to man, because though he is white, whiteness is not his essence. But if all statements are accidental, there will be nothing primary about which they are made, if the accidental always implies predication about a subject. (4.5.1007a21-b1)

According to Aristotle, thus, to refer to secondary qualities alone is the best mark of metaphysical indeterminacy. And to refer to secondary qualities alone is exactly what the Cyrenaics do when they use such neologisms as 'I am being whitened' (when they undergo a sensation of white, with reference to what is usually believed to be, for instance, a white chair). Again, despite his mocking tone, this is exactly the main point of Colotes' argument: the Cyrenaics should restore real objects in their metaphysics and, for that matter, in their neologisms if they wanted to make life possible to live.[24]

6. THE ANONYMOUS AND PHILODEMUS

I now turn briefly to two other passages that may lend support to my indeterminacy reading of the Cyrenaics. The first passage is a brief extract from the Anonymous' Commentary on Plato's *Theaetetus*. In that dialogue, while he explains the real meaning of Protagoras' maxim that man is the measure of all things, Socrates makes the example of the blowing wind (*Tht.* 152b1-3), which is felt as cold by someone and as hot by someone else. According to Protagoras' relativism, both perceivers are correct and legitimate in their different affections. Socrates now asks Theaetetus the following metaphysical question: "the wind itself, by itself, is cold or not cold? (152b5-6)." In commenting on the question, the Anonymous remarks:

Something is the agent, something else is the patient. But, if people undergo affections that are opposed to the thing in itself, they will agree that the intrinsic feature of the agent is not defined (*mê einai hôrismenên tên tou poiêsantos idiotêta*);[25] if it were so, the same thing at the same time will not produce different affections. Because of this, the Cyrenaics say that only affections are apprehensible, while external things are not. That I am being burnt, they say I apprehend; that the fire is such as to burn is obscure (*adelon*): if it were such, all things will be burnt by it.

(col. LXV, 19–35=SSR IV A 214)

By suggesting a linkage, both terminological and conceptual, with the active and passive elements that are so central in the theory of perception endorsed by the subtler thinkers at *Theaetetus* 156a–157c, the Anonymous commentator remarks that, by being affected by the same object in different ways, it has to follow that "the intrinsic feature of the agent is not defined."[26] Material objects, therefore, are not ontologically determinate, since they (such as the wind of Socrates' example) may appear F to someone and not-F to someone else. Socrates' wind in itself is neither cold nor not-cold. It is simply neutral, that is, it does not possess any ontological feature of its own. On the basis of this explanation, the Cyrenaic view that affections alone are apprehensible relies on external objects being inapprehensible because ontologically indeterminate. The fire in itself is not caustic, because, if it were so, everybody would be burnt by it. It has to be noted here that the kind of indeterminacy that is ascribed to the Cyrenaics is mild, that is, objects are understood to be indeterminate as far as their secondary qualities are concerned.[27]

There is another source that has been brought to light by Tsouna as containing reference to the Cyrenaics. The passage in question does not name the Cyrenaics directly. However, Tsouna believes (quite correctly, I think) that the passage refers to the Cyrenaics.[28] The passage in question is by Philodemus of Gadara, an Epicurean philosopher, whose work *On Choices and Avoidances* (the title is conjectural) is preserved in a papyrus found in Herculaneum (PHerc. 1251, 23 columns). The papyrus is badly damaged so reconstruction by editors is often difficult. Philodemus probably wrote his treatise on choices in the first half of the first century BC, when the Cyrenaic school had already been dead for at least a century. A sensitive philosopher like Philodemus is capable to highlight the various developments that the Cyrenaic school carried out in the elaboration of its philosophy over the space of more than two centuries. This is particularly probable in so far as the Cyrenaics, especially the later sects of the school, extensively rivalled the Epicureans with their theories on pleasure and the end. These Cyrenaic doctrines are likely to have been well known by those Epicureans, like Philodemus, who aimed to argue against them.

The main point Philodemus seems to be addressing in his text is a root-and-branch rejection of those philosophical doctrines that do not relate

The Cyrenaics as Metaphysical Indeterminists 125

choices about actions to rational calculation and knowledge. In his attack against what he believes are irrational views that ground decisions for acting on factors that have nothing to do with reason and knowledge, Philodemus singles out a family of doctrines that are undoubtedly Cyrenaic in their core. The passage goes thus:

> (Col. II) They claim that as for truth no judgement is superior to any other. They believe in fact that the great *pathos* of the soul occurs as a result of pain and that thus we make our choices and avoidances by observing both bodily and mental pain (. . .)
>
> (Col. III) Some people denied that it is possible to know anything. They also added that if nothing on whose basis one should make an immediate choice is present, one should not choose immediately. Some other people made affections [*pathē*] of the soul as the moral ends and as not in need of any additional judgement based on further criteria. In doing so they granted to everybody an authority, which was not accountable, to get pleasure in whatever they cared to name and to do whatever contributed to it. Others held the view that what our school calls grief or joy are totally empty notions because of the manifest indeterminacy (*aoristia*) [of things]. (=SSR IV H 30)

The view that the affections of the soul are the ends of life (col. III) is the kernel of Cyrenaic ethics.[29] At the same time, Philodemus' words that affections are "not in need of any additional judgement based on further criteria" is an explicit reference to the Cyrenaic idea that only affections are knowable and, from an epistemological standpoint, perfectly legitimate. In linking Cyrenaic ethics and epistemology in the way he does in the passage, Philodemus is concerned about the conceptual linkage he sees as operating between the ethics of the Cyrenaics and their epistemology. Since they maintain that affections are the only source of knowledge, it will be correct for the Cyrenaics to postulate that people decide what course of action they will take in light of the affections they have. Given his rationalistic approach to ethics and knowledge, that one decides what action to perform on the basis of one's affections is a problematic view to adopt for Philodemus. While discussing these views, he also refers to a third group of people who appear to have criticized the Epicureans on the ground that what the Epicureans call grief or joy are "totally empty notions because of the manifest indeterminacy [of things]" (end of col. III). These people are highly likely to be exponents of later Cyrenaic sects, such as the Hegesians or the Theodorians, as Tsouna & Indelli and Dorandi have persuasively shown.[30]

Philodemus' attribution to the Cyrenaics of the view that things are indeterminate is quite remarkable. Philodemus attributes such indeterminacy to the Cyrenaics by making an example that has to do with ethical concepts, such as joy or grief, on which the Epicureans centred their ethical speculation. Although the attribution of indeterminacy to the Cyrenaics is made by suggesting an ethical example central to Epicurean thinking, Philodemus' attribution need not to be restricted to ethical cases at all. The attribution of the view that things are manifestly indeterminate comes at the end of Philodemus' reasoning against the Cyrenaics. This attribution appears to be the almost natural outcome of the whole argument Philodemus has been constructing in columns II and III, which is purported to criticize the philosophical views of the Cyrenaics.

I take such an argument to be the following. The Cyrenaics ground knowledge on affections; such affections cannot be further elaborated by reason and so are purely subjective. In being so, these affections grant to each of us the authority to take pleasure in whatever we believe (quite incorrectly, according to Philodemus) to be pleasurable. We thus decide for a particular course of action on the basis of our subjective affections. This is possible—that is the conclusive point when indeterminacy comes in—because things in the world are manifestly indeterminate: they are not in themselves pleasurable or painful, white or black and so on. On the basis of the conceptual reconstruction of Cyrenaic philosophy that Philodemus provides us with (at least on the ground of the interpretation I am offering), affections are for the Cyrenaics the basis of knowledge and the guide for action because things in the world are ultimately indeterminate.

7. CYRENAIC NEOLOGISMS AND INDETERMINACY

I have now constructed a case for showing that, in contrast with the sceptical reading, an alternative interpretation of the philosophy of the Cyrenaics is available. On the basis of the indeterminacy interpretation that I recommend, for the Cyrenaics only our affections are knowable not because we are somehow epistemologically incapable to arrive at the very nature of things, but, rather, because things in themselves are indeterminate. The responsibility here is on things, not on the knower. By drawing parallelisms with both ancient and contemporary conceptions of indeterminacy, I have suggested to interpret metaphysical indeterminacy mainly as tantamount to denying existence to material objects. I have shown that there is nothing in the sources that rules out the idea that the Cyrenaics could have actually been committed to indeterminacy. Even the passage from Sextus (*M*. VII 191–2) that is classically taken to expound the core of Cyrenaic subjectivism does not prevent us from assuming that the subjectivism endorsed by the Cyrenaics cannot in principle be rooted into a metaphysics of indeterminacy. On the contrary, other texts of Sextus and other important sources on the Cyrenaics do appear to commit them to indeterminacy.

A commitment to indeterminacy helps explaining those famous Cyrenaic neologisms we have often encountered in the course of the present investigation. When the Cyrenaic says: 'I am being whitened' or 'I am being sweetened,' the sceptical exegete tends to take these sentences as an original way for expressing the epistemological subjectivism so inherent to Cyrenaic philosophy. With their neologisms, the sceptical argument goes, the Cyrenaics express the ultimate epistemological fact that we could know properly our internal states only, that is, how things affect us. But I find this argument not quite convincing. What strikes any reader (both modern and ancient) who hear Cyrenaic neologisms is the fact that, while proffering them, the Cyrenaics get rid of any reference to objects in the world. When I see a table as white or when I taste the honey as sweet, I usually say: 'I see that white table' or 'I taste this honey as sweet.' In both sentences there are two elements: the 'I,' which refers to the person undergoing the affection (in this case, me), and the object that causes the relevant affection in me (table, honey). In the Cyrenaic neologism, like in our standard sentences reporting how we perceive things, the 'I' is there: so, on this respect, no Cyrenaic originality. The striking novelty of the Cyrenaic neologism lies in the expression 'to be whitened or sweetened,' which fully replaces the talk of objects typical of our everyday language with a language that has no reference at all to objects.[31]

My point here is not that I want to deny the salient characteristic of Cyrenaic epistemology (that is, its subjectivism), but, rather, to root it into a peculiar kind of metaphysics (that is, indeterminacy). Since things are radically indeterminate and are not, strictly speaking, existing items, the Cyrenaics may well maintain to be confronted with a world of undifferentiated matter affecting them in purely subjective ways. Differently from current treatments of metaphysical indeterminacy (which, as is plainly evident in Van Inwagen's case, well accommodate strong versions of realism within them), the focus on the role of the subject could be the main feature of the metaphysics of indeterminacy as this was developed by Greek philosophers (this remark applies, although in different way, to both the Cyrenaics and Pyrrho).

On the contrary, to insist on the sceptical reading would mean to single out the epistemological view, deprived of any metaphysical connotation, as the main and only feature of Cyrenaic subjectivism. But this would mean more problems than originality for the Cyrenaics: how could the Cyrenaic proffering the expression 'I am being whitened' escape the danger of solipsism? How could that Cyrenaic know that there are other people in the world apart from him? In a Wittgensteinian fashion, how could that Cyrenaic know the very nature and content of his own affections if he could be the sole existent being in the world? Could he build up a credible way to detect and understand his own affections if he has no way to escape his solipsism?[32]

To say that the Cyrenaics accompany their epistemology with a traditional outlook of the material world is, I believe, a too unwarranted answer to these questions, also given the fact that an alternative reading is there, a reading that I claim is more promising to make sense of Cyrenaic philosophy as a whole. If we want to understand the Cyrenaics as sceptics, we should be prepared to look at them as sceptics in the sense that Richard Bett has attached to Pyrrho (although, as shown, Bett does not think the Cyrenaics to be sceptics of this kind). They would have anticipated, in different way and perhaps with different aims, Pyrrho's metaphysical thesis. And this new perspective would help us not only rethinking the philosophical importance of the Cyrenaics in Greek philosophy, but also reconsidering the history and development of ancient scepticism in a new light.[33]

NOTES

1. I champion O'Keefe (2013) and, more essentially, his chapter in this volume as the kind of sceptical interpretation I aim to resist; see also Warren (2013). O'Keefe (2011) is an interesting attempt to highlight the different epistemological commitments of Pyrrhonists and Cyrenaics.
2. Unless otherwise stated, all translations of Cyrenaic sources are my own and are taken from the Appendix 'Cyrenaic testimonies in translation,' to be found in Zilioli (2012), pp. 185–96. I often supply the appropriate reference to the canonical work of Giannantoni on the Socratics: *Socratis et Socraticorum Reliquiae*, Naples 1990 (*SSR*).
3. I do not take any position in the recent debate, triggered by Casin (2010), whether the sceptic has to believe what appears to him (a blatant case of Moore's paradox), since this is not immediately relevant to my own characterization of the term 'sceptic' in this contribution.
4. On the passage, see O'Keefe, chapter 6 in this volume. Although the term has wide circulation in Hellenistic philosophy, Klaus Döring has founded a first occurrence of the verb '*katalambano*' in the *Phaedrus* (250d1), hence allowing the possibility that in the account of Cyrenaic philosophy he provides us with Sextus actually reports the original Cyrenaic position *ipsissima verba*: Doring (1988), 29.
5. Lee (2010), 22.
6. On four-dimensionalism (which goes back to the important work of David Lewis), see Sider 2001; on stage-theory, see Hawley (2001). See below for metaphysical indeterminacy.
7. Rosen and Smith (2004). More recently, see the papers grouped under the section 'Metaphysical Vagueness' in *Oxford Studies in Metaphysics* 6 (2011), eds. K. Bennett and D.W. Zimmerman, and French (2014).
8. For a view of the material world that denies the existence of both things and persons, see Unger (2006a and 2006 b).
9. The passage (*PE* 14.18.1–5) goes like this:

    Pyrrho himself has left nothing in writing; his pupil Timon, however, says that the person who is to be happy must look to these three points: first, what are things by nature? Second, in what way ought we to be disposed towards them? And finally, what will be the result for those who are so disposed? He [Timon] says that he [Pyrrho] reveal that things are equally indifferent and unstable and indeterminate; for this reason neither our sensation nor our opinions tell the truth or lie. For this reason, then, we should not trust them, but should be without opinions and without inclinations and without wavering, saying about each single thing that it no more is than is not or both is and is not, or neither is nor is not. Timon says that the result for those who are so disposed will be first speechlessness, but then freedom from worry (Bett's translation).

The passage is highly disputed, even for textual reasons: see Bett (1999, 14–36) who reviews all the rival interpretations. I side with him when he suggests that the metaphysical interpretation he recommends provides an overall reading of the passage that makes more sense of it than any rival reading. Against Bett, see mainly Brunschwig (1994).

10. See his critical remarks at my interpretation of the Cyrenaics as metaphysical indeterminists in chapter 9 of this volume. Although he thinks that a "a sizeable portion of the evidence for the Cyrenaic position is compatible with Zilioli's interpretation," he concludes that "the traditional interpretation of the Cyrenaics, as focused on our lack of knowledge of anything beyond the *pathê*, is after all correct."
11. In Zilioli (2012, 86–90), I have shown how the subtler thinkers' theory of perception and powers at *Theaetetus* 156a3–157c3 could be read as a theory of metaphysical indeterminacy (on the point, see Bett 1999, 132–4). On Aristotle's discussion of the principle of non-contradiction as mainly aimed at showing the implausibility of metaphysical indeterminacy, see Zilioli 2012, 97–8 (against this, see Bett 1999, 123–31).
12. One may further speculate over the conceptual relationship between mild and radical indeterminacy, and even wonder whether the most coherent form of metaphysical indeterminacy is the radical one or whether mild indeterminacy could be conceptually reduced to radical indeterminacy: on the point, see Rosen and Smith (2004), 195–8; Van Cleeve (1985), 102–5.
13. Tsouna (1998),82; see also 75–88.
14. Zilioli (2012), 76–83.
15. Both Bett and O'Keefe (this volume, chapter 9 and chapter 6, respectively) highlight the overt epistemological tone of Sextus' passage (and of other passages dealing with the Cyrenaics, such as those from Plutarch, Cicero, Aristocles). In interpreting Sextus' passage (and others) as committing the Cyrenaics to metaphysical indeterminacy, I do not want to deny the epistemological flavour of those sources. Rather, I aim to emphasise that a metaphysical reading of some sections or lines of those passages is also available (or at least possible), even if the epistemological tone in those passages looks preponderant. In the prosecution of Sextus' passage (*M.* VII 194, quoted at p. 120), the sentence 'what is external and productive of the affection perhaps is a being, but it is not a *phainomenon* for us' is a clear example of the metaphysical reading I have in mind. On the other hand, as far as Sextus' reliability as a source is concerned, the overt epistemological tone of his main report on the Cyrenaics (*M.* VII 191–200) too often betrays a technical jargon (such as the talk of places, distances, motion, changes and so on at *M.* VII 195) and that is likely to be due to Sextus' genuinely sceptical approach.
16. O'Keefe in this volume (chapter 6) objects to me that I take '*huparchein*' in Sextus' passage in a too particular sense, i.e. implying that "sound (alongside everything other than the *pathê*) does not exist as a proper or determinate being, while allowing that it exists indeterminately" (p. 102). I take my reading of '*huparchein*' in Sextus' passage to be fair enough. In addition I well accept Harold Tarrant's suggestion (in Tarrant 2014, 127) that, to make my indeterminacy case stronger, I should have ventured to translate '*huparchein*' in Sextus' passage as 'to be present [to one]." Both Bett and O'Keefe (this volume, chapter 9 and chapter 6 respectively) warn me that my reading of Sextus' passage does not seem to help the case of indeterminacy, since the passage is taken to deny that anything other than affections really exists. As Bett puts it: "if there is really *nothing* beyond the *pathê*, there is not even an indeterminate reality" (p. 167), this volume. Let me briefly recapitulate my reading

of Sextus' passage on sound for the sake of clarity. On my interpretation, Sextus attributes to the Cyrenaics the following view: only *pathê* exist, what causes them does not. On this understanding, sound (that is, a material item like chairs and tables) does not (properly) exist. And this type of not-existence can be interpreted as a commitment to metaphysical indeterminacy exactly in light of what I have shown in section 3 of this chapter: the radical version of metaphysical indeterminacy actually amounts to denying existence to material objects. On the passage, see also Rowe, this volume, p. 40.

17. Sextus' passage goes on like this: "By denying the existence of every sensory object [*aisthēton*], the schools of Democritus and Plato deny the existence of sound as well, for sound is a sensory object." Following Tsouna (1998, 80), O' Keefe (this volume, chapter 6) suggests that in the passage on sound Sextus is not concerned with historical accuracy in reporting the view of the Cyrenaics, since he attributes the same (untenable) view to Plato and Democritus. On my part, I am happy to recognize the dialectical context in which Sextus puts the passage on sound. I am not inclined, however, to take the views reported by him in that passage as a pure dialectical game to attack the implicit belief of the professors of art and music in the existence of sound. In effect, to disregard the philosophical content of Sextus' passage on sound simply in light of the dialectical context in which he puts it would be tantamount to distrusting Sextus' main report on the Cyrenaics (that is, *M.* VII 191–200) because in that report Sextus betrays too often his sceptical approach in reporting the views of the Cyrenaics. In short, although he puts it in a dialectical context, the view on sound Sextus attributes to the Cyrenaics needs to be taken seriously. In addition, the attribution of the same view to Democritus and Plato need not be understood simply as a polemical concession in the dialectical context of the passage. In attributing to Democritus and Plato that view, Sextus may have had in mind that long section of Plato's *Theaetetus* (156a-160e), where the subtler thinkers are made to argue that material items (such as sound) do not exist, since the world is just a dialectical process between active and passive powers. F.M. Cornford (1935, 49–50) famously held that the perceptual and metaphysical theory expounded at length at *Theaetetus* 155c-157e is actually Plato's theory of the sensible world (more recently Ademollo (2011, 225) has seen Democritus behind that section of the dialogue—against this, see Rowe, this volume, chapter 2).

18. O'Keefe (this volume, chapter 6) objects to me that I read this passage, as the one on sound in Sextus, in terms of types of existence and not, as he does, in terms of mere existence. In addition, he notes that, even if my reading of it is plausible, the passage itself will not support my metaphysical indeterminacy thesis, since in the passage "the Cyrenaics are asserting that we *cannot know* about the being of external things, rather than asserting that external things *are not* proper beings" (p. 103). I reply to O'Keefe by saying that I do not deny that Sextus' passage has mainly an epistemological concern. Yet, the very final line of the passage "What is external and productive of the affection [*to d'ektos kai tou pathous poiētikon*] perhaps is a being [*tacha men estin on*]" well allows a metaphysical reading, and one that interprets the mere denial of being for what is external to the percipient as a commitment to a radical form of metaphysical indeterminacy (see note 16, above).

19. My translation modified, following the suggestion of Kechagia (2011), 253–4.

20. Another passage of Aristocles on the Cyrenaics (Eusebius, *PE* 14.19.1–3) is susceptible to be interpreted along the two philosophical alternatives I am here discussing.

21. See Tsouna (1998), 83; Kechagia (2011), 260, 264. O'Keefe (this volume, chapter 6) labels the second option as 'object identity skepticism.' Against Warren (2013), O'Keefe argues that Colotes' argument commits the Cyrenaics

to 'object identity skepticism,' I agree with him on this overall reading of Colotes' passage (although in footnote 5, p. 112, he seems to imply that our reading of the passage differs). What I ultimately disagree him with is whether 'object identity skepticism' leads to what he calls 'global object identity skepticism,' the idea that, as he puts it, "this object identity skepticism extends to the structure of the world in general" (p. 110). Since O'Keefe's 'global object identity skepticism' is something very close to what I call 'metaphysical indeterminacy,' rather unsurprisingly I think that 'object identity skepticism' leads quite naturally to 'global object identity skepticism,' whereas O'Keefe thinks that, given the evidence, we should suspend our judgement on the question.

22. Plutarch, *Against Colotes* 1120e-f.
23. According to Aristotle, those who deny the principle of non-contradiction "seem (...) to be stating something indeterminate (*to aoriston*)" (4.5.1007b27–8). He also says that those who believe that all appearances are true deny the principle of non-contradiction because "they believed that things-that-are are merely perceptibles; and in these things the nature of indeterminacy [*he tou aristou phusis*] is an important constituent" (1010a3–4).
24. For an alternative reading of Colotes' passage, see Warren (2013).
25. A similar view is ascribed by the Anonymous to the followers of Pyrrho: "the Pyrrhonists say that everything is relative, inasmuch as nothing exists in its own right but everything is relative to other things. Neither shape nor sounds nor objects of taste and smell or touch nor any other object of perception has a character of its own" (col. LXIII, 3–11).
26. In Zilioli (2013), in line with attempts further back in time (Grote and Zeller), I make a case for identifying the subtler thinkers of the *Theaetetus* (at 156a3) with the Cyrenaics. On a more recent and more sophisticated attempt to see Aristippus and the Cyrenaics behind the subtler thinkers of the *Theaetetus*, see Rowe in this volume (chapter 2).
27. While in his chapter O'Keefe does not comment on this passage as a possible source for committing the Cyrenaics to metaphysical indeterminacy, Bett (this volume, chapter 9) warns me not to take the Anonymous' report too seriously because it looks as internally inconsistent. The quality and perspicuity of the Anonymous' commentary has often been disputed but the general view among scholars nowadays is that it is rather insightful on many passages of Plato's *Theaetetus*. At the same time, I do not see any inconsistency in the Anonymous' passage on the Cyrenaics: he may have been inaccurate in using '*adelon*' when referring to the causticity of the fire, but I find his overall argument quite straightforward. For another criticism of my reading of this passage, see Lampe (2014a).
28. Indelli and Tsouna (1995), *ad locum* and (1998), 146–7.
29. See, e.g., DL II 85.
30. Tsouna-Indelli, *ad locum*; Winiarczyk (1981), 44–5 (T 66 on Theodorus) and Dorandi, chapter 10 in this volume. While agreeing with me that Philodemus' passage refers to the Cyrenaics, both O'Keefe and Bett (this volume, chapter 6 and chapter 9 respectively) object that the attribution of "the manifest indeterminacy [of things]" is made with reference to "others," hence not to the Cyrenaics. The objection does not hold, I think, for the reason that "others" does refer to the Cyrenaics, that is, to a later sect of the school. Philodemus mentions 'others' because in the passage he is likely to be dealing with all the different sects of the Cyrenaic school, since his aim is to offer an exhaustive assessment of Cyrenaic philosophy as a whole (in Zilioli (2012), chapter 8, I have shown the substantial doctrinal continuity among all those Cyrenaic sects; contra, see Lampe 2014b).
31. O'Keefe (chapter 6, this volume) for the sceptical interpretation of the Cyrenaic jargon.

32. Elsewhere (Zilioli 2012), in particular chapters 5–7, I have argued that an appeal to metaphysical indeterminacy helps answering these questions for the Cyrenaics, as well as explaining some other important aspects of their philosophy (in particular, of their philosophy of language) that, if explained along the traditional lines, would otherwise be completely inexplicable.
33. I thank Richard Bett for a set of written comments on the paper and Tim O'Keefe for having accepted my invitation to contribute to this volume a sort of counter-paper on the Cyrenaics. I also thank both of them for having dealt in their chapters (although critically) with my historical and metaphysical interpretation of the Cyrenaics.

REFERENCES

Ademollo, F. (2011), *The Cratylus of Plato. A commentary*. Cambridge: Cambridge University Press.
Bennett, K. and Zimmerman D.W. eds (2011), *Oxford Studies in Metaphysics 6*, Oxford: Oxford University Press.
Bett, R. (1999), *Pyrrho, his antecedents, and his legacy*. Oxford: Oxford University Press.
Brunschwig, J. (1994), 'Once again on Eusebius on Aristocles on Timon on Pyrrho,' *Papers in Hellenistic Philosophy*, in Brunschwig, J. (ed.). Cambridge: Cambridge University Press, 190–211.
Casin, P. (2010), *The demands of reason*. Oxford: Oxford University Press.
Cornford, F.M. (1935), *Plato's theory of knowledge*. London: Routledge and Kegan Paul.
Doring, K. (1988), *Der Sokratesschüler Aristipp und die Kyenaiker*. Mainz: Akademie der Wissenschaften und die Literature.
French, S. (2014), *The Structure of the world*. Oxford: Oxford University Press.
Giannantoni, G. (1990), *Socratis et Socraticorum Reliquae*. Naples: Bibliopolis.
Hawley, K. (2001), *How things persist*. Oxford: Oxford University Press.
Indelli, G. and V. Tsouna. (1995), *Philodemus. On Choices and Avoidances*. Naples: Bibliopolis.
Kechagia, E. (2011), *Plutarch against Colotes*. Oxford: Oxford University Press.
Lampe, K. (2014a), "Review of Ugo Zilioli, *The Cyrenaics*," *The Classical Review* 64, 53–6.
———. (2014b), *The Birth of Hedonism. The Cyrenaic philosophers and Pleasure as a way of life*, Princeton: Princeton University Press.
Lee, M.K. (2010), 'Antecedents in early Greek philosophy,' *The Cambridge Companion to Ancient Scepticism*, Richard Bett (ed.). Cambridge: Cambridge University Press, 13–35.
O'Keefe, T. (2011), 'The Cyrenaics vs. the Pyrrhonists on Knowledge of Appearances,' *New Essays on Ancient Pyrrhonism*, Diego Machuca (ed.). Leiden: Brill, 27–40.
———. (2013) "Review of Ugo Zilioli, *The Cyrenaics*," *Notre Dame Philosophical Reviews*, November 4, 2013 (http://ndpr.nd.edu/news/39081-the-cyrenaics/).
Rosen, G. and Smith, J.J. (2004), 'Worldly Indeterminacy: a rough guide,' *Australasian Journal of Philosophy* 82, 185–198.
Sider, T. (2001), *Four-dimensionalism*. Oxford: Oxford University Press.
Tarrant, H. (2014), "Review of Ugo Zilioli, *The Cyrenaics*," *Journal of the Platonic Tradition* 18, 126–8.
Tsouna, V. (1998), *The epistemology of the Cyrenaic school*. Cambridge: Cambridge University Press.

Unger, P. (2006a), 'There are no ordinary things,' *Philosophical Papers* 2, P. Unger (ed.). Oxford: Oxford University Press, 3–36.
Unger, P. (2006b), 'Why there are no people,' *Philosophical Papers* 2, P. Unger (ed.). Oxford: Oxford University Press, 53–112.
Van Cleeve, J. (1985), 'Three versions of the Bundle-theory,' *Philosophical Studies* 47, 95–107.
Warren, J. (2013), 'The Cyrenaics,' *Routledge Companion to Ancient Philosophy*, F. Sheffiled, J. Warren (eds.). London and New York: Routledge, 409–22.
Winiarczyk, M. (1981), *Diagoras Melius Theodorus Cyrenaeus*. Leipzig: Teubner.
Zilioli, U. (2012), *The Cyrenaics*. Durham: Acumen. Reprinted in New York and London: Routledge, 2014.
———. (2013), 'The Wooden Horse: The Cyrenaics in the *Theaetetus*,' *The Platonic art of Philosophy*, G. Boys-Stones, D. El Murr, C.J. Gill (eds.). Cambridge: Cambridge University Press, 154–71.

8 Diodorus Cronus on Perceptible Minima*

Francesco Verde

1. ARISTOTLE

The main textual evidence illustrating Diodorus' interest in perceptible minima is constituted by two passages from Alexander of Aphrodisias' commentary on Aristotle's *On Sense and Sensibilia*.[1] I begin by quoting the original passage of Aristotle on which Alexander is commenting:

> That every sensible object is a magnitude, and that nothing which it is possible to perceive is indivisible, may be thus shown. The distance whence an object could not be seen is indeterminate, but that whence it is visible is determinate. We may say the same of the objects of smelling and hearing, and of all sensibles not discerned by actual contact. Now, there is, in the interval of distance, some extreme place, the last from which the object is invisible, and the first from which it is visible. This place, beyond which if the object be one cannot perceive it, while if the object be on the hither side one must perceive it, is itself necessarily indivisible. Therefore, if any sensible object be indivisible, such object, if set in the said extreme place whence imperceptibility ends and perceptibility begins, will have to be both visible and invisible at the same time; but this is impossible.[2]

Aristotle's dense argument seeks to show that the sensible object, *to aisthêton*, is a magnitude (*megethos*),[3] and that it is impossible for such an object to be indivisible (*adiaireton*). What is indivisible thus cannot be perceived, and perception is strictly speaking possible only of magnitudes that, insofar as they are the subject of perception, are divisible. According to Aristotle, the distance (*apostêma*) from which an object cannot be seen is indeterminate (*apeiron*), whereas the distance from which it can be seen is determinate (*peperasmenon*). This is true not only for sight, but also for smell and hearing.[4]

In order to understand exactly what Aristotle means by the "indeterminacy" and "determinacy" of the distance, one needs to take into account the existence of a "point" (literally, a "something": *ti*), relating to the distance, which is at the same time "last" (*eschaton*) and "first" (*prôton*): last, because it indicates the space or interval from which you can no longer see the object, and first, insofar as it relates to the same space or interval from which, conversely, the object in question can be seen. It is therefore clear, given that the point *qua* last represents the limit of the distance from which an object cannot be seen, that the distance will be indeterminate, while when treated as first the point will indicate a determinate distance from which the object can be seen. The indeterminacy and determinacy of the distance are thus connected respectively to character of this point, which marks a real division; it is the limit indicating the threshold of perceptibility of an object. Being at the same time first and last, such a "something" must necessarily be indivisible (*adiaireton*): beyond it the object will not be visible, whereas from the other side it will.

To justify the indivisibility of this "something," Aristotle considers the possibility of locating an object precisely at this point: if the point were divisible, this would lead to the absurd conclusion that the object would be both visible and invisible. If the point taken as limit were divisible, an object located at the point would actually turn out to be simultaneously (*hama*) visible and invisible, which is impossible. The threshold of perceptibility is a limit and, as such, cannot be thought of as divisible. Apart from anything else, if it were divisible, not only would the object located at the point be visible and invisible at the same time, but the distance (*apostêma*) would be simultaneously determinate and indeterminate, which would contradict what Aristotle himself has said, namely that the distance from which an object is not visible is indeterminate, while the distance from which it is visible is determinate. The indeterminacy and determinacy of the distance depend precisely on thinking of the "something" solely as a limit.

2. ALEXANDER OF APHRODISIAS

In his commentary on Aristotle's *On Sense* Alexander of Aphrodisias preserves two very interesting and significant testimonia including mention of the name Diodorus:

(I) Hence, even if there is something imperceptible, there is no largest imperceptible just as there is no smallest perceptible either even if there is something imperceptible. Moreover if every magnitude is potentially perceptible (for the imperceptible is not such by its nature but because of the weakness of the perception), there would not be any magnitude imperceptible by its own nature. Consequently there would not be a largest <imperceptible>. But if there is no <magnitude> which is by its own nature the smallest perceptible nor any which is the largest imperceptible there would not be any magnitude which was by its own nature the smallest, as Diodorus thinks he shows.[5]

(II) It seems by means of this that he [*scil.* Aristotle] himself was the first to use and enquire into the account concerning things without parts, which was enquired into either by Diodorus or by someone else. But he discovered it and used it soundly whereas those who were presumptuous in relation to it took it from him and failed to use it in the way they should. For he showed by means of it that what comes about as partless in relation to perception is not impossible, but is <impossible> in nature and in things, because there is no partless perceptible because there cannot even be a distance which is partless between the ultimate perceptible and the first imperceptible. For this is the limit which holds together continua. And a part of a body whether perceptible or imperceptible cannot be partless. With reference to this the <argument> was used by those who reason falsely,[6] since the part of a body is a body. For this reason there cannot be in their case either <a body> that is the largest imperceptible or the smallest perceptible one by its own nature, because this magnitude[7] has to be partless but every magnitude is divisible to infinity.[8]

The second testimony (II) refers to the passage from Aristotle's *On Sense* that I have just examined; the first (I), for its part, is concerned with the problem of the perception of the extremely small and the extremely large,[9] and relates closely to Aristotle's observations in *On Sense* 449a 20–449a3. Aristotle had argued (446a 4–5) that the extremely small (*ta mikra*) cannot be perceived; Alexander, in his comments on these contexts, maintains that even if there were something imperceptible, there would not necessarily be either a maximum perceptible or a minimum. What is not perceptible is not such by nature, but only because of the "weakness" of our perception (*dia tên tês aisthêseôs astheneian*); for this reason, if every magnitude were potentially (*dunamei*) perceptible, there could not be a magnitude that was imperceptible by its own nature. The essential point here is that by its own nature (*têi hautou phusei*) there is neither a minimum perceptible (*elachiston ti estin aisthêton*) nor a maximum imperceptible (*megiston anepaisthêton*); the fact is that perceptibility and imperceptibility depend, ultimately, on the limited capacity of our senses. If this is so, Alexander concludes, given that there is no magnitude that is by its own nature the minimum perceptible, in the same way it cannot be shown, as Diodorus thinks he has shown, that there is a magnitude that is minimal by its own nature (*elachiston ti on têi hautou phusei megethos*).

The second passage (II) concludes Alexander's commentary; and the name of Diodorus appears again. After commenting on *On Sense* 449a 20–449a 31, Alexander claims that Aristotle was the first to deal with the question of indivisible magnitudes or, more precisely, of what is without parts (*peri tôn amerôn*), an issue raised also by either Diodorus or someone else (*eite kai hup'allou tinos*). We should, I think, take seriously the possibility that Alexander's form of words here refers to Epicurus or the Epicureans, who in fact did deal with magnitudes without parts. Unlike Diodorus, and the other philosopher, or philosophers, whose name Alexander deliberately fails to mention, Aristotle allegedly dealt with partless things in a correct and sound way (*hugiôs*), whereas the others, in their arrogance (unpremeditated, of course, given that Aristotle was the first to interest himself in the full complexity of the issue of partlessness), dealt with the issue in an unsuitable way (*ou deontôs*).

We need to consider the reasons why Alexander would have regarded Aristotle's treatment of partless things as correct. Aristotle has shown that in itself (*di'hautou*) it is not impossible that what happens in perception involves partlessness; but this is not something occurring in nature (*en têi phusei*) or in things themselves (*en tois pragmasin*). There is no such thing as a partless perceptible, given that there cannot be a perceptible and partless distance (*diastêma*) intermediate between the extremity of the perceptible and the first imperceptible. What we are dealing with is a limit or, better, a "boundary" (*horos*), which joins the last perceptible and the first imperceptible and makes them continuous with one another. Alexander here takes up Aristotle's argument in *On Sense* 449a 20–449a 31, where we found him saying that there is a "something" which is both last and first, and therefore necessarily indivisible, since if it were divisible, an object located at it would be simultaneously visible and invisible, and so at once perceptible and imperceptible (which is absurd). Alexander concludes with a further demonstration of the error of those who believe that there are partless perceptibles. Unlike those who reason falsely (*hoi paralogizomenoi*),[10] Aristotle dealt correctly with the topic of indivisibles because he showed that a part (*meros*) of a body (perceptible or imperceptible) cannot be partless. This is the reason why by their own nature neither a largest imperceptible nor a smallest perceptible could exist: if they did, there would have to be partless magnitudes too, but this is impossible, since every magnitude (*megethos*) is divisible (*diaireton*) *ad infinitum* and cannot, therefore, be something lacking parts.

3. DIODORUS CRONUS

From Alexander's account some important information emerges about the question of perceptible minima as raised by Diodorus. From the first passage (I), we can infer that Diodorus asserted the existence of a magnitude minimal (*elachiston*) by nature; though the passage hints in this direction, Alexander does not explicitly attribute to him a theory of a perceptible minimum, even while he confirms that Diodorus' assertion of minimum magnitudes, something that is in perfect agreement with our other testimonia on Diodorus' *amerê* ("things without parts").[11] However, as we saw, the context does have something more to tell us about Diodorus' minimal magnitudes, insofar as it represents Diodorus as an example of someone holding a doctrine opposed to Aristotle's. While Aristotle denied the existence of a magnitude that by its own nature—and this is a crucial addition—was the minimum perceptible or the maximum imperceptible, Diodorus by contrast allowed for the existence of a minimum that was such by its own nature. If there is to be a relationship between Diodorus' minimal magnitude and the perceptible minimum rejected by Aristotle, it is very likely that Alexander was in fact attributing to Diodorus the idea of a perceptible magnitude which is by its own nature smallest.

Further, we can understand why Diodorus' treatment of "the account concerning things without parts" discovered by Aristotle, was, unlike Aristotle's, "not correct or sound." The validity of the Aristotelian treatment derives from the fact that Aristotle considered it impossible that "in nature and in things themselves" there could exist an *ameres pros aisthêsin*, a magnitude "without parts for perception"; *per differentiam*, one can infer that Diodorus acknowledged the existence of a partless (and so a minimum) perceptible that is such by its own nature and that actually exists "in nature and in things themselves."[12] This is confirmed by Aristotle's firm assertion—probably in opposition to atomistic doctrines, or views going back to the early Academy (Xenocrates')[13]—of the point that a part of a body is still a body; given that, according to Aristotle, it is impossible to perceive a body that is without parts, it is equally impossible that something partless (which, from the Aristotelian point of view, is not body) be a constituent part of a body. One can conclude, once again *per differentiam*, that Diodorus, along with those Alexander describes as reasoning incorrectly, will in all probability have asserted, as Aristotle denied (since he treated every magnitude as infinitely divisible *qua* continuous) the existence of perceptible minima (as such indivisible) as constituent parts of a body. I believe, then, that a careful analysis of the passages from Alexander allows us to conclude that Diodorus in fact envisaged a minimum/partless perceptible, as well as the (non-perceptible) *amerê*, things without parts, which he used in his arguments on motion, essentially for dialectical purposes not necessarily related (as we shall see) to kinetic issues.

Before I turn to the problem of the role of the theory of perceptible minima in the philosophy of Diodorus, I shall first briefly discuss the Epicurean doctrine of perceptible minima as presented in Epicurus' *Letter to Herodotus*, in order to help bring out any convergences with or divergences from the Epicurean approach.

4. EPICURUS

Without going into the complex details of the Epicurean theory of minimal parts,[14] I quote section 58 and the beginning of section 59 from the *Letter to Herodotus*:

> As for the minimum in sensation, we must grasp that it is neither of the same kind as that which admits of traversal, nor entirely unlike it; but that while having a certain resemblance to traversable things it has no distinction of parts. Whenever because of the closeness of the resemblance we think we are going to make a distinction in it—one part on this side, the other on that—it must be the same magnitude that confronts us. We view these minima in sequence, starting from the first, neither all in the same place nor touching parts with parts, but merely in their own peculiar way providing the measure of magnitudes—more for a larger magnitude, fewer for a smaller one.
>
> This analogy, we must consider, is followed also by the minimum in the atom: [59] in its smallness, obviously, it differs from the one viewed through sensation, but it follows the same analogy (tr. Long and Sedley).

According to Epicurus, the minimum perceptible or, more literally, the minimum in perception (*to te elachiston to en têi aisthêsei*) is the last magnitude perceptible to our senses.[15] Perception is thus unable to penetrate beyond this minimum magnitude. However this perceptible minimum has an ambivalent character. It is at the same time similar and dissimilar to what is capable of having, or being subjected to, "traversals" (*to tas metabaseis echon*): on the one hand, it has something in common with what can be "traversed"; on the other, it is not differentiated into parts (it contains no *dialêpsis merôn*). These features may appear contradictory; however in my view Epicurus simply means that the perceptible minimum is *perceived as* lacking parts, whereas, being an extended magnitude, it is in its turn constituted by "parts"—that is, atoms, which obviously enough are not objects of perception for Epicurus.

According to Epicurus, we can observe (*theôroumen*) these perceptible minima one after another (*hexês*). Being the smallest "parts" graspable by perception, they cannot be in contact with one other, since if they were they would have parts; but this is impossible in the case of minimal magnitudes. Although these minima are not in contact, we succeed in observing them one after another,[16] each in their singularity (*en têi idiotêti*). Being the smallest perceptible parts, they will be the unit of measurement of the (limited) body that such minima constitute. Since we are dealing with minimal magnitudes, they must be of the same magnitude or, at least, must appear such to the percipient; obviously a larger number of perceptible minima will make up larger magnitudes, and conversely smaller magnitudes will be constituted by a smaller number of perceptible minima[17].

The beginning of *Letter to Herodotus* 59 explains the purpose of the Epicurean treatment of perceptible minima: the atomic minimum (*to en têi atomôi elachiston*) differs from the perceptible minimum only by smallness (*mikrotêti*), and we are to conceive of the former by analogy with the latter.[18] In other words, we are not to think of the atomic minimum as an immaterial version of the perceptible minimum: the minimum in the atom differs from the minimum in perception only for reasons relating to size. In this sense, the atomic minimum is the absolutely minimal magnitude, as compared to the *elachiston en têi aisthêsei*; the atomic minimum functions as unit of measurement (*katametrêma*) of the size of atoms, and is responsible for the (limited) number of different weights, shapes and magnitudes that atomic bodies have. Like atoms, atomic minima are not perceptible; thus in order to legitimise their existence within atoms, Epicurus is forced to theorise about—or, better, to recognize, thanks to perception, the existence of—perceptible minima, which he will then be able to connect, by analogy, with atomic minima. The relationship of analogy is thus the fundamental element linking perceptible entities with realities that are equally existent but not direct objects of perception.

5. CONCLUSION: DIODORUS AND PERCEPTIBLE MINIMA

Although they have not, to my knowledge, been the subject of any specific scholarly treatment, Diodorus' perceptible minima have been variously interpreted. As Alan Towey[19] suggests, the range of interpretations may usefully be divided into two. On the one hand, some interpreters (Mau, Denyer, Sedley) have thought of perceptible minima as an idea used by Diodorus in order to "draw an analogy between perceiving something and conceiving of it." On this view, Diodorus will have accepted that something that can be perceived as lacking parts, although actually divisible, cannot be conceived of as having parts. On the alternative view (Sorabji's), Diodorus used the idea in connection with the problem "that a smallest visible size and a largest invisible size differ from each other by an atomic magnitude."[20]

Such interpretative hypotheses all possess a fair measure of plausibility, but none can be said to be certain, given that Alexander's testimony provides us with rather less than a full account of the matter. If we hold to what Alexander says, I think there is no doubt that Diodorus had talked about perceptible minima, just as it is certain, to go by our other evidence, that he acknowledged the existence of things without parts, *amerê*, for genuinely dialectical purposes. The thorniest problem is to understand, first, why Diodorus introduced such minima; and second, what their role is in the context of his philosophy, and whether they had some sort of relationship with the more familiar Diodorean doctrine of *amerê* (and if so what that relationship was). That Diodorus allowed the existence of perceptible minima in my view has no tendency to indicate that he had an actual physics[21] in which such magnitudes figured as part of a positive theory. On the contrary, it is very likely that, from a methodological point of view, the perceptible minimum fulfilled a function similar to that of *amerê*, about which we have good information from other sources:[22] in short, the main reason for Diodorus' introduction of perceptible minima will have been dialectical and polemical. From this point of view, as in the case of partless things, it is not at all impossible that the target of Diodorus' arguments was Aristotle himself. This receives some confirmation from Alexander, when he deliberately opposes Aristotle and Diodorus, two people who disagreed quite sharply about the existence of a perceptible minimum. As Nicholas Denyer has argued, the fact that Diodorus may not have been interested in maintaining a specific physical doctrine does not mean that his dialectical arguments, for example on movement, lacked any internal consistency. To assert the existence of a perceptible minimum does not mean believing it to have a physical function; it is used "to prove his atomism coherent, not to prove his atomism true."[23] According to Denyer's interpretation, this may mean at least two things: on the one hand, Diodorus needed the perceptible minimum to consolidate—if not, directly, his attacks on the reality of motion, then other—dialectical arguments (not least against Aristotle), which, as we will see, are likely to have concerned the veracity of perception;[24] on the other hand, he needed it to provide a more coherent basis for the doctrine of *amerê*, things without parts.

It may be useful, however, to reflect further on the latter point. If there is a connection between the minimum perceptible, *elachiston aisthêton* and the partless, *amerê*, then there must be some sort of analogy between them. Were that the case, then *mutatis mutandis* the originality of the Epicurean approach would be severely compromised. David Sedley[25] has looked closely at the relationship between Diodorus' minimum and Epicurus' *elachiston en têi aisthêsei*,[26] concluding that the existence of perceptible minima, although convincingly refuted by Aristotle, "was rescued by Diodorus as providing proof of his doctrine of theoretical minima,"[27] and that there is "a remarkable coincidence" between Diodorus and Epicurus on the point.[28]

I think it very likely that there was a close relationship between Diodorus' and Epicurus' positions, and that Diodorus' perceptible minimum may to some degree have influenced the Epicurean doctrine as this is presented in *Letter to Herodotus* 58 (unless the influence is the other way around). But we need to ask exactly what form this influence took. Given what can be inferred from Alexander's evidence, we need to use a great deal of caution in this context, and we cannot conclude with any degree of certainty that Diodorus introduced the idea of a perceptible minimum as proof of, or as "auxiliary concept"[29] to, his things without parts (*amerê*). This is not to say that the minimum perceptible in Diodorus has nothing to do with what he has to say about things without parts; but there is no justification for supposing the connection between them to involve analogy or inference. If this is correct, then evidently, if Diodorus influenced Epicurus in this context, as it might appear he did, such influence would probably have been limited to the mere idea of a perceptible minimum, which Epicurus could actually have taken over from Diodorus (though once again the question who influenced whom remains a controversial one). Thus, given the present state of the evidence, we can say that the analogical procedure that makes the "minimum in perception" the starting point from which to infer the features and functions of the atomistic minimum is genuinely Epicurean. Alexander's testimony remains significant insofar as it tells us both that Diodorus introduced a perceptible minimal magnitude, and that he had a "dialectical relationship" with Aristotle,[30] very likely centred on issues not directly related to movement, but rather connected to issues about perception, as is already to some degree suggested by Sorabji's interpretation.[31]

If, moreover, Alexander mentions Diodorus in his commentary on Aristotle's *On Sense*, it is very probably because Diodorus was closely concerned with the problem of perception from what was, once again, a dialectical perspective, and for the purposes of polemic and refutation. This perhaps receives some confirmation from the interest Diodorus showed in the sorites paradox, the authorship of which is usually attributed to Eubulides.[32] Sextus Empiricus preserves a Diodorean paradox concerning movement based on the distinction between motion "by predominance" (*kat'epikrateian*) and motion pure and simple (*kat'eilikrineian*), clearly exploiting the modality of the sorites argument.[33] One of the best known formulations of the sorites paradox was illustrated by the grains forming a heap, and in a rather complex section of *On Sense*, Aristotle uses (446a 1) the example of perceiving the parts of a grain of millet[34]—which could well be a coincidence, but there seem to be rather a lot of coincidences in the present context. Diodorus could well have used the argumentative strategy of the sorites argument and allowed the existence of perceptible minima just to raise arguments against the Aristotelian approach to issues about perception.

This is evidently a hypothesis that, if confirmed, would constitute a significant confirmation of the suggestion that Diodorus might have brought in perceptible minima not as an "auxiliary concept" or as a proof of a doctrine of things without parts, but in order to raise arguments against the possibility or reliability of sensory perception. In addition, it would help to confirm the originality of the Epicurean methodology described in *Letter to Herodotus* 58–59, even though it remains highly plausible that there is a relationship of influence, in whichever direction, between Diodorus' and Epicurus' perceptible minima.

Appendix
Epicurus on Infinite in Thought (*Letter to Herodotus* 57)

Finally, as I pointed out previously,[35] I would like to return very briefly to the *Letter to Herodotus* 57, because this is a very significant paragraph for Epicurus's doctrine of minimal part and, more particularly, for the Epicurean notion of infinite (in thought). In order to examine carefully this point, it is necessary to understand closely the content of a section of the paragraph. For this reason I take the opportunity to correct the Italian translation I offered in Verde (2013) 46,[36] which contains a misprint.[37] The correction is important for the general purposes of the present essay (especially regarding its Epicurean section), and to advance our understanding of what "kind" of infinite Epicurus refers to in his treatment of minimal parts.

Here is the relevant part of the text, followed by the Italian translation of it that I proposed; for convenience I put the English translation first:

ἄκρον τε ἔχοντος τοῦ πεπερασμένου διαληπτόν, εἰ μὴ καὶ καθ' ἑαυτὸ θεωρητόν, οὐκ ἔστι μὴ οὐ καὶ τὸ ἑξῆς τούτου τοιοῦτον νοεῖν, καὶ οὕτω κατὰ τὸ ἑξῆς εἰς τοὔμπροσθεν βαδίζοντα εἰς τὸ ἄπειρον ὑπάρχειν κατὰ <τὸ> τοιοῦτον ἀφικνεῖσθαι τῇ ἐννοίᾳ.

Since what is limited has a distinguishable extremity, although it is not observable in itself, it is not possible not to think that what is in sequence to this is not of this kind, and that it thus follows that proceeding forward in sequence in this way one reaches the unlimited in thought.

Dal momento che ciò che è limitato possiede un'estremità distinguibile, benché non sia osservabile di per se stessa, non è possibile non pensare che anche ciò che è successivo a questa non sia di tal genere e che, così, risulti che procedendo successivamente in avanti si giunga in tal modo all'infinito con il pensiero.

The fourth "non" in the translation must be eliminated, the correct Italian translation being "non è possibile non pensare che anche ciò che è successivo a questa sia di tal genere"/"it is not possible not to think that what is in sequence is of this kind."

The underlying sense of the context is, I think, that the sensible minima we can see on the surface of a (perceptible) body are all of the same kind: if sensible minimum *a* were different from sensible minimum *b*, we would not have a sequence of (identical) minimal parts, but *a* would be bigger than *b* or vice versa.

We also need to notice the οὐ that follows οὐκ ἔστι μὴ, at least in manuscripts B and P¹ of Diogenes Laertius. The difficulty of the passage lies in understanding what exactly is governed by this οὐ.[38] (1) If we take it as not applying to second proposition (καὶ οὕτω κατὰ τὸ ἑξῆς κτλ.), with, e.g., Bignone,[39] Arrighetti,[40] Conche[41] and Morel,[42] the sense will be: "it is not possible not to think that what is in sequence to this is . . . and (it is not possible) to reach the unlimited in thought." (2) If on the other hand we suppose that it does apply to the second proposition (with, e.g., Isnardi Parente[43] and Long-Sedley[44]), the sense will be "it is not possible not to think that what is in sequence to this is . . . and (it is not possible not) to reach the unlimited in thought."

According to my (corrected) translation, what Epicurus must be saying (given the way I take him to be reasoning in the context as a whole) is that the parts in sequence are all of the same kind and it is thus possible to reach the unlimited, though only in thought. Thus I think interpretation (2) is more compelling than (1).

But the question now is why Epicurus should talk about the unlimited here. I believe that on his view we can only *think* of what is unlimited: we can reach it by successively adding these partless extremities to one another, but this is empirically/physically impossible. We can perceive only a limited body. Thus Epicurus says at the beginning of *Letter to Herodotus* 57 that, since we always perceive limited bodies, it is impossible for a limited body to be constituted by an infinite number of "parts" (*apeiroi ogkoi*, "[an] unlimited [number of] bodies"). He thus rejects the empirical possibility of infinite divisibility, and maintains that the only way to reach the unlimited is in thought, by adding partless extremities (the perceptible minima) in sequence, one after another, and another . . .

NOTES

  * I profoundly thank Tiziano Dorandi and Emidio Spinelli for reading an earlier version of this chapter, to my great advantage. I wish to thank also Christopher Rowe for improving and checking my English; I am also very grateful to Ugo Zilioli for inviting me to contribute to this volume.
1. That Alexander quotes Diodorus' philosophical position does not in my view constitute a compelling reason for supposing first-hand knowledge of Diodorus on Alexander's part (a different view is taken by Gemelli Marciano (2007), 272 n. 195).
2. Aristotle, *On Sense and Sensibilia* 449a 20–31, tr. Beare in Barnes 1984.
3. Aristotle, *On Sense and Sensibilia* 445b 8–10.
4. On this point see Cosenza (2013), vol. II, 355 n. 117.

5. Alexander of Aphrodisias, *On Aristotle's* De sensu 122 16–23 Wendland (= *SSR* II F 9, part), tr. Towey.
6. In Alexander's text "those who reason falsely" are those responsible for paralogisms, that is, roughly speaking, arguments that are not grounded in *endoxa* but on premises or assumptions that are somehow peculiar to the sciences to which they belong and may either be true or not. Aristotle examines paralogisms mainly in his *Sophistical Refutations*. On the paralogism as such, see Aristotle, *Topics* I 1 101a 5 ff.; *Prior Analytics* II 15 64b 13 ff.; *Posterior Analytics* I 12 77b 16 ff.
7. See Towey (2000), 188 n. 521.
8. Alexander of Aphrodisias, *On Aristotle's* De sensu 172 28–173 10 Wendland (= *SSR* II F 9), tr. Towey, slightly modified.
9. I believe it possible that this question has something to do with Anaxagoras (cf. Simplicius, *On Aristotle's* Physics 164 16 = 59 B 3 DK).
10. See above, n. 6.
11. See *SSR* II F 8–17. On the relationship between the Epicurean doctrine of minimal parts and Diodorus' hypothesis of *amerê*, see, e.g., Mau (1954–1955), esp. 110–111, Furley (1967), 131–135, Sedley (1977), esp. 84–89, and Verde (2013), 210–237.
12. The "partless bodies" attributed to Diodorus by Simplicius (*On Aristotle's* Physics 926 19–21 Diels = *SSR* II F 9; see also *SSR* II F 8) and by other sources are not necessarily related to the Diodorean minimum/partless perceptible as reported by Alexander.
13. I refer here especially to Xenocrates' doctrine of indivisible lines, on which see fragments F 44–67 Isnardi Parente (2012). See also Verde (2013), 129–184.
14. In passing, I call attention to the fact that the doctrine of atomic minima was probably at the heart of debates and discussions in the Epicurean Garden from the very beginning. This shows its importance for the philosophical debate of the time. In *PHerc.* 1012, which contains a "philological" work by the Epicurean Demetrius Laco, we also find a mention of the doctrine of minima (Coll. XLVIII–L Puglia), along with a mention of the name of Metrodorus (XLIX 8 Puglia). It is reasonable to infer from this that Metrodorus too had a view on the idea, as may be confirmed by a fragment of *PHerc.* 439 (= O '253' = *PHerc.* 1824) published by R. Janko, that forms part of the roll that probably contained Metrodorus' *Against the Dialecticians*. The topic of the fragment may be atomic and / or molecular physics. See Janko (2008), 5–95 (esp. 64–65), Verde (2011), and Dorandi in this volume, chapter 10, p. 175.
15. See Verde (2013), 48–57.
16. Cf. on this matter Epicur. *Hrdt.* 57. Here Epicurus maintains that what is in sequence to the extremity of a finite body will be inevitably of the same kind. This paragraph, moreover, is very significant because Epicurus also argues that, by proceeding along this sequence, it is possible to reach infinity in thought. I briefly return on *Hrdt.* 57 in the *Appendix* (below, 143–4).
17. The Italian translation of the conclusion of the *Letter to Herodotus* 58 (τὰ πλεῖω πλεῖον καὶ τὰ ἐλάττω ἔλαττον: «le maggiori [*scil.* le grandezze / the magnitudes] quelle [*scil.* parti / parts = perceptible minima] maggiori e le minori quelle minori») that I provided in Verde (2013), 49 (and in Verde (2010) 47) needs to be clarified. This text does not mean that larger minima are unities of measurement for larger magnitudes, and vice versa. If so, minimal magnitudes would not be such: it cannot exist a minimum (either atomic or perceptible) that is larger and smaller. Epicurus argues that a higher number of minimal (perceptible) magnitudes are the measures of a larger magnitude (the same applies to smaller magnitudes).

18. Analogy and inference from signs play highly significant roles in the field of Epicurean epistemology, allowing us to infer from perceptible objects or "events" to the existence and peculiar features of entities that are not directly perceptible, like atoms and minimal parts. Philodemus' *On Signs* tells us how this works, and about the debate between Epicurean and Stoics on the matter. For a first survey on the topic see Allen (2001), Study IV, and Manetti (2013), 233–257.
19. Towey (2000), 188 n. 523.
20. Sorabji (1983), 345–348.
21. On this topic, Döring (1972), 129 rightly talks of "Diodors *Hypothese* von den ἀμερῆ" (italics mine); see also Muller (1988), 187–188, and Sedley (1999), 355–411, esp. 356. There is an interesting passage of Eustathius (12 Wehrli = 121 Taifakos = 11 Dorandi) referring to Diodorus and a text of the Peripatetic Clearchus of Soli (probably from his *Arcesilaus*), which may point to an interest on Diodorus' part in science (and astronomy in particular), but is insufficient on its own to prove it. On this matter see Denyer (2002), 597–600, and now Tsitsiridis (2013), 85–86 and 92–93.
22. See above, n. 11.
23. Denyer (1981), 37.
24. See Muller (1985), 136 (4. Fr. 119).
25. Sedley (1977), 86–87.
26. I record, in passing, that Diogenes Laertius (X 27) mentions an *Against the Megarians* among Epicurus' best books. Diogenes (X 24) also tells us that Metrodorus wrote an *Against the Dialecticians*: see Spinelli 1986, and Tepedino Guerra 1992, though the latter maintains that the work in question is the *Against the Sophists*. See Dorandi in this volume, chapter 10.
27. Sedley (1977), 87.
28. On the *status quaestionis* on the relationship between Diodorus and Epicurus, see Montoneri (1984), 131 and n. 25 (with further bibliography).
29. Giannantoni (1990), vol. IV, 80.
30. On this topic, see Mau (1954–1955) 109 (reminding us that according to Diogenes Laertius II 109 = *SSR* II B 8, Eubulides was in dispute with Aristotle), and Giannantoni (1980), 125–133. We should also note that another passage from Alexander of Aphrodisias (*On Aristotle's* Metaphysics 84 16–18 Hayduck = 9 Wehrli) makes it very likely that the *Against Diodorus* of the Peripatetic Phanias was a work precisely aimed against Diodorus Cronus. If this attribution were shown to be right, it would confirm the polemical relationship between the school of Aristotle and Diodorus.
31. See Sorabji (1983), 346.
32. Diogenes Laertius II 108 = *SSR* II B 13.
33. Sextus Empiricus *Against the Mathematicians* X 113–117 = *SSR* II F 14 (cf. also Fronto *On Eloquence* II 16 = *SSR* II C 9).
34. See Cosenza (2013), 267–273.
35. See above n. 16.
36. See also Verde (2010), 47.
37. I thank Jan Opsomer for drawing my attention to this point.
38. Morel (2011), 135 n. 47.
39. Bignone (1920), 92–93.
40. Arrighetti (1973), 52.
41. Conche (1987), 111 and 151 n. 8.
42. Morel (2011), 68.
43. Isnardi Parente (1983), 166.
44. Long-Sedley (1987), vol. I, 39.

BIBLIOGRAPHY

Allen, J. (2001), *Inference from Signs: Ancient Debates about the Nature of Evidence*, Oxford, Clarendon Press.
Arrighetti, G. (ed.) (1973), *Epicuro: Opere*, Turin, Einaudi.
Barnes J. (ed.) (1984), *The Complete Works of Aristotle: The Revised Oxford Translation*, Princeton, Princeton University Press.
Bignone, E. (ed.) (1920), *Epicuro: Opere, frammenti, testimonianze sulla sua vita*, Bari, Laterza.
Conche, M. (ed.) (1987), *Épicure: Lettres et Maximes*, Paris, Presses Universitaires de France.
Cosenza, P. (ed.) (2013), *Aristotele: Parva Naturalia, Volume II (Del senso e dei sensibili)*, Naples, Loffredo.
Denyer, N. (1981), 'The Atomism of Diodorus Cronus,' *Prudentia* 13, 33–45.
Denyer, N. (2002), 'Neglected Evidence for Diodorus Cronus,' *Classical Quarterly* 52, 597–600.
Furley, D.J. (1967), *Two Studies in the Greek Atomists, Study I: Indivisible Magnitudes*, Princeton/ New Jersey, Princeton University Press.
Gemelli Marciano, M.L. (2007), *Democrito e l'Accademia: Studi sulla trasmissione dell'atomismo antico da Aristotele a Simplicio*, Berlin/New York, de Gruyter.
Giannantoni, G. (1980), 'Aristotele, Diodoro Crono e il moto degli atomi,' in F. Romano (ed.), *Democrito e l'atomismo antico*, Atti del Convegno Internazionale, Catania 18-21 aprile 1979, *Siculorum Gymnasium* 33, Catania, 125–133.
Giannantoni, G. (1990), *Socratis et Socraticorum Reliquiae*, 4 voll., Naples, Bibliopolis. [=SSR]
Isnardi Parente, M. (ed.) (1983), *Opere di Epicuro*, Turin, UTET.
Isnardi Parente, M. (ed.) (2012), *Senocrate-Ermodoro: Testimonianze e frammenti*, Revised and up-to-date edition by T. Dorandi, Pisa, Edizioni della Normale.
Janko, R. (2008), 'New Fragments of Epicurus, Metrodorus, Demetrius Laco, Philodemus, the *Carmen De Bello Actiaco* and Other Texts in Oxonian *Disegni* of 1788–1792,' *Cronache Ercolanesi* 38, 5–95.
Long, A. A. and D.N. Sedley (eds.) (1987), *The Hellenistic Philosophers*, vol. 1: *Translations of the Principal Sources with Philosophical Commentary*, Cambridge, Cambridge University Press.
Manetti, G. (2013), *In principio era il segno: Momenti di storia della semiotica nell'antichità classica*, Milan, Bompiani.
Mau, J. (1954–1955), 'Über die Zuweisung zweier Epikur-Fragmente,' *Philologus* 99, 93–111.
Montoneri, L. (1984), *I Megarici: Studio storico-critico e traduzione delle testimonianze antiche*, Catania, Edizioni CUECM.
Morel, P.-M. (ed.) (2011), *Épicure: Lettres, maximes et autres textes*, Paris, Flammarion.
Muller, R. (ed.) (1985), *Les Mégariques: Fragments et témoignages*, Paris, Vrin.
Muller, R. (1988), *Introduction à la pensée des Mégariques*, Paris/Bruxelles, Vrin/Ousia.
Sedley, D.N. (1977), 'Diodorus Cronus and Hellenistic Philosophy,' *Proceedings of the Cambridge Philological Society* 203, 74–120.
Sedley, D.N. (1999), 'Hellenistic Physics and Metaphysics,' in K. Algra, J. Barnes, J. Mansfeld, M. Schofield (eds.), *The Cambridge History of Hellenistic Philosophy*, Cambridge, Cambridge University Press, 355–411.
Sorabji, R. (1983), *Time, Creation and the Continuum: Theories in Antiquity and the Early Middle Ages*, Ithaca/New York, Cornell University Press.
Spinelli, E. (1986), 'Metrodoro contro i dialettici?,' *Cronache Ercolanesi* 16, 29–43.

Tepedino Guerra, A. (1992), 'Metrodoro «Contro i Dialettici»?,' *Cronache Ercolanesi* 22, 119–122.
Towey, A. (ed.) (2000), *Alexander of Aphrodisias: On Aristotle's "On Sense Perception,"* Ithaca/New York, Cornell University Press.
Tsitsiridis, S. (2013), *Beiträge zu den Fragmenten des Klearchos von Soloi*, Berlin/Boston, de Gruyter.
Verde, F. (ed.) (2010), *Epicuro: Epistola a Erodoto*, Introduction by E. Spinelli, Rome, Carocci.
Verde, F. (2011), 'Minimi in movimento? Note sulle coll. XLVIII-L Puglia del *PHerc.* 1012 (*Demetrii Laconis Opus incertum*),' *Cronache Ercolanesi* 41, 51–63.
Verde, F. (2013), Elachista: *La dottrina dei minimi nell'Epicureismo*, Leuven, Leuven University Press.

9 Pyrrho and the Socratic Schools
Richard Bett

The seminal article "Socrates in Hellenistic Philosophy," by Tony Long,[1] includes no mention of Pyrrho, and this is no accident. There is no evidence of Pyrrho having regarded Socrates as an intellectual or ethical inspiration, as so many others did in the century or more after his death. Similarly, one would be hard pressed to find any kind of link between the two in terms of philosophical "succession"—not that some did not try, as we shall see. But it does not follow, of course, that there were no connections between Pyrrho and one or more of the various groupings known (with greater or lesser propriety) as the "Socratic Schools"; such connections might take the form of an actual influence, in one direction or the other, or a looser resemblance in ideas or attitudes. My purpose in this chapter is to see to what extent these can actually be established. This is not the first time I have approached this topic; in my book *Pyrrho, his Antecedents, and his Legacy*,[2] I spent some time exploring the relations between Pyrrho's thought and that of numerous other groups or individuals. But my focus there was explicitly backward-looking—I was trying to get clear on what already existing ideas in Greek philosophy may have helped to shape Pyrrho, rather than the influence he may have had on others—and it was not directed particularly at the thinkers who are the subject of this volume (though it did touch on several of them). Thus, although I find that on a number of points I have not changed my mind in the years since completing that book, I hope nonetheless to have something new to offer in this chapter.

Any consideration of Pyrrho is heavily dependent on the evidence of his disciple and biographer Timon of Phlius. And in this case there is a considerable number of fragments of Timon that are of interest. Timon's *Silloi*, in hexameter verse, consisted largely of satirical vignettes of other philosophers, and their concise and memorable character made them ripe for quotation;[3] as a result, we have fragments on most Greek philosophers up to and including his own time, and members of the Socratic schools are among them. These portraits are not, of course, philosophical arguments; but they do incorporate pointed, often acerbic philosophical verdicts, and hence tell us something about the attitude of Pyrrho's immediate follower, if not necessarily Pyrrho himself, towards the thinkers in question. Timon's fragments

I. TIMON ON THE SOCRATICS, TIMON ON PYRRHO

We may begin, indeed, with a fragment of Timon on Socrates himself:[4]

> But from them the sculptor, blatherer on the lawful, turned away,
> Spellbinder of the Greeks, who made them nitpicking arguers,
> Looking down his nose, rhetoricians' snot, sub-Attic ironist.[5]

The first line is quoted by Clement (*Strom.* 1.14.63.3) and Sextus (*M* 7.8), and both tell us that it refers to the turn away from physics and towards ethics with which Socrates is widely associated; "from them" refers, then, either to physical topics or to physicists themselves. One might think that this would be a positive development in Pyrrho's or Timon's view, since another fragment of the *Silloi* praises Pyrrho for not troubling himself with questions about the nature of the universe (DL 9.65). But the tone of the present fragment makes very clear that concentration on ethics, at least in Socrates' manner, is no improvement. *Ennomoleschês* is plausibly interpreted by Sextus as referring to Socrates' ethical turn; I have translated this by "blatherer on the lawful" because compounds ending in-*leschês* or cognates regularly seem to denote trivial or pointless chatter. *Muktêr*, literally "nostril," can also be used for sarcasm or verbal sneering, and here seems to be personified as the one who does the sneering—hence my "looking down his nose." And the next word *rhêtoromuktos*, is a verbal adjective from the same root—so, "blown out of the nose"[6]—in connection with rhetoricians; and Diogenes Laertius, who quotes all three lines (2.19) shows by his immediately following words that he understands it to indicate that Socrates was rhetorically trained. If Diogenes is not misreading, LSJ's "blown (i.e. trained) by rhetoricians" seems correct, except that it is far too polite; I hope my "rhetoricians' snot" gets closer to the tone. The remaining terms in the fragment, considered by themselves, seem capable of a positive or a negative interpretation; but if I am on the right lines about the ones considered so far, I think we can assume that the negative predominates. In particular, *akribologous*, which I have rendered by "nitpicking arguers," might be understood more positively as "precise in argument/language." But in combination with the image of Socrates as a sneerer, it seems much more naturally to belong to a view of Socrates—which one can get from a certain reading of Plato (though this is obviously not what Plato intended), and which is shared by many American undergraduates when they first encounter Plato's portrait of him—as playing with his interlocutors by means of over-subtle and manipulative forms of argument. If Timon's attitude is even moderately reflective of Pyrrho's (supposing he had a view about Socrates at all), we can hardly suppose that Pyrrho saw Socrates as a guiding light.

What, then, of the many diverse philosophers who did think of Socrates as a hero? Do they fare any better at Timon's hands? For the moment I leave aside the Academy and concentrate on the other Socratics. Another fragment of Timon, quoted by Diogenes in his life of Euclides of Megara (2.107), reads "But I do not care about these wafflers (*phledonôn*), nor about anyone else: not Phaedo, whoever he was, nor Euclides the contentious (*eridanteô*), who implanted in the Megarians a mania for quarrel (*erismou*)." Diogenes says that the opening line refers to "the rest of the Socratics." It is not quite clear how broadly this term is supposed to extend, or what the distinction is between "these wafflers" and "anyone else"; but at least we have here a broad swipe at the Megarians, Phaedo and an indeterminate number of other Socratics. Antisthenes comes in for related criticism as an "all-producing waffler"; according to Diogenes (6.12), this is directed against his prolific number of books. Menedemus of Eretria, named by Diogenes as a pupil of Phaedo and previously of the Megarian Stilpo (2.125–6), seems to do no better. The line of Timon that Diogenes quotes about him (2.126) is textually problematic in the first half, but we then have him called *ôphruômenos*, "supercilious," and *aphrosibombax*. Some have taken the latter as meaning "mocker of fools" or the like,[7] relying on a verb *bombazô* that the Suda tells us means "rip apart" or "mock." But in this case the very same attitude singled out for criticism in *ôphruômenos* (which is definitely negative) would be immediately turned into something positive (at least from Timon's perspective),[8] and this seems too jarring; some additional disparagement seems far more likely, and several translations along these lines have been offered. LSJ and Goulet-Cazé[9] render "a puffing, bustling fellow" and "fanfaron [braggart]" respectively, while Aldobrandini[10] chose "insipienter strepens," "foolishly making a big noise." To continue the list, Aristippus receives the following thumbnail sketch: "such was the luxurious nature of Aristippus, feeling around falsehoods" (DL 2.66), a probable reference to his reported advocacy of bodily pleasures.[11] Finally, Xenophon and Aeschines are skewered with these lines: "A feeble pair or triad of discourses, or even more—such is Xenophon or the powerful Aeschines, not beyond being persuaded to write" (2.55).[12]

Numerous Socratics, then, receive just as rough treatment at Timon's hands as does Socrates himself.[13] Again, if Timon was even roughly in accord with Pyrrho about this, it is hard to imagine that Pyrrho thought of them as kindred spirits. Moreover, in several cases this has something to do either with the person's superior attitude or with his pointless and/or disputatious manner of discussion—both of which were also features of Timon's portrait of Socrates. Now, at this point it is natural to ask, what *would* be an acceptable attitude or manner of discussion from Timon's or Pyrrho's perspective? We have already seen that physics is not an acceptable topic, but that this would not be a ground for criticizing Socrates—or, one might add, the Socratics mentioned in the previous paragraph. A more helpful answer is suggested by a fuller look at the fragments of Timon about Pyrrho.

First, the fragment that points to Pyrrho's avoidance of physical speculation in fact ranges more widely than this; the complete set of lines in Diogenes (9.65) is:

> Pyrrho, old man, how and whence did you find a way out
> From servitude to opinions and empty-mindedness of sophists,
> And loosened the bonds of every deception and persuasion?
> You were not concerned to enquire what winds
> Hold sway over Greece, from where everything comes and into what it passes.[14]

Although the last two lines particularly mention meteorological and cosmological questions, the remainder of the passage seems to have no such restriction; the sophists who engage in deception and persuasion and are slaves to opinions can, we may assume, be "empty-minded" about any topic at all. Another passage quoted by Aristocles (in Eusebius, *Praep. evang.* 14.18.19) describes Pyrrho as

> ... the man without vanity and unbroken
> By all the things by which both the unknown and the celebrated among mortals are overpowered
> Empty hosts of people, weighed down on this side and that
> By affections, opinion, and pointless laying-down of the law.

We also have some lines from Timon's poem *Indalmoi* (*Images*) explicitly addressed to Pyrrho:

> This, Pyrrho, my heart longs to hear
> However you, a man, conduct yourself with the greatest ease and tranquility
> Always heedless and uniformly unmoved
> Paying no attention to the whirls of sweet-voiced wisdom.[15]

The composite picture suggested by these fragments is in many respects the polar opposite of the sorts of image Timon creates of Socrates and of the Socratics who receive treatment in the surviving materials. Pyrrho does not give himself airs or look down on others; indeed, he pays very little attention to others.[16] He is also not a victim of "opinion" (*doxa*), which I take to refer, as in Plato and the Stoics, to a misguided or inferior set of beliefs, which one might very well mistakenly regard as much more worthwhile than they really are. And because he avoids theoretical speculation of any kind, which is no doubt at least part of what is meant by "pointless laying-down of the law" (*eikaiês nomothêkês*), he does not get involved in the tricky, unstable and, it may be assumed, disputatious discussions that all three fragments seem to allude to, and of which Timon elsewhere accuses Socrates and several Socratics. Calm and imperturbability is the overriding attitude with which Pyrrho is here credited, and this seems to derive both from his steering clear of philosophical debate and from his not caring, quite generally, what others think—about him or about anything else.

II. PYRRHO AND THE CYNICS

If a number of Socratics conspicuously fail to meet this standard, are there others who do better, and who might therefore share more common ground with Pyrrho? One group that has traditionally been considered a Socratic school, and that seems to escape criticism in the surviving fragments of Timon, are the Cynics. We did see that Antisthenes is described as a "waffler." But despite the alleged historical link between Antisthenes and Diogenes of Sinope (DL 6.21), it seems clear from the list of Antisthenes' titles in Diogenes Laertius' life (6.15–18), as well the meager evidence on his thought, that he had philosophical or other theoretical interests—in logic,[17] say, or epistemology[18] or rhetorical theory[19]—that the Cynics did not remotely share, and that might make the charge of being a "waffler" seem particularly appropriate to someone of Timon's cast of mind. Timon's suspicion of Antisthenes does not, then, imply a suspicion of the Cynics. And in fact we can find considerable links—biographical, philosophical and even literary—between Timon and Pyrrho on the one side and the Cynics on the other; this has been well documented by others,[20] and a brief discussion should suffice.

One obvious point that links them is the avoidance of theoretical speculation. Diogenes Laertius reports it as a matter of contention whether Cynicism can be called a philosophical school (*hairesis*) at all, as opposed to simply a way of life (6.103); and though he is willing to call it a school, he immediately adds that the Cynics had nothing to do with logic or physics, confining themselves entirely to ethics—a claim that is quite consistent with the other evidence. Moreover, their ethical teachings seem to have been confined to a few broad tenets, such as "live according to virtue" or "live naturally," rather than any kind of detailed argumentation such as we find in Aristotle or the Stoics. The main interest of Cynicism lies in the ways they try to exemplify these tenets in an actual life. Indeed, in this respect they are probably even more anti-theoretical than Pyrrho. For although Pyrrho did not trouble himself with philosophical debates, and took no interest in most of the things with which philosophers generally concern themselves, he is reported, in a much discussed passage of Aristocles (in Eusebius, *Praep. evang.* 14.18.1–5), to have held that a happy life depended on having successfully answered the question "what are things like by nature?" There is, then, at least a minimal amount of theorizing to be found in his record. We shall return to this passage, and will see how it does not necessarily contradict Pyrrho's generally anti-theoretical stance. For now, we can simply observe that he too, like the Cynics, seems to have been mostly known for a set of practical attitudes, and for living a certain kind of life, rather than for an elaborate edifice of theory.

As for what those practical attitudes were, there is again a considerable overlap. The many anecdotes about Pyrrho and about Diogenes of Sinope and other Cynics, in Diogenes Laertius and elsewhere, show a common disregard for conventional mores and for conventional views of what is important in life. The anecdotes about the Cynics perhaps tend to emphasize a deliberate flouting of convention more than the pure indifference to it that we find in Pyrrho; but for both Pyrrho and the Cynics, not caring what people think is a prominent feature of their image and one that I would assume to have some historical basis, regardless of the veracity of any individual story. Other important aspects of the Cynic outlook are the ability to endure hardships and a state of self-sufficiency that has one needing as little as possible; both these, but especially the latter, are the features of Cynicism that can most easily be understood as having a Socratic inspiration. Again the emphasis is a little different in what we hear about Pyrrho. As we have seen, Timon emphasizes his extraordinary calm and tranquillity, and this is also born out in many of the anecdotes. But preserving one's calm in all circumstances must (unless one is exceptionally lucky) include self-sufficiency and an indifference to hardship. And in fact a few of the anecdotes on Pyrrho do suggest this dimension. Diogenes tells us that he did not even frown when his wound was treated with ancient surgical techniques (9.67). And both Diogenes (DL 9.68, citing Posidonius) and Plutarch (*Prof. Virt.* 82E-F) report a story about his observation while on a ship in a storm—he saw a pig calmly munching its food and pointed to this as a model for the wise person to emulate; the suggested ideal seems to include imperviousness to life's ups and downs and making do with the basics.

We have, then, a broad similarity of outlook. Taken just by itself, this might be attributed to a general *Zeitgeist* rather than to a specific influence. That there is some influence—and from the Cynics on Pyrrho rather than the other way around, since Diogenes of Sinope was at least a generation older than Pyrrho—is made much more likely by the fact that the group of philosophers that Alexander took with him on his expedition to India included both Pyrrho and a Cynic, Onesicritus. While there, both are reported to have visited some "naked wise men" (DL 9.61; Strabo, *Geography* 15.1.63–5); we have no indication that they did so together, but in both cases there seems to have been some kind of attempt at philosophical exchange. What, if anything, they learned from these encounters is very unclear, but that is not my concern here; the point is that they are likely to have talked about them, and about other matters, with one another, which makes it very natural, given the numerous points of contact we have just observed, to suppose that some measure of Cynicism may have rubbed off on Pyrrho.

To this we can add that Timon's writing shows a clear debt to Cynicism, which would make excellent sense if Pyrrho already felt a connection with the Cynics. *Tuphos*, "vanity" or "humbug," is a common term of Cynic invective,[21] and Timon appropriates it; besides using it of Zeno of Citium (DL 7.15), he turns it around and, as we saw, gives Pyrrho the supreme compliment *atuphos*, "without vanity," as well as situating Xenophanes, a leading figure in the *Silloi*, on a higher plane than most by calling him *hupatuphos*, "partly free from vanity" (Sextus, *PH* 1.224). Long has also argued convincingly that the satirical poems of the Cynic Crates were an important inspiration behind Timon's *Silloi*.[22] In addition, Timon suggests his approval of Cynicism by attributing to Anaxarchus, Pyrrho's teacher (DL 9.61) and one of the few philosophers in the *Silloi* besides Pyrrho to receive a partially positive review, *kuneon menos*, "Cynic [or dog-like] strength" (Plutarch, *De virt. mor.* 446b-c).

Finally, there is an interesting connection between Anaxarchus and the Cynic Monimus. Sextus reports that some people took Anaxarchus and Monimus to have abolished the criterion of truth because "they likened what there is to stage-painting and supposed them to be like the things that strike us while asleep or insane" (*M* 7.88). Given the context in which Sextus makes this remark—his review in the first book of *Against the Logicians* of those who might be considered to have argued against the existence of a criterion of truth—it is easy to take this as the expression of an extreme epistemological scepticism, especially since it is juxtaposed with the view of Metrodorus of Chios, which clearly does fit that description. But Sextus does not endorse the reading of Anaxarchus' and Monimus' view as a denial of the criterion, and in fact his words taken literally do not point towards this interpretation. The point is not that *we have no way of knowing* whether we are dreaming, or insane, or caught up in some staged scenario, rather than simply viewing reality head-on. Instead, the claim is that *what there is* (*ta onta*) has the status of a stage-set or a dream or a hallucination. The point is to downgrade reality itself, not to cast doubt on our access to it; it is the world that is being called insubstantial. Now, one could read this as a serious metaphysical claim, and if one did so, one might see a correspondence between this view and what some, including myself, have held that Pyrrho believed, namely that reality is indeterminate; more on this later. But whatever one thinks about Pyrrho's position, I doubt that this is the best way to understand the position of at least Monimus, because, as we saw, the Cynics do not seem to have involved themselves in metaphysical reflections of any kind. It seems to me more likely that the view, in Monimus' hands and very possibly also in Anaxarchus', amounts to what Shakespeare meant when he wrote "All the world's a stage" or what has generally been meant by "Life is but a dream."[23] In this case the point is to emphasize the fleeting and insubstantial character of our lives. Elsewhere Sextus reports that Monimus stated that "everything is *tuphos*" (*M* 8.5), and the remark about stage-painting, etc., on this latter reading, would amount to much the same thing. If this is correct, however, we still have a connection with Pyrrho and Timon, given the points that we explored earlier.

III. PYRRHO AND THE MEGARIANS

We can, then, with some plausibility associate Pyrrho with the Cynics. What of the other Socratic schools or movements? Here I find it much more difficult to make connections, and my discussion of the fragments of Timon has already pointed to some of the reasons. I shall consider the Megarians, together with a very brief mention of Phaedo, and then the Cyrenaics, ending with a quick look at Pyrrho's relation to the Academy.

We have seen that Timon labelled Euclides, the purported founder of the Megarian school, as "contentious" and blamed him for passing on a "mania for quarrel" to the Megarians in general; this is precisely one of the major characteristics that we found to be a black mark on many Socratics, in Timon's view, and to place them in stark contrast with the serene and tranquil Pyrrho. And indeed, most of our evidence about the Megarians makes this verdict (coming from Timon) very understandable. In a passage that has excited considerable scholarly discussion, Diogenes Laertius says that Euclides' followers "were called Megarians, then Eristics, and later Dialecticians" (2.106). In light of this passage and other evidence, some have argued for a Dialectical School who separated themselves from the Megarians proper;[24] but, as several have pointed out, it is highly unlikely that any group would have claimed for themselves the label Eristic. Still, the many logical paradoxes associated with Euclides' follower Eubulides, such as the liar and the Sorites (see especially DL 2.108), which set the tone for much of what we know about this group or groups, are precisely the kind of thing that would have earned the name "eristic" in many people's eyes, and that Timon and Pyrrho would have wanted nothing to do with. Timon and Pyrrho would have had no more sympathy for the logical enquiries of Diodorus Cronus and Philo into, for example, the truth conditions for conditional sentences (Sextus *M* 8.115–17), or for the worries about definition and predication associated with Stilpo and with the Megarians in general (DL 2.119, Plutarch *Adv. Col.* 1120a-b, Simplicius *In Phys.* 120.12–17), or for Diodorus' arguments against motion (Sextus *M* 10.85–120); to their way of thinking, all of this would qualify as *tuphos*.[25]

So much for logic and dialectic (and a touch of physics): what about ethics? Diogenes tells us in passing (in his life of Aristo of Chios) that the Megarians adhered to the unity of the virtues; virtue, according to them, is "one but called by many names" (7.161). In his life of Euclides, Diogenes records what looks like a related view, or perhaps a more accurate statement of the same view; Euclides is said to have held "that the good is one but called by many names—sometimes practical wisdom, sometimes god, at other times mind, etc.; but he did away with the things opposed to the good, saying that they are not" (2.106). Cicero attributes to the Megarians in general (but initially Euclides) a view that is related but seemingly a little different, that "only that which is one and alike and always the same is good" (*Acad.* 2.129, cf. Lactantius *Inst.*, 3.12.9), and associates the Megarians with the

Eleatics on this basis. A more sweeping Eleaticism, not restricted to views about the good, is also ascribed to "Stilpo and the Megarians" by Aristocles (in Eusebius, *Praep. evang.* 14.17.1), according to whom they maintain "that what is is one, and the other is not, and that nothing at all is generated or destroyed or in motion."

The Megarian-Eleatic connection has long been suspected,[26] and indeed the ideas about the unity of the virtues and/or the good seem easy enough to relate to Socratic themes, irrespective of any Eleatic-style views about changelessness. Now, if the Megarians did believe in an Eleatic changeless one being, this would not put them any closer to Pyrrho or Timon; though Timon does express some rare qualified approval for Parmenides, Melissus and Zeno, it is certainly not because of their monistic metaphysics.[27] But even without the Eleatic twist, these views have no discernible connection with anything in the evidence for early Pyrrhonism. One might think that ethical ideas (stripped of metaphysics) would be easier to relate to Pyrrho's largely practical orientation. But that his outlook is fundamentally practical is precisely the problem. Whether or not virtue or the good is one, and whether there are such things as anti-goods,[28] are questions belonging to the *theory* of value; the surviving testimonies on Pyrrho show no interest in such questions.[29]

So far we have seen nothing to suggest that Pyrrho and Timon were indebted in any way to Megarian thinking. On the other hand, Timon is said to have spent time with Stilpo (DL 9.109). Admittedly this is before his association with Pyrrho; but at least it may encourage the thought that Stilpo could have taught Timon something enduring, which was also more congenial to the ideas of Pyrrho than the things we have seen so far. And, although this may be just coincidence, it is worth noting that Stilpo is not singled out for criticism in any surviving passage of Timon. In addition, the biographical tradition makes a connection, or several different connections, between the Megarians and Pyrrho. At the start of Diogenes' life of Pyrrho we read that he studied with "Bryson son of Stilpo" (9.61); the Suda under Pyrrho also gives Bryson as his teacher, this time calling him a student of the Megarian Clinomachus; and the Suda under Socrates calls Bryson a student either of Socrates himself or of Euclides, and again names him as Pyrrho's teacher. Besides being inconsistent in various ways, these reports are in certain respects chronologically impossible or very difficult; Pyrrho's teacher could not have been a *son* of Timon's teacher, and Socrates's student could hardly have been a teacher of Pyrrho. But clearly some effort is being made to connect Pyrrho with the Megarians, and thereby also with Socrates. Who Bryson was is also something of a mystery,[30] and the philosophical views that are ascribed to someone of that name (that obscenity is impossible and that squaring the circle is possible)[31] seem very far from the concerns of Pyrrho. But still, these numerous hints of a Pyrrho-Megarian connection may prompt us not to close the question just yet.

If the unity of the good was too theoretical a topic for Pyrrho, there are also reports about the ideals and attitudes of Stilpo, in particular, that seem to belong much more in Pyrrho's sphere of interest. A letter of Seneca (*Ep.* 9.1) associates Stilpo with "those to whom the highest good seemed to be a soul free of suffering." *Impatiens* must be a Latin version of *apathês*, and *apatheia* is one of the terms used for Pyrrho's ideal (e.g., Plutarch, *Prof. virt.* 82E-F, Aristocles in Eusebius, *Praep. evang.* 14.18.26). Plutarch also mentions the reputation he had for "mildness and moderate feeling" (*praotêtos kai metriopatheias, Adv. Col.* 1119C); both feature in later Pyrrhonist accounts of the sceptics' *telos* (DL 9.108, alongside *apatheia*; Sextus, *PH* 1.25, 30), which are clearly descendants of the ideal laid out by Pyrrho. Long draws attention more specifically to a "Cynic style" in Stilpo's ethical remarks,[32] of which the most striking example is his reaction to the destruction of his property in the siege of Megara by Demetrius Poliorketes; when an effort was made to restore it, he said that he had not lost anything truly his own (*mêden tôn oikeiôn*), since he still had his education, his reason and his knowledge (DL 2.115).[33] In a similar vein he is reported to have argued that exile is not an evil, because it cannot deprive you of the things that really matter (Stobaeus 3.40.8, which is presented as an excerpt from a work *On Exile* by the Cynic Teles (third century BC)). As we saw earlier, the Cynics attitudes have much in common with Pyrrho's, and the same could clearly be said of these ideas of Stilpo's. But this, of course, just draws attention to the fact that there is nothing distinctively Megarian about the outlook that these various texts record for Stilpo. If Pyrrho or Timon learned anything from Stilpo or other Megarians[34]—and the biographical snippets mentioned in the previous paragraph suggest that we cannot rule this out—it was not significantly different from what they could have learned from the Cynics themselves. In the end, then, their connection with the Megarians, to the extent that it existed, seems to be of little philosophical importance.

As a brief coda to this discussion, I return to the case of Phaedo. We have seen that Timon lumps Phaedo in dismissively with the Megarians and other unspecified Socratics; we have also seen that he appears to have harsh words for Menedemus of Eretria, whose philosophy clearly belongs in the tradition of the Megarians but who is also said to have studied with Phaedo. We know little enough about Phaedo's own philosophical activity, except that he wrote dialogues.[35] But nothing in the cluster of points I have just mentioned would encourage one to think that Pyrrho's thought was in any way indebted to Phaedo. They do, however, have one thing in common: their native city, Elis. And this apparently made it irresistible for someone to decide that Pyrrho belonged to the "Elean" school founded by Phaedo, as duly recorded in Strabo's *Geography* (9.1.8). This also had the effect of bringing Pyrrho into the fold of Socratics, which was surely part of the point; we saw another example of this in the muddled reports about Pyrrho, Bryson and the Megarians. Clearly there were some to whom it mattered a great deal to give Pyrrho a Socratic pedigree. Biographically, there is no reason to believe the Phaedo connection. But the more important point is that it is uphill work, philosophically, to connect Pyrrho with Socrates or with most of those who legitimately belong in some line of succession from him; that might serve as a summary of my argument so far.

IV. PYRRHO AND THE CYRENAICS

I turn now to the Cyrenaics. We have seen that Timon briefly makes Aristippus a target, and there is no evidence of a biographical connection between any Cyrenaic and either Timon or Pyrrho. This might suggest that the two groups simply had nothing to do with one another. But Ugo Zilioli has recently argued that underlying the Cyrenaics' often-reported claim that "only the *pathê* are apprehensible"[36] was a metaphysical view of the indeterminacy of things, a view that is very similar to one attributed by some scholars, including myself, to Pyrrho.[37] On this reading of the crucial passage of Aristocles mentioned earlier, Pyrrho answered the question "what is the nature of things?" by saying "things are in themselves indeterminate," and on that basis recommended a withdrawal from all opinions about how things really are that ascribe fixed and definite characteristics to those things. The avoidance of physical and other theorizing would stem from this; one would resist the attempt to pin down the way things are—in the way that physicists, for example, try to do—not because of any epistemological qualms, but because one has come to the single, global realization that there is *no* determinate way things are. The Cyrenaics, on Zilioli's interpretation, thought much the same. If, like many, one thinks that the older Aristippus, the original Cyrenaic, had largely or exclusively ethical concerns, and that the view that only the *pathê* are apprehensible was not part of the Cyrenaics' outlook before the younger Aristippus, then one might infer that Pyrrho influenced the younger Aristippus. But Zilioli argues for this having been part of Cyrenaicism from the start, and so in his view the Cyrenaics' indeterminacy thesis anticipated Pyrrho's.[38] He does not say whether there was any influence in this direction, and in view of the silence in our sources about any relations between them (and Timon's apparent hostility), one might think otherwise. But this would be quite compatible with Zilioli's view and mine, because Zilioli finds important inspiration for Cyrenaic metaphysics in the "secret doctrine" attributed to Protagoras and others in the first main portion of Plato's *Theaetetus*, which I also argued to be an important source for Pyrrho's ideas.[39] One might, then, suppose that the Cyrenaics were thinking independently along the same lines and were influenced by the same earlier text; the similarity between the two views would be non-accidental without the one having prompted the other.

Should we accept this account? Unfortunately, I cannot go along with Zilioli's interpretation of the Cyrenaics as metaphysical indeterminists. I quite agree with him that such views were around in the period; indeed, that is part of what I hoped to establish in my reading of Pyrrho. And it is true that one explanation for why nothing could be apprehended beyond the *pathê* might be that the underlying world beyond the *pathê* had no determinate qualities to be apprehended. Thus a sizeable portion of the evidence for the Cyrenaic position is compatible with Zilioli's interpretation—and that is of considerable interest in itself. For example, when Diogenes Laertius reports that the Cyrenaics abandoned physics because of its *akatalêpsia* (2.92), that is consistent with their having believed in an indeterminate reality.[40] However, a number of other texts cannot be explained away in this fashion. The sources consistently place epistemological uncertainty at the root of the position; the objects causing the *pathê* are inapprehensible because *we cannot tell* how they are, not because there is no definite way they are.

Sextus Empiricus summarizes the Cyrenaic position in his survey of views about the criterion of truth in *Against the Logicians*. He says that the *pathê* are apprehensible but that "the externally existing thing" is inapprehensible, "the soul being too weak to discern it" for various reasons (*M* 7.195). A little later, speaking of a perception as of something white, he says "for each person grasps the *pathos* that is his own, but on the question whether this *pathos* comes about in him and in his neighbor from a white thing," one is not in a position to say (*M* 7.196). Similarly, Aristocles says of the Cyrenaics "when burned or cut, they said that they recognized that they were affected (*paschoien*) in some way; but whether what was burning was fire, or what was cutting was iron, they were not able to say" (in Eusebius, *Praep. evang.* 14.19.1). Cicero says of them that "they say that nothing external is apprehensible; they apprehend only things they experience with internal touch, like pain, or pleasure; and they don't know what has which color or sound—their experience is just that they are affected in some way" (*Acad.* 2.76).[41] And Plutarch says that "they say that they are sweetened and bittered and chilled and heated and lightened and darkened, each of these *pathê* having its own, incontrovertible (*aperispaston*) evident character (*enargeian*) in itself; but whether honey is sweet, the young olive-shoot bitter, the hail cold, the unmixed wine warm, the sun lightening, or the night air dark" is the subject of unresolvable disagreement (*Adv. Col.* 1120E-F). The testimony of these four authors is quite consistent: what makes for the inapprehensibility of the external objects is our own cognitive limitations, not the intrinsically undifferentiated character of reality. All four authors say that we are unable to tell whether these external objects have certain specific features. But if the point was that reality was in itself indeterminate, we *would* be able to answer this question; the answer would be that the objects (supposing there are differentiable objects in the first place) do *not* have these features—or their opposites, or any definite features at all.[42]

So I think that the traditional interpretation of the Cyrenaics, as focused on our lack of knowledge of anything beyond the *pathê*, is after all correct. Now, one might of course seek to reconnect the Cyrenaics with Pyrrho by rejecting the metaphysical interpretation of his thought as well. Many scholars have read the Aristocles passage on Pyrrho as ascribing to him the view that the answer to the question "what is the nature of things?" is "we cannot tell what the nature of things is."[43] But, while this would bring Pyrrho into a notable point of agreement with the Cyrenaics, it would remain true that the other distinctive element of the Cyrenaic view has no counterpart in the evidence on Pyrrho. In addition to stressing that we cannot tell how things are beyond the *pathê*, the Cyrenaics are constantly reported as asserting that the *pathê* themselves are apprehensible. We do not find this said of Pyrrho; in fact, an interest in the character of the *pathê* seems to be completely absent from the testimonies on Pyrrho. And this, coupled with the lack of a reported connection between any Cyrenaic and either Pyrrho or Timon, leads me to think that Pyrrho's intellectual milieu did not include the Cyrenaics as a significant factor—even if his thought was more epistemologically inclined than I and others have argued it to be.[44] Once again, connecting Pyrrho with the Socratics is tough!

V. PYRRHO AND THE ACADEMY

I close with a brief mention of the Academy, mindful of the fact that we are supposed to be talking about the *minor* Socratic schools. I have already mentioned the idea that Plato was an important influence on Pyrrho, and I will not repeat my argument of some years ago that we should think of Pyrrho as a sort of "Plato without the Forms."[45] Whatever the truth of this, Timon appears to have no more time for Plato's Academic successors than he does for the other Socratics we have been considering.[46] Speusippus is called "good at teasing" (Plutarch, *Dion* 17, 4), and Diogenes quotes a line about the Academics in general—a line that he says is meant as disparagement, though this would be easy enough to guess—referring to "the Academics' unsalted broad talk (*platurêmosunês analistou*)," i.e. prolixity with nothing to liven it up (4.67). There is, of course, an additional dig at Plato, and/or the Academics' slavish imitation of Plato, in the coinage *platurêmosunês*. We have somewhat more to work with when it comes to Arcesilaus, Timon's younger contemporary and the head of the Academy who seems to have turned it in a sceptical direction. A line of Timon that Diogenes quotes to illustrate his own claim that Arcesilaus was "critical and outspoken (*epikoptês . . . kai parrêsiastês*, 4.33-4) is severely corrupt, allowing us to extract only the words "adding to his reproaches (*epiplêxesin egkatameignus*)" and not giving us an adequate sense of its tone.[47] But an unbroken sequence of four lines, also quoted by Diogenes (4.42) leaves us in no doubt about Timon's attitude; I quote the translation of Long and Sedley,[48] which I cannot improve on:

> Having spoken thus, he [Arcesilaus] plunged into the crowd of bystanders.
> And they like chaffinches round an owl gawped at him,

> Showing up his vanity because he pandered to the mob.
> There's nothing big in this, you miserable fellow. Why do you give yourself
> airs [*platuneai*, another Platonic dig] like a fool?

But if Arcesilaus is thus dismissed by Timon, the spokesman for early Pyrrhonism, it does not follow that he did not himself owe something to Pyrrho, or even that Timon did not recognize this. And the remaining two fragments allude to precisely this point. One, introduced by Diogenes simply as Timon's words about Arcesilaus, reads "But here, having leaden Menedemus under his chest, he will sink, or all-horn Pyrrho or Diodorus." The other, which immediately follows in Diogenes' text, is said to have Arcesilaus speaking the following words: "I will swim to Pyrrho and to tortuous Diodorus" (4.33).[49] There is room for considerable discussion about the character of the scene depicted here, and the ways in which it plays on Homeric themes; a number of possibilities have been proposed. But clearly part of Timon's point is that Arcesilaus is in some way a philosophical imitator of Pyrrho (whether or not he recognized this about himself), and of others too. In this Timon was not alone; in the same context Diogenes quotes a line of Ariston of Chios in which Arcesilaus is described, with a slightly different cast of characters, as "Plato in front, Pyrrho behind, Diodorus in the middle."[50] Here the Homeric reference is very clear—Arcesilaus is portrayed as a philosophical chimera (cf. *Il.* 6.181)—and Timon's message is essentially the same. And this no doubt explains why Arcesilaus' adoption of some element of Pyrrho's outlook does not raise him in Timon's estimation. Someone who combines elements of Pyrrho with elements of such unsavory characters (as Timon would view them) as "crooked Diodorus," a descendant of the Megarian tradition, or Menedemus, is fundamentally missing, and misusing, Pyrrho's message; you cannot emulate the argumentative styles of these two and still be an authentic follower of Pyrrho. If Arcesilaus follows Pyrrho to some degree, he also betrays him; this would be Timon's attitude.

We do not have to share Timon's sarcasm and scorn to see some truth in his depiction of Arcesilaus. That he learned something from Pyrrho is not implausible; already in antiquity the Pyrrhonists and the Academic sceptics were regarded as having a good deal in common, and it would not be surprising if some connection between the two traditions went back to the beginning.[51] However, everything that we know about Arcesilaus from such sources as Cicero and Sextus makes clear that, unlike Pyrrho, he relished the play of opposing arguments in intricate debate; and there is no indication that he took tranquility as his goal. On both counts, from Timon's perspective, Arcesilaus' avoidance of definite belief—the aspect of his thought that is most likely to owe something to Pyrrho—would turn out to be contaminated with alien elements that made it quite worthless.

If the purpose of this survey had been to accumulate as many Socratic connections for Pyrrho as possible, then it would not have been a success.

We have seen a link with the Cynics, and with Cynic-inclined aspects of the Megarian Stilpo's practical thought; and we have seen the sceptical Academy regarded as appropriating Pyrrho to some degree, but nonetheless ridiculed by the Pyrrhonist tradition itself. That is not much. However, I hope that there has been some interest in precisely the project of working out how much—or, as it has turned out, how little—Pyrrho has to do with the traditions tracing themselves back to Socrates.[52]

NOTES

1. *Classical Quarterly* 38 (1988), 150–71; reprinted with a new Postscript in A.A. Long, *Stoic Studies* (Cambridge: Cambridge University Press, 1996), 1–34.
2. Oxford: Clarendon Press, 2000.
3. For a brief account of the poem's contents, as far as we can reconstruct them, see my "Timon of Phlius" in the *Stanford Encyclopedia of Philosophy* (online). A much fuller discussion can be found in Dee L. Clayman, *Timon of Phlius: Pyrrhonism into Poetry* (Berlin: Walter de Gruyter, 2009), esp. chapters 3 and 4.
4. This Long does mention in "Socrates in Hellenistic Philosophy" (150–2 in the original publication).
5. *Ek d'ara tôn apeklinen ho laxoos, ennomoleschês*
   Hellênôn epaoidos, akribologous apophênas,
   Muktêr rhêtoromuktos, hupattikos eirôneutês. (Translations are my own unless otherwise specified.)
6. See *mussomai* in LSJ.
7. See most recently Clayman, *Timon of Phlius*, 102, "roaring at those without intelligence."
8. As pointed out by Di Marco, *Timone di Fliunte: Silli* (Rome: Edizioni dell'Ateneo, 1989), 179. Di Marco's own interpretation, "oggetto di ammirazione per gli stolti," relies in turn on a use of *bombax* in Aristophanes, *Thesm.* 45 that LSJ reports as meaning "prodigious," and Di Marco reads as an expression of wonder. But a glance at the context—Euripides' old unintellectual relative's reaction to Agathon's servant's pompous announcement that Agathon is about to compose a drama—suggests precisely the opposite; *bombax* there is surely dismissive, not admiring (see the note ad loc. in the Budé edition).
9. Diogène Laërce, *Vies et doctrines des philosophes illustres*, Traduction française sous la direction de Marie-Odile Goulet-Cazé (Paris: Librairie Générale Française, 1999).
10. *Laertii Diogenis De vitis, dogmatis et apophthegmatis eorum qui in philosophia claruerunt, libri X*. Th. Aldobrandino interprete (Rome, 1594).
11. So Di Marco, who points out that *amphaphoôntos*, "feeling around," can sometimes have an erotic connotation.
12. Reading *apithês* as passive with Goulet-Cazé and Di Marco. As Di Marco points out, *apithês* is naturally read at first with *is*, and hence as active—"the not unpersuasive force of Aeschines"—but it then becomes clear that it has to be taken with *grapsai*, and that the point is Aeschines' susceptibility to being persuaded to write the "feeble" works with which the first line credits him and Xenophon; and now, of course, the epic-sounding *Aischinou . . . is*, "the power of Aeschines," comes across as ironic.

13. There is also a fragment on one Ctesibius of Chalcis, named by our source Athenaeus (4.162f) as a *gnôrimos* of Menedemus. *Gnôrimos* can sometimes be used to refer to pupils, although it can also mean "acquaintance" in a more general sense. Giannantoni includes him in *SSR* (*Socratis et Socraticorum Reliquiae*, ed. G. Giannantoni 4 vols. (Naples: Bibliopolis, 1990), III H); but even if he was a pupil of Menedemus, we know nothing whatever about his thought, and so it is doubtful whether he can be said to qualify as a Socratic. Still, it is interesting that, at least on its face, this line is less unequivocally critical than the others I examine in this paragraph; Ctesibius is called "dinner-mad" (*deipnomanes*) but is also said to have an "undaunted heart" (*kradiên d'akuliston*).
14. For this and the other fragments of Timon quoted in this paragraph, I use the translations in my *Pyrrho, his Antecedents, and his Legacy*, 70–71; see also the footnotes on those pages for some minor textual issues.
15. This is part of a sequence of seven lines that can be assembled from DL 9.65 together with Sextus *M* 11.1 and *M* 1.305. The remaining three lines compare Pyrrho to the sun.
16. It is not clear that the same can be said of Timon himself. As we saw (see n.8 and accompanying text), an epithet meaning "mocker of fools" would surely be a commendation in his hands; indeed, much of the *Silloi* would seem to earn *him* just such an epithet. And he can hardly be said to be free from contention with other thinkers, when he spends so much time penning derisive portraits of them. Timon, then, seems in some respects to fall considerably short of the ideal that he presents Pyrrho as attaining.
17. Note the title *Truth* (DL 6.16), and the theory of the *oikeios logos* for each thing; on the latter, see Aldo Brancacci's chapter in this volume.
18. Note the title *On Opinion and Knowledge* (DL 6.17).
19. Note the title *On Diction or on Styles* (*peri lexeôs ê peri charaktêrôn*) (DL 6.15).
20. See Aldo Brancacci, "La filosofia di Pirrone e le sue relazioni con il cinismo," in G. Giannantoni (ed.), *Lo scetticismo antico* (Naples: Bibliopolis, 1981), 213–42; A.A. Long, "Timon of Phlius: Pyrrhonist and Satirist," *Proceedings of the Cambridge Philological Society* 24 (1978), 68–91, revised version in A.A. Long, *From Epicurus to Epictetus: Studies in Hellenistic and Roman Philosophy* (Clarendon Press: Oxford, 2006), 70–95.
21. On this see Long, Timon of Phlius" and Fernanda Decleva Caizzi, "*Tuphos*: contributo all storia di una concetto," *Sandalion* 3 (1980), 53–66.
22. "Timon of Phlius."
23. Henry Wadsworth Longfellow opens his poem "A Psalm of Life": "Tell me not, in mournful numbers, Life is but an empty dream"; instead we are told to think "Life is real! Life is earnest!" By contrast, Lewis Carroll's poem "Life Is But a Dream" endorses the sentiment. The general idea can of course be found in ancient Greek literature (thanks to Kurt Lampe for this point); see, e.g. Pindar, *Pythians* VIII, 95–6, Aristophanes, *Birds* 687 (although both these texts compare *human beings*, rather than life itself, to dreams).
24. This was originally argued by David Sedley, "Diodorus Cronus and Hellenistic Philosophy," *Proceedings of the Cambridge Philological Society* 23 (1977), 74–120, and developed in Theodor Ebert, *Dialektiker und frühe Stoiker bei Sextus Empiricus: Untersuchungen zur Entstehung der Aussagenlogik*, Hypomnemata 95 (Vandenhoeck & Ruprecht: Göttingen, 1991). For some doubts, see Jonathan Barnes, "A big, big D?," *Classical Review* 43 (1993), 304–6, reprinted as "Logic and the Dialecticians" in Jonathan Barnes, ed. Maddalena Bonelli, *Logical Matters: Essays in Ancient Philosophy II* (Clarendon Press: Oxford, 2012), 479–84. James Allen, "Megara and Dialectic" (working title of a paper presented at the 2013 Symposium Hellenisticum),

has recently urged caution about taking any talk of "schools" too much at face value, while nonetheless suggesting that there may be a philosophical point to distinguishing a later group of "dialecticians," including Diodorus Cronus, from the original group inspired by Euclides of Megara; the difference would have to do with their greater logical sophistication. In what follows I ignore this issue, assuming that it would not have concerned Pyrrho and Timon.

25. We have two mentions of Diodorus in the surviving fragments of Timon—one of them calling him "crooked" (*skolion*), which seems consistent with my argument in this paragraph. However, he features not as a subject in his own right, but as someone to whom Arcesilaus is indebted; I return to this near the end.
26. See Giannantoni, *SSR* vol. 4, especially note 5, also notes 4 and 9, which include detailed reviews of the scholarship on the topic.
27. On these fragments and their bearing on the relations between Pyrrho and the Eleatics, see my *Pyrrho, his Antecedents, and his Legacy*, chapter 3.4.
28. It is not entirely obvious what issue is being addressed in the words "he did away with the things opposed to the good, saying that they are not." But one obvious possibility is that Euclides wants to conceive of bad as merely the absence of good—a privation, in Aristotle's terms—rather than as having a substantial existence in its own right.
29. The notorious lines from Timon's *Indalmoi* that speak of "the nature of the divine and good" (*hê tou theiou te phusis kai t'agathou*), quoted by Sextus at *M* 11.20, may be thought to conflict with this claim. If one takes them to represent Pyrrho's literal position, and reads them in the most dogmatic possible way, then Pyrrho holds that the nature of the divine and the good is eternal (*aiei*, with existential *esti* understood). This is still not exactly a view about the *unity* of the good, but it would easily accommodate such a view. However, we do not have to read the lines in this way—they can be understood less dogmatically, and in any case Sextus (who is our only source for these lines) gives no indication that Pyrrho is even the speaker—and we have strong reason not to do so, given the difficulty (I would say, impossibility) of fitting such a reading with everything else we are told about Pyrrho. For a brief discussion, which takes account of recent literature and is open to a number of possibilities, see section 6 of my "Pyrrho" in the *Stanford Encyclopedia of Philosophy* (online); for a detailed and much more opinionated account, see my "What did Pyrrho think about 'The Nature of the Divine and the Good'?," *Phronesis* 39 (1994), 303–37.
30. There may have been more than one person of that name; for an attempt to make sense of the evidence, see Giannantoni, *SSR* vol 4, note 10.
31. Both are attested in Aristotle. For the first, see *Rhet.* 1405b6–11, for the second *An. post.* 75b37–76a1, *Soph. el.* 171b16–22, 172a2–7. Giannantoni, *SSR* also includes relevant passages from the commentary tradition (vol. 1, II S, 9–11).
32. "Timon of Phlius," 78–9 in the revised version. Russell Dancy, in his article on Stilpo in the *Encyclopedia of Classical Philosophy*, ed. Donald J. Zeyl (Greenwood Press; Westport, Conn., 1997) cites Diogenes Laertius and the Suda as reporting that Stilpo actually studied with Diogenes the Cynic. As far as I can see, this is simply false. But that does not prevent there being a Cynic side to his thought.
33. Numerous other reports or remarks about this incident are collected in Klaus Döring, *Die Megariker: Kommentierte Sammlung der Testimonien* (B.R. Grüner: Amsterdam, 1972), texts 151B-I.
34. The Megarians in general are said to have strived for *aochlêsia*, "freedom from disturbance" (Alexander of Aphrodisias (?), *Supplement to On the Soul*

150.34–5). As Döring notes (*Die Megariker*, p.154), the reliability of this is questionable, seeing that in the same sentence the Academics are said to have an ideal of *aproptôsia*, "lack of precipitancy." However, in view of the picture of Stilpo that we have just seen, it is not inherently implausible.

35. See, however, Livio Rossetti's contribution to this volume; also Rossetti's earlier "Ricerche sui 'dialoghi Socratici' de Fedone e di Euclide," *Hermes* 108 (1980), 183–200, and George Boys-Stones, "Phaedo of Elis and Plato on the Soul," *Phronesis* 49 (2004), 1–23. As far as I can see, none of the very interesting speculations about Phaedo's thought in these papers gives any plausibility to a philosophical connection between Phaedo and Pyrrho.

36. I leave *pathos* untranslated throughout. A *pathos* is a way in which someone or something is affected. "Passion" and "emotion" are sometimes acceptable renderings, but in this case, where ordinary sense-perceptions are also examples of *pathê*, they would clearly not be appropriate. "Affection" is impossibly archaic; today the word does not remotely mean what it needs to mean in this context. I have sometimes experimented with "effect," but this often leads to vagueness about what kind of effect is at issue.

37. Ugo Zilioli, *The Cyrenaics* (Durham: Acumen, 2012; reprinted in London and New York: Routledge, 2014); and see my *Pyrrho, his Antecedents, and his Legacy*, chapter 1. Other proponents of a metaphysical reading of Pyrrho include Fernanda Decleva Caizzi, *Pirrone: Testimonianze* (Naples: Bibliopolis, 1981), text 53 with commentary; A.A. Long and D.N. Sedley, *The Hellenistic Philosophers* (Cambridge: Cambridge University Press, 1987), vol.1, commentary on section 1.

38. *The Cyrenaics*, p.100.

39. *Pyrrho, his Antecedents, and his Legacy*, chapter 3, esp. section 3.

40. *Pace* Tim O'Keefe in his review of Zilioli's book, *Notre Dame Philosophical Reviews* 2013.04.14. In general, though, my criticism runs along similar lines to O'Keefe's.

41. I use the translation of Charles Brittain in Cicero, *On Academic Scepticism* (Indianapolis/Cambridge: Hackett, 2006).

42. Zilioli points to three other texts in support of his interpretation. One is PHerc 1251, plausibly conjectured to be Philodemus' *On Choices and Avoidances*, Col. II and III (=*SSR* IVH30), which speaks about those who took the *pathê* of the soul as ends (*telê*), and then says "others held the doctrine that what we call grief and joy are entirely empty because of the manifest indeterminacy." Zilioli comments "Philodemus' attribution to the Cyrenaics of the view that things are indeterminate is quite remarkable" (93). But while the attribution to the Cyrenaics of the view that the *pathê* are *telê* is highly plausible, the view concerning indeterminacy is attributed to "others"; hence I see no support here for his claim. Second, the Anonymous Commentator on the *Theaetetus*, col.65, 18–39, commenting on *Tht.* 152b1–3, mentions a view according to which "the peculiar character of the producer [i.e., what produces a *pathos*] is not determined (*mê hôrismenên*)" and shortly afterwards says "Hence the Cyrenaics say that only the *pathê* are apprehensible, whereas the external things are inapprehensible. For that I am being burned, they say, I apprehend, but that the fire is such as to burn is unclear; for is it was such, everything would be burned by it." The problem with this is that it is internally inconsistent. The last portion, "for if it was such, everything would be burned by it" is an argument for the conclusion that the fire does *not* have the intrinsic character of being "such as to burn"; but if this is the case, "that the fire is such as to burn" is not "unclear (*adêlon*)" but false. The Anonymous is trying to connect the Cyrenaics with an indeterminacy view (something that, as we saw

earlier, can indeed be detected in the *Theaetetus*), but failing, in part because he is too honest about what the Cyrenaics actually thought; his description of the Cyrenaic view (just like all the texts cited in this paragraph) puts the focus on an epistemological problem, not on metaphysical indeterminacy. Finally, Zilioli cites Sextus M 6.52–3, which attributes to the Cyrenaics the view that nothing beyond the *pathê* exist. But, first, this does not seem to help his case; if there is really *nothing* beyond the *pathê*, there is not even an indeterminate reality. And second, this passage of Sextus is in a polemical context in which he makes suspect claims about the views of Democritus and Plato as well; we should not take seriously his claim about the Cyrenaics, which contradicts many other sources, including himself in *Against the Logicians*. On this see Voula Tsouna, *The Epistemology of the Cyrenaic School* (Cambridge: Cambridge University Press, 1998), 80–1, and my "A Sceptic Looks at Art (but not Very Closely): Sextus Empiricus on Music," *International Journal for the Study of Skepticism* 3, no.3 (2013), 155–81, at 177–8.
43. See, e.g., M.R. Stopper, "Schizzi Pirroniani," *Phronesis* 28 (1983), 265–97; and the introduction to Sextus Empiricus, *Outlines of Scepticism*, translated by Julia Annas and Jonathan Barnes (Cambridge: Cambridge University Press, 1st edition 1994).
44. The Suda, under Theodorus the atheist, reports that Theodorus studied with Pyrrho (and Bryson) and cultivated an ideal of *adiaphoria*. If this is true, then Pyrrho had an influence on at least one Cyrenaic. However, the report is not paralleled by any other information and seems suspect. Elsewhere we are consistently told that the Cyrenaics had pleasure as their *telos*. Given their other views, it may very well be that they were indifferent to many things about which others would care (see DL 2.94–6 on Hegesias); but that is not the same as pursuing indifference as an end in itself.
45. *Pyrrho, his Antecedents, and his Legacy*, 143.
46. Timon's verdict on Plato himself appears to be more mixed—as one might expect if Pyrrho learned something from him, even while repudiating other elements of his thought (such as the Forms); see *Pyrrho, his Antecedents, and his Legacy*, 140.
47. See the commentary of DiMarco (*Silli*, p.187) for the unacceptability of all proposed emendations.
48. *The Hellenistic Philosophers*, text 3E.
49. There are textual issues in both fragments. I adopt the texts and the translations in Clayman, *Timon of Phlius*; see pp.109–10 for discussion of the textual variants and the kind of scene to which these fragments may have belonged.
50. Diogenes Laertius, in introducing all these quotations (4.33), himself endorses the idea that Arcesilaus adopted the approaches of Pyrrho, the dialecticians (probably Diodorus, cf. n.24) and the Eretrians (i.e. Menedemus). However, it is not clear that he has any warrant for this beyond the lines of Aristo and Timon that he is about to quote.
51. For a subtle and careful exposition of this point of view, see David Sedley, "The Motivation of Greek Skepticism," in Myles Burnyeat, ed., *The Skeptical Tradition* (Berkeley/Los Angeles/London: University of California Press, 1983), 9–29.
52. I thank Ugo Zilioli for inviting me to the conference in Soprabolzano where this chapter was first presented, and to the participants at that meeting for their helpful reactions.

10 Epicureanism and Socraticism
The Evidence on the Minor Socratics from the Herculaneum Papyri
Tiziano Dorandi

1. INTRODUCTION

At the XVIIth International Congress of Papyrology, held in Naples in May 1983, Gabriele Giannantoni read a paper entitled "The Minor Socratics in the Herculaneum Papyri." Thirty years after Giannantoni's work, it is necessary, I believe, to review the issues in light of the continuous and undoubted progress that has been made in the interpretation of the Herculaneum papyri, which has not only resulted in improvements to the transmitted text of some fragments, but has also brought to light some hitherto unknown testimonia and allowed us to discard others.

Following the example of Giannantoni's paper, I have organized my contribution into three main sections: Megarians, Cyrenaics and Cynics. These sections are preceded by a further two sections, one on Philodemus as a biographer of Socrates and the Socratics, the other aimed at explaining a reference by Philodemus to "the whole of Socratic literature." Bibliographical references are limited to the most significant contributions and do not pretend to be exhaustive.

The aim of this contribution is to present the material for a collection of testimonia on the Socratics from the Herculaneum papyri that will both complement the similar collection that Acosta Méndez and Angeli have provided for Socrates, and also serve as a sort of prelude to a comprehensive investigation into the often sharp polemic aimed by Epicurus and his followers at Socrates and the Socratics (see, e.g., Acosta Méndez-Angeli 1992 and Clay 2003).

2. PHILODEMUS AS BIOGRAPHER OF SOCRATES AND THE SOCRATICS

One of the main works of Philodemus of Gadara (first century BC) was without doubt the *Collection of the philosophers* (*Suntaxis tôn philosophôn*). As with all the Philodemus' works, parts of the *Collection* are preserved in the Herculaneum papyri alone (Longo Auricchio 2007 and Longo

Auricchio-Indelli-Del Mastro 2012: 340–1). The title is a conjecture based on comparison with Diogenes Laertius (10.3). We have sections from some books: PHerc. 1021 and 164 (Plato and the Academy); PHerc. 1018 (the Stoa); PHerc. 1780 (the Garden); PHerc. 327 and 1508 (the Abderites and the Pythagoreans?); PHerc. 495 and 558 (Socrates and the Socratics).

Philodemus put together a historical work, based on a sound chronology, that followed the pattern of the familiar Hellenistic genre of *Successions of the philosophers*. He conceived the *Collection* as a teaching manual, written not only for the members of the Epicurean school but also for cultivated Roman society. It was written with a wide readership in mind, and with the aim of presenting a history of philosophy compiled *sine ira et studio* by an Epicurean curious about the life and times of the members of other philosophical schools.

The meagre remains of the book on Socrates, preserved in two exemplars (PHerc. 495 and 558) are available in the edition by Giuliano (2001). Giulano has convincingly shown (*contra* Giannantoni 1983a: 133–5, but see also Gallo 2002) that the book on Socrates belongs to Philodemus' *Collection*. In fragment 1 col. 1.4–5, PHerc. 495 we read the names of Socrates and Xanthippe, without being able to infer anything about the context. The name Socrates is found again in *sottoposto* ['substratum'] 1, column 1.1–2 of the same papyrus and in frr. 1.6 (preceded by the name of Satyrus of Callatis) and 11–2, as well as in the *titulationes* ['headings'] of fr. 1 δίκ]η Σωκράτ(ους) and of *sottoposto* 1 to fr. 17 of PHerc. 558. Λυσίου in fr. 2, col. II 4, PHerc. 495, probably refers to the episode in which Socrates rejects the defence that Lysias had written for him. According to Giuliano (2001: 56–7), the mutilated remains of fr. 5, PHerc. 495, refer to the last moments of Socrates' life. The *titulatio* of PHerc. 558 fr. 11 introduces a chapter on the sayings, *apophthegmata*, of Socrates; that of PHerc. 558, fr. 12, *sottoposto* 1 col.1, (Σωκράτου]ς μαθη[τ]αί), indicates the beginning of the section on the Socratics. The name of Aeschines of Sphettus appears next to that of Socrates in fr. 3.3–6 and 8 of PHerc. 495: ἐπεὶ | [δ' Αἰ]σχίνης ἑωρᾶτο πιε||ζούμ]ενος ὑπὸ τῆς πενίί[ας. The motif of Aeschines' poverty (cf. Diogenes Laertius 2.62) perhaps also figures in PHerc. 495 fr. 6, col. 1.2–5 (ἀφελὶ[κομένου δ' Αἰσχίνου διὰ | [τὴν ἀπορ]ίαν). In fr. 7.5–6 of the same roll, there appears the name of the Cynic Diogenes (καὶ Διογ[έ]ν[ης | ἔσκ]ωπτον). Crönert referred the mention of Dionysius and Dion in fr. 7.9–10 to the disagreement between Plato and the tyrant of Syracuse (the city itself appears to be mentioned in PHerc. 558, fr. 8, col. 2.7). Philodemus talks of Plato, together with Xenophon, in PHerc. 495, fr. 9.2–5, in a context relating to the moments after Socrates' death: τινες [Ξενο]ιφῶντι [μετ]ὰ τ]ἡ[ν Ἀθηνῶν ἁλω]ισιν στρατευσ[α]μέν[ωι εἰς] | τὴν Ἀσίαν, Πλάτωνι δ[έ ≈ PHerc. 558 fr. 15 col. 1.1–3 μένωι εἰς τὴ]ν Ἀσίαν, Πλά[τωνι δ' εἰς Σικ]ελίαν [π]λεύ[σαντι. The Διοσκούρους (most likely Xenophon's sons) are referred to in PHerc. 495, fr. 11.5–6 together with some unknown disciples of Plato (Πλάτωνος [μ]αθητῶ[ν]). The name Plato

170 *Tiziano Dorandi*

is mentioned more than once in PHerc. 558 *sottoposto* 1.1, fr. 12–6–7 and fr. 14.1–2 (ἐ]ξ Ἀκαδη[μείας] | Πλάτωνι [). A reference to Megara or the Megarians is perhaps to be found PHerc. 558 fr. 4 *sottoposto* 1.3 Μεγα[ρ. Usener found trace here of the tradition preserved by Aulus Gellius (*Attic Nights* 7.10, 1–4) of the nightly visits of Euclides to Athens, but this looks like a fantasy.

3. "ALL THE RECORDS OF SOCRATES" (HAPANTA TA SÔKRATIKA MNÊMONEUMATA)

In a personal comment added at the end of a transcription of the 'Character' of the εἴρων by a certain Aristo (who I still believe to be the Peripatetic philosopher Aristo of Ceos; *contra* see Ranocchia 2007, which identifies him as the Stoic Aristo of Chios), Philodemus refers in support of his position to ἅπαντα τὰ Σωκρατικὰ μνημονεύματα ("all the records of Socrates"). The passage (Philodemus, *On Vices* 10, PHerc. 1008, col. 23.36–8 Jensen; see also Ranocchia 2007, 278–9, 351–2 and 2010 = testimonium 5 Acosta Méndez-Angeli) ends abruptly, so that we do not know what Philodemus was recovering here from the Socratic literature or what use he was making of it. Acosta Méndez-Angeli (1992, 111–2) suggests that the reference to "all the records of Socrates" is explained

> if we suppose that such records to have included multiple examples of Socrates and of his behaviour as *eirôn* and *alazôn*. These could have consisted of the canonical sources on Socrates, the vast literature that emerged from Socratic circles after the death of the master and by other literary and philosophical documents that were hostile to him.

Rossetti too (1993, 268–74) thinks that Philodemus will have been referring to works by Socratics no longer available to us. If Philodemus did not himself have direct access to the old Socratic literature, Rossetti proposes, it will at least have been available to Aristo, so that the passage can be seen as "one of those rare attempts to take account of this kind of literature in a systematic way" (Rossetti 1993, 271).

Philodemus' reference to "the records of Socrates" is further evidence of his interest in Socratic literature and its authors and protagonists, for whom he had already reserved a book of the *Collection*. Rossetti suggests additionally that in the "character" copied by Philodemus in *On Vices* 10, PHerc. 1008, col. 22.35–7, Aristo was alluding to the lost *Aspasia* of Aeschines of Sphettus: the *eirôn*, we read, "parades ideas he identifies as wise and then attributes them to others, such as Socrates to Aspasia or to Ischomachus." I take no position on this identification, since it outside the limits of the present essay, focused as it is on the polemics of Epicurus and his followers against the Socratic schools.

4. THE MEGARIANS: THE POLEMICS, FROM EPICURUS DOWN TO PHILODEMUS

The Megarians were one of the targets of Epicurus' criticisms; Diogenes Laertius (10.27) cites a work of his *Against the Megarians*, nothing of which survives. Verde (2013: 210–37) examines the connections between Epicurus and Diodorus, with some original results. There is, however, clear evidence of a polemic against Megarian theories of language in Book 28, and possibly in Book 14, of the *On Nature*.

4.1 The Polemic against the Megarians: Epicurus' On Nature Books 14 and 28.

Book 28 of his *On Nature* finds Epicurus engaged in a discussion with his pupil Metrodorus in the presence of other members of the Garden. Metrodorus takes no part in the discussion, his arguments being presented by Epicurus himself. The tone of polemic against the Megarians is clear even from the first surviving fragments of the book, and was further developed in the final part through the use of the weapons of ridicule and scorn (Leone 2003). The discussion turns on two fundamental issues:

1. The correct usage of our linguistic tools in philosophical investigation, as a guarantee of the precision of our concepts, and
2. Whether, within what limits, and through what sort of process of verification it will be possible for the philosopher to use ordinary language, without this resulting in the loss of such precision and running into ambiguity.

Epicurus and Metrodorus thought long and hard about how to achieve that accuracy and precision in the use of philosophical terminology when dealing with objects and concepts lying outside the range of direct apprehension by the senses. In his attempt to elaborate a specific, technical language of philosophy, Metrodorus did not succeed in doing without terms of ordinary language. Although he was well aware of the risks implicit in the multiple conventions of ordinary language, characterised as it is by generic and polysemic and thus ambiguous terms, and by the lack of an exact and univocal correspondence between words and objects, Metrodorus was not careful enough in dealing with those risks and was thus caught in contradictions. Epicurus had discussed the views of his pupil and arrived at his own philosophy of language (see *Letter to Herodotus* 37 and 75–6). The use of ordinary language, Epicurus maintains, is not only legitimate for the philosopher but actually advisable, in order to facilitate communication between individuals of the same group and between one generation and another. Ordinary language is useful for designating both perceptual and non-perceptual objects; in the latter case, ordinary words originally linked to perceptible objects are used metaphorically. In order to avoid the kind of ambiguity always latent in ordinary language, Epicurus thought it should be subject to adaptation—an expedient that had not occurred to Metrodorus—and the sort of verification that would allow an assessment to be made of its correctness and the truth or falsity of the beliefs it expresses. Epicurus conceived of tools that would be infallible because grounded upon the evidence of phenomena and of our preconceptions (*prolêpseis*): *ouk epimarturêsis*, lack of corroboration, which declares a belief false if unconfirmed by perceptual evidence; *antimarturêsis*, judging as false those beliefs that go against perceptual evidence; and *epilogismos*, reckoning or calculation, which measures and evaluates the truth or falsity of practical or theoretical beliefs on the basis of the consequences that flow from them.

We find a fundamental testimony on Epicurus' polemic in fr. 13, cols 4 inf. 3–5 sup. 15. Epicurus to Metrodorus:

> I am convinced that I see them clearly in the way in which we used to distinguish them, as you took the meaning, and not in the senses in which certain people would understand them. But perhaps this is not the moment to prolong the discussion by citing these cases? Quite so, Metrodorus. For I expect you could cite many cases from your own past observations, of certain people taking words in various ridiculous senses, and indeed in any sense rather than their actual linguistic meanings. Whereas our own usage does not flout linguistic convention, nor do we alter names with regard to things evident. (Sedley 1973)

Epicurus here contrasts two opposed linguistic practices: the correct one, adopted by the Epicureans, which consists in using the words of ordinary language in their commonest sense, without this altering the relationship between names and visible objects, and avoids any ambiguity thanks to the procedures of verification just listed; and a second, incorrect, practice, employed by his adversaries, which is the butt of Epicurus' sarcasm. These adversaries go beyond linguistic conventions, deny the connection between names and things, and rely uncertainly on the vagueness (*koinotês*) and indefiniteness (*adialêpsia*) of ordinary language to give words false and ridiculous meanings. Metrodorus himself is likely to have contributed to such criticism in his work *Against the Dialecticians*. In his *On Ambiguity* Epicurus (fr. 13 cols 5 inf.— 6 sup.) demonstrated and criticised other mistakes by his adversaries relating to the attribution of false meanings to the words of ordinary language.

David Sedley (1973) has maintained that the frequent allusions in book 28 to past discussions of linguistic questions will have referred to *On Ambiguity*. By contrast, Leone (1987: 67–93) has suggested connecting the methodological remarks on the correct usage of our means of expression—as a guarantee of the coherence and precision of our beliefs—with the end of book 14 of *On Nature*, as a kind of riposte to those who, exactly because of that "vagueness" and "indefiniteness" of ordinary language, were trapped in error about the real content of the beliefs (*doxai*) of others, hence becoming *sumpephorêmenoi*, "muddlers" (among these "muddlers" one should probably include Plato (Verde 2013, 344–5). Leone (1987: 74) is persuaded that in book 14 (written in 301/300 BC):

> the polemic . . . relating to the incorrect usage of the means of expression and the consequences that it carries with it is directed against those Megarian or Dialectical adversaries whom Epicurus, some years later, would criticise afresh, and more decisively, in a book of his main work [i.e., 28, dated to 296/5] that was entirely devoted to linguistic and epistemological questions.

The suggested relation between the two books of *On Nature* is rejected by Tepedino (1990). She believes that the work to which Epicurus refers, along with *On Ambiguity*, in the course of his treatment of the theories of language in book 28 of *On Nature*, is not Book 14 of the same treatise but rather Metrodorus' *Against the Dialecticians* (on which see section 4.3 below): "A reference to this book seems to me to be evident in fr. 13, cols IV inf., 4 ff.—V sup., when Epicurus admits sharing the same view as his pupil about the 'distinction' of names, saying 'as you took the meaning', ὡς σο [ὶ ἐνο]εῖτο" (Tepedino 1990, 25).

In *On Nature* Book 28 Epicurus does not refer to his adversaries by name, limiting himself to using expressions like "some people," "someone," or "those people." Sedley (1973) identifies "someone" (τίς) with Diodorus Cronus or one of his followers. Epicurus accuses him of having maintained a contradictory view before accepting an opposed and generally wiser one; and the identification with Diodorus Cronus will be confirmed by his remark, cited above, about "certain people taking words in various ridiculous senses, and indeed in any sense rather than their actual linguistic meanings" (fr. 13, col. 5 sup. 5–8), which finds a parallel in Diodorus' subjectivist theory of meanings, denying ambiguity but allowing for "obscurity" (*obscuritas*: Aulus Gellius, *Attic Nights* 11.12.1–3 = SSR II F 7 = SVF II 152. See Verde 2013: 216–7):

> Chrysippus said that every word is ambiguous by nature (*omne verbum ambiguum natura*), since two or more meanings can be understood from it. But Diodorus Cronus said "No word is ambiguous. No one says or thinks anything ambiguous, and nothing should be held to be being said beyond what the speaker thinks he is saying. When you have

understood something other than what I had in mind, I should be held to have spoken obscurely, rather than ambiguously. For the characteristic of an ambiguous word would have had to be that whoever said it was saying two or more things. But no one is saying two or more things if he thinks that he is saying one. (tr. Long and Sedley)

This explanation did not persuade Giannantoni (1983b, 19), who claimed that

> the polemic was not directed against the thesis about conventional language but rather against the incorrect usage of linguistic tools and, hence, against the kind of *amphibolia* [ambiguity] hidden behind the so-called 'Megarian arguments', which were either invented by Eubulides or taken up by him and which the 'dialecticians' who modelled themselves on him continued to propose.

Thus identifying Epicurus' main adversary as Eubulides of Miletus, Giannantoni went on to insert the relevant testimony among the fragments of the latter (*SSR* II B 18).

In favour of Sedley's (1973) view, Leone (1987: 76) suggests a comparison with the final columns of book 14 of *On Nature*: "The doctrines of Diodorus, the heterogeneous background to which included Zeno's aporiai, Democritus' doctrines and Aristototelian critiques, might perhaps justify the reference to Diodorus as *sumpephorêmenos* [a 'muddler']."

4.2 Who Is Eubulides in the Herculanean Poetics (author unknown)?

Crönert (1906: 190–1, s.v. Eubulides) proposed to link the name of Eubulides in a badly damaged fragment of PHerc. 128 (fr. 6 = *SSR* II B 7: ἀλλ' ἡμ[εῖς] | Εὐβουλίδ[ην), attributed by Crönert himself to Philodemus' *Poetics*, with "the dialectician Eubulides" that Athenaeus (10.437d-e = *SSR* II B 1) appears to treat as author of a comedy entitled *Revellers*. But this remains highly speculative, and in general the identity of the Eubulides mentioned in PHerc. 128 remains uncertain, as does the paternity of the work to which the fragment belongs. The handwriting, datable to the second century BC, is plainly incompatible with the attribution of the work to Philodemus (Janko 2008: 83, n. 375; Romeo 1993: 285–8).

4.3 *Metrodorus of Lampsacus,* against the Dialecticians

One of the most interesting results of Cavallo's (1983) research into the palaeography of the Herculaneum papyri is the demonstration that five papyri catalogued as PHerc. 225, 418, 1084, 1091 and 1112 in fact belong to a single roll, copied in the middle or second half of the third century BC (Del

Corso 2013: 146). Starting from Cavallo's results, Emidio Spinelli (1986) has investigated the content of these fragments and succeeded in identifying not only the author but also the possible title of the work.

The extent of the roll grows if we accept the recent finding by Janko (2008: 56 and 57 n. 200) that PHerc. 390, 456, 1108 and perhaps 1103, all written by the same hand, also belonged to the same volume. PHerc. 1607 and 1645 could also be added. Janko (2008: 64–5) has moreover for the first time published PHerc. 439 = PHerc. 1824, also written by the same hand, its main theme being "atomic and/or molecular physics." This could explain the presence of Metrodorus' name in PHerc. 1012, col. 49, in a section devoted to the doctrine of minima (Verde 2013: 316–24). The fact that all the fragments are the product of just one scribe, using a somewhat peculiar kind of graphic language does not, however, in itself guarantee that they all derive from the same roll. The possibility that they belong to different rolls or works remains just as likely.

The portions of text preserved are limited. There are, however, some key elements that turn out to be useful for determining the authorship and title of the work:

1. In one fragment (PHerc. 1084, fr. 1.5) Epicurus is mentioned by name, which would rule out his being the author of the work. The presence of Epicurus' name in PHerc. 255, fr. 6.7 is uncertain (in the original, in fact, we read ε. [. . .] ωι—see Longo Auricchio 2005: 8).
2. The names of Megarian philosophers appear frequently: Alexinus, Diodorus, Eubulides, Euphantus, Stilpo. The context of references to them appears always to be "polemical enough to make one think that they are the specific subject/target of the work" (Spinelli 1986: 32).
3. In other fragments we find the names of other philosophical figures: Antidorus, Aristippus, Memnon, Plato and Timocrates the Epicurean.

In PHerc. 418 fr. 6 (*SSR* II C 2; II O 19; IV A 133; see also Spinelli 1986, 34) we find the following:

> . . . And the same work also says of this person 'Stilpo', nicknamed by some such as 'the drunkard', and Aristippus grazes in freedom, for the most part indulging his innate delight in the pleasures of sex, and Alexinus, who asks for five minas [as payment], and Antidorus, who is always being charged with something else.

The initial lacuna prevents us from establishing who the author of the quotation is. But since Epicurus and Metrodorus are joint authors of the attack on the linguistic doctrines of the Megarians in book 28 of *On Nature*, and since Metrodorus is credited with a treatise *Against the Dialecticians*, Spinelli has concluded that he, Metrodorus, is likely to be the author of the work in question. The hypothesis, Spinelli says (1986: 33), is confirmed by the close verbal correspondences between a fragment of PHerc. 418 (fr. 5.12–4, "all the wonderful, ingenious and brilliant works of the mind" (. . . τὰ καλὰ [πάν]|τ[α] καὶ σοφὰ καὶ περιτ[τὰ | τῆς] ψυχῆς ἔργα . . .) and a quotation from Metrodorus (fr. 6 Körte) in Plutarch's *Against Colotes* (1125b):

> and the sage Metrodorus thinks that this is as it should be, when he says that all the wonderful, ingenious and brilliant inventions of the mind (*ta kala panta kai sopha kai peritta tês psuchês exeurêmata*) have been contrived for the sake of the pleasure of the flesh or for the sake of looking forward to it, and that any accomplishement that does not lead to this end is worthless. (tr. Einarson and De Lacy)

Taking all this evidence into account, Spinelli proposes—with appropriate caution—that the papyrus in question gives us fragments of Metrodorus' *Against the Dialecticians*.

The attribution to Metrodorus seems to me unobjectionable; as for the identification of the work, Spinelli's thesis is likely enough, but does not exclude other possibilities. Tepedino (1992) has highlighted the fact that the content of some of the fragments is undoubtedly ethical. On her view this would not fit with a work like *Against the Dialecticians*, which, on her reconstruction, dealt exclusively with linguistic matters; Metrodorus there discussed the problem of finding a correct philosophical terminology for the world beyond the senses. The presence of ethical fragments, and of the names of various philosophers accompanied by criticism of their behaviour, leads Tepedino to suggest that this roll preserves one of the nine books of Metrodorus' *Against the Sophists*. In it, Metrodorus would have described, among other things, "the behaviour of his adversaries and their moral doctrines, although not these exclusively" (Tepedino 1992: 122).

A piece of evidence in favour of Tepedino's identification may come from the new edition of fr. 1 of PHerc. 255 by Janko (2008: 56–7 = O '247,' after Spinelli 1986: 38–9). The fragment contains: "an important discussion of mankind's early progress in discovering laws and new ideas and comments ironically on the self-proclaimed 'immortality' of their inventors, a theory that goes back to Prodicus and was taken up the Stoic Persaeus."

Once Metrodorus' paternity of the book is accepted (whatever title the work may have had), its importance for the reconstruction of the debate between first-generation Epicureans and at least the Megarians is incontestable (Longo Auricchio 2005).

4.4 Hermarchus against Alexinus

A page from Book 2 of Philodemus' *Rhetoric*, well known to scholars of the Megarians, and included in the collections both of Döring and of Giannantoni), provides us with a long excerpt from a *Treatise in Epistolary form* ('Ἐπιστολικόν) by Hermarchus against Alexinus (PHerc. 1674, cols.

44.19–49.19). The text of the papyrus (sometimes lacunose) was re-edited by Longo Auricchio (1975 and 1985), who has also included it in the edition of the fragments of Hermarchus (1988: 74–5, 100–1, 151–3 = fr. 36). More recently it has drawn the attention of Chávez Reino (2004) and Chandler (2006: 39–40, 107–17, 201–3).

Hermarchus' *Treatise*, addressed to an unknown Theopheides and dated to the period of Menecles' archonship (267/6 BC), is directed against Alexinus, who, in his *On Education* (*Peri agôgês*), had charged the rhetorical sophists (i.e., the epideictic orators) with having studied many useless things—his targets including their preoccupation, stylistic and otherwise, with Homer's work. Hermarchus sees Alexinus' attitude as ambivalent because, in certain aspects, his criticism of the rhetorical sophists boils down simply to complaining of a degree of freedom in their arguments that, in his view, proceeded not from a scientific basis but rather from one of probability and conjecture. Here are some significant moments in Hermarchus' confrontation with Alexinus' views:

> So while Alexinus uttered nonsense like this, (Hermarchus,) arguing against the assumption which pervades the whole work, says 'if one must interpret the argument concerning useful things as equivalent to that which concerns the kind of things from which financial profit originates for those able to twist speeches in any sense and constitutes total control, then regard it as completely insane . . . [lacunas].
>
> For let us pass over the fact that rhetoric tends not to trip up intelligent and reasonable men in affairs which involve crowds, cross-examinations, informers, oaths, and false testimonies. For it is better to lose a lot of money, or a piece of land [scorning] a juror while avoiding totally with the faculty of the soul the most important and greatest fears, than to have these fears and win all court cases. . . . [lacunas]
>
> . . . Not to practise court cases not [to have] experience in rhetorical art but to avoid [those who] offer (it). . .
>
> . . . Worthy to admire the rhetoricians for being useful citizens, his argument does not constitute novelty in itself. For we could interpret cooks and shopkeepers as doing something useful for us, but . . . [lacunas]
>
> For even an uneducated man who is completely [unacquainted] with writing, let al.ne devoid of rhetorical experience, is able to find out what is advantageous for the people and to express it clearly.
>
> And moreover, [how] should one interpret the fact that some rhetorical speech is accomplished not in accordance with [science] but with experience and conjecture? For, naturally, one should not think that by this expression is meant that the speeches do not contain dialectical syllogisms; for this is the case not only with *some*, but with *all* speeches, despite the fact that Alexinus is not too willing to concede this. In any case, Alexinus accuses Eubulides on one occasion of dismissing speeches which don't contain syllogisms; for he says that we understand the facts even without these (tr. Chandler).

In this testimony (and in another on Metrodorus, fr. 20 Körte = Phld. *Rhet.* II cols 49.27–52.10) Margherita Erbì (2011: 192) sees a surprising example of the way in which Philodemus, in recalling those who led the way in support of his argument about the status of the art of rhetoric appears

> to be revealing an attempt to bend the words of the original masters to his own purposes.... Philodemus tries to give prominence to the reference to sophistic rhetoric in the letter ..., but cannot disguise the fact that the letter might appear to have been written with no relation to the question in the context of which he cites it.

4.5 *Eubulides and the Megarians in Philodemus'* Rhetoric

Eubulides the Megarian is mentioned, with Demosthenes, in Book 3 of the *Rhetoric* (PHerc. 1056, col. 4.7–17 = SSR II B 2; see Erbì 2008: 198–201).

In a polemic aimed at the Stoic Diogenes of Babylon, Philodemus aims to show that the great political orators were engaged in maintaining and strengthening their position. He uses Themistocles, Pericles and Demosthenes as examples, referring to the training Demosthenes underwent with Plato and Eubulides to improve his communicational skills. His efforts to overcome his stutter, and his difficulties in pronouncing the Greek letter *rho*, are documented by Philodemus with anecdotes that are also preserved by other sources: pseudo-Plutarch, Diogenes Laertius, and pseudo-Lucian. Diogenes Laertius also cites (along with other authors) three anonymous comic verses (Adesp. com. fr. 149 Kassel-Austin), in which Demosthenes is pictured addressing his deficiency by listening to Eubulides. In his identification of Demosthenes' two teachers, Philodemus seems to underline two aspects of the orator's personality that are congenial to the image of him that he aims to project: "oratorical training focused on performance, and a philosophical and political education" (Erbì 2008: 199).

Finally, in an unidentified book of the *Rhetoric* (PHerc. 1015 fr. 24.3–5 = fr. 89 Döring = SSR II C 13), we find, in a lacunose context, a mention of "the Megarian dialecticians" (ἔγωγ' ἂν | τοὺς [Μ]εγα[ρ]ικοὺ[ς διαλεκτικού[ς), in which Giannantoni proposed to find a reference to Alexinus.

5. ARISTIPPUS AND THE CYRENAICS

The testimonies on Aristippus and the Cyrenaics are limited but nonetheless important. Diogenes Laertius (10.136–8) draws an important contrast between the doctrine of pleasure of the Epicureans and that of the Cyrenaics, based on the distinction between kinetic and katastematic pleasures (see Nikolsky 2001).

To start with, we need to reject the hypothesis, originally made by Sbordone and then adopted by Giannantoni, that in some extremely lacunose fragments (fr. c³, c⁴) of Πρὸς τοὺς [(PHerc. 1005) Philodemus was proposing a comparison of Epicureans and Cyrenaics on the subject of happiness; this on the basis of the reading] Κυρηνα[ιο . . . In the new edition of the text (fr. 41.5–7), Angeli (1988: 144, 200–1) has convincingly reconstructed a reference not to Cyrenaics but rather to the *Main Tenets* = *Kuriai doxai* of Epicurus.

5.1 Epicurus as "Reader" of Aristippus according to Philodemus' Testimony

In a fragmentary section of Πρὸς τοὺς [(PHerc. 1005, fr. 111 Angeli), which preserves epistolary extracts, Philodemus cites a letter of Epicurus addressed to an unknown person, asking for some books to be sent to him that he had listed: ". . . the work of Aristippus *On Socrates*, the *Eulogy of Plato* by Speusippus, Aristotle's *Analytics* and his books *On Nature*, in fact the ones we chose."

The fragment has attracted attention especially as evidence of the diffusion of Aristotle's school treatises in the Epicurean era (for a presentation of the issues, see Verde 2013: 3–9. On the fragment of Philodemus: 5–9). The report that Epicurus knew Aristippus' book *On Socrates* has to be read in light of what Diogenes Laertius (2.84–5) says about the Cyrenaic's literary production:

> Some also maintain that he (Aristippus) wrote six Books of Essays; others, and among them Sosicrates of Rhodes, that he wrote none at all. According to Sotion in his second book, and Panaetius, the following treatises are his: . . . *To Socrates* . . . (tr. Hicks).

Angeli's new reconstruction allows us to make a new assessment of the value of the catalogue made by Sotion and Panaetius, "on whose reliability scholarship has up to now not been positive" (Angeli 1988: 239–40.) It cannot be ruled out that the request for Aristippus' book *On Socrates* was dictated by Epicurus' need for first-hand information on Socrates and his thought for polemical purposes.

5.2 Metrodorus against Aristippus

Metrodorus refers twice to Aristippus (PHerc. 418 fr. 5.8 and fr. 6.9–13=SSR IV A 72). In the second fragment (Spinelli 1986: 34–5), the example of Aristippus follows that of Stilpo and is followed by that of Alexinus and Antidorus. The author quoted by Metrodorus appears to establish a close connection between Stilpo's drunkenness and Aristippus' innate hedonism, especially in relation to the pleasures of sex (see section 4.3 above).

5.3 An Anecdote on Aristippus in Philodemus' Rhetoric

An anecdote about Aristippus already familiar from Diogenes Laertius (2.71) resurfaces in a lacunose passage from Book 7 of Philodemus' *Rhetoric* (PHerc. 1004, col. 41= fr. 13 Acosta Méndez-Angeli). The fragment is included in the collections of Mannebach (fr. 100b) and Giannantoni (*SSR* IV A 11), but the text has been wholly updated by Acosta Méndez and Angeli (1992: 160, 186 and 254–60), who have uncovered closer analogies with Diogenes Laertius.

Philodemus reports an anecdote about Aristippus reported by an unknown author in a treatise *On Law-Courts* (Περὶ δικαστηρίων, new reading by Acosta Méndez-Angeli):

> In the treatise *On Law-Courts* he recalled the person who defended Aristippus for free (προῖκα)—he could not speak in his own defence—and asked him what advantage he had got from Socrates; to which he replied 'to be able to find fighting talk like that (τ[[ε]]ὸ τοιούτους εὑ-[ρ]ίσκειν λόγ[ους] μαχομέ[νο]υς).

Diogenes Laertius offers some variants, but the overall meaning is the same: "An advocate, having pleaded for him and won the case, thereupon put the question, 'What good did Socrates do you?' 'Thus much,' was the reply, 'that what you said of me in your speech was true'" (Hicks' translation).

On the general meaning of the anecdote, Acosta Méndez and Angeli share the view of Gomperz (1866/1983: 32–3, 696–7), who saw in the phrase "for free" a reference to Aristippus' persuasive capacities—capacities he had acquired by associating with Socrates, thanks to which he was able to persuade the logographer to defend him for free: "If we compare the disinterested attitude of the latter [i.e. the logographer] with Aristippus' tendency to lecture for a fee, that makes the addition 'for free' still more allusive" (Acosta Méndez-Angeli 1992: 257). The context in which the anecdote is located allows us to identify further nuances. After having presented, in the initial part preserved from the book, the anti-rhetorical discourses (*logoi*) of his Stoic adversary, Diogenes of Babylon, Philodemus begins his refutation, which is aimed at demolishing the Stoic conception of rhetoric as scientific knowledge rather than technique pure and simple. In the column immediately preceding the one containing the anecdote (col. 40), Philodemus appears to be dealing with the impudence of the orators that manifests itself either through insult salted with humour, or through irony understood as a more persuasive and subtler expedient than humour. If the distinction is Philodemus,' the use of the anecdote could be explained as an exemplification of irony as a kind of technique of allusion. If on the other hand the subject of rhetorical abuse (*loidoria*) is part of what Diogenes of Babylon says, Philodemus' response and the citation of the anecdote will need to be understood as a further distinction between rhetoric and philosophy, the superiority of the latter being measured by its usefulness. Aristippus was well able to deploy the criteria of truth consistent with the authentic practice of philosophy.

5.4 *The Cyrenaics and Hegesias in Philodemus'* On What to Choose and Avoid (Περὶ αἱρέσεων καὶ φυγῶν)?

Philippson (1941/1983: 288–9, 279–80) saw in columns 2–3 of PHerc. 1251 (a book with no author or title, but most probably Philodemus' *On What to Choose and Avoid*) a polemic aimed at Theodorus of Cyrene. Philippson's hypothesis has recently been challenged, on good grounds, by Voula Tsouna and Giovanni Indelli (1995: 21–3, 118–26). On the basis of a new reconstruction of the text, the two scholars reach a somewhat aporetic conclusion: "The author probably refers to various sceptical sects . . ., and in particular the Cyrenaics (possibly col. 2.5–11, probably col. 2.11–15, and certainly col. 3.6–14), Hegesias (col. 3.14–18), and perhaps the Pyrrhonians (cols 2.5–11, 3.2–6)" (21).
Philodemus writes:

> (col. 2) . . . and they claim that in truth no (judgement) takes precedence over any other, being persuaded that the great affection of the soul occurs as a result of pain and that thus we accomplish our choices and avoidances by observing both [sc. bodily plus mental pain]. For it is not possible that the joys arise in us in the same way and all together, in accordance with some expectation . . . [lacunas] (col. 3) and some people denied that it is possible to know anything. And further, they added that if nothing is present on account of which one should make an immediate choice, then one should not choose immediately. Some other people, having selected the affections of the soul as the moral ends and as not in need of additional judgement based on further criteria, granted to everybody unchallengeable authority to take pleasure in whatever they cared to name and to do whatever contributed to it. And yet others held the doctrine that what we call grief or joy are totally empty notions because of the manifest indeterminacy of things.
> (tr. Tsouna-Indelli)

Philodemus does not name any philosopher, simply reporting different views on the topic of our "choices and avoidances by observing bodily and mental pain." The main theme of column 2 seems to be a sceptical argument, or, alternatively, it may relate to Cyrenaic ethics. The sceptics did in fact maintain that "we act partly by following the indications of our nature, especially our affections (πάθη)," while some Cyrenaics admitted that affections are the only things which we can know and the only appropriate guides for action, and further, they defined the moral goal by reference to two affections, namely pleasure which we pursue as the supreme good, and pain which we avoid as the supreme evil. (Tsouna-Indelli 1995, 118–9)

The affinities between the two positions make it difficult to establish whether the author was referring to the Sceptics or to the Cyrenaics. In column 3, Philodemus lists three positions each of which is maintained by a group of philosophers, continuing his presentation of sceptical views. The first section is obscure, but its meaning is probably "since no knowledge is possible on the grounds of which a choice could be justified, and since only the affections of the present moment can be our guides for action, we should not make choices unless such affections occur." The second section reports what is certainly a Cyrenaic position: "moral choice is performed by attending to the affections of the present moment which are the ultimate criteria for action. The author adds that adherence to this view causes an unrestrained pursuit of any pleasure that one would care to name." The third section, attributed by Tsouna and Indelli to Hegesias (Tsouna-Indelli 1995, 125–6), "consists in the claim that long-term grief or joy are 'empty concepts'" (123).

The attribution to Theodorus has not survived the new reading of the papyrus. At the same time the Cyrenaic substrate of a large part of the report is confirmed, and Hegesias appears as the most likely author of the third and final thesis (Zilioli 2012: 91–4).

5.5 Theodorus in a Passage from Philodemus' Rhetoric

In a lacunose and mutilated fragment at the end of Book 2 of the *Rhetoric* (PHerc. 1079 = SSR IV H 12 = fr. 63 Wyniarczyk; the passage is not included in Mannebach's collection), after having examined the views of a philosopher whose name is lost, Philodemus recorded (for the purposes of assessment: ? ἐγ[κρῖνα]ι) what the anonymous philosopher calls Theodorus of Cyrene's own questions on the same topics (τὰς τοῦ | [Κυρην]αίου Θεοδώρου | [περὶ τ]ῶν αὐτῶν, ὥς φη[σιν αὐ]τός, ἠρωτημέ|[νας]); in particular, the question that Theodorus puts first. Sadly, the papyrus breaks off at this point and we are left guessing as to what this question was.

5.5.1 Not Theodorus the Godless

Mayer (1910: 547–62, 560–1) had maintained, on the basis of a daring reconstruction of the text and a series of deductions from it, that a large section of a book, perhaps Book 10, of the *Rhetoric* (PHerc. 1669) of Philodemus reflects elements of Cyrenaic doctrine; and that the encomiast of rhetoric against whom Epicurus' polemic is directed here ought to be identified with Theodorus the Godless. This hypothesis is presently undemonstrable, apparently receiving no concrete support from the texts as they stand (Giannantoni 1983a: 140).

6. EPICUREANISM AND CYNICISM

The crude and continuing polemics of the Epicureans against the Cynics have been investigated as a whole by Marcello Gigante (1992). But on some specific points—a testimony on Antisthenes' notion of *homonoia*, and a contribution from Philodemus towards the reconstruction of the *Republic* of Diogenes of Sinope—there has recently been substantial progress.

6.1 Epicurus, Metrodorus and Polystratus

The Cynics were the targets of heavy criticism on the part of Epicurus and his immediate pupils. Metrodorus took over and further developed Epicurus' precept that the wise man "will not play the dog/behave like a Cynic either . . . or beg"; he rejected the Cynics' mendicant way of life, reassessing poverty in relation both to beggary and to wealth. He also discussed the best way to become rich (*chrêmatizein*) according to nature (*kata phusin*), in the lost treatise *On Wealth*, which we can reconstruct through the lacunose testimony of Book I of Philodemus' work of the same name (PHerc. 163, col. 50.2–38), and the more joined-up testimony of *On Household Management* (PHerc. 1424, col. 12.25–43: see Gigante 1992: 29–53; Tsouna 2012: 34–5).

In *On Household Management*, Philodemus quotes an extract from Metrodorus' work *On Wealth* directed against those who maintained that the Cynics choose the lightest and easiest way of life, insofar they have eliminated as far as possible anything that does not bring us a life that is frugal, peaceful, free from disturbance, and realised in a pragmatic way with the minimum of effort. This is obtained, they claim, by the person who succeeds in procuring what he needs to meet the demands of daily life, and it suffices for the philosopher too; all the rest is vain.

Polystratus (died 219/8 BC), the second successor of Epicurus as scholarch, attacked the Cynics and the Sceptics in his work *On Irrational Contempt* (PHerc. 336/1150) and in the first book of *On Philosophy* (PHerc. 1520). Polystratus' polemic is directed above all against the Antisthenic brand of Cynicism, which Polystratus combats by rejecting the assimilation of the human world to that of the animals that was central to the Cynic idea of living "in accordance with nature" (Gigante 1992: 79–89). Polystratus "launches a fundamental attack on the thesis that the beliefs of human beings are false, and that we have to reject them because fine and disgraceful have no more value for human beings than they do for animals" (88).

6.2 Antisthenes in Philodemus

With Philodemus the polemic against the Cynics gains a new vigour. I begin with a presentation of the testimonia in Philodemus relating to Antisthenes, some of which turn out to be unique.

6.2.1. Philodemus on the Cynic-Stoic Succession

In a passage of Philodemus *On Stoics* (PHerc. 155 and 339, col. 12.1–4 Dorandi = SSR V A 138), which is lacunose at the beginning, the name of Antisthenes appears with that of Diogenes, confirming the Socratic influence on those Stoics who wanted to be labelled as Socratics: "(Some say that the Stoic school) at the beginning took its form (from Socrates) and from Antisthenes and from Diogenes, which is why they want to be called Socratics (Σωκρατικοί) too." This brief testimonium connects immediately with the long debate about the relationship between Cynicism and Stoicism, which is sufficiently well treated in Goulet-Cazé 2003.

6.2.2. Antisthenes' Physics

Antisthenes' *Physics*, mentioned in Diogenes Laertius' catalogue with the title *On Nature*, drew attention from both Epicurus and Philodemus. Philodemus (PHerc. 1005 fr. 110 Angeli=SSR V A 184) preserves a fragment of a letter, probably by Epicurus, of which we have only the words "in fact I arranged for you to be brought a copy of Antisthenes' *Physics*." It is impossible to say who Epicurus is writing to here; the context seems similar to that of the other letter of Epicurus where he asked for books by Aristippus, Aristotle and Speusippus to be sent to him (see section 5.1 above).

Philodemus comes back to Antisthenes' *Physics* in two places in his *On Piety*. In the first (PHerc. 1428, fr. 21 = SSR V A 179; see also Cicero, *On the Nature of the Gods* 1.32), he reports that to combat the popular religion of custom (the gods are many), Antisthenes opposes the reality of nature (in reality there is just one god). Philodemus thus appears not to reject religion, but rather to explain it (Brancacci 1985/6: 218–9): "According to Antisthenes in his *Physics* it is said that many gods exist by convention, but only one in reality" (tr. Obbink). The second fragment brought to light by Obbink (PHerc. 1077 col. 19, 533–41 Obbink) presents Antisthenes together with Prodicus, Diagoras, and Critias (col. 19, 524–6) as "another of Epicurus' *Paradebeispiele* of atheists" (Obbink 1996: 359–60).

> For indeed they (*i.e.* Prodicus, Diagoras and Critias) explain the names of the gods by changing letters, just as Antisthenes, substituting the most common, ascribes the particular to imposition and even earlier through some act of deceit (tr. Obbink).

6.2.3 Socrates, Antisthenes and the Stoics on Homonoia.

In a passage from Book 3 of the *Rhetoric* (PHerc. 1506, col. 18.9–28 = SSR V A 69 = Fr. 17 Acosta Mendez-Angeli 1992: 162, 188–9, 269–72),

Philodemus continues his attack on the Stoic Diogenes of Babylon. The latter maintained that the rhetorician cannot be a good ruler, even if he is an expert in the art of ruling, unless he himself is a philosopher, and that consequently only the Stoic philosopher is the perfect orator: the Stoic philosopher-orator is able to reconcile whole communities, and single individuals, just as the musician can bring one lyre into agreement with many others. Against Diogenes, Philodemus refers to Antisthenes' notion of "like-mindedness" (*homonoia*), and putting it in the context of the life-experiences and thoughts of Socrates and of the Stoics Zeno, Cleanthes and Chrysippus:

> Why then did Socrates, who managed to settle things between one person and another, appear not to have been able to reconcile his one person with the masses; and neither did Antisthenes, nor Zeno, nor Cleanthes, nor Chrysippus, nor anyone else who has progressed in the sorts of ways they have progressed?

Aldo Brancacci (2011: 83–91) has clarified the meaning of *homonoia* in Antisthenes, arguing against the interpretation of it as "like-mindedness with oneself" (*homonoia heautôi*), and showing that *homonoia* for Antisthenes has a political as well as an ethical meaning. He focuses on the expression "to settle things between one person and another," in which he sees Philodemus as recognising in Socrates and, through him, in Antisthenes and the Stoics, "a real and fundamental feature of the Socratic conception of dialectic and rhetoric" (89). After Democritus (fr. 250DK), Antisthenes is the first philosopher to attribute a central importance to the notion of *homonoia* interpreted in light of a broadened conception of logical coherence: coherence between thought and action, between thought and life, points—so Brancacci concludes—to

> a rigorous connection between thoughts and reasonings . . ., one that, when conceived in connection with the Socratic *beltistos logos* (his "best account"), and with the entire philosophy of Antisthenes himself, takes on the sense of moral coherence too. . . . At the same time it is extended into interpersonal relationships, in a way that already points towards the ethical and political meaning of *homonoia*, understood as the foundation of the life of a citizen.
> (Brancacci 2011: 90).

6.3 Diogenes of Sinope

The testimonies from Herculaneum on Diogenes of Sinope have been collected by Giannattasio (1980). The main source is Philodemus, from whom we are able to recover a wide range of citations from Diogenes' *Republic*.

6.3.1 Diogenes' Republic

Philodemus makes a considerable contribution towards the reconstruction of some sections of Diogenes' *Republic* (*Politeia*), of which he gives a detailed, though probably much doctored, account in his *On the Stoics* (PHerc. 155 and 339: Dorandi 1982). In recent years this testimony has been fundamentally re-examined by Goulet-Cazé (2003) and Husson (2011), and in the book by Bees (2011, with a collection of fragments), a book abounding in innovative but not always persuasive readings (see the objections set out in Goulet-Cazé forthcoming). I have offered a detailed account of these studies (Dorandi, forthcoming), focusing on the partiality of Philodemus' judgment in relation to the contents of Diogenes' *Republic*, and on the goals Epicurus set himself in writing his treatise *On the Stoics*. In the present essay I shall limit myself to giving a brief rehearsal of Philodemus' presentation of Diogenes' *Republic*, along with that of Zeno of Citium, united as these were, as he says, by innumerable shameless proposals.

Philodemus begins with a well argued defence of the authenticity of the two works, doubts about which had been raised by some more recent Stoics with the aim of freeing their school from a legacy so weighed down by the influence of Cynic views (cols 15.13–17). In this chapter, he points to some precepts of Diogenes: the uselessness of weapons, the suggestion that knucklebones be used as currency, the acceptance of cannibalism. All these elements, he says, were taken up by Zeno too in his *Republic*.

More information on the contents of both works comes from the long doxographical excursus that follows (cols 18–20). Here Philodemus sets about presenting a complete list of the bad ideas that are shared by Diogenes and Zeno (ἀ|ρέ[σ]κ[ει] τοίνυν τοῖς παναγέσι | τού[το]ις, col. 18.4–6). The complex structure of this section has been well explained by Goulet-Caze (2003: 47–51). The members of the two *Politeiai* would be allowed

1. to say what they liked in public,
2. to wear a double cloak;
3. to establish equality between men and women (in dress, by taking part in the same activities, by exercising naked),
4. to refuse to recognise existing cities and laws as true cities and true laws,
5. to enjoy full sexual freedom, whether the men or the women (masturbation in public; incestuous sexual relations, both heterosexual and homosexual; open unions and the sharing of children; sexual abuse of partners),
6. to dine communally, and perhaps to eat the dead (to leave them unburied; to indulge in parricide),
7. to express a negative judgement on humanity, and
8. not to have any trust in friends.

I am convinced that Philodemus' work is fundamental for the reconstruction of both Diogenes' *Politeia* and of Zeno's. But at the same time we need to remember that the Epicurean Philodemus as usual shows an extremely polemical and partisan attitude, which leads him to highlight, to his own advantage, only the most scabrous and questionable aspects of Cynic-Stoic thinking. It is quite possible that he was still reading the two works, but extracted from them only what interested him, and frequently modified or deliberately misunderstood the sense, perhaps even the content, in order to make it suit the demonstration of his own theses. Philodemus is too much of a polemicist for us to trust him blindly. On many aspects, however, he remains the only source we have of Cynic-Stoic "political" thought; thus we cannot do without his testimony, but we do have to use it with the necessary caution.

6.3.2 The Other Texts from Herculaneum

The remaining, meagre testimonia (Giannattasio 1980: 134, 149–51) are of no use. In the first (Philodemus *On the Gods* I, PHerc. 26, col. 21.27–9 = fr. 2), the restoration of the name of Eudoxus of Cyzicus, against whom Diogenes the Cynic is supposed have launched a harsh polemic (Diels), is not confirmed by autopsy of the papyrus (Angeli 1981: 53, n. 170). The other two (fr. 4–5) that Crönert had identified in fragments of the *Vita Socratis Herculanensis* (see section 2 above) of Philodemus, and the one we find in the *Stoicorum historia* of the same author, are too fragmentary for us to provide us with anything concrete.

6.4 Colotes' Criticism: Menedemus the Cynic or Menedemus of Eretria?

Crönert's hypothesis (1906: 8–11, 162–70) that Colotes' polemic in what remains of his books *Against Plato's* Lysis (PHerc. 208) and *Against Plato's* Euthydemus (PHerc. 1032) was directed against the Cynic Menedemus (so too Kechagia 2011, 59) has been questioned by Concolino Mancini (1976: 61–7), who identifies the Menedemus in question as Menedemus of Eretria. More recently Francesca Alesse (2003: 101–6) has re-opened the whole issue, raising the question not only whether the Cynic Menedemus was the target of Colotes' polemic but even whether there was ever a Cynic called Menedemus in the first place. Her results are inconclusive. It is not certain that Colotes in fact attacked the Cynic Menedemus—whose existence, nonetheless, we should not doubt. The target of Colotes' criticism, as Crönert had already recognised, is "the Socratic conception of education, and of the relationship between friends, *philoi*, as simultaneously and dialectical, resulting in reciprocal moral and intellectual progress" (106). Colotes sees in the Socratic doctrine of educational *philia* or erotic *paideia* a sort of alternative version of Epicurus' ideas on friendship from which the Epicureans should keep their distance.

7. TOWARDS A CONCLUSION

It is now the moment to offer a brief account of the conclusions reached in this essay for the reconstruction of certain moments in the lively skirmishes between Epicureans and minor Socratics.

If the whole book Philodemus devoted to Socrates and the Socratics in the *Collection of the philosophers* had survived, we would have had a comprehensive idea of the "historical" reading of the Socratic schools from the Epicurean side. What we have is, however, is reduced to some scattered names and a few sentences. Even Philodemus' reference to "all the records of Socrates" remains obscure because of the lacunose nature of the text.

The attacks on the Megarians began with Epicurus. In Book 28 of the *On Nature* there is clear evidence of criticism from Epicurus and Metrodorus of the linguistic theories of the Megarians, whether those of Diodorus Cronus or of Eubulides. Traces of that polemic also surface in the final section of Book 14.

Metrodorus contributed to the polemic against the Megarians (in *Against the Dialecticians* or in a book of *Against the Sophists*), or so it seems, by opposing their positions on ethics too.

Hermarchus continued the fight, attacking Alexinus' ideas on rhetoric in a treatise in epistolary form of which Philodemus preserves some extracts.

The identification of the Eubulides attacked in a *Poetics* (author unknown) preserved in PHerc. 128 with the Megarian philosopher of the same name is uncertain.

The Cyrenaics too were a target of the Epicureans.

If Epicurus asked for a copy of Aristippus' work *On Socrates*, Metrodorus offered a criticism of some of the doctrines in it together with those of the Megarians.

Philodemus cites an anecdote on Aristippus (known also to Diogenes Laertius), in the context of a polemic against the Stoic Diogenes of Babylon; in his book *On What to Choose and Avoid*, he condemns the interpretations of the Cyrenaics, and of Hegesias in particular, while he refers to Theodorus the Godless in a lacunose passage of the *Rhetoric*.

The hostile relationship between Epicureanism and Cynicism is on a wider front. Here too the attacks began with Epicurus himself and his immediate disciples Metrodorus (on Cynic thinking on household management and on wealth), Polystratus (on "Cynicising"), and Colotes (on the views on friendship of a certain Menedemus, perhaps the Cynic).

Antisthenes was of particular interest to Philodemus, who not only occupies himself more than once with his (Antisthenes') *Physics* in theological contexts, but is also a precious witness to the transformation undergone by the concept of *homonoia* with Antisthenes (and the Stoics).

The majority of the information we have on Diogenes of Sinope's *Republic* comes once again from Philodemus. His testimony is to be handled with extreme caution in light of Philodemus' highly polemical attitude, but it remains all the same of undoubted importance for the reconstruction of parts of the work and for aspects of the "political" thinking of the Cynics and of the Stoic Zeno of Citium.

A final caveat is here necessary. My conclusions are based on the texts of Epicurus, Metrodorus, Colotes, Hermarchus, Polystratus and Philodemus as these appear in the editions currently available of their works. I am well aware that the progress of research on the Herculaneum rolls, and above all the use of new microscopes and of multi-spectral photography, will improve these texts in many places (see, e.g., Macfarlane 2003 on PHerc. 1084, belonging to Metrodorus). I am happy to run this risk nonetheless, thirty years after Giannantoni, I wanted to run this risk because

> [i]f, taking into due account the diversity of judgments and perspectives, we link these polemics to those we can reconstruct in relation to those other great movements in Hellenistic philosophy, the sceptical and the Stoic . . . we must conclude that the themes of Socraticism continue to be at the centre of the debate, and that Socrates . . . is the main reference-point of that debate. This seems to me destined to bring about a wide-ranging revisions to our thinking about the history of philosophy in this period.
>
> (Giannantoni 1983a, 145–6)

I hope that this essay of mine will have served at least to help lay the foundations on which, perhaps in the not too distant future, a new and updated collection of all the Herculeanean evidence can be put together; one that will contribute towards the writing up of those "wide-ranging revisions to our thinking" that Giannantoni predicts.*

NOTES

* I wish to thank Livio Rossetti, Emidio Spinelli, and particularly Francesco Verde for their helpful suggestions. I also thank Ugo Zilioli for having invited me to the conference, held in the peace of Soprabolzano.

BIBLIOGRAPHY

Acosta Mendez, E. and Angeli, A. 1992. *Testimonianze su Socrate*. Napoli: Bibliopolis.
Alesse, F. 2003. "La polemica di Colote contro il 'socratico' Menedemo." *Cronache Ercolanesi* 33: 101–6.
Angeli, A. 1981. "I frammenti di Idomeneo di Lampsaco." *Cronache Ercolanesi* 11: 41–101.
Angeli, A (ed.). 1988. "Filodemo, Agli amici di scuola" (PHerc. 1005). Edizone, traduzione e commento. Napoli: Bibliopolis.
Bees, R. 2011. *Zenons Politeia*, Leiden, Brill.
Brancacci, A. 1985–1986. "La théologie d'Antisthène." Φιλοσοφία 15–16: 218–29.
Brancacci, A. 2011. "Antistene e Socrate in una testimonianza di Filodemo (T 17 Acosta Méndez-Angeli)." *Cronache Ercolanesi* 41: 83–91.

Cavallo, G. 1983. *Libri scritture e scribi a Ercolano*. Napoli: Macchiaroli.
Chandler, C. 2006. *Philodemus On Rhetoric Books 1 and 2: Translation and Exegetical Essays*. New York/London: Routledge.
Chávez Reino, A.L. 2004. "La cita de Hermarco y de Alexino en Filodemo, Rhet. II (PHerc. 1674), col. XLIV 19-XLIX 27." *Emerita* 72: 249–66.
Clay, D. 2003. "The Trial of Socrates in Herculaneum." *Cronache Ercolanesi* 33: 89–100.
Concolino Mancini, A. 1976. "Sulle opere polemiche di Colote." *Cronache Ercolanesi* 6: 61–7.
Crönert, W. 1906. *Kolotes und Menedemos*. Leipzig: Avenarius.
Del Corso, L. 2013. "Ercolano e l'Egitto: Pratiche librarie a confronto." *Cronache Ercolanesi* 43: 139–60.
Dorandi, T. 1982. "Filodemo. *Gli Stoici* (PHerc. 155 e 339)." *Cronache Ercolanesi* 12: 91–135.
Dorandi, T. (forthcoming). "Les *Républiques* de Diogène et de Zénon dans le témoignage de Philodème: Nouvelles remarques et réflexions." In *Les trois Républiques: Platon, Diogène de Sinope et Zénon de Citium*, S. Husson & J. Lemaire (eds.). Paris: Vrin.
Döring, K. 1972. *Die Megariker: Kommentierte Sammlung der Testimonien*. Amsterdam: Gruner.
Erbì, M. 2008. "Demostene nella *Retorica* di Filodemo: l'immagine del ῥήτωρ ἔμπρακτος." *Cronache Ercolanesi* 38: 193–219.
Erbì, M. 2011. "La retorica nell'Epicureismo: Una riflessione." *Cronache Ercolanesi* 41: 189–205.
Gallo, I. 2002. "Una trattazione biografica di Socrate nei Papiri Ercolanesi." *Studi Italiani di Filologia Classica* 95: 59–62 = Id., *Studi di Papirologia Ercolanese*, 265–8. Napoli: D'Auria.
Giannantoni, G. 1983a. "I Socratici minori nei papiri Ercolanesi." *Elenchos* 4: 133–46.
Giannantoni, G. 1983b. "La polemica antimegarica nel XXVIII libro *Della natura* di Epicuro," *Cronache Ercolanesi* 13: 15–9.
Giannattasio Andria, R. 1980. "Diogene Cinico nei papiri ercolanesi." *Cronache Ercolanesi* 10: 129–49.
Gigante, M. 1992. *Cinismo e Epicureismo*. Napoli: Bibliopolis.
Giuliano, F.M. 2001. "PHerc. 495 — PHerc. 558 (Filodemo, *Storia di Socrate e della sua scuola*?). Edizione, commento, questioni compositive e attributive." *Cronache Ercolanesi* 31: 37–79.
Gomperz, Th. 1866/1993. "Die herculanensischen Rollen. III," *Zeitschrift für die österreichische Gymnasien* 17: 691–708 = Theodor Gomperz, *Eine Auswahl herkulanischer Kleiner Schriften* (1864–1909) hrg. von T. Dorandi, 27–44: Leiden/New York/Köln: Brill.
Goulet-Cazé, M.-O. 2003. *Les Kynika du Stoïcisme*, Stuttgart: Steiner.
Goulet-Cazé, M.-O. (forthcoming). "La *République* de Zénon: Essai d'interprétation éthique." In *Les trois Républiques: Platon, Diogène de Sinope et Zénon de Citium*, S. Husson & J. Lemaire (eds.). Paris: Vrin.
Husson, S. 2011. *La République de Diogène le Cynique. Une cité en quête de la nature*. Paris: Vrin.
Janko, R. 2008. "New Fragments of Epicurus, Metrodorus, Demetrius Laco, Philodemus, the *Carmen de bello Actiaco* and Other Texts in Oxonian disegni of 1788-1792." *Cronache Ercolanesi* 38: 5–95.
Kechagia, E. 2011. *Plutarch against Colotes: A Lesson in History of Philosophy*. Oxford: Oxford University Press.
Leone, G. 1987. "La chiusa del XIV libro *Della natura* di Epicuro." *Cronache Ercolanesi* 17: 9–76.

Leone, G. 2003. "Rileggendo il XXVIII libro *Della natura* di Epicuro: riflessioni e proposte." *Cronache Ercolanesi* 33: 159–64.
Longo Auricchio, F. 1975. "I filosofi megarici nella *Retorica* di Filodemo." *Cronache Ercolanesi* 5: 77–80.
Longo Auricchio, F. 1985. "Testimonianze della *Retorica* di Filodemo sulla concezione dell'oratoria nei primi maestri epicurei." *Cronache Ercolanesi* 15: 39–41.
Longo Auricchio, F. 2005. "Novità nella biblioteca ercolanese nell'ultimo trentennio." *Cronache Ercolanesi* 35: 5–13.
Longo Auricchio F. 2007. "Gli studi sui testi biografici ercolanesi negli ultimi dieci anni." In *Die griechische Biographie in hellenistischer Zeit*, 219–55, M. Erler & S. Schorn (eds.), Berlin/New York, De Gruyter.
Longo Auricchio F.-Indelli G.-Del Mastro G. 2012. "Philodème de Gadara." In *Dictionnaire des Philosophes Antiques*, Va, 334–59, R. Goulet (ed.). Paris: CNRS Éditions.
Macfarlane, R.T. 2003. "New Readings Toward Electronic Publication of PHerc. 1084." *Cronache Ercolanesi* 33: 165–7.
Mayer A. 1910. "Aristonstudien." *Philologus Suppl.* 11: 483–610.
Nikolsky, B. 2001. "Epicurus on Pleasure." *Phronesis* 46: 440–65.
Obbink, D. 1996. *Philodemus On Piety. Part 1*. Oxford: Oxford University Press.
Philippson R. 1941/1983. "Der Papyrus Herculanensis 1251." *Mnemosyne* 9: 284–92 = *Studien zu Epikur und den Epikureern*, 275–83. Hildesheim: Olms.
Ranocchia, G. 2007. *Aristone Sul modo di liberare dalla superbia nel decimo libro De vitiis di Filodemo*. Firenze: Olschki.
Romeo, C. 1993. "Il PHerc. 128." In *Ercolano 1738–1988. 250 anni di ricerca archeologica*, 285–8. Roma: Bretschneider.
Rossetti, L. 1993. "Sulle tracce della letteratura socratica antica." *Giornale Italiano di Filologia* 45: 263–74.
Sedley, D. 1973. "Epicurus, *On nature*, Book XXVIII." *Cronache Ercolanesi* 3: 5–83.
Spinelli, E. 1986. "Metrodoro *Contro i Dialettici?*." *Cronache Ercolanesi* 16: 29–43.
Tepedino Guerra, A. 1990. "Il contributo di Metrodoro di Lampsaco alla formazione della teoria epicurea del linguaggio." *Cronache Ercolanesi* 20: 17–25.
Tepedino Guerra, A. 1992. "Metrodoro *Contro i Dialettici?*." *Cronache Ercolanesi* 22: 119–22.
Tsouna, V. 2012. *Philodemus on Property Management*. Atlanta, GA: Society of Biblical Studies.
Tsouna-McKirahan, V.-Indelli, G. 1995. *[Philodemus], [On choices and Avoidances]*. Napoli: Bibliopolis.
Verde, F. 2013. *Elachista. La dottrina dei minimi nell'Epicureismo*, Leuven: Peters.
Zilioli, U. 2012. *The Cyrenaics*, Durham: Acumen; reprinted in London and New York: Routledge, 2014.

11 Socrates, Alcibiades and Antisthenes in PFlor 113[1]

Menahem Luz

Socrates' closest pupils often described his direct and personal approach to philosophical teaching whereby he drew his followers to a love of philosophy through displaying his love for them as their teacher. The role of *eros* in his educational method is an important theme in the writings of his pupils: Plato, Xenophon, Aeschines and Antisthenes.[2] While the last two are known only from sparse fragments, our store of knowledge is happily supplemented by the discovery of a second century AD papyrus roll acquired in Egypt at the beginning of the last century. Preserved today in the University of Florence, it proved to be the remains of a new and completely unknown composition of the Roman period discussing success and failure in the arts and sciences as well as philosophy.[3] As an appendage to this discussion are added two previously unknown anecdotes concerning the failure of Socrates and Antisthenes to influence the moral behaviour of a favourite pupil by means of philosophical love. In the case of Socrates, this was said to be his beloved student, Alcibiades (col. II *ll*. 19–26)—and in that of Antisthenes, an unnamed lad whom he had befriended (*ll*. 26–36). The subject of this paper is to examine the anecdotes in their context in the hope of discovering their origin and meaning.

While the four surviving columns of this papyrus were published shortly after their discovery,[4] later scholarly research concentrated almost entirely on the second column with its discussion of the two new anecdotes.[5] Although sections of them have even been re-edited in more recent years,[6] the remaining three columns have been examined only sporadically and selectively since their initial publication.[7] However, while a revision of the complete text is unfortunately well beyond the scope of this paper, one still needs to take cognizance of cols. I, III-IV in order to clarify the philosophical framework of the anecdotes in col. II. The latter's argument is, as I will attempt to show, introduced by a preceding section in cols. I-II and possibly continued in the discussion of cols. III-IV. By extracting the section on the anecdotes from its contextual framework, one may easily misjudge its integral purpose. Furthermore, although each anecdote naturally lends itself to being treated as a separate testimony, this approach could also prejudge the issue of their unity of origin. In the following paper, I propose to return to the method established by Italo Gallo by treating them both as a single continuous text. Aldo Brancacci has recently analysed the Antisthenean anecdote of the papyrus as part of a much wider question: its place in gnomic and *chriastic* literature as evidence of the philosopher's original writings.[8] Many of these conclusions can be adopted for other sections of the papyrus as well. After a short survey of the nature of the composition in the papyrus, its date and provenance, I will attempt to set these two anecdotes in their contextual setting, closing with a discussion of their relationship with the philosophical tradition of the philosophers mentioned in them.

1. NATURE OF THE COMPOSITION

In style and language, the papyrus as a whole shows a few unique forms.[9] However, there is no agreement over the work's exact date of composition.[10] Whatever the case, it supposedly looks back to an earlier tradition, referring to Socrates and Antisthenes as well known personalities of the past (II *l.* 19–36). Moreover, its reference to the ancients (οἱ ἀρχαῖοι) in general (col. III *l.* 26) could be a sign that the author follows an anecdotal, or even doxographical convention known to him through writers of the Hellenistic or even Greco-Roman era. In addition, his Socratic anecdotes have some unusual characteristics of presentation so that a question needing to be addressed is whether the author, extracted them from their original source himself, or *via* this later tradition.

Formally speaking, one if not two sentences of the text suggest that its original format was that of a dialogue held between at least two anonymous speakers.[11] However, it is now generally accepted, perhaps with more certainty than is warranted, that the composition was originally written in the form of a *diatribe*, but one where the speaker sometimes employed a semi-rhetorical mannerism of addressing himself to an imaginary or abstract figure as exemplified in many a Cynic-Stoic *sermo* of the Hellenistic and Greco-Roman periods.[12] Although this still does not help determine its exact date, Croenert's general comparison with this specific genre of literature—particularly with the moral diatribes of the 2nd century BC Teles—found subsequent approval. He does not refer to specific passages for comparison, but we may recall Teles' use of Bion's dialogic debates with imaginary speakers in his περὶ αὐταρκείας (fr. II) and his dramatic anecdotes concerning Socrates' meals with Alcibiades.[13] However, we should recall that many of these motives continue to characterise later authors of diatribes as well other literary genres. Whatever its final date of composition and style (dialogue or diatribe), the author clearly relies on later literary traditions in addition to his testimonies concerning fifth-fourth century BC Socratics.

2. SUBJECT OF COMPOSITION

Setting aside problems of precise date and even genre of this new composition, questions have also been raised concerning its general theme and purpose. Since it includes two anecdotes that discuss the success and failure of Socrates and Antisthenes to persuade certain pupils to lead a moral life, Comparetti considered it to be an anonymous treatise on moral education.[14] However, since the anecdotes are also introduced with a reference to "a method of persuasion" (μεθόδω<ι> πείθειν, col. II. 17–18),[15] Croenert insisted that the composition's real subject was "On Persuasion" and has been unfortunately followed in this.[16] We should first note that the author cited the anecdotes in order to question the efficacy of persuasion in practical, moral issues rather than to discuss the meaning of "persuasion" *per se*.[17] In other words, his discussion comprises no examination of the concept and essence of persuasion itself, but of its success and failure in moral education as part of a much wider issue. Moreover, the speaker replies to the objections of an imaginary, or real conversant with the words: "it is you who say that they (*viz.* philosophers) are the ones who are most capable of (using) a method of persuasion" (λέγεις σὺ ὅτι αὐτοὶ μεθόδω<ι> πείθειν μάλιστα δύνα\|νται; II. 17–18). However, the speaker immediately continues: "Socrates' words do not seem to me to be even/also out of character" (καὶ οὐκ ἀπὸ τρόπου δέ μοι \| δοκεῖ ὁ Σωκράτης εἰπεῖν) when he agreed that he had failed to make Alcibiades a better person (19–26).[18] In other words, the use of a regular "method" of persuasion was a notion raised by the speaker's conversant who is refuted with the following anecdote showing how even/also Socrates sometimes failed.[19] The speaker thus considered that the latter's admission of his failure to impart virtue in this specific instance was characteristic of his philosophy ("not out of character") since success and failure of "persuasion" are *not* the outcome of a methodological lesson in imparting virtue—as was apparently upheld by his conversant—but as part of the success or failure of transferring Socratic values in a non-methodological manner.[20] Sometimes these could be unlearned once the teacher's personal influence was no longer felt: in Alcibiades' case, in the company of others at night-time (II *l.* 25) and for Antisthenes' it was when his friend was dining with rivals in love (*ll.* 29–32). In both cases, the issue involved was the failure of either philosopher to succeed in convincing their ward of moral values rather than the essence of persuasion itself. We should secondly note that the topic of success and failure in moral education is only one aspect of a more general discussion of success and failure in this composition. The anecdotes are in fact introduced by a discussion of how the successful could be the expert and knowledgeable—but sometimes could also be the one who stumbles on a solution by pure chance (ἐν [ἴ]οτε δ' ὁ τυχών), or at other times, even fails by chance. This notion is demonstrated by means of four introductory analogies where success and failure often depend on chance even in the hands of the knowledgeable, thus leading up to the two anecdotes where the failure of the two philosophers is discussed.[21] However, before analysing their unity of purpose and theme, it would be best to set forth each analogy separately:

1. As the text is broken at the top of col. II, the background of the first analogy (*ll.* 1–5) is uncertain, but it clearly refers to people who keep packs of dogs and snares out all night ([νυ]|κτερεύοντας κύνας καὶ πάγα[ς] | οὐκ ὀλίγους).[22] Since a comparison is made (*ll.* 3–5) between its conclusions and those of the next analogy concerning success and failure of the doctor (*ll.* 6–11), this first analogy may have discussed success and failure in hunting.[23]
2. The second analogy (*ll.* 6–11) refers to success in healing, describing how the doctor aims at treating the patient medically, *viz.* using medical methodology (ὁ μὲν γὰρ ἰα|τρὸς στοχάζεται τοῦ ἰατρικῶς | θεραπεῦσα[ι τ]ὸν κάμνοντα), but sometimes a person is lucky having applied something that made the patient healthy on his own (ἐν[ί]|οτε δ' ὁ τυχὼν προσενέγκας τι | ταὐτομάτου ὑγία ἐποίησεν | τὸν ἄνθρωπον).[24] This topic obviously does not involve the concept of persuasion in treatment,[25] but as in the following analogies, its intention is to explain the efficacy of treatment which is sometimes achieved by art, and other times by chance.
3. A shorter analogy on cases of failure and success in wrestling reaches similar conclusions (*ll.* 11–17): the same occurs in the case of a wrestling-throw (τὸ δ' αὐτὸ καὶ ἐ|πὶ τοῦ παλαίειν γείνεται). One person preparing himself for athletics (ὁ μὲν | γὰρ παλαιστρικῶς σκευαζόμε|νος)—*viz.* is trained as an expert in the wrestling-school[26]—but at some time made a throw too late/slowly (βραδέως δ' ἐνίοτε κατέβα|λεν).[27]
4. Finally, there is a brief mention of failure to hit the mark in fighting (*ll.* 15–17). Although tagged on to the previous one concerning athletics, it reflects a situation where a man aims actually to attack and injure a rival: another person may hit out with wood or stone, but struck the heel (τῷ ξύλῳ ἢ | λίθῳ παίσας [ε]ἰς τὸ σφυρὸν κατέβαλεν) of the adversary. Here too the aim is contrasted with an unintentional effect. Although not specific, the attacker was presumably aiming at some more vital part of his rival's body, but his expertise failed him for once.

What is common to the last three analogies is the idea that sometimes an expert does not succeed in achieving the results desired and sometimes they are achieved by pure chance (ἐν[ί]οτε δ' ὁ τυχών). Although much of the contents of the hunting analogy is fragmentary and uncertain, the author clearly states that the following medical analogy is to be considered identical to it in principle.[28] Moreover, he also compares the hunting analogy to a yet earlier, but now *missing* analogy, whose contents can only be surmised,[29] but whose purpose must have conformed to the same pattern.[30] If the *missing* analogy was similar to the hunting analogy which is said to be "identical" in purpose (στοχάζεται) to that of the medical one—*i.e.*, where success of treatment results not only through medical care (τοῦ ἰατρικῶς | θεραπεῦσαι), but also by chance (ταὐτομάτου)—then the *missing* analogy which is compared to the hunting analogy must have had a principle similar to the medical one as well. In other words, we are speaking of at least four separate analogies with the missing analogy as a possible fifth—and all expressing the same philosophical principle concerning success through knowledge/chance. It is unfortunate that the exact point of comparison in col. I (the missing analogy) is too fragmentary to be reconstructed from the surviving text. However, we can make out a reference in it to someone who is "polite. . . . by chance . . . sometimes" that could hypothetically indicate its broad context.[31] However, this is not of critical importance to my argument since it is clear that the speaker regarded the four surviving analogies as leading to similar if not identical conclusions concerning knowledge and chance.[32]

Besides their common topic of success/failure in relation to knowledge/chance, we should also note the style of the surviving analogies: general and schematic, but not totally identical in formulation. The medical analogy discusses success *and* failure in a general sense while the others describe cases of failure alone, but though formulated as particular, they are not specifically defined cases as with the anecdotes. Their role in the argument is as inductive examples resembling Socratic *epagogai* and used as a form of *elenchos* refuting the opinion of the speaker's dialogic or imaginary conversant (*ll.* 17–18). Although no final conclusion is presented, we may deduce from their argument:

1. that a strict *methodos* of action sometimes proves no less successful than chance;
2. and sometimes even that fails where chance succeeds.

It is only at this point that the author finally introduces his "anecdotes," but not as additions to his list of general analogies, but as specific events concerning Socrates, Antisthenes and their respective pupils. This difference is apparent not only from their formulation, but also from their content:- whereas the anecdotes record only the failure of these philosophers—thus corresponding only to the third and fourth analogies—the philosophers' success "at other times" must have been presupposed, or was possibly discussed later in the composition.[33] Thus, although this work has been claimed to discuss "the efficacy of the art of persuasion," we see that this is only one aspect of a much wider issue concerning practical success acquired by chance or method. On the formal level, the author sets out a list of inductive *epagogai* in the manner of a Socratic argument, but not in search of universal definition as in the Platonic dialogues, but culminating in a discussion of the failure of the Socratics in some particular instances.

3. THE ANECDOTES

Similar to the introductory analogies, the two anecdotes comprise a single argument, each describing a philosopher who gives an adequate reply to critics in order to explain his failure to instill morality in a particular pupil. Although they have most recently appeared as two separate fragments (col. II *ll*. 19–26, 26–36), I present them as a continuous discussion as they appear in Italo Gallo, but taking into account more recent work on the text with some minor adjustments of my own:[34]

(19) καὶ οὐκ ἀπὸ τρόπου δέ μοι | (20) δοκεῖ ὁ Σωκράτης εἰπεῖν πρὸς | τὸν λέγοντα ὅτι "Ἀλκιβιάδην, | ὦ Σώκρατες, οὐ δύνασαι βελτ{ε}ί-|ω ποιῆσαι τοσοῦτον χρόνον συ{ν}-| σχολάζοντα"—"ἃ γὰρ ἄ[ν], ἔφη, τὴν | (25) ἡμέραν διδάξω, ἕτεροι τὴν νύ|κτα ἀναλύουσιν." φασὶ δὲ καὶ Ἀν|τισ[θένη] μειρακίου τινὸς ἐρᾶν | καί τινας βουλομένους θη|ρεύειν αὐτὸ ἐπὶ δεῖπνον παρα- | (30) τιθέναι λοπάδας ἰχθύων καὶ | δὴ εἰπεῖν τινας πρὸς Ἀντισθέ|ν[η διό]τι [35] παρευημεροῦσιν αὐ|τ[ῷ] [36] οἱ ἀ]ντερασταί"—"καὶ μά[λ]α, | [ἔφη οὐ θα]λαττοκρατοῦμαι δή·[37] | (35) [ἀλλὰ γ]ὰρ ὁ μὲν [38] ἀξιοῖ αὖ τ᾽ α[ἰ]τεῖν | [ἐγώ·δ᾽ ἀπέ]χεσθαι τῶν τ[οιούτων].

The following is my own translation:

(19) Socrates' words do not seem to me to be even out of character when he said to someone who claimed that:
"You, Socrates, are incapable of making Alcibiades a better person although he is spending such a length of time under you as a codisciple."[39]
"Yes," he said, "for what I would (25) teach him during the day, there are others who unravel it at night."
Yet they say that even Antisthenes was in love with a particular lad and certain persons wishing to catch[40] (the youth) at dinner (30) set out plates of fish. Then there were those who related this to Antisthenes:

"That is the reason that your rivals in love abound in his company."[41]
"And rather," he said, "I am not truly beaten at sea[42] (35) for while he may think that it is worth ordering these (fish), I myself withdraw from that sort of thing . . . "

The column continues further (*ll*. 37–43) and although only a few fragmentary words can be made out, the following reconstruction has been suggested as Antisthenes' final reply to the suitors:[43]

(37) [αὔριον δ᾽ ἂν παρ]αθῇ λο[πάδας ἄλλος τις] | [οὐκ ἂν π]άλιν ο‡χ[οιτο μ]ε[τὰ τούτου].

"(37) [But if someone else] sets out plates [tomorrow], (38) he (the lad?) would not go off with him a second time."

However, even if this imaginative reconstruction of the few remaining letters is correct, most scholars consider line *l.* 36 to be the natural conclusion of the anecdote.[44] Furthermore, this specific restoration does not cap the previous joke and raises many mute questions regarding whose actions are described—and why they should be so.[45] The "punch-line" of this section is obviously Antisthenes' claim that he was "not truly beaten at sea" ([οὐ θα]λαττοκρατοῦμαι δή), presumably by the abundance of rivals swarming around the lad, a point to which I shall return below.

4. THE ANECDOTES' CONTEXTUAL UNITY

Whether or not the author compiled these two accounts out of several sources (*l.* 26, φασί) or one needs further discussion, but, on a *contextual* level, both anecdotes make an identical point: how each philosopher failed to educate his particular ward. Furthermore, both are based on similar philosophical *presuppositions* concerning the philosopher's criticism of that ward. If what Socrates attempted to teach Alcibiades by day was to be "unravelled" at night by Alcibiades' suitors, his teaching is most likely to have touched on some aspect of *erotika*. Although he is not said to have been in love with Alcibiades in the papyrus, this tradition may be presupposed from a reading of Plato,[46] but equally from the fragments of Aeschines[47] and Antisthenes as well.[48] Moreover, Plutarch uses the tradition recorded in our anecdote to describe how Alcibiades slipped away from Socrates in order to enjoy himself with others although still pursued by his teacher.[49] We can thus understand why the next section of the papyrus opens with the remark that *even* or *also* Antisthenes (καὶ Ἀν|τισ[θένη]) was said to have been in love (ἐρᾶν) with some unnamed lad. If the meaning is that he *too* was in love, then it would clearly infer "as well as Socrates," from which we would understand that Socrates was meant to have been in love with Alcibiades in this papyrus tradition as well. On the other hand, if it meant "*even* Antisthenes," then the implication would merely introduce what seems out of character for that philosopher. However, even if the second option is correct, it is clear from the many contextual parallels underlying the anecdotes, that the author of the papyrus composition saw them as similar. The text does not directly state that Antisthenes tutored the lad as had been said of Socrates two lines earlier when the latter admitted that he taught (διδάξῳ) Alcibiades. However, two points can be inferred from the context of the discussion (*ll.* 35–36):

1. the lad's set of values in demanding those sorts of delicacies ([ἀλλὰ γ] ἀρ ὁ μὲν ἀξιοῖ [τα]ῦτ᾽ α[ἰ]τεῖν) were in contradiction to Antisthenes' *own* set of values (ἐγώ·δ᾽ ἀπέ]χεσθαι τῶν τ[οιούτων]).

2. Although this does not not necessarily mean that the boy had studied those values with him, it is clear from the description of Antisthenes as a romantic suitor that he at least once had the opportunity to instill them.[50]

Obviously, the whole situation is ironic, but for the irony to work, the account must be based on these presuppositions. It must then be a subtextual assumption that Antisthenes had personally known the lad from the period prior to that described albeit on a presumably non-sexual level. As a philosopher and teacher, he would be expected to have attempted to instill his philosophical *values*, which the lad blatantly disregarded at the rivals' dinner.

There are thus both dramatic and philosophical parallels to be drawn between this account and the previous one describing how Alcibiades "unlearned" Socrates' lessons. Both anecdotes describe a philosopher's chagrin when a particular ward was involved with a third party at some sort of *nocturnal* activity (*l.* 25) or *deipnon* (*l.* 29). Each is meant to harbour similar presuppositions concerning his wards' failure to grasp his philosophy. Implicit erotic overtones are made in the Socratic anecdote and, as we have seen, are the explicit back-drop of the Antisthenean scene where the "rivals in love" catch the lad (θη|ρεύειν αὐτό) in order to succeed with him (παρευημεροῦσιν). However, these should not be perceived as two separate themes, the erotic and the educative, but as a single theme: *viz.*, Socratic *eros* as a philosophical means of education. As a single theme, it explains not only Socrates' relations with Alcibiades but also those of Antisthenes and his failed ward. Moreover, this theme neatly dove-tails into the preceding discussion of the papyrus: that there is no strict *method* for success and failure. In the following accounts of Socrates and Antisthenes, the philosophers were inconsistently successful especially when their wards were beyond the sphere of their philosophical *eros*.

This common literary and philosophical theme of the two anecdotes could suggest that the author of the papyrus text drew on a single philosophical tradition rather than compiled two separate accounts that he found in different sources. Similarities from the classical period easily come to hand. On the one hand, Antisthenes' speech in Xenophon's *Symposium* describes his own *paideia* under Socrates, where it is claimed that his companionship with his teacher was successful and worthy of his teacher's love.[51] By contrast, the account in the Antisthenes anecdote tells of his companion's failure to live up to his teacher's love. Several dramatic points and even phrases actually recall details from Xenophon's account. In the papyrus, the boy's *esteem* (ἀξιοῖ) for fish delicacies was apparently valued above love for his teacher (*ll.* 32–35) whereas, in Xenophon, Antisthenes values Socrates as the one who is highest in his esteem (ὃ πλείστου ἐγὼ τιμῶμαι).[52] Furthermore, the description of how Antisthenes spent the leisure time of his day with Socrates recalls detailed phrases in our anecdotes.[53] In the latter, Socrates admits that he himself actually *taught* (διδάξω) Alcibiades to be a better person (*l.* 25) as one of the codisciples under him (*ll.* 23–24). This immediately reminds us of the Antisthenean argument that virtue was itself teachable (διδακτή; *D.L.* vi. 10) an issue often contrasted with the *aporetic* Socrates known to us from Plato.[54] Furthermore, the anonymous conversant in the papyrus presupposes that his teaching was supposed to make Alcibiades a better (βελτ{ε}ί[ω ποιῆσαι) person (*l.* 22–23).[55] In other words, Socrates is here conceived as *teaching* practical morality, rather than searching for it aporetically. It can thus be tolerably argued not only that the first anecdote reflects the dramatic and philosophical presuppositions of the second, but that it is also more akin to an Antisthenean Socrates rather than a Platonic one.[56]

Although Antisthenes' anti-hedonist stand is detailed in many ancient sources, modern scholarship has shown that this applied only to non-philosophical love whether that be sexual or physical.[57] His infamous remark that he would shoot Aphrodite dead could he but catch her does not really contradict the applicaton of the verb ἐρᾶν to him in the papyrus text—nor does his role as an *erastes*.[58] His understanding of that sexually charged term, *eros*, was to be identified with philosophical *eros*, *that was attainable only between the morally good*. This philosophical, spiritual love was intended to be between only a good person worthy of love (ἀξιέραστος) and the moral who are his friends.[59] Although this theme was probably treated in one of Antisthenes' *Hercules* compositions, it is clear from its main surviving fragment that physical pleasures were criticised there as well.[60] The lad in the papyrus fragment is like Alcibiades, apparently not worthy of love. Antisthenes closes the papyrus anecdote with a declaration that *he himself* would abstain from such things ([ἀπέ]χεσθαι τῶν τ[οιούτῶν]) as the lad demanded. Besides its metaphorical meaning ("withdraw") in response to the previous metaphor of defeat at sea, the term literally refers to Antisthenes' abstention:[61] first on the dramatic level, from the fish delicacies—but also on a moral level from the successes of the *anterastai*. Antisthenes should thus likely be credited with referring to abstention from their presumably erotic intentions as well.

This involved multi-layered meaning of the text could indicate that some serious literary and philosophical writer lies behind the source of the anecdote. This is also apparent from the striking metaphor of defeat at sea. The passive use of the verb θαλαττοκρατοῦμαι is highly unusual, but has been plausibly explained with reference to a fragment of the Old Comedy, *The Sicilians*, attributed to the late fifth century, Demetrius (I).[62] The latter describes Athens' naval concessions to Sparta in 404 BC at the close of the Peloponnesian War: "Spartans cast down our walls (ἡμῶν τὰ τείχη κατέβαλον) and took our triremes hostage so that Peloponnesians would no longer be beaten at sea (μηκέτι θαλαττοκρατοῖντο)" (*PCG* V p. 9–10 *Demetrius I* fr. 2). Our anecdote is clearly a parody of these lines although scholars do not agree on its terms of reference.[63] However, once accepted as a parody as they suggest, then Comparetti's reading of the negative in the anecdote ([ἔφη οὐ θα]λαττοκρατοῦμαι) would be the best equivalent to the negative of the original line in the play—and in a manner that was instantly recognizable to ancient readers.⁶⁴ Whether we accept this restoration or not, Antisthenes' bon mot in the anecdote is certainly in keeping with his characteristic style of parodying dramatic lines in order to make a philosophical point.⁶⁵ Important for the philosophy in the present instance are his Homeric metaphors of prudence (φρόνησις) resembling "a city wall most safe" (τεῖχος ἀσφαλέστατον)—or "the walls of the soul" remaining unshakable (ἀσάλευτα) and unbreached (ἀρραγῆ).⁶⁶ We should thus recall that the lines parodied in the comedy mention not only the threat of a Peloponnesian naval power, but also the destruction of Athens' Long Walls. The context of the anecdote thus fits nicely into this philosophical parody: the lad may submit to fish delicacies and even the success of rivals in love, but Antisthenes' mind is *not* to be defeated at sea *for its walls are impregnable*. Whether he intended to identify himself with Athens or Sparta politically as has been suggested, the main thrust of the argument would thus be this philosophical point.

Although the lad (μειράκιον) whom Antisthenes supposedly held in such regard is nameless, he does resurface in a whole cycle of anecdotes and in a manner that explains his fishy background. We hear of a young man from the Pontos (Ποντικὸς νεανίσκος) in Antisthenes' company who announced that he would esteem the philosopher properly (πολυωρήσειν αὐτοῦ ἐπαγγελλομένου) only after his cargo of salt-/smoked fish (τάριχη)⁶⁷ had arrived (*D.L.* vi. 9). In response to this misjudged scale of priorities, Antisthenes dragged the lad off to a grain-store where he would learn that esteem for a philosopher was obtainable merely with a sack of flour purchased on credit (vi. 9).⁶⁸ Regarding the drama of the situation, it would seem that the lad was supposed to have been a *potential* pupil who procrastinated because of concerns closer to his commercial interests. As in our papyrus anecdote, this story describes Antisthenes and a lad who set fish delicacies high in his esteem. One further piece of irony should not be overlooked: the lad's "order" of plates of fish in the papyrus (λοπάδας ἰχθύων, *l.* 30) introduces an additional meaning to the subtext. The expression "fish" (ἰχθύς) was also used as slang scorn for the "ignorant and witless" (τοὺς ἀμαθεῖς καὶ ἀνοήτους) just as was "salt/smoked fish" (τάριχος) in the sense of "dolt."⁶⁹ In the papyrus, the subtext would thus refer to plates of "witless dolts" while in the Pontic anecdote, the lad could also be scorned as expecting a ship of fools (πλοῖον . . . ταρίχων). In fact, Antisthenes use of the term gave rise to the anecdote how he himself once took a τάριχος through the market-place.⁷⁰ In this context, we can better understand his most famous banter with the same or another Pontic lad (τὸ Ποντικὸν μειράκιον) who wished to study with him: that he had better bring his wits (νοῦς) about him to do so.⁷¹ To this same cycle belongs the story of a whole group of (witless) Pontic lads (Ποντικοὶ νεανίσκοι) in Antisthenes' company: the latter encountered them (περιτυχών) by chance when they came to visit Athens because of "Socrates' fame," but instead he cunningly led them off to Anytus, thus indirectly leading to the latter's downfall.[72] This involved story belongs to the same cycle of Pontic lads as the other two anecdotes: two about Pontic νεανίσκος/ νεανίσκοι and one concerning a Pontic μειράκιον. As a cycle, it would naturally open with his encounter with them as a group "upon arrival" in the port, from where he was said "to lead them off" to Athens. The other two anecdotes describe meetings with one or two of them apart and in the context of teacher and potential pupil. All are typical of the wit and philosophy generally associated with Antisthenes himself. Gabriele Giannantoni included the papyrus fragment in his section on Antisthenes' περὶ παιδείας along with two of the Pontic anecdotes concerning study.[73] This cycle was probably expanded and developed during the Hellenistic period, but it apparently stems from genuine ideas associated with the philosopher's work concerning the requirements of education—and expressing scorn for dolts. While the home-land of the μειράκιον in our papyrus anecdote is not indicated, he apparently belongs to this same cycle concerning a pupil or potential pupil who failed to grasp the virtues held by Antisthenes.[74]

5. CONCLUSION

The question may now be asked whether the papyrus composition is a compilation of different sources or traditions—or whether there is an underlying unity to its structure. We have seen that the introductory analogies comprise a single argument with a specific idea to be set forth:- that success can be accomplished not only by means of a *method*, but also by chance, and that even a *method* may sometimes fail. The anecdotes were also shown to have a single structure and idea behind them. Formally speaking, they both prove the same point as the analogies: that the philosophers sometimes failed to instill virtue in spite of the fact that they had something to teach. However, in addition to this conclusion, the point made in the anecdotes is that it was the Socratic method of erotic *paideia* which sometimes failed—but presumably sometimes achieved its goal of instilling virtue, albeit that this is not explained in the surviving text. This point is thus a logical deduction to be derived from the introductory analogies. The uncertainty of Socrates' philosophical success also surfaces in the dialogues of Plato, particularly in the form of an epistemological dilemma.[75] However, Plato's portrayal of Socrates' searching for moral definitions through a strict dialectical *method* of *elenchus* and *logos*, runs counter to the criticism raised in the papyrus analogies. An aporetic Socrates knows only that he does *not know*, but yet asserts that knowledge through *elenchus* and definition will make a better person. By contrast, the papyrus anecdotes maintain:

1. that Socrates does claim to *"teach"*—and thus must be presumed to *know*;

2. while Antisthenes *knows* at least what is "worthy of esteem," it was argued that he was also meant to have tried to teach this to his failed love.

In whatever way this composition concluded, it is clear that the analogies and anecdotes comprise a single unit whether as dialogue, or as diatribe. However, even as diatribe, it contained important dialogic sections that are—or are *meant* to be—derived from historical conversations. It would thus appear that they either derive, or are at least *are meant* to derive, from some previous philosophical dialogue(s). From what we know of Antisthenes' style employed in the meager fragments of his dialogues, they also featured episodic conversations in direct speech sometimes interrupted by Antisthenes himself.[76] Although the two anecdotes of the papyrus have sometimes been compared to *chriastic* citations from noted philosophers,[77] they are not handed down as mere bon mot just for the sake of humour, but make valid philosophical points that are an integral part of the whole composition. Furthermore, we have seen that there are indications that the analogies introducing the anecdotes may have been excerpted or summarised from an originally longer argument. The same may be said of the anecdotes themselves. What has been described as the author's clumsy construction of the second anecdote could possibly indicate that the passage has been excerpted from a more explicit account, or at least more polished account.[78] To a certain extent, this is true of the first anecdote as well where Socrates' addressee and Alcibiades' companions are not given names. However, granted the discussion of Socrates' relationship with Alcibiades and the general sympotic background in both sections of the anecdote, it is also likely that the author's original source extracted his citation from a number of Antisthenean works including some sort of feast. In fact, the final sections of this papyrus text returns us to the subject of a drunken feast (col. III *ll.* 15-29) although its connection with the allusions in the two anecdotes in col. II is now lost.[79] However, given the allusion to the *deipnon* attended by Antisthenes' lad—and that presumably attended by Alcibiades in the first anecdote—the question arises whether the author's source could also have used a literary description of a symposium for his material.[80] Whatever the case, the Antisthenean material surfacing in sections of this composition was used by the author as part of a wider debate concerning success and failure, chance and knowledge, philosophical teaching and pleasure. Much of it slips quite easily into the background of early Socratic thinking although the philosophical provenance of the entire composition still eludes us.

NOTES

1. I would like to thank: Susan Prince for kindly giving me access to the proofs of her forthcoming work on Antisthenes; Giyora Hon and Carl S. O'Brien generously forwarding me bibliographical material; and the observations of an anonymous reader.

2. On Plato: Kahn (1998), 21. On the Socratics: Rossetti (1976), 29–76; Brancacci (2004/1991), 35–55. On the historical Socrates: Vlastos (1997), 38–41, 245–247; O'Connor (2011), 60–64.
3. PFlor. II. 113 = Mertens-Pack³ no. 2584. Analysis of its date and physical appearance, accompanied by a digital photograph and bibliography, are on internet site of the Florence Academy: http://www.accademiafiorentina.it/paplett/scheda.asp?id=7.
4. Comparetti (1908), no. 113 pp. 19–26, accompanied by a b/w photograph of the entire papyrus (Tav. III); reviewed by: Croenert (1908), col. 1201 and Koerte (1920), 239. This papyrus is associated with acquisitions made in Egypt in 1901–1904 (Comparetti (1908), notiz. prelim.; Messeri-Savorelli (2006), 203).
5. Gallo (1980), 229–235, accompanied by a b/w photograph of col. II, *ll*. 19–38 (Tav. X); reviewed in West (1982), 807; details and bibliography of this section of the papyrus in *LDAB* 4657 (http://www.trismegistos.org/ldab/text.php?quick=4657).
6. (1) Socrates in Funghi—Caizzi (1999), 718–720. (2) Antisthenes in: Prince (forthcoming), test. 175; Brancacci (2004), 226–32; Giannantoni in *SSR* 2, V A fr. 175; Guida (1989), no. 18 2T pp 238–40; Decleva-Caizzi (1966), fr. 192 & n. p. 128.
7. Following the preliminary edition by Comparetti (1908), 19–26, a few alternative reconstructions were suggested by Croenert (1908), col. 1201, largely followed by Koerte (1920), 239 with a different interpretation of its content in Edwards (1929), 93–94. A modern edition of the entire text has yet to appear.
8. Brancacci (2004), 232–48 has examined a number of such fragments as part of Cynic and Socratic literature (pp. 221–3).
9. E.g.: συν-|σχολάζοντα (col II. *l*. 24), παρευημερούσιν (*l*. 32), θαλαττοκρατούμαι (*l*. 34; see below, n. 53; Gallo (1980), 233; van Leeuwen (1909), 70).
10. Comparetti (1908), 20: "qualche minor sofista dei tempi Plutarchei," but drawing on much earlier material from the fourth century BC, but for Croenert (1908), col. 1901 followed by Koerte (1920), 239: it belongs to a Stoic-Cynic oration of the Hellenistic period, Edwards (1929), 93 specifying second century BC or later. For Gallo (1980), 228 and West (1982), 806–8, it could belong to anywhere between the late Hellenistic and early imperial periods, but mainly Antisthenean and Cynic in spirit.
11. Comparetti (1908), 19 concludes that it was either a letter or a dialogue between two speakers (col. II. *ll*. 17–20 (λέγεις σύ. . . . μοι | δοκεῖ) with a *paragraphus* mark at *ll*. 17–18). We may also note col. I. *l*. 9 (συνέφη) indicating a response to an account related in a previous sentence although this could admittedly have been part of a narrated analogy rather than a response to the narration itself. The restoration οὐ μόνον δ᾽ [ἔ-]| γωγε . . . ὁρῶ (*ll*. 4–5) as an intensive reference to the speaker's own opinion could also indicate a dialogue.
12. A "stoisch-kynischen Diatribe" (Croenert (1908), 1201) with "fingierten Zwischenreden" of an anonymous "Predigten" (Koerte (1920), 239); and a "testo diatribico" with "un (fittizio) interlocutore" (Guida (1989), 239; similarly Funghi—Caizzi (1999), p. 719). Edwards (1929), 93 is more cautious, describing it as "a continuous reply to some interlocutor (real or imaginary)."
13. See perhaps: Teles fr. II 7.1–8.6 (= Fuentes González (1998), 134), 17.1–20.1 (= pp. 140–142). Croenert (1908), 1201 and Koerte (1920), 239 mention Teles' style in reference to the jests ascribed to Socrates and Antisthenes (col. II *ll*. 19–36) and its allegorical style (cols. I. 5, III. 14 and the framm. stacc. of col. IV).
14. Comparetti (1908), 19 ("una discussione filosofica intorno alla παιδεία o educazione"), followed by Edwards (1929), 94 ("the virtue of method in ethical

15. Perhaps, also col. III. *l.* 10: διὰ τὸ μεθ[οδικῶς πείθειν] marked by Comparetti (1908), 239 with a question mark.
16. Croenert (1908), col. 1201: "Diatribe Περὶ τοῦ πείθειν," accepted by: Koerte (1920), 23. This view is also followed by Guida (1989), 238 ("*Diatriba de suadendo (?)*") and with more certainty by Funghi—Caizzi (1999), 279 ("Diatriba *de suadendo*").
17. Funghi—Caizzi (1999), 279: its object is "l'efficacia dell'arte persuasiva"; Guida (1989), 239 "*del valore del metodo nel convincere e nell' educare.*"
18. For this meaning of τρόπος (= ἦθος), compare Teles (Fuentes González (1998), 88).
19. Cf. Guida (1989), 239: "l'inadeguatezza del metodo nell' opera di persuasione."
20. Funghi—Caizzi (1999), 279.
21. While Edwards (1929), 94 was correct that the subject of the whole composition is much broader than persuasion by itself, his suggestion that "the moral" is that "empirical and material methods are preferable to mere theory" lies counter to the conclusion of the analogies in cols. I-II: that the empirical and the methodological often lead to the *same* results.
22. It is unclear if [νυ]κτερεύοντας describes the masters (who keep dogs and nets all night), or their dogs (who are awake all night by the nets), but if the latter then we should read πάγα[ις].
23. Possible mention of wolves (λύκοι, *l.* 6) and dogs (κύνες) can also be made out in *col.* I *ll.* 3, 4, but the reconstruction in Croenert (1908), col. 1201 and Koerte (1920), 239 is highly speculative.
24. Edwards (1929), 94 interprets ὁ τυχών as the "chance-comer," but the analogy could equally refer to the same doctor—who sometimes succeeds and sometimes fails—as to an outsider who succeeds without using medical art. Later, in a dislocated fragment of the papyrus (col IV *framm. staccato*), reference is made to a person who heals drunkards by chance.
25. As in Pl. *Gorg.* 456b.
26. Croenert (1908), col. 1201: ὁ μὲν γὰρ παλαιστρικὸς δοξαζόμε|νος, but this misses the point of the argument concerning one who is trained as wrestler, but sometimes fails in the ring. However, the argument is clear even without the second word.
27. From the tense of κατέβαλεν we may understand that it was a single (failed) move and not a *continuous* series (κατέβαλλεν) which would imply a methodology of slow moves.
28. *ll.* 5–6: "but also in the (following) medical treatments the identical situation applies (ἀλλὰ καὶ ἐπὶ τῶν | ἰατρείων ταὐτόν)."
29. It may have filled the bottom of the hopelessly fragmentary col. I, extending to part of the 20 lines missing from the top of col. II, but leaving space for the following hunting analogy (*ll.* 1–3).
30. Cf. col II *ll.* 3–5: "Not only do *I* personally see *that* case (τοῦτο) produced in (situations) *such as these* (ἐπὶ τῶν τοιούτων)" where *such as these* refers to the previous hunting analogy (*ll.* 1–2)—and not to the following medical analogy said to be "identical with it *as well*" (ἀλλὰ καί . . . ταὐτόν; *ll.* 5–6). The comparison of *"that"* (τοῦτο) case with the hunting analogy must then refer to a yet earlier example that had the same intent as situations "such as these."
31. Reconstruction of col. I is highly speculative (Koerte (1920), 239), but we can make out disjointed arguments: "a person polite" (ὁ ἀστεῖο[ς) . . . is "by chance" (τύχῃ, col, I *ll.* 34–35) . . . "sometimes. . . . polite" (ὁ ἀσ[τεῖος | . . . ἐνίοτε, I. *ll.* 39–40). Possibly, the theme was the efficacy of aiming at urbanity and politeness, *sometimes* achieved by *chance* and sometimes by being very

good (βελτιστ[..], l. 32), but only as an analogy and *not* as suggested in order to explain the "instruction . . . of the ἀστεῖος or *urbanus*" (Edwards (1929), 94).
32. The frag. col. I ll. 2–9 has been restored suggesting a sixth analogy: dogs (κυνες) when wolfs attack (λυκοι ἐπιτίθοιν[το]), would drive them off ([ἀπώ]σαισαν), but would fail to help (οὐκ ἂν βοηθή|σ[ειαν]) their master against men (αν[. . .]) known to them (Koerte (1920), 239). However, this is still very speculative. If it introduced the hunting analogy, this would make it much longer than any of the following analogies and if the restoration *is* correct, it would rather have served as an independent analogy or discussion.
33. This anomaly raises the question whether both anecdotes and analogies were part of a longer or fuller discussion from which the papyrus is an *epitome* or extract.
34. For the text of ll. 19–25, I follow Funghi—Caizzi (1999), 2T with minor changes regarding punctuation and sublinear notation. For ll. 25–36, I follow Guida (1989), 2T, except for a few readings (noted below) where, on comparison with the photographs (above, n. 3–5), I prefer either Gallo (1980) or Comparetti (1908).
35. διότ]ι Guida: νῦν δ]η or ἤδ]η Gallo. All photographs show the top of Guida's ι and the digital photograph (above, n. 3) shows a dot that is perhaps part of the top of a τ.
36. αὐ|τ[ῷ Gallo (but lacks a space for a letter in the lacuna): αὐ|τ[οῖς Comparetti, Decleva-Caizzi: αὐ|τ[ὸν Guida (but παρευημεροῦσιν needs a dative, e.g., Philo, Quod Deus. 3.6). Here the singular would refer to their success with the lad rather than with plates of fish in the plural.
37. [ἔφη οὐ θα]λαττοκρατοῦμαι Comparetti: [ἔφη οὐ θαλ]αττοκρατοῦμαι Gallo: [ἔφη θαλ]αττοκρατοῦμαι Guida ("οὐ spatio non admittitur"), but digital magnification of Comparetti's *Tavola* III (above, n. 4) does show room for [ἔφη οὐ θα] between the left margin (indicated by l. 33) and the vertical of a λ visible in Comparetti, but not seen in modern photographs (!).
38. [ἀλλὰ γ]ὰρ ὁ μὲν Guida: [ἐγώ εἰ γ]ὰρ ὁ μὲν Comparetti: [ἐγώ εἰ γ]ὰρ μὲν Gallo. Guida's restoration is *lectio facilior* in this context.
39. This does *not* mean "frequento uno maestro" rather than Socrates' "condiscepolo" (Gallo (1980), 232, n. 23; Edwards (1929), 94), but rather that Alcibiades was one of a group of συμμαθηταί gathered *under* Socrates. Cf. the tradition in: SSR VA 12; Prince (forthcoming), t. 12B on Antisthenes and his "codisciples."
40. "to catch (θη|ρεύειν)" as one does fish (cf. Plu. 949d).
41. παρευημερεῖν: the rivals were either abounding numerically, or flourishing successfully (almost only in Philo, *e.g.*, de Op. 80.2, de Spec. 2. 160), reflecting their success with the lad (above, n. 36). A more frequent form εὐημερεῖν ("have a good time with") is contextually better, but see below.
42. For θα]λαττοκρατοῦμαι as passive, "*I am beaten at sea*," see PCG I fr.2 (Guida (1989), 239; Brancacci (2004), 226); as a *middle*, "*have mastery over the sea*" (Gallo (1980), 239), it is otherwise unsupported.
43. Croenert (1908), col. 1201, adopted by Brancacci (2004), 227–228.
44. Guida (1989), p. 238 n. ("*hac linea videtur terminari chria*"); Decleva-Caizzi (1966), fr. 192; Giannantoni in SSR 2, VA fr. 175. Gallo (1980), 234–235 thinks that Croenert's reconstruction is ingenuous though the fragmentary lines could well be a continuation of the anecdote.
45. If the subject is the *lad*, it would mean that he would not go out again on another's invitation (but why?)—and if it is another suitor, it would mean that the *latter would* not go with him a second time if, for instance, the fish was "spoilt or done badly" (Brancacci (2004), 228). However, the reason has to be an adequate philosophical response, depending on the previous statements that the lad's esteem for such dishes is not Antisthenes', and not for any accidental reason.

46. In *Symp.* 216d-218e, Socrates is described as regularly displaying *erotic* feelings for the beautiful (ἐρωτικῶς διακεῖται) in general (216d) albeit under philosophical restraint. That he was Alcibiades' only admirer worthy of him, see: *Symp.* 218c (ἐμοῦ ἐραστὴς ἄξιος γεγονέναι μόνος); *Alcib.* I 103a, 135e.
47. In Aeschines' *Alcibiades* this is even clearer (SSR 2 VI A 53 p. 610 (74): Krauss, fr. 3: ἐγὼ δὲ διὰ τὸν ἔρωτα ὃν ἐτύγχανον ἐρῶν 'Ἀλκιβιάδου), Socrates explaining his ἔρως and τὸ ἐρᾶν as a means for interrogating Alcibiades (VI A 53, p. 610, SSR 53 (74)). Kahn (1994), 93 suggested that "no one before Aeschines proposed to understand the protreptic and educational influence of Socrates in terms of *eros*."
48. Prince (forthcoming), sec. 14A; Luz (2014), 179, 187–189.
49. Plu. *Vit. Alc.* 6 where Antisthenes is cited as one of his sources. In our anecdote, others unravel Socrates' teaching by night (ἕτεροι τὴν νύ|κτα ἀναλύουσιν) as a spin on the unraveling of Penelope's web (νύκτας δ' ἀλλύεσκεν; Od. 2 105, 19 150, 24 140).Thus, Socrates as Penelope has rival suitors. See also: Funghi – Caizzi (1999), 720; Prince (forthcoming), 124, 159–160.
50. He is described not only as in love (ἐρᾶν) with the lad, but as one who had rival suitors ([ἀ]ντερασταί) to compete with him for the lad's attention. In other words, Antisthenes was seen by certain people (τινας) to be a failed *erastes* himself and that he once had spent time with the lad.
51. *Symp.* viii.5–6 (Socrates' love for Antisthenes), iv.42–44 (Antisthenes' on his debt to Socrates), viii.5–6 (Socrates' love for Antisthenes).
52. *Symp.* iv.44. Although Xenophon undoubtedly fictionalized Antisthenes' speech as he did others (Dorion (2011), 1–23; Danzig (2005), 331–357), its language and concepts are to be ultimately derived from Antisthenes' writings on love and education (Prince (forthcoming), 13A; Brancacci (2004), 228, 229 n. 22) as other authors that Xenophon used (B. Huss (1999) 381).
53. Cf. συ{ν}|σχολάζοντα . . . παρευημεροῦσιν (*ll.* 23–24, 32) with σχολάζων συνδιημερεύειν (*Symp.* IV.44). Although συ{ν}σχολάζοντα refers to Alcibiades, it presupposes the tradition of Antisthenes as one of the συμμαθηταί under Socrates (above, n. 39).
54. Plato not only makes Socrates deny any ability to teach (*Ap.* 19d-e, 24b-d), but depicts him failing to teach virtue *inductively*—or at least not in the accepted sense of *didaxis* (*Meno* 71b, 81e).
55. This has been compared to Xenophon's reply to the charge that Socrates' gave lessons (*Mem.* I 4.1) where he contrasts Socrates' "protreptic" ability with his "educational" inability (Funghi—Caizzi (1999), 279). However, our anecdote has Socrates claim *to have* educative ability, but *did not succeed* protreptically.
56. Brancacci (2004), 227 has also suggested that the second anecdote is derived from a work by Antisthenes—and that that the discussion of Socrates in the first anecdote also originated in such a work.
57. Cf. SSR 2, V A 118–122, 124, 127; Brancacci (2004), 54–55.
58. Cf. SSR 2, V A 123. He apparently compared *eros* to the "divine disease" attacking mind and body: *viz.* epilepsy and seizures. His maxim—"I had rather go mad than enjoy myself (ἡσθείην)" makes special reference to quick sexual encounters (122). Although the Stoa also considered emotions a *pathos* especially *eros*, our text is not characterized by its technical vocabulary (Luz (1994), 114–121).
59. D.L. VI.105 (= SSR VA 135.10); vi. 12 (134): the ἀξιέραστος is wise and a friend to whoever is like himself (cf. Xen. *Symp.* viii.14–15 (the soul as more worthy of love (ἀξιεραστοτέρα) for a moral lover), viii.3-4 (Antisthenes' love for Socrates), viii.5–6, iv.42–44). A discussion of these passages in: Prince (forthcoming), sec. 13A-14A; Brancacci (2004), 229–230; Huss (1999), 381.
60. Although Hercules' love of Achilles was mentioned in Antisthenes' *Hercules* (Brancacci (2004), 228–229), the Syriac Prometheus testimony of this work makes it clear that the hero was criticised for his worldly aspirations (Luz (1996), 98–99, 101–103).

61. Literally, "abstain" ([ἀπέ]χεσθαι), but it could also imply that I know when to pull out (ἀποίχεσθαι) when I am at sea.
62. Guida (1989), 239; *FAC* I Demetrius pp. 9–10 (Σικελικοί), also known as Σικλελα (*CGF* fr. 77 p. 50).
63. Whether as positive or negative—"I am (*not*) beaten at sea" (above, n. 37)— Antisthenes' parody refers either to uncertain historical events (Decleva Caizzi (1966), 128 n. 19; Gallo (1980), 234), or to the situation at Athens when it was rarely defeated at sea during the Peloponnesian War (Guida (1989), 239), or even to Sparta defeated at sea throughout most of it (Brancacci (2004), 230–231).
64. The play itself was presented some time after the defeat of the Thirty and restoration of democracy in Sept. 403 BC (*PCG* V p. 9–10 *Demetrius I* fr. 3: a *demos* free and untrammeled by tyrants) and thus possibly at the *Lenaea* of 402 BC.
65. See: Luz (2000) 88–95. Antisthenes' philosophy that αἰσχρὸν τό γ' αἰσχρόν, κἂν δοκῇ κἂν μὴ δοκῇ is a parody of a relativist line from Euripides' lost *Aeolus* (fr. 19N) in which incest had been justified (Plut. *Quomodo Adul*. 33c): "What is shameful if the perpetrators think it not so?" (τί δ' αἰσχρὸν εἰ μὴ τοῖσι χρωμένοις δοκεῖ;). Other sources are quoted only as anecdotes not as a citation (*SSR* 2, V A 195).
66. D.L. vi.13; *SSR* 2, V A 134, 106, 107.
67. The noun τάριχη could refer to any salted/smoked delicacy (meat or fish), but the Pontic origin of the cargo would perhaps suggest "fish" rather than salted meat.
68. As it stands, the anecdote has multiple layers: 1. The Pontic lad procrastinated because he patently esteemed a cargo of delicacies over Antisthenes; 2. But πολυωρία ("esteem"/also "a treat") could be obtained for the price of grain; 3. This could be purchased even with credit when the cargo arrives. Although the theme of the true value of commodities is characteristically Cynic, it already appears as Antisthenean in Xenophon (Brancacci (2004/1991), 37–40).
69. Plu. *Sol Animal*. 975b5 (cf. Pl. *Tim*. 92b6); Ar. fr. 200 (= Athen. 3. 89).
70. Plu. *Praec.ger. reipubl*.811b (θαυμάσαντος γάρ τινος, εἰ δι' ἀγορᾶς αὐτὸς φέρει τάριχος, "ἐμαυτῷ γ'," εἶπεν·) cites this "memorable" (μνημονευόμενον) anecdote as if to prove that if something need be done, one better do it oneself. However, as τάριχος also meant "dolt," then Antisthenes would have been dragging off one of his foolish listeners through the *agora* since no one else would do so.
71. *DL* vi.3: to study under him he would require one book and his wit, one pen and his wit, and one notebook and his wit (βιβλαρίου καινοῦ καὶ γραφείου καινοῦ καὶ πινακιδίου καινοῦ) with the famous play on the words καινοῦ (new) and καὶ νοῦ (and his wit).
72. D.L. vi.10: they must have supposedly come after Socrates' death and thus the act of vengeance on his accuser, Anytus.
73. *SSR* II V A xxv fr. 175, 171, 172 and *SSR* IV n. 25 (pp. 248–249), 38 (pp. 265–385).
74. This conclusion does not rule out the suggestion of Brancacci (2004), 228 that the first anecdote concerning Socrates originated in the same work as the second. Antisthenes' dialogues were much more episodic in structure than those of Plato with Antisthenes himself sometimes addressing the reader *in persona* and different speakers participating at different points (Luz (1996), 89–103).
75. On his failure to define: knowledge of knowledge (*Charm*. 175b-c); political excellence (*Meno* 100b-c); virtue by means of dialectical and endeictic methods (*Protag*. 360e-361b). This is a theme raised also in several of the doubtful dialogues (*Theag*. 130c; *Alcib*. I 133d-e).

76. In the Prometheus scene—originally part of one of Antisthenes' *Hercules* compositions—the hero is addressed by Prometheus following a scene describing his conversation with Chiron and Achilles with Antisthenes' interrupting the discussion of both scenes in order to make remarks of his own (Luz (1996), 89–103). The effect would thus have resembled a (diatribic) narration with dialogic elements.
77. Because or their form and witty repartee, they have been compared to *chriastic* literature (Decleva-Caizzi (1966), 128 n. 192) which were often taught by rote without real knowledge of their original purport (Bastianini (2004), 249; Funghi (2004), 369–370). However, the second anecdotes' heterogonous form is not of a purely doxographical *chreia*, (Brancacci (2004), 226–227).
78. Brancacci (2004), 226–228 gives structural reasons for thinking that the Antisthenes anecdote is a summary or excerpt of a longer text.
79. Koerte (1920), 239 actually suggested that the sympotic discussion in *col.* III is a continuation of this *deipnon* theme although the background is unclear.
80. On other evidence for a sympotic description in Antisthenes, see: Prince (forthcoming), sec. 64–65. I hope to deal elsewhere with the question of a sympotic episode in Antisthenes' work that preceded both Plato and Xenophon.

BIBLIOGRAPHY

Bastianini, G. 'PSI 85 e la definizione di <<chreia>>' in: M.S. Funghi (ed.), *Aspetti di Letteratura Gnomica nel Mondo Antico* (Firenze: Olschki 2004), 249–261.
Brancacci, A. 'Il contributo dei papiri alla gnomica di tradizione cinica' in: M.S. Funghi (ed.), *Aspetti di Letteratura Gnomica nel Mondo Antico* II (Firenze: Olschki, 2004), 221–248.
Brancacci, A. 'Érotique et Théorie du plaisir chez Antisthène' in: Goulet-Cazé, Marie-Odile (ed.), *Le cynisme ancien et ses prolongements acte du colloque international du CNRS Paris 22–25 Juillet 1991* (Paris: PUF, 2004), 35–55.
Comparetti, D. *Papiri letterari ed epistolari* (Milan, 1908), in: D. Comparetti—G. Vitteli, *Papiri greco-egizii* II (Milan: Hoepli, 1908–1911).
Croenert, W. ('C'), *Deutsches Literarisches Zentralblatt* 59 (1908), col. 1199–1202.
Danzig, Gabriel 'Intra-Socratic Polemics: The *Symposia* of Plato and Xenophon' in *GRBS* 45 (2005), 331–357.
Decleva-Caizzi, F. *Antisthenis Fragmenta* (Milane-Varese: Cisalpino, 1966).
Dorion, L.-A. 'The Rise and Fall of the Socratic Problem', in: D.R. Morrison (ed.), *The Cambridge Companion to Socrates* (Cambridge: Cambridge University Press, 2011), 1–23.
Edwards, W.M. 'Διάλογος, Διατριβή, Μελέτη' in: Powell, J.U.—Barber, E.A. *New Chapters in the History of Greek Literature Second Series* (Oxford: Clarendon, 1929), 88–124.
Fuentes González, P.P. *Les Diatribes de Télès* (Paris: Vrin 1998).
Funghi, M.S. '<<CHREIA>> di Diogene e <<Detti dei Sette Sapienti>>' in: M.S. Funghi (ed.), *Aspetti di Letteratura Gnomica nel Mondo Antico* (Firenze: Olschki, 2004), 249–261.
Funghi, M.S.—Caizzi, F.D. *CPF* I vol 1*** (Firenze, 1999), no. 95 2T.
Gallo, I. *Frammenti Biografici da Papiri* II: La biografia dei filosofi (Roma: Ateneo e Bizzarri, 1980).
Giannantoni, G. *Socratis et Socraticorum Reliquiae* 2 (Naples: Bibliopolis, 1990).
Guida A. *CPF I* vol 1* (Firenze, 1989), no. 18 2T.
Huss, B. *Xenophon's Symposium: ein Kommentar* (Leipzig: Teubner 1999).

Kahn, C.H. 'Aeschines on Socratic Eros', in P.A. Vander Waerdt (ed.), *The Socratic Movement* (Ithaca-London: Cornell University Press, 1994), 87–106.

Kahn, C.H. *Plato and the Socratic Dialogue* (Cambridge: Cambridge University Press, 1998).

Koerte, A. 'Anonyme Diabribe' in *Archiv* 43 (1920), 239.

Luz, M. 'Antisthenes' Prometheus Myth', in J. Glucker-A. Laks (eds.), *Jacob Bernays un philologue juif* (Villeneuve d'Ascq: PUF, 1996), 89–103.

Luz, M. 'The Erlangen Papyrus 4 and Its Socratic Origins.' *JPT* 8 (2014), 187–189.

Luz, M. "Knowledge of Knowledge in Plato's Charmides", in K. Boudoris (ed.), *Greek Philosophy and Epistemology, Vol. II* (Athens: Ionia Publications, 2000), 181–204.

Luz, M. 'The Transmission of the Antisthenes' *Hercules* in Hellenistic Literature', in K. Boudouris (ed.), *Hellenistic Philosophy* II (Athens: IAGP, 1994), 114–121.

Messeri-Savorelli, G. 'Comparetti e il volume II dei <<Papiri Fiorentini>>' in Cerasuolo, S.—Chirico, M.L.—Cirillo, T. (eds.), *Domenico Comparetti 1835–1927, Convegno internationale di studi, Napoli-Santa Maria Capua Vetere 6–8 giugno 2002* (Napoli: Biblipolis, 2006), 195–214.

Prince, S. *Antisthenes of Athens Texts Translation and Commentary* (Ann Arbor: University of Michigan Press, forthcoming).

O'Connor, D.K. 'Xenophon and the Enviable Life of Socrates' in: D.R. Morrison (ed.), *The Cambridge Companion to Socrates* (Cambridge: Cambridge University Press, 2011), 48–74.

Rossetti, L. 'Il momento conviviale dell'eteria socratica e il suo significato pedagogico' *Ancient Society* 7 (1976), 29–76.

Van Leeuwen, J. 'Ad Aristophanis Comici Fragmenta Nuper reperta' *Mnemosyne* 37 (1909), 67–70.

Vlastos, G. *Socrates Ironist and moral philosopher* (Ithaca: Cornell University Press, 1997).

West, S. 'Gallo, Frammenti biografici da papyri. 2' *Gnomon* 54 (1982), 807.

Contributors

Richard Bett is Professor of Philosophy and Classics at Johns Hopkins University. His scholarly work has focused particularly on the ancient sceptics. He is the author of *Pyrrho, his Antecedents and his Legacy* (Oxford, 2000), and has translated Sextus Empiricus' *Against the Ethicists* (Oxford, 1997, with Introduction and Commentary), *Against the Logicians* (Cambridge, 2005, with Introduction and Notes) and *Against the Physicists* (Cambridge, 2012, with Introduction and Notes). He is the editor of *The Cambridge Companion to Ancient Scepticism* (Cambridge, 2010). He has also published articles on Plato, Socrates, the Sophists, the Stoics and Nietzsche.

Aldo Brancacci is Professor of Ancient philosophy at the University of Rome "Tor Vergata." Among his books: *Oikeios logos. La filosofia del linguaggio di Antistene*, Naples 1990 (*Antisthène. Le discours propre*, Paris 2004); *Studi di storiografia filosofica antica*, Florence 2008; *Musica e filosofia da Damone a Filodemo*, Florence 2008. He edited *Platon, source des Présocratiques*, Paris 2002; *Philosophy and Doxography in the Imperial Age*, Florence 2005; *Democritus: Science, The Arts, and the Care of the Soul*, Leiden-New York 2007; *La Repubblica di Platone*, "Giornale Critico della Filosofia Italiana," Florence 2010.

Tiziano Dorandi is Directeur de recherche at CNRS (Centre J. Pépin/UPR 76). His interests include papyrology, the Herculaneum Papyri, textual criticism, ancient biography and ancient philosophy. He has just published the long-awaited new edition of Diogenes Laertius' *Lives of Eminent Philosophers* (Cambridge 2013).

Kurt Lampe is Lecturer in the department of Classics and Ancient History at the University of Bristol. He has published articles on Plato, Xenophon, Aeschines of Sphettus, and the Old Academy, and *The Birth of Hedonism: The Cyrenaic Philosophers and Pleasure as a Way of Life* (Princeton 2014).

Menahem Luz (also Mervyn Lewis) is emeritus lecturer in the department of Philosophy of the University of Haifa. He has translated and annotated *Aristotle On the Soul* (1989; Heb.) and is completing an annotated translation of *Metaphysics* i-ii. He has published widely on Antisthenes, Plato and Neoplatonic studies.

Tim O'Keefe is Associate Professor of Philosophy at Georgia State University. He is the author of the books *Epicurus on Freedom* (Cambridge 2005) and *Epicureanism* (Durham and Berkeley, 2009), as well as articles on subjects such as Epicurean friendship, Lucretius on the fear of death, Aristotle's cosmology, and the spurious Platonic dialogue *Axiochus*.

Livio Rossetti is Emeritus Professor of Ancient Philosophy at the University of Perugia. He has authored *Le dialogue socratique* (Paris 2011) and coedited (with A. Stavru) *Socratica 2005* (Bari 2008) and *Socratica 2008* (Bari 2010). The main focus of his current and past research is Socrates and the Socratic circle. He is now writing a new monograph on Parmenides and Zeno, to appear in 2015.

Christopher Rowe, Emeritus Professor of Greek, Durham University. His recent publications include *Plato and the Art of Philosophical Writing* (Cambridge 2007), *The Last Days of Socrates: Euthyphro, Apology, Crito, Phaedo* (a new translation, with notes: London 2010), *Plato's Republic* (a new translation, with notes: London 2012), and *Socrates and his Circle: Readings in the First-Generation Socratics* (edited with George Boys-Stones: Indianapolis 2013). He is currently working on a new translation of Plato, *Theaetetus* and *Sophist* for CUP.

Voula Tsouna is Professor of Philosophy at the University of California, Santa Barbara and a Fellow of the National Endowment for the Humanities and of the Onassis Foundation. Her publications include: *Philodemus on Choices and Avoidances*, Naples 1995 (co-authored with Giovanni Indelli); *The Epistemology of the Cyrenaic School* (Cambridge 1998); *The Ethics of Philodemus* (Oxford 2007), as well as several articles on Plato and the Hellenistic and Roman Philosophers.

Francesco Verde is a Post-doctoral Researcher in the History of Ancient Philosophy at University "La Sapienza", Rome. His interests focus mainly on ancient atomism and ancient physics from Aristotle to Epicurus. In addition to several papers on ancient thought, he has published an Italian translation with a commentary of Epicurus' *Letter to Herodotus* (Rome 2010), an anthology of ancient texts on the notion of freedom, fate, and grace from the Stoics to Augustine (Rome 2010), "*Elachista*: La dottrina dei minimi nell'Epicureismo" (Leuven 2013) and *Epicuro* (Rome 2013). He has also edited (with S. Marchand) *Épicurisme et Scepticisme* (Rome 2013).

Ugo Zilioli has been an Irish Research Council fellow at Trinity College, Dublin, and, more recently, a Marie Curie Intra-European Fellow at the University of Pisa. He has mainly written on Protagoras (*Protagoras and the Challenge of Relativism*, London & Aldershot 2007) and on the Socratic schools (*The Cyrenaics*, Durham 2012 and London-New York 2014; *The Circle of Megara*, London and New York, forthcoming). He has also contributed articles on Donald Davidson's notion of truth, Derek Parfit's idea of the self and Joseph Margolis' engagement with ancient relativism.

Index

Ademollo, F. 40–1
Aeschines of Sphettus: 46, 63–77;
    Alcibiades 71–6, 84, 87–8, 89,
    207; *Aspasia* 69–71; *Miltiades*
    56, 63–7
Alcibiades 15–17, 194, 198
Alexander of Aphrodisias *On Aristotle's*
    De Sensu 122 16–23: 135; 172
    28–173 10: 136
'All the Records of Socrates' 170–1
Anonymous Commentary on Plato's
    Theaetetus 65, 19–35: 108, 124
Antisthenes: and Socrates 45–6, 47–8,
    50–3, 198–200; and the Cynics
    48, 50, 56–7; and the dialectical
    method 47–8; and ethics 48–9;
    and Homer 48, 201; and moral
    education 197; 199–203, 208;
    and *philosophein* 47, 54; and
    Plato 49, 50–2; and the Stoics
    48, 51–2, 54; and virtue 51–2;
    200; *Works* 44–5
Aristippus: 28–30, 46, 92; an anecdote
    on him in Philodemus *Rhetoric*
    180–1 (*see also* Cyrenaics); and
    the early Cyrenaics 30–1
Aristocles of Messene (in Eusebius,
    Preparation for the Gospel
    14.19.1–5) 105, 118
Aristotle, *Metaphysics* 4, 5–6: 123; *On*
    Sense and Sensibilia 449a20–31:
    134
Aulus Gellius, *Attic Nights* 11.12.1–3:
    173–4

Bett, R. 101, 118–19, 159, 166–7
Boys-Stones G. 84–5, 88–9, 97
Brancacci, A. 185, 193, 207, 208, 209

Colotes the Epicurean 187–8; *see also*
    Plutarch
Critias 15–17
Cynics xiv, 153–5, 183–7; *see also*
    Antisthenes
Cyrenaics xiv, 178–83; and Aristippus
    28–30; as committed to
    indeterminacy 100–3, 119–28;
    and Plato's *Theaetetus* 31–6;
    and Pyrrho 159–61; as sceptics
    99, 103–11; 114–16; 127–8;
    their subjectivism, 99, 114, 116,
    126–7; *see also* indeterminacy

Denyer, N. 140–1
Diodorus Cronus: minimal parts
    137–8; 140–2; and things
    without parts 137–8; 140–1
Diogenes Laertius 2.71: 180–1
Diogenes of Sinope' *Republic* 186–7
Dorion, L. 90, 97, 207

Epicurus: 171–4, 179, 183; and the
    doctrine of infinity in thought
    143–4; and the doctrine of
    minimal parts 138–40; and
    Epicureanism 168–91
Epicurus' *Letter to Hedorotus* 57:
    143–4; 58–9: 139; *On Nature*
    Books 14 & 28: 171–174
Eubulides 174, 178
Euclides 41, 156

Foucault, M. 62–3; 77; and
    governmentality 63–4, 67–8, 73,
    76; and subjectivation 63–4, 68,
    73; and veridiction 63–5, 68, 73

Gallo, I. 193, 197

Hegesias 181–2
Hermarchus of Mytilene, *Against Alexinus* 176–8

indeterminacy: in ancient thought 118–9; in contemporary thought 116–8; and the Cyrenaics 100–3, 118–28; and global object identity scepticism 110–11, 131; and Pyrrho 119, 159–61

Long, T. 149, 155

Megarians xiv, 27, 156–9, 171–8
Menedemus the Cynic 187–8
Menedemus of Eretria 187–8
Metrodorus of Lampsacus 171–4, 179, 183; *Against the Dialecticians* 174–6
metaphysical indeterminacy *see* indeterminacy

oikeios logos 47, 56

Panaetius 43–4
Phaedo: 82–90, 94–5, 158–9; *Zopyrus* 83–5, 93–6
Philodemus of Gadara 168–91; *Collection of Philosophers* 168–70; *On Choices and Avoidances* (PHerc. 1251), cols. 2–3 103, 125, 181–2; *On Vices* 10 (PHerc. 1008) col. 23–36–8 170–1; *Rhetoric* 7 (PHerc. 1004), col. 41 180–1
Plato: *Charmides* 11–15; *Symposium* 15–17; *see also* Socratics and *Theaetetus*
Plutarch: *Against Colotes* 1120c-d 105, 107–8, 121

Polystratus 183
Pyrrho: and the Academy 161–3; and the Cynics 153–5; and the Cyrenaics 159–61; and indeterminacy 159–61; and the Megarians 156–9; and the Socratic schools 149

scepticism: external world scepticism 104; global object identity scepticism 110–11; object identity scepticism 103, 106–9; object property scepticism 103, 104–6
Sedley, D. 140–1
Sextus Empiricus *M.* 6.53: 101–2, 120; 7.191–2: 114; 7.194: 102–3, 104, 111, 120; *PH* 215: 116
Socrates: 43–4, 83–6, 88–90; and the education of Alcibiades 198–8, 202–3; and *eros* 198–9; as 'stupidus, bardus and libidinosus' 85
Socratic dialogues 43–4
Socratic question 90–1
Socratics 168–91; as dramatic characters in Plato's dialogues 3–6; and the Socratic schools xiii–xiv, 26; their philosophical views in Plato's dialogues 6–11
Socratic schools xiii–xiv, 26–8, 149
Stilpo 157–8

*Theaetetus*156a3-c3, 32, 129; 155d5–156a3, 33; 179c1-d1, 40
Themistius *On Virtue* 43 Mach (=SSR V A 96) 53, 54
Theodorus the Godless 182–3
Tsouna, V. 38–9, 104–5, 106, 119

Van Inwagen, P. 117, 127

Warren, J. 105–6